ACT 26 THE RUMINATING WOMAN

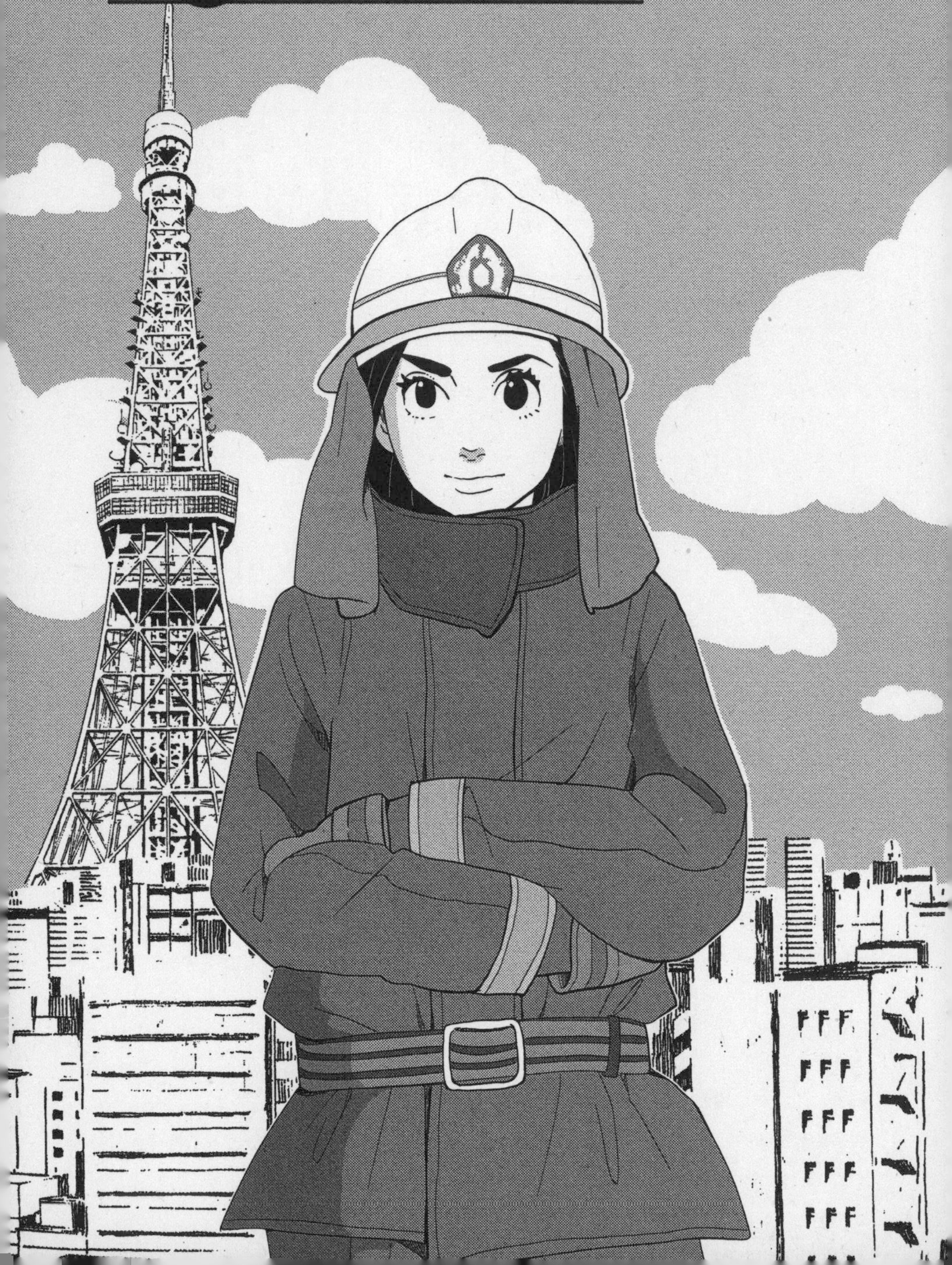

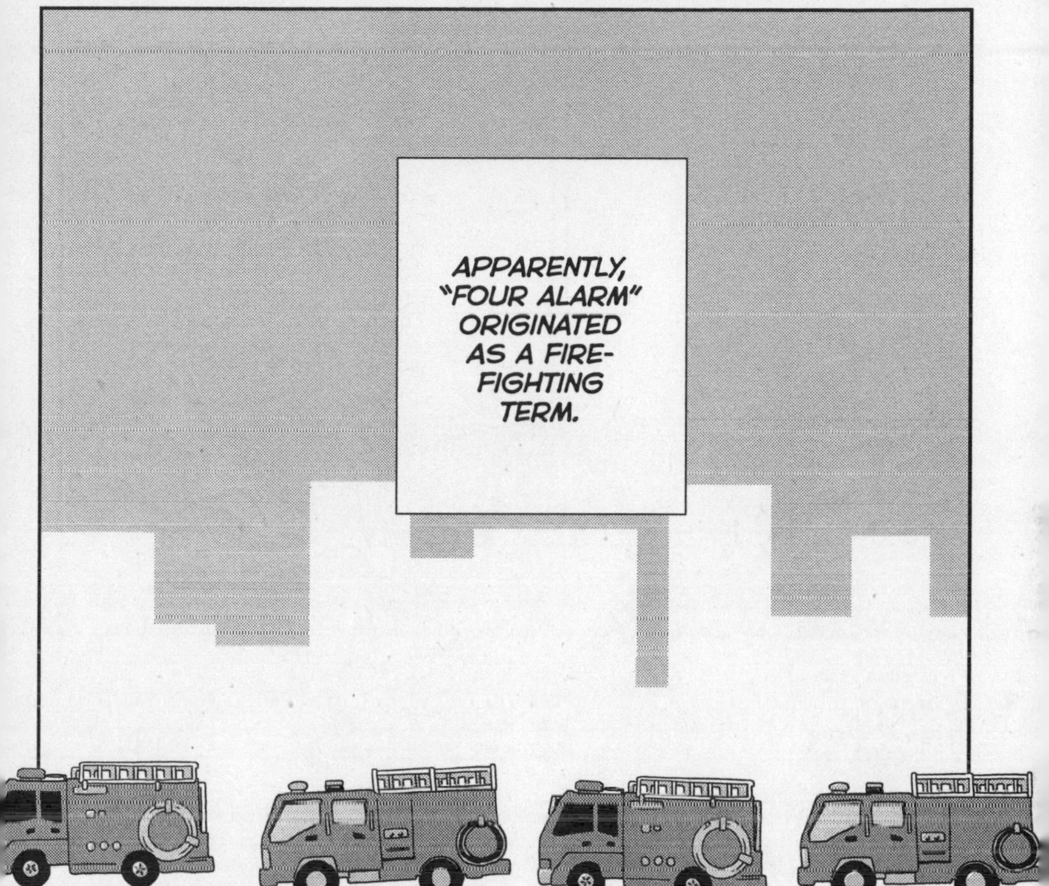
APPARENTLY, "FOUR ALARM" ORIGINATED AS A FIRE-FIGHTING TERM.

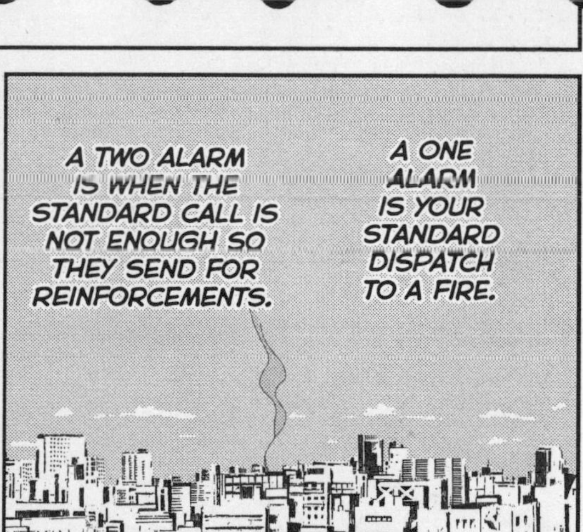
A ONE ALARM IS YOUR STANDARD DISPATCH TO A FIRE.
A TWO ALARM IS WHEN THE STANDARD CALL IS NOT ENOUGH SO THEY SEND FOR REINFORCEMENTS.

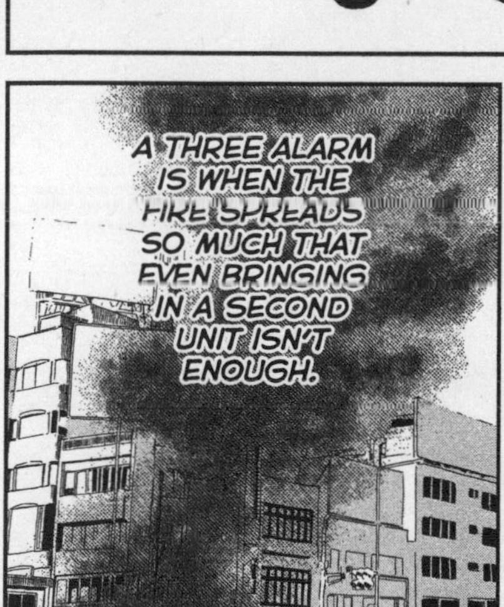
A THREE ALARM IS WHEN THE FIRE SPREADS SO MUCH THAT EVEN BRINGING IN A SECOND UNIT ISN'T ENOUGH.

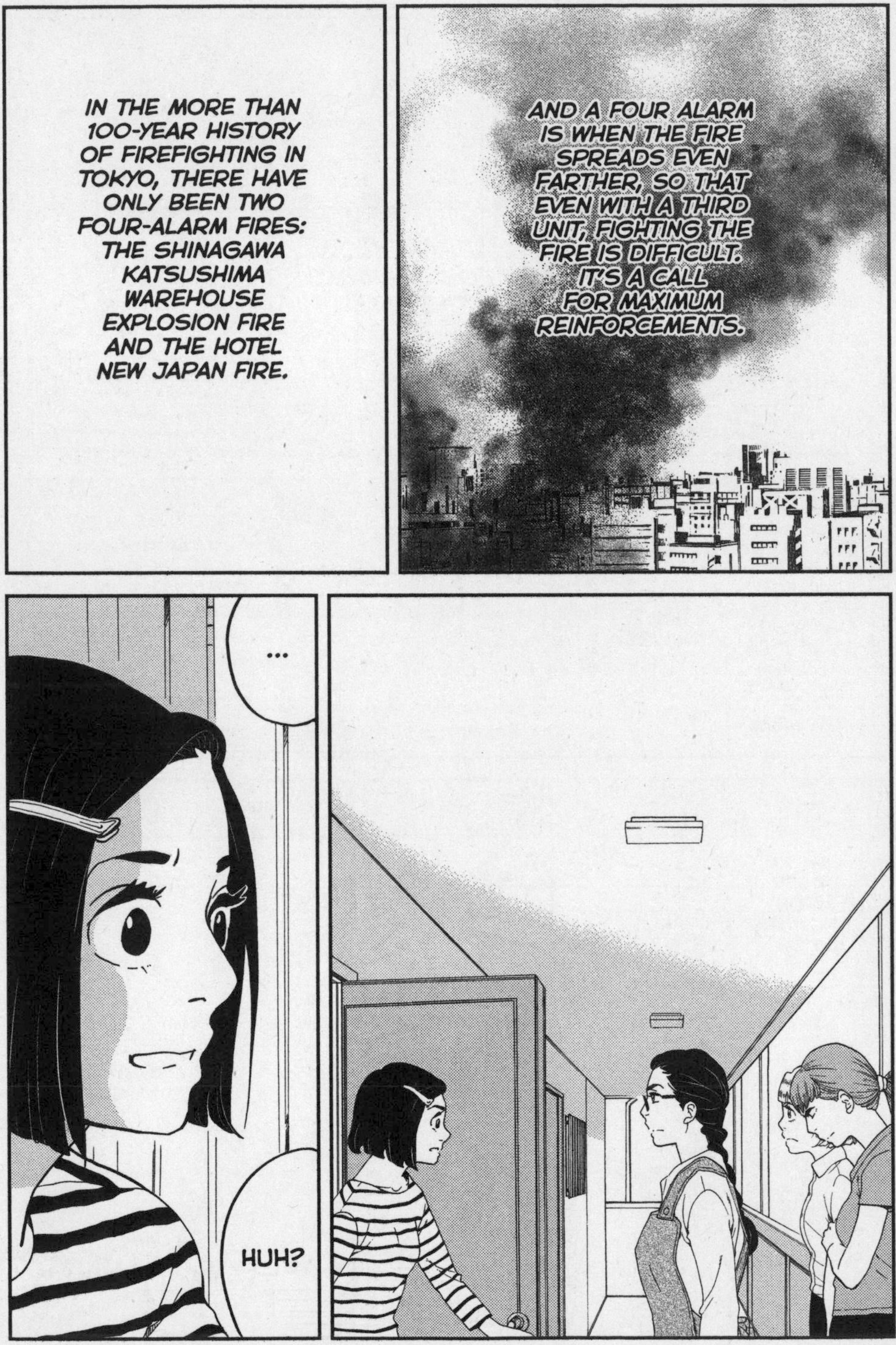
AND A FOUR ALARM IS WHEN THE FIRE SPREADS EVEN FARTHER, SO THAT EVEN WITH A THIRD UNIT, FIGHTING THE FIRE IS DIFFICULT. IT'S A CALL FOR MAXIMUM REINFORCEMENTS.
IN THE MORE THAN 100-YEAR HISTORY OF FIREFIGHTING IN TOKYO, THERE HAVE ONLY BEEN TWO FOUR-ALARM FIRES: THE SHINAGAWA KATSUSHIMA WAREHOUSE EXPLOSION FIRE AND THE HOTEL NEW JAPAN FIRE.
...
HUH?

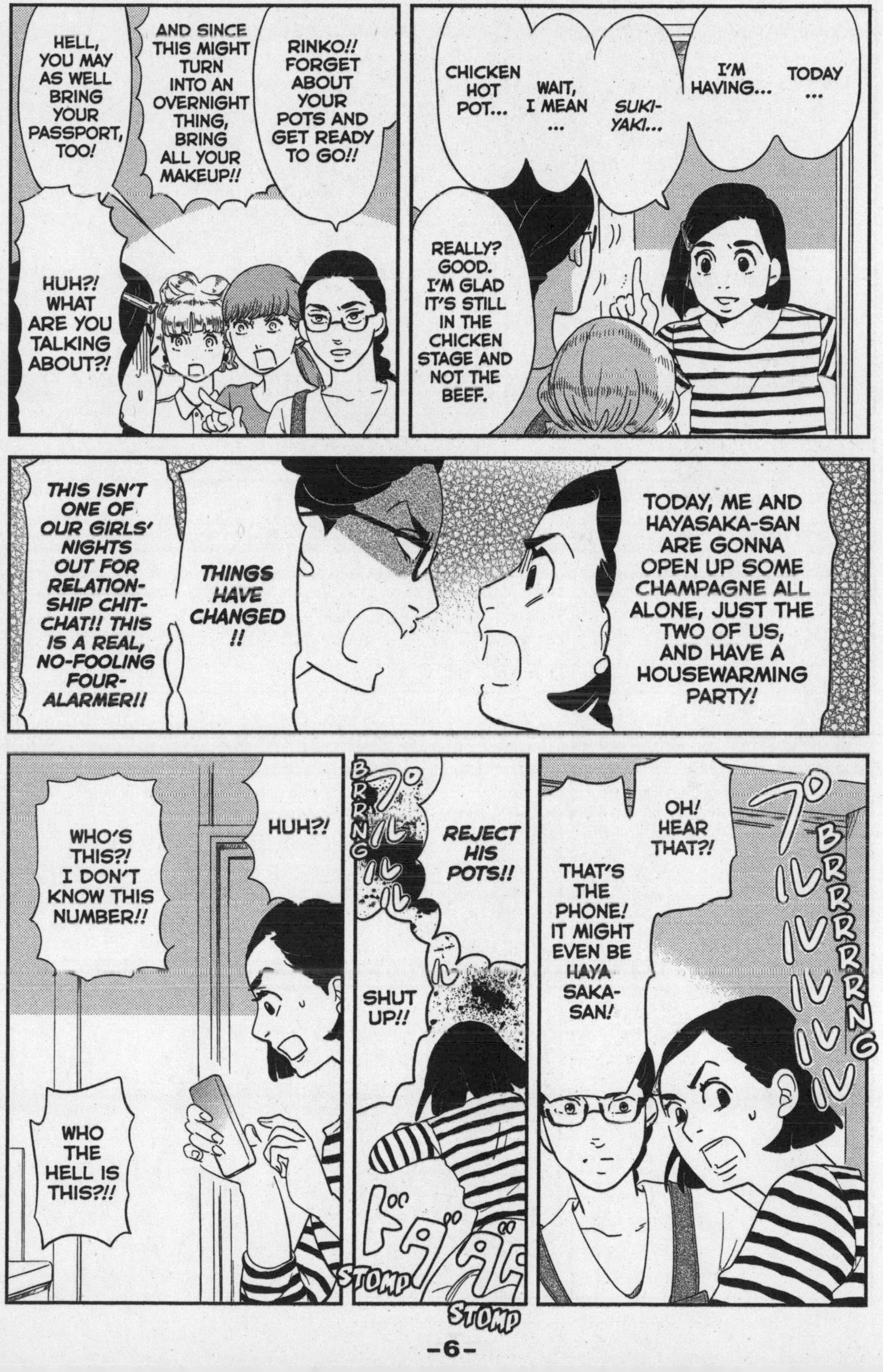
TODAY ...
I'M HAVING...
SUKI-YAKI...
WAIT, I MEAN ...
CHICKEN HOT POT...
REALLY? GOOD. I'M GLAD IT'S STILL IN THE CHICKEN STAGE AND NOT THE BEEF.
RINKO!! FORGET ABOUT YOUR POTS AND GET READY TO GO!!
AND SINCE THIS MIGHT TURN INTO AN OVERNIGHT THING, BRING ALL YOUR MAKEUP!!
HELL, YOU MAY AS WELL BRING YOUR PASSPORT, TOO!
HUH?! WHAT ARE YOU TALKING ABOUT?!
TODAY, ME AND HAYASAKA-SAN ARE GONNA OPEN UP SOME CHAMPAGNE ALL ALONE, JUST THE TWO OF US, AND HAVE A HOUSEWARMING PARTY!
THINGS HAVE CHANGED!!
THIS ISN'T ONE OF OUR GIRLS' NIGHTS OUT FOR RELATION-SHIP CHIT-CHAT!! THIS IS A REAL, NO-FOOLING FOUR-ALARMER!!
BRRRRRRNG
OH! HEAR THAT?!
THAT'S THE PHONE! IT MIGHT EVEN BE HAYA SAKA-SAN!
BRRNG
REJECT HIS POTS!!
SHUT UP!!
STOMP
STOMP
HUH?!
WHO'S THIS?! I DON'T KNOW THIS NUMBER!!
WHO THE HELL IS THIS?!!

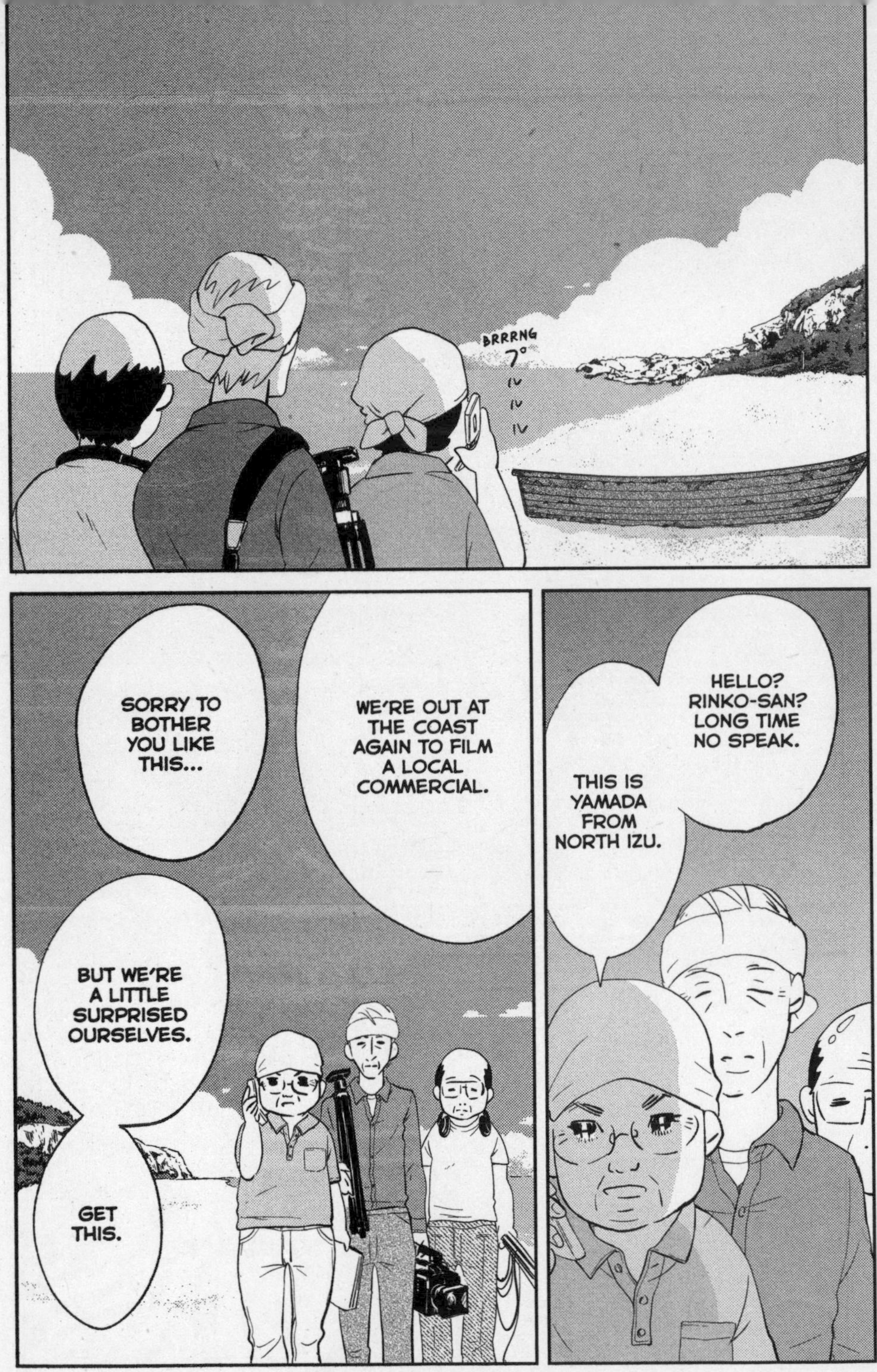
BRRRNG
HELLO? RINKO-SAN? LONG TIME NO SPEAK.
THIS IS YAMADA FROM NORTH IZU.
WE'RE OUT AT THE COAST AGAIN TO FILM A LOCAL COMMERCIAL.
SORRY TO BOTHER YOU LIKE THIS...
BUT WE'RE A LITTLE SURPRISED OURSELVES.
GET THIS.

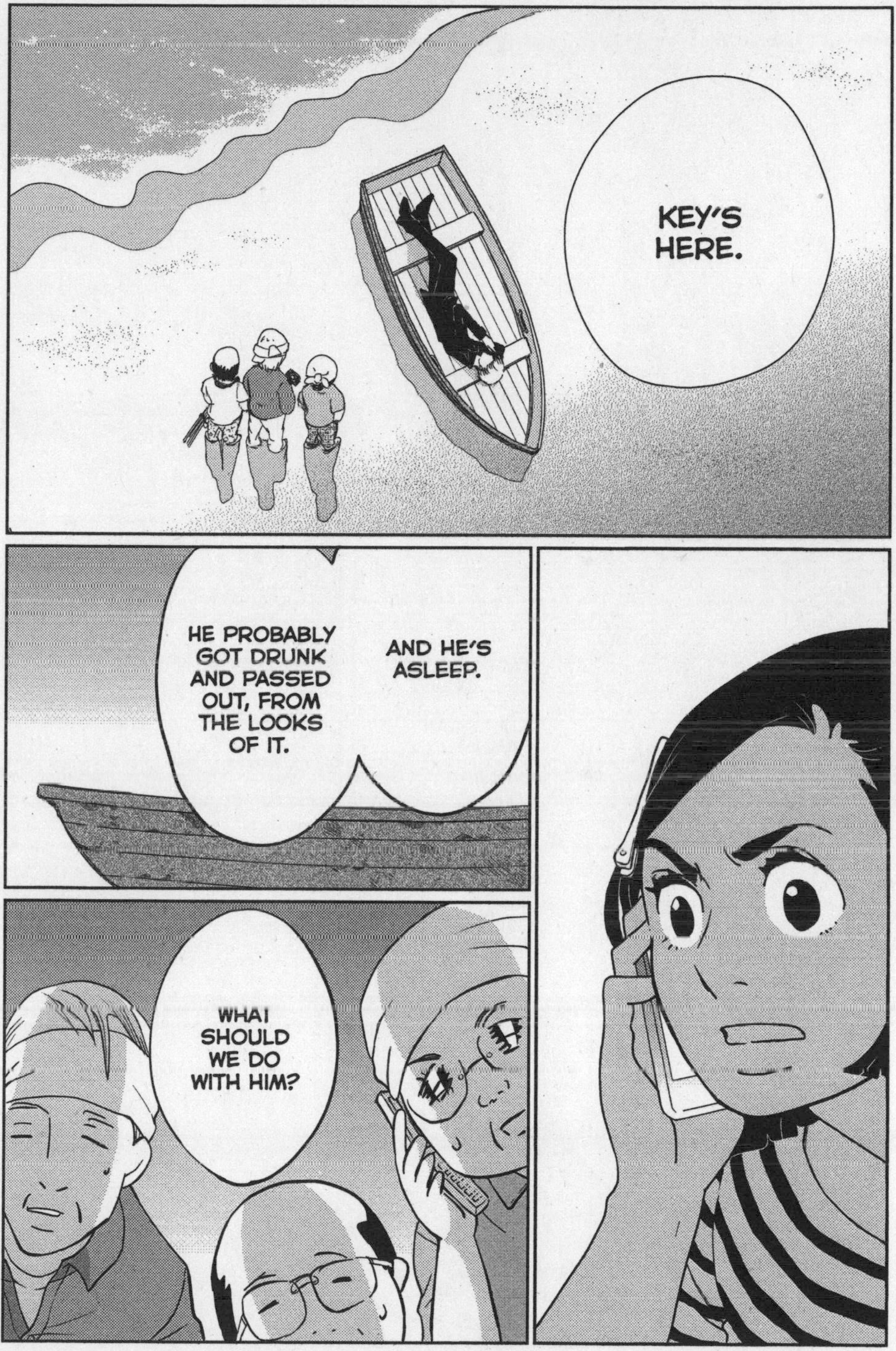
KEY'S HERE.
HE PROBABLY GOT DRUNK AND PASSED OUT, FROM THE LOOKS OF IT.
AND HE'S ASLEEP.
WHAT SHOULD WE DO WITH HIM?

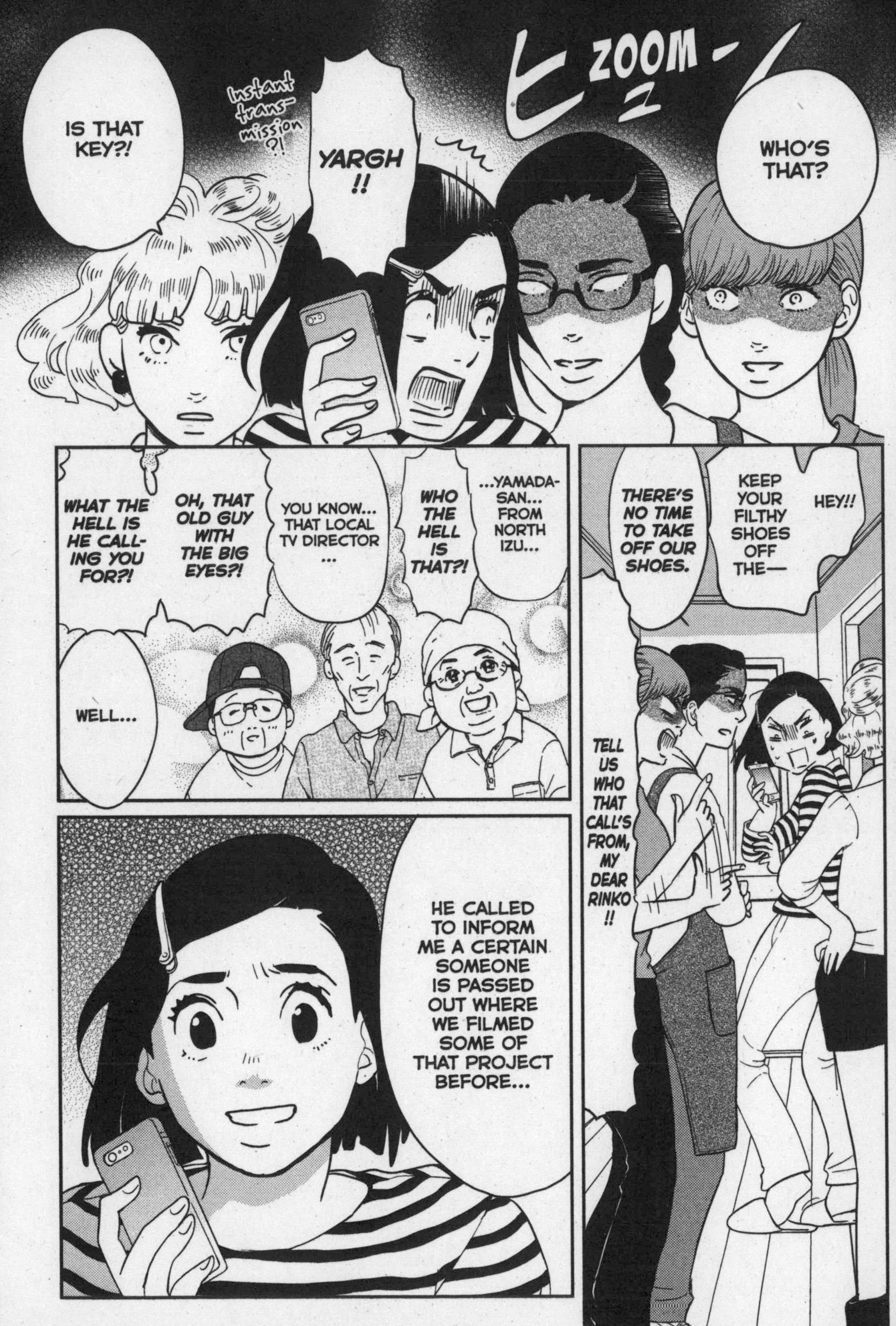
WHO'S THAT?
ZOOM
YARGH!!
Instant trans-mission?!
IS THAT KEY?!
HEY!!
KEEP YOUR FILTHY SHOES OFF THE—
THERE'S NO TIME TO TAKE OFF OUR SHOES.
TELL US WHO THAT CALL'S FROM, MY DEAR RINKO!!
...YAMADA-SAN... FROM NORTH IZU...
WHO THE HELL IS THAT?!
YOU KNOW... THAT LOCAL TV DIRECTOR...
OH, THAT OLD GUY WITH THE BIG EYES?!
WHAT THE HELL IS HE CALLING YOU FOR?!
WELL...
HE CALLED TO INFORM ME A CERTAIN SOMEONE IS PASSED OUT WHERE WE FILMED SOME OF THAT PROJECT BEFORE...

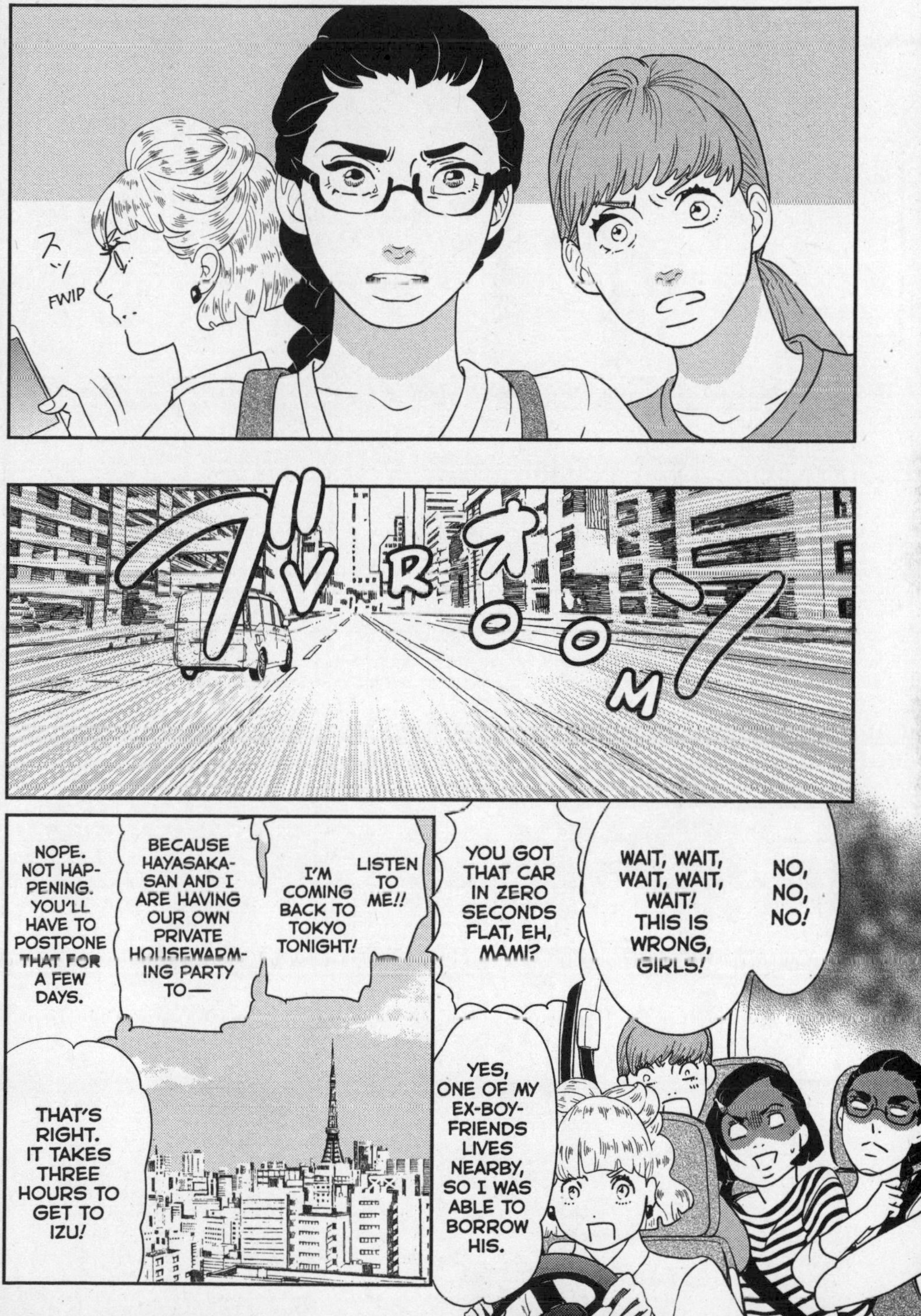
スッ
FWIP
ブオーン
VROOOM
NO, NO, NO!
WAIT, WAIT, WAIT, WAIT, WAIT! THIS IS WRONG, GIRLS!
YOU GOT THAT CAR IN ZERO SECONDS FLAT, EH, MAMI?
YES, ONE OF MY EX-BOY-FRIENDS LIVES NEARBY, SO I WAS ABLE TO BORROW HIS.
LISTEN TO ME!!
I'M COMING BACK TO TOKYO TONIGHT!
BECAUSE HAYASAKA-SAN AND I ARE HAVING OUR OWN PRIVATE HOUSEWARMING PARTY TO—
NOPE. NOT HAP-PENING. YOU'LL HAVE TO POSTPONE THAT FOR A FEW DAYS.
THAT'S RIGHT. IT TAKES THREE HOURS TO GET TO IZU!

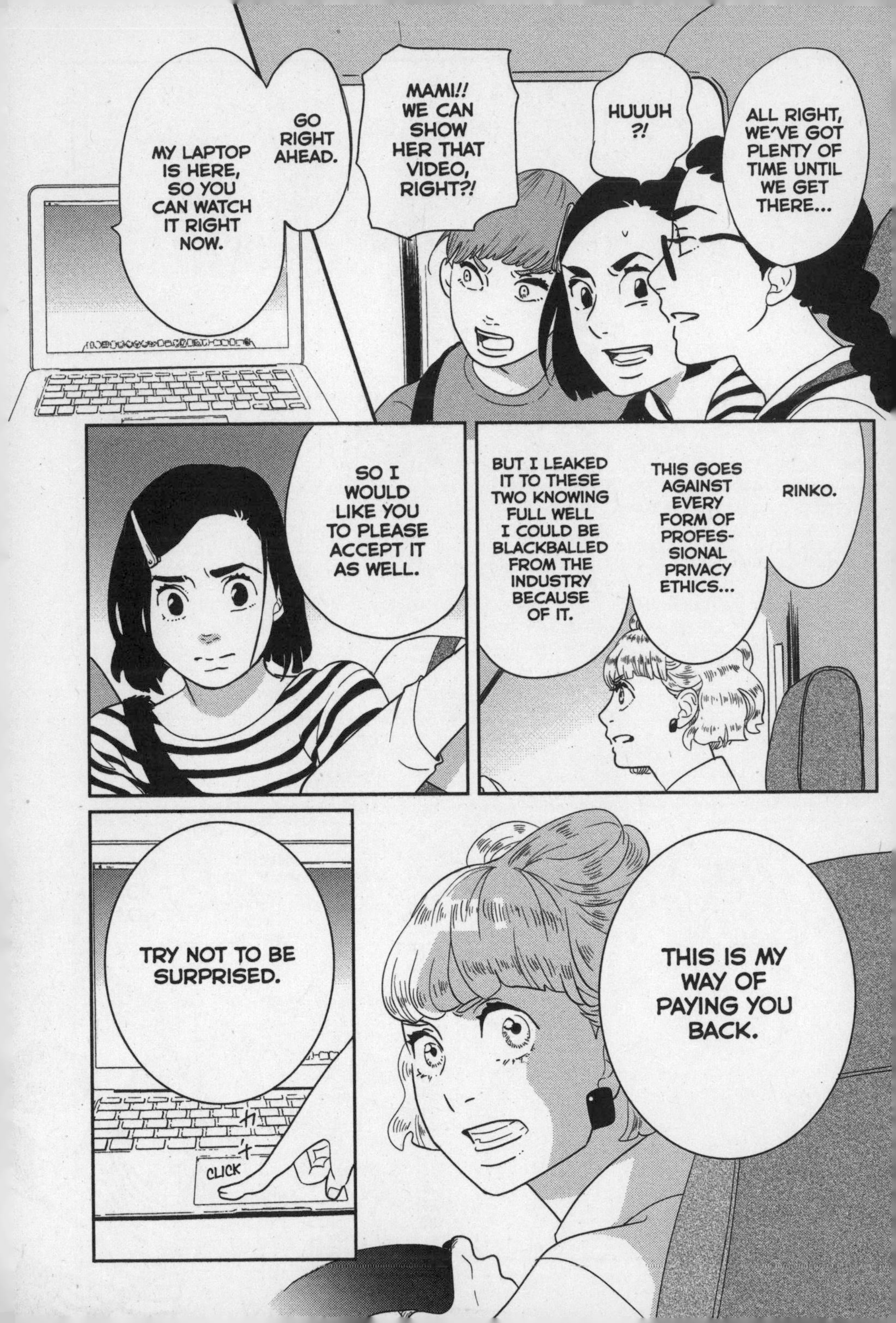
ALL RIGHT, WE'VE GOT PLENTY OF TIME UNTIL WE GET THERE...
HUUUH ?!
MAMI!! WE CAN SHOW HER THAT VIDEO, RIGHT?!
GO RIGHT AHEAD.
MY LAPTOP IS HERE, SO YOU CAN WATCH IT RIGHT NOW.
RINKO.
THIS GOES AGAINST EVERY FORM OF PROFES-SIONAL PRIVACY ETHICS...
BUT I LEAKED IT TO THESE TWO KNOWING FULL WELL I COULD BE BLACKBALLED FROM THE INDUSTRY BECAUSE OF IT.
SO I WOULD LIKE YOU TO PLEASE ACCEPT IT AS WELL.
THIS IS MY WAY OF PAYING YOU BACK.
TRY NOT TO BE SURPRISED.
CLICK

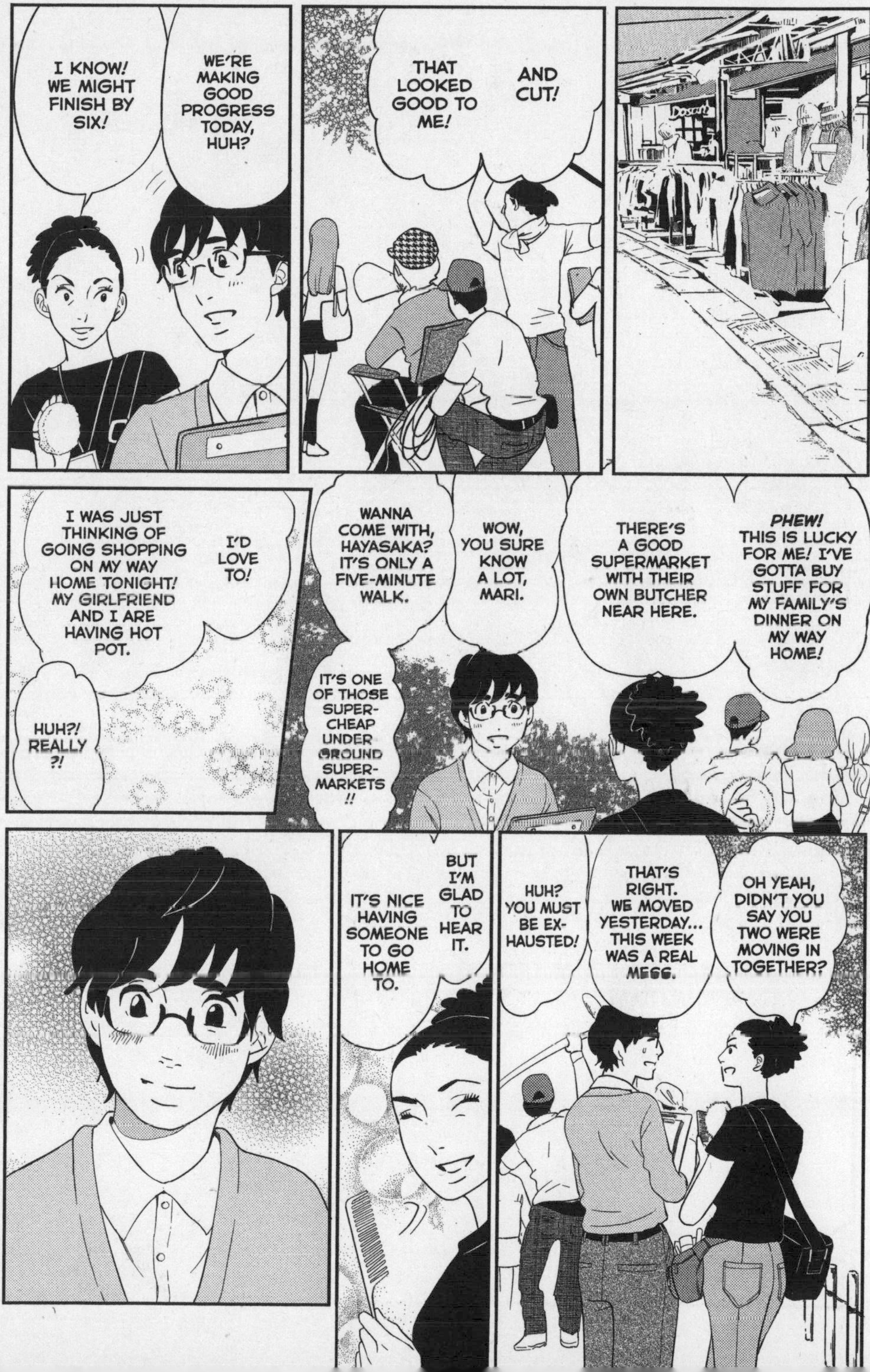
AND CUT!
THAT LOOKED GOOD TO ME!
WE'RE MAKING GOOD PROGRESS TODAY, HUH?
I KNOW! WE MIGHT FINISH BY SIX!
PHEW! THIS IS LUCKY FOR ME! I'VE GOTTA BUY STUFF FOR MY FAMILY'S DINNER ON MY WAY HOME!
THERE'S A GOOD SUPERMARKET WITH THEIR OWN BUTCHER NEAR HERE.
WOW, YOU SURE KNOW A LOT, MARI.
WANNA COME WITH, HAYASAKA? IT'S ONLY A FIVE-MINUTE WALK.
IT'S ONE OF THOSE SUPER-CHEAP UNDERGROUND SUPERMARKETS!!
I'D LOVE TO!
I WAS JUST THINKING OF GOING SHOPPING ON MY WAY HOME TONIGHT! MY GIRLFRIEND AND I ARE HAVING HOT POT.
HUH?! REALLY?!
OH YEAH, DIDN'T YOU SAY YOU TWO WERE MOVING IN TOGETHER?
THAT'S RIGHT. WE MOVED YESTERDAY... THIS WEEK WAS A REAL MESS.
HUH? YOU MUST BE EX-HAUSTED!
BUT I'M GLAD TO HEAR IT.
IT'S NICE HAVING SOMEONE TO GO HOME TO.

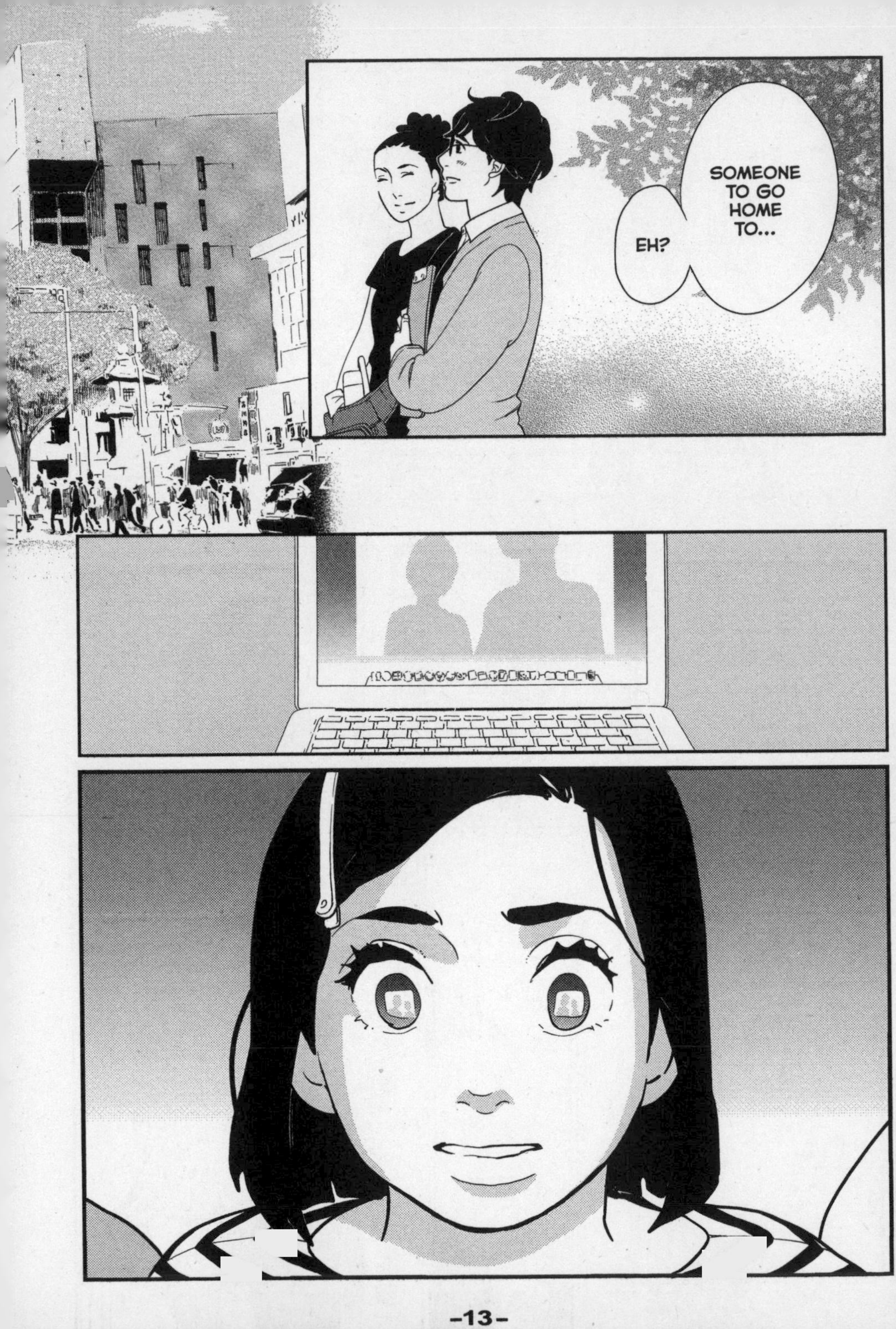
SOMEONE TO GO HOME TO...
EH?

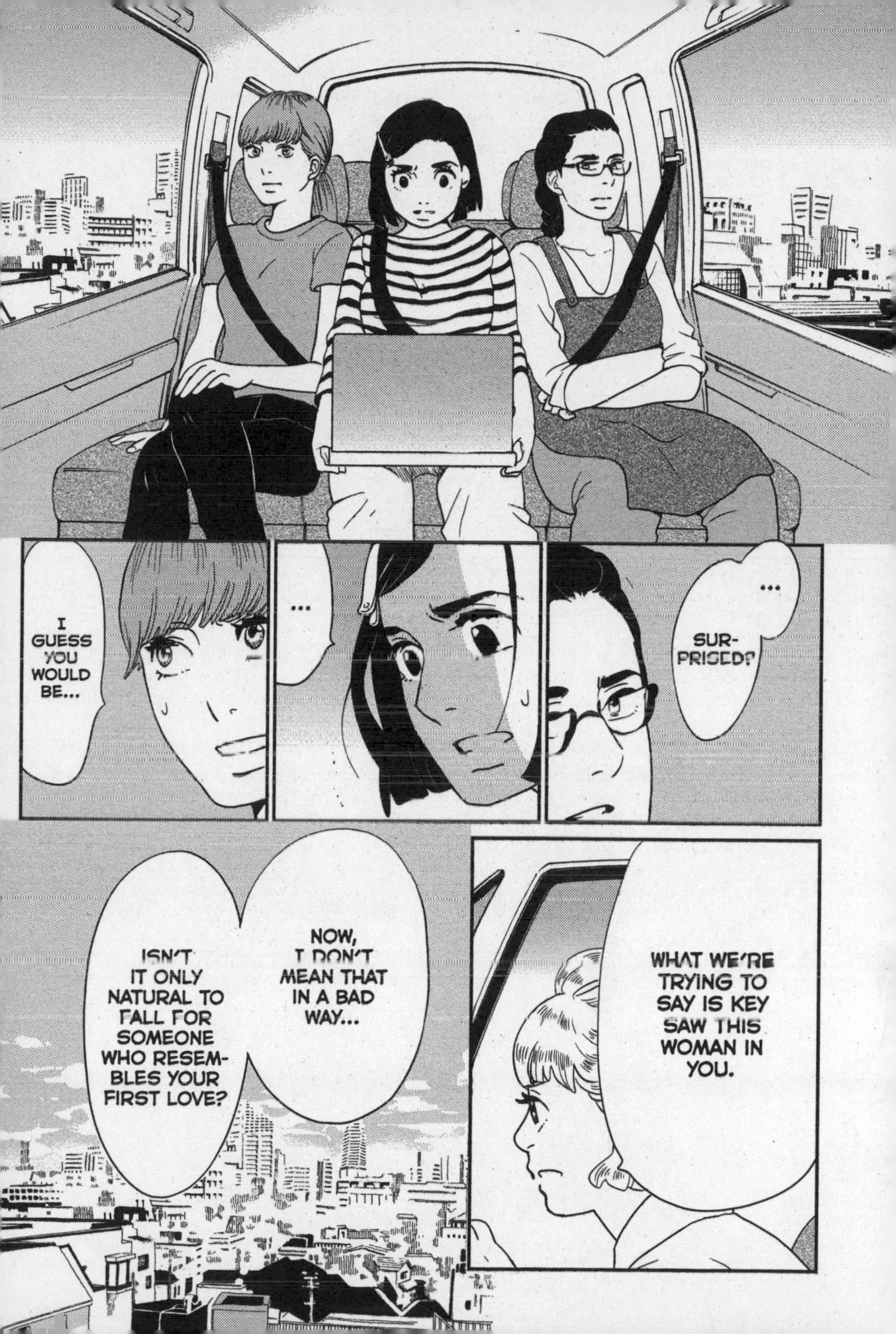
...
SUR-PRISED?
...
I GUESS YOU WOULD BE...
WHAT WE'RE TRYING TO SAY IS KEY SAW THIS WOMAN IN YOU.
NOW, I DON'T MEAN THAT IN A BAD WAY...
ISN'T IT ONLY NATURAL TO FALL FOR SOMEONE WHO RESEM-BLES YOUR FIRST LOVE?

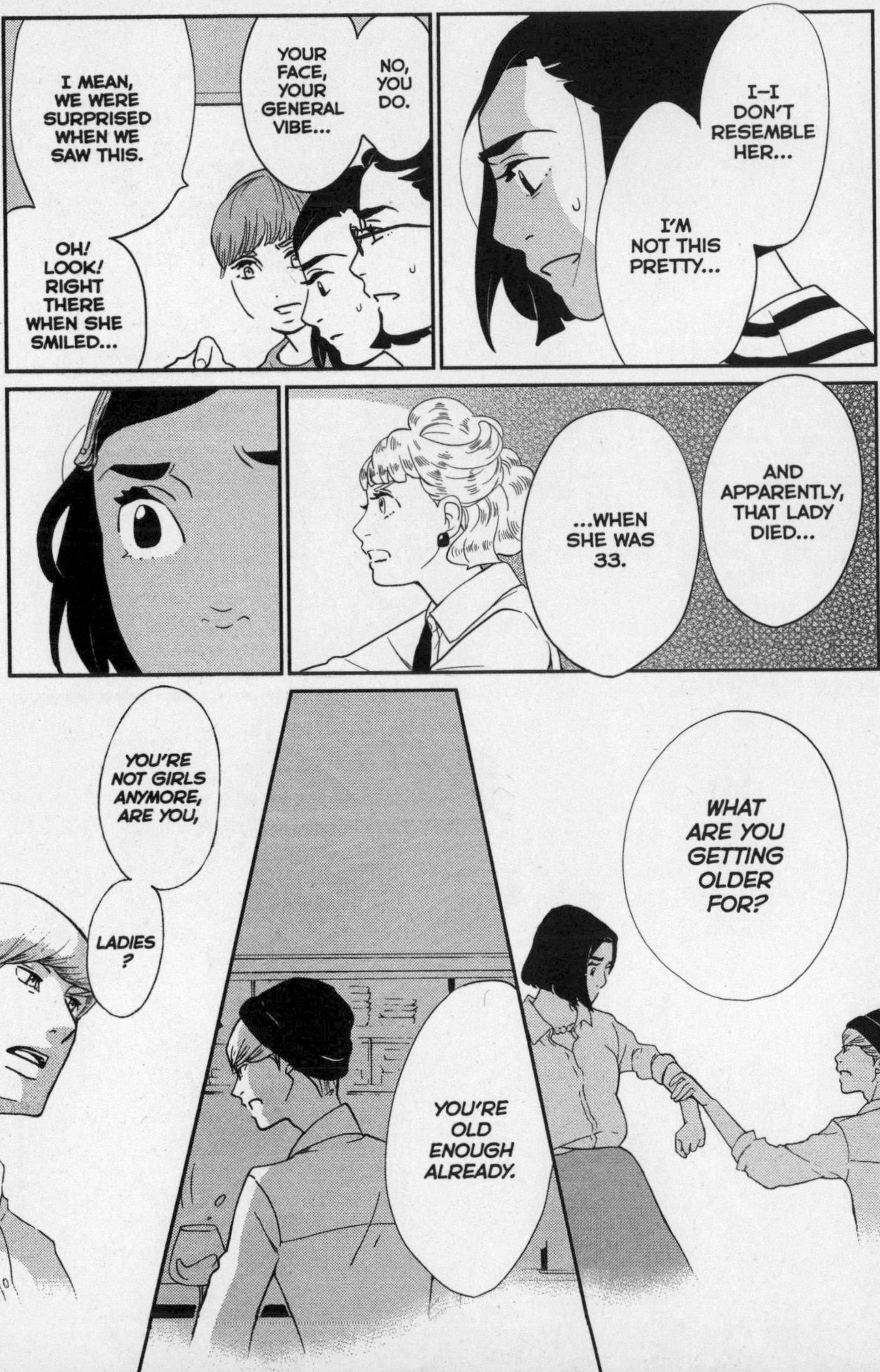
I—I DON'T RESEMBLE HER...
I'M NOT THIS PRETTY...
NO, YOU DO.
YOUR FACE, YOUR GENERAL VIBE...
I MEAN, WE WERE SURPRISED WHEN WE SAW THIS.
OH! LOOK! RIGHT THERE WHEN SHE SMILED...
AND APPARENTLY, THAT LADY DIED...
...WHEN SHE WAS 33.
WHAT ARE YOU GETTING OLDER FOR?
YOU'RE NOT GIRLS ANYMORE, ARE YOU,
LADIES?
YOU'RE OLD ENOUGH ALREADY.

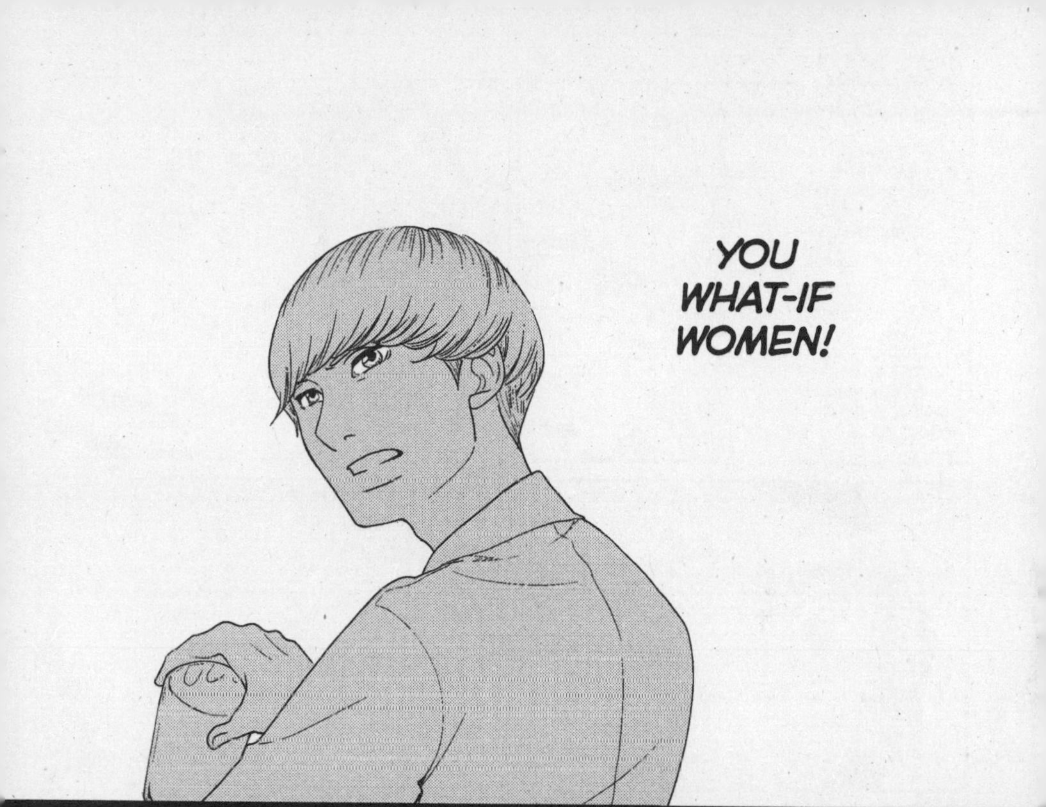
YOU WHAT-IF WOMEN!
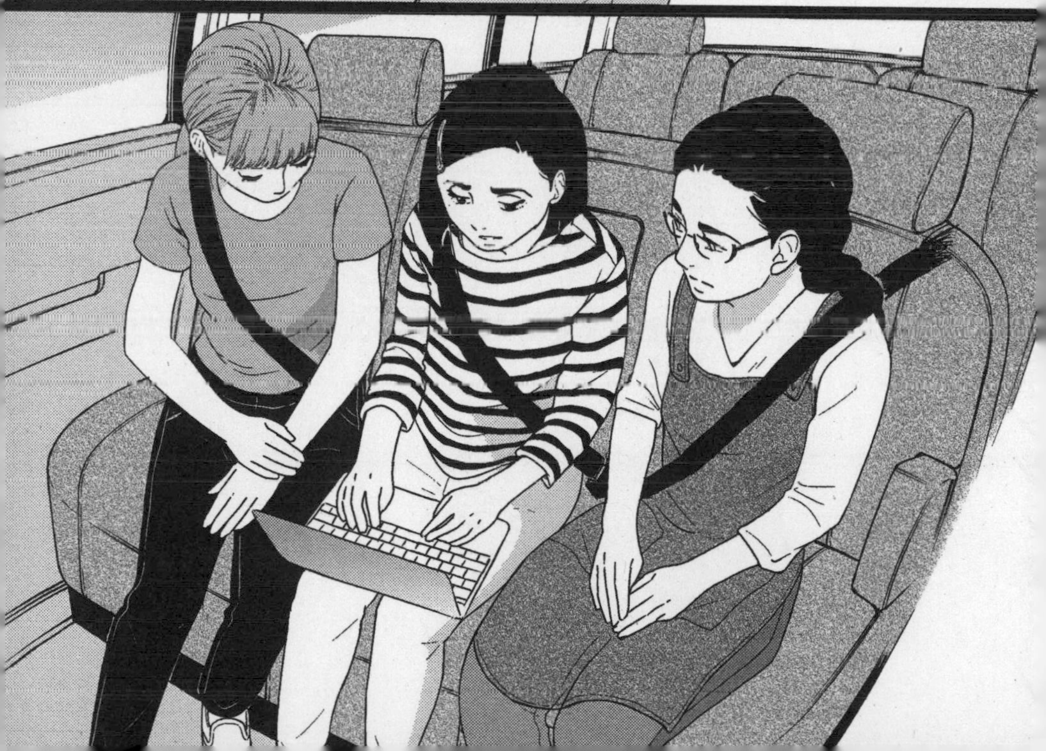

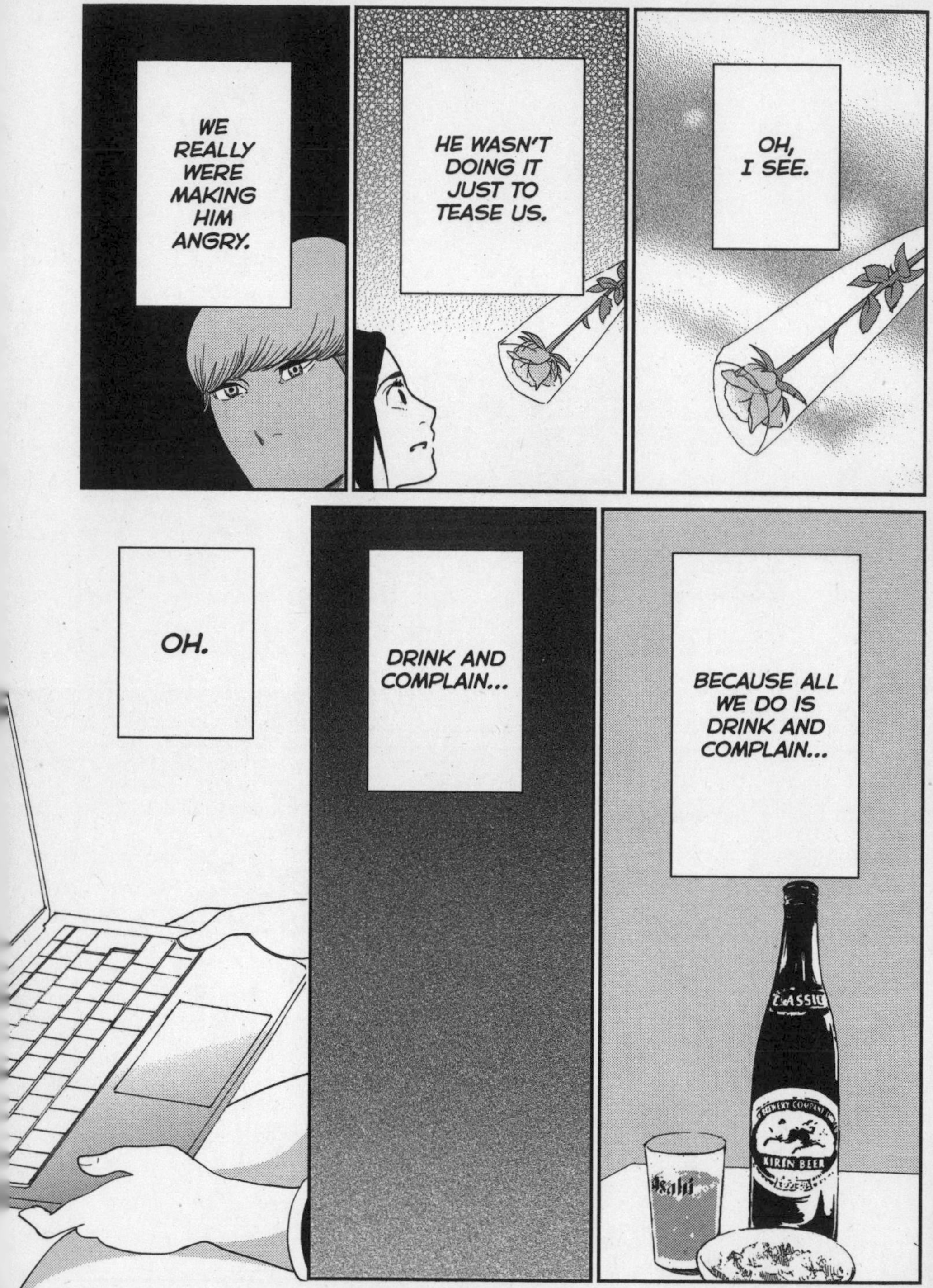
OH, I SEE.
HE WASN'T DOING IT JUST TO TEASE US.
WE REALLY WERE MAKING HIM ANGRY.
BECAUSE ALL WE DO IS DRINK AND COMPLAIN...
KIRIN BEER
DRINK AND COMPLAIN...
OH.

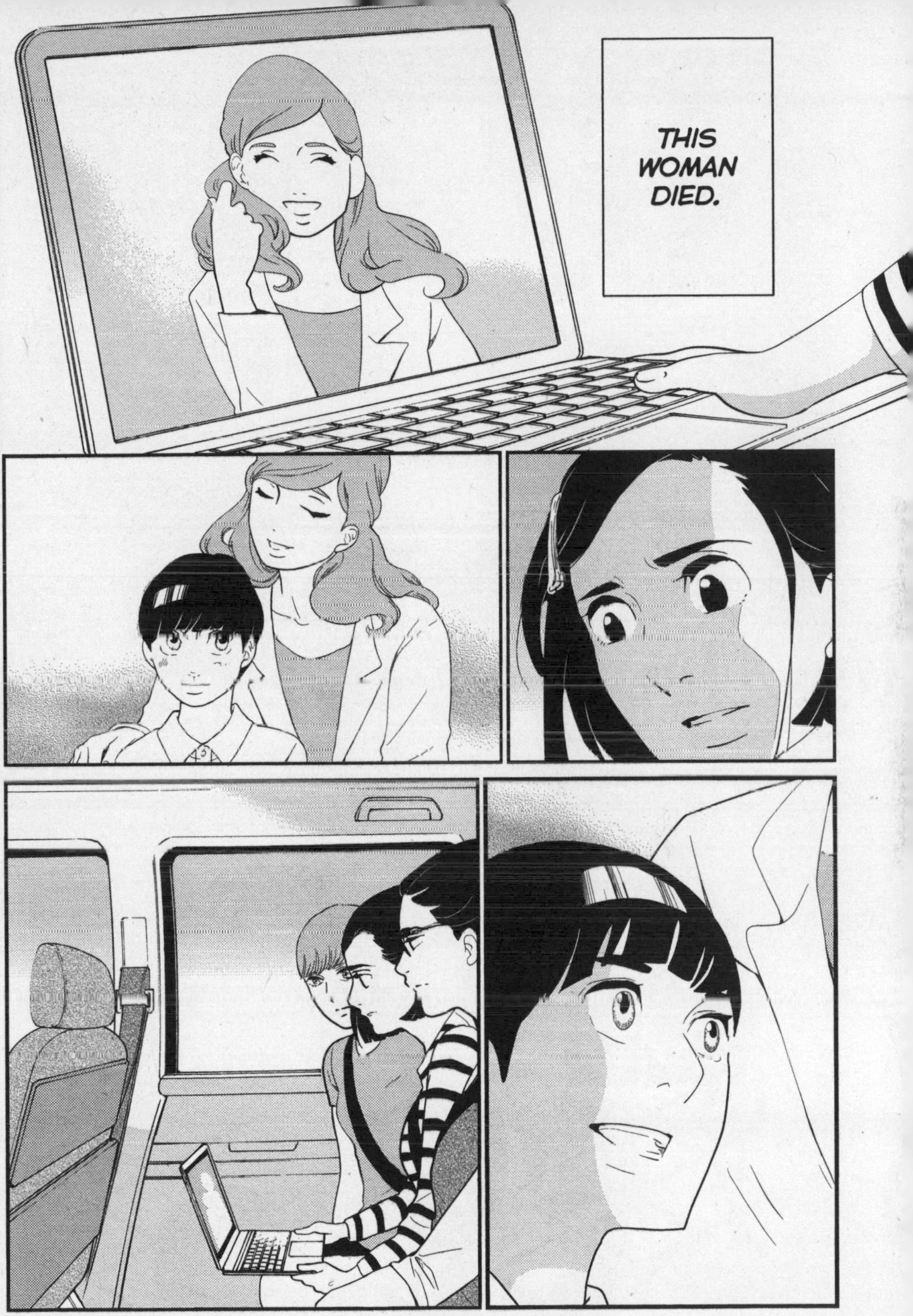
THIS WOMAN DIED.

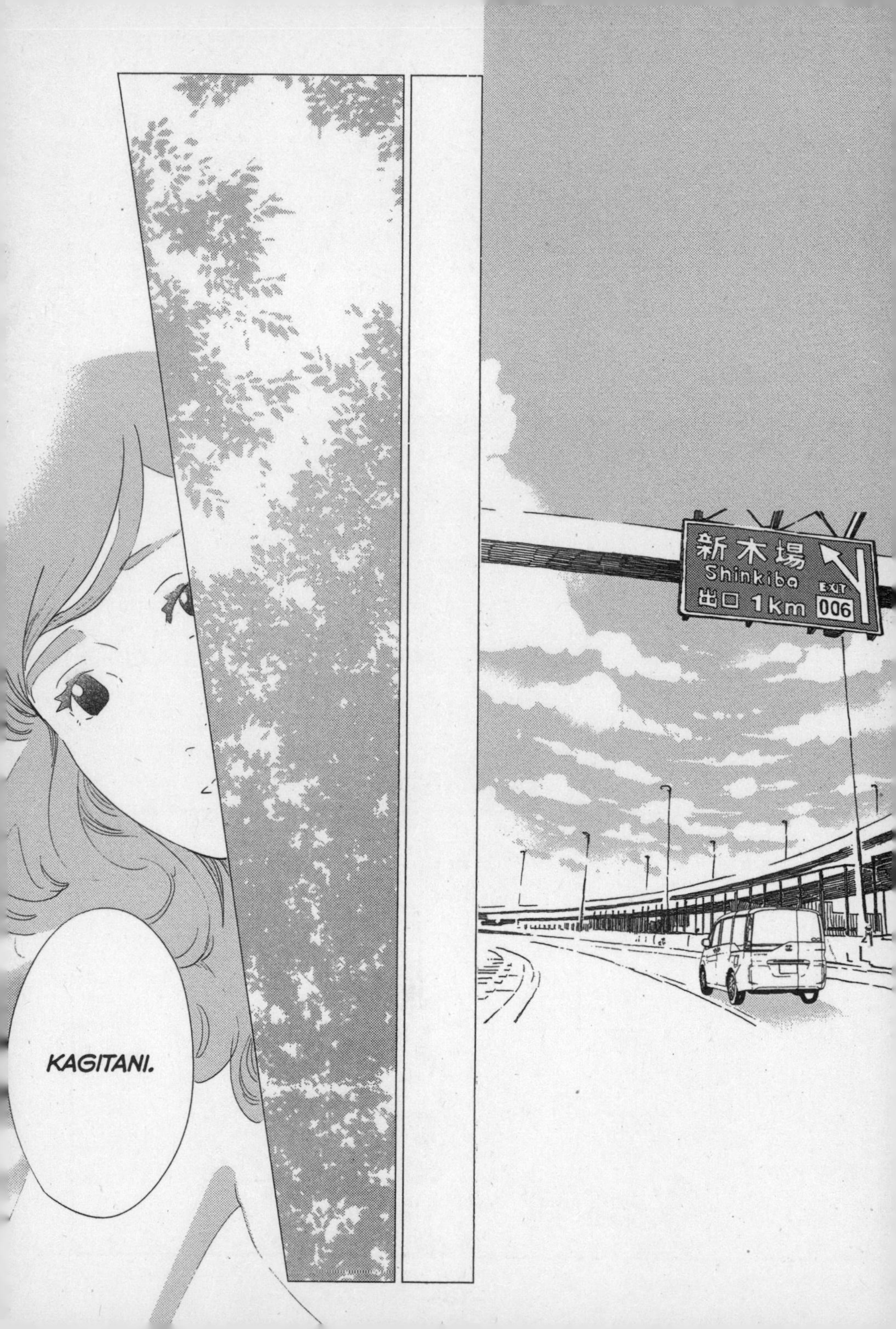
新木場
Shinkiba
EXIT
出口 1km
006
KAGITANI.

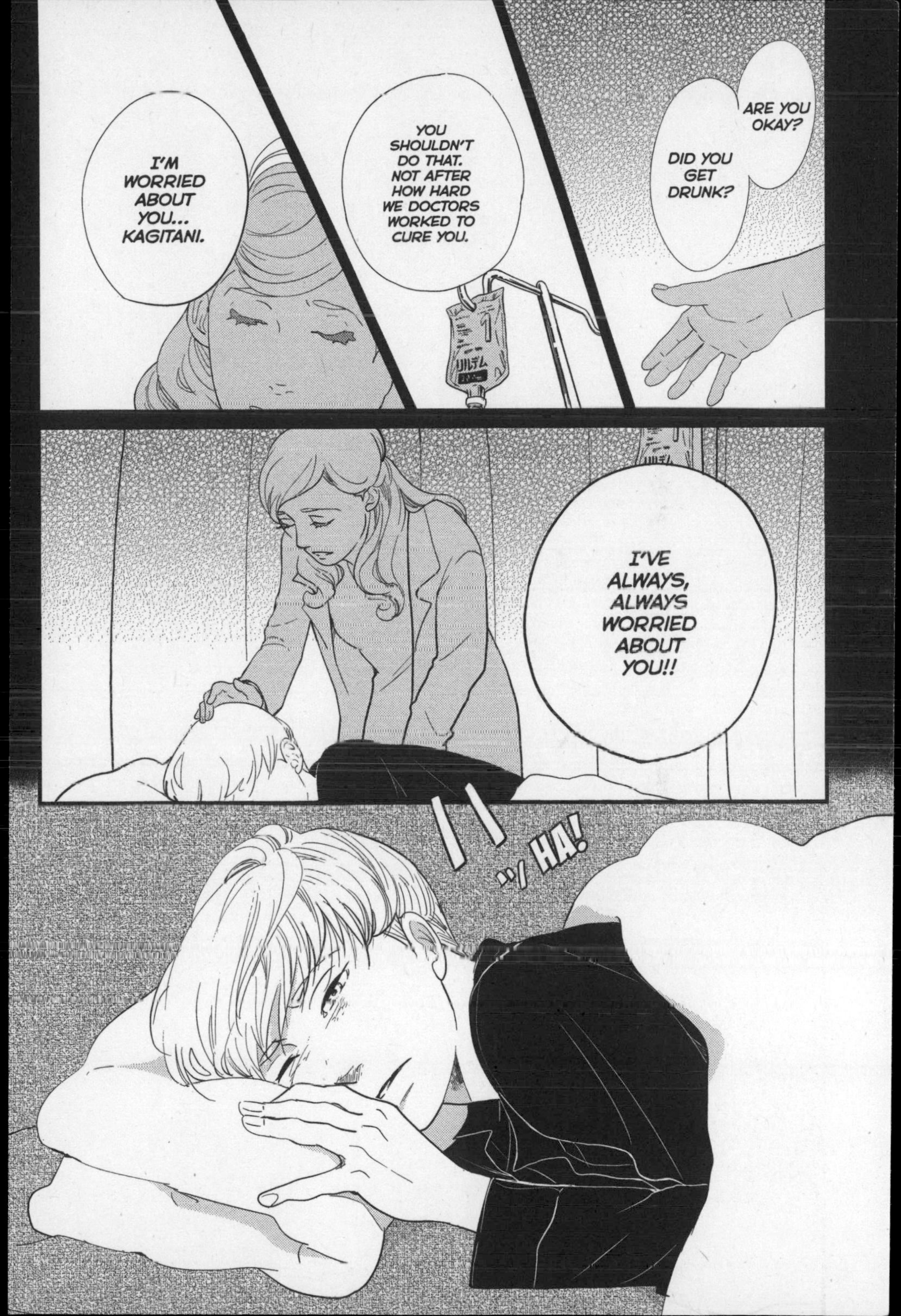
ARE YOU OKAY?
DID YOU GET DRUNK?
YOU SHOULDN'T DO THAT. NOT AFTER HOW HARD WE DOCTORS WORKED TO CURE YOU.
リルデム
I'M WORRIED ABOUT YOU... KAGITANI.
I'VE ALWAYS, ALWAYS WORRIED ABOUT YOU!!
HA!

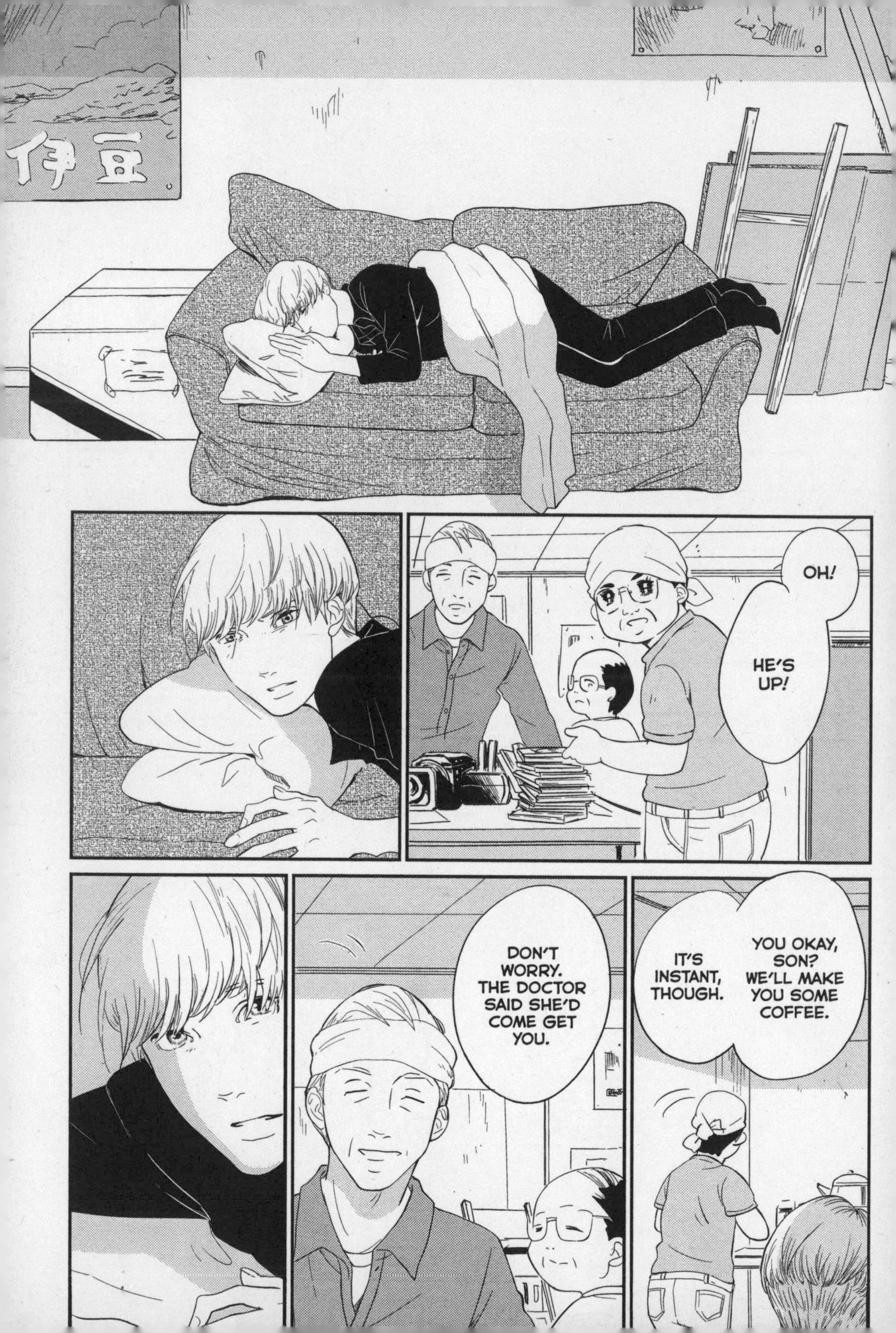
伊豆
OH!
HE'S UP!
YOU OKAY, SON? WE'LL MAKE YOU SOME COFFEE.
IT'S INSTANT, THOUGH.
DON'T WORRY. THE DOCTOR SAID SHE'D COME GET YOU.

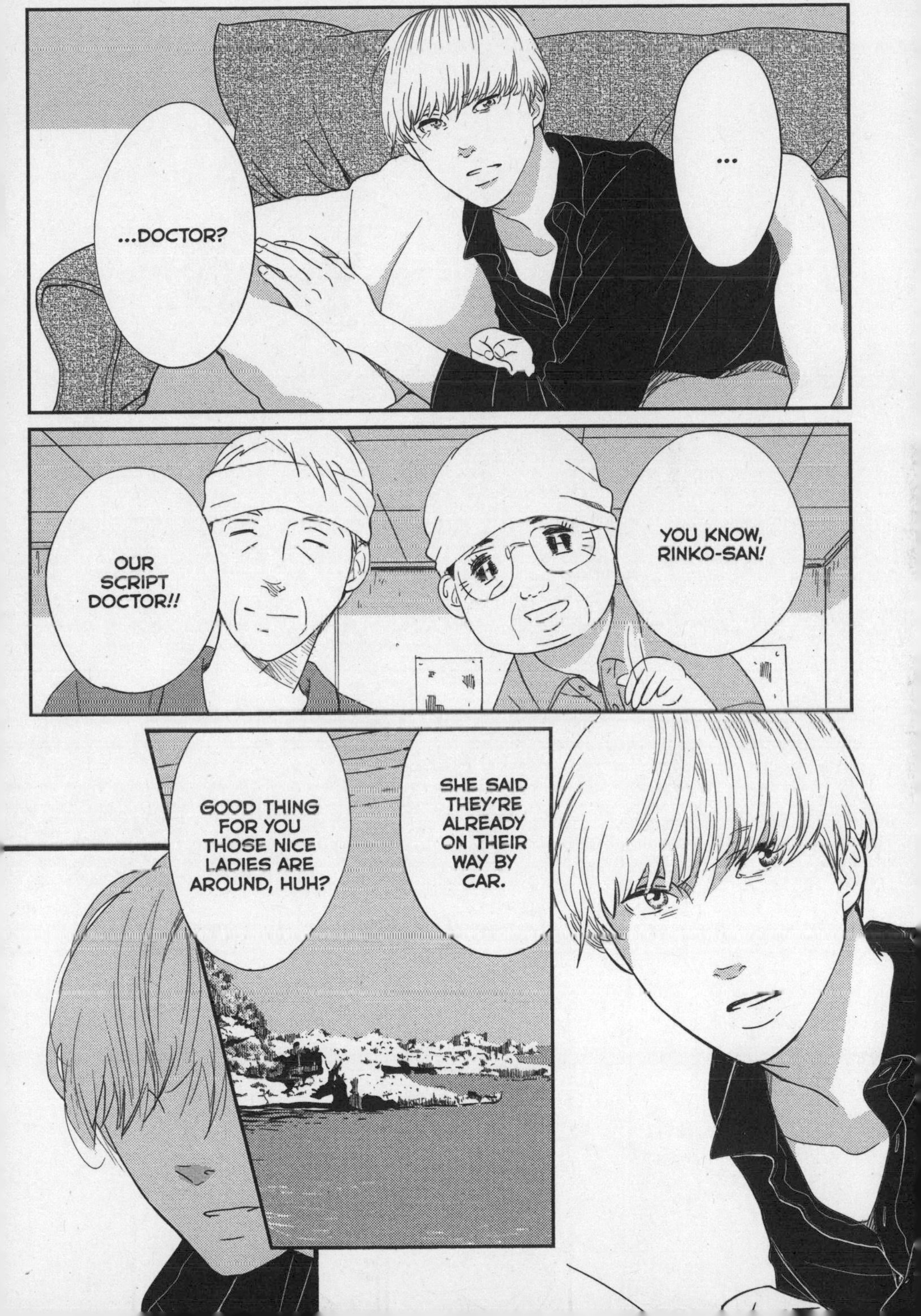
...
...DOCTOR?
YOU KNOW, RINKO-SAN!
OUR SCRIPT DOCTOR!!
SHE SAID THEY'RE ALREADY ON THEIR WAY BY CAR.
GOOD THING FOR YOU THOSE NICE LADIES ARE AROUND, HUH?

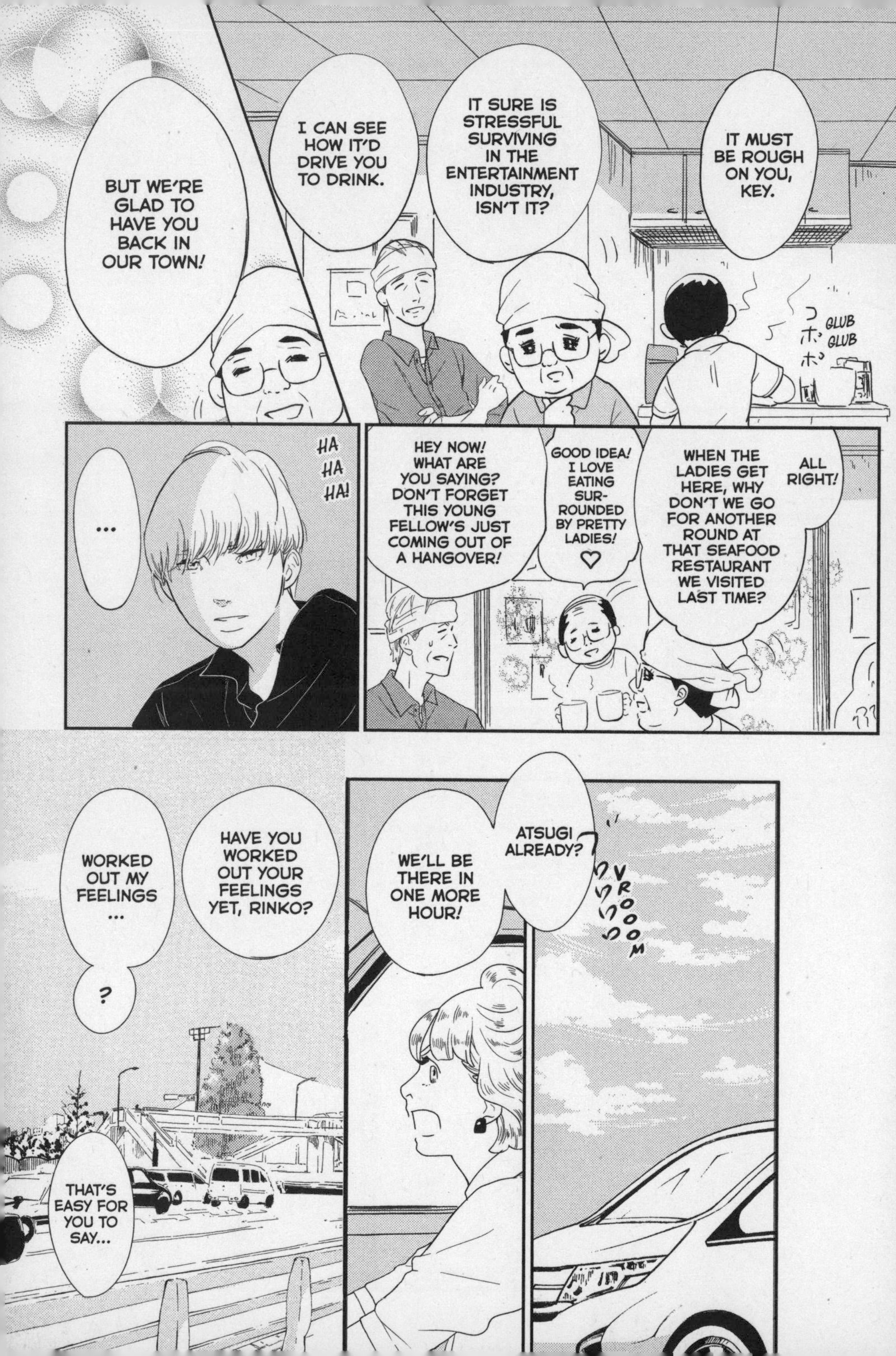
IT MUST BE ROUGH ON YOU, KEY.
コポポ
GLUB GLUB
IT SURE IS STRESSFUL SURVIVING IN THE ENTERTAINMENT INDUSTRY, ISN'T IT?
I CAN SEE HOW IT'D DRIVE YOU TO DRINK.
BUT WE'RE GLAD TO HAVE YOU BACK IN OUR TOWN!
ALL RIGHT!
WHEN THE LADIES GET HERE, WHY DON'T WE GO FOR ANOTHER ROUND AT THAT SEAFOOD RESTAURANT WE VISITED LAST TIME?
GOOD IDEA! I LOVE EATING SUR-ROUNDED BY PRETTY LADIES! ♡
HEY NOW! WHAT ARE YOU SAYING? DON'T FORGET THIS YOUNG FELLOW'S JUST COMING OUT OF A HANGOVER!
HA HA HA!
...
ATSUGI ALREADY?
VROOOOM
WE'LL BE THERE IN ONE MORE HOUR!
HAVE YOU WORKED OUT YOUR FEELINGS YET, RINKO?
WORKED OUT MY FEELINGS ...
?
THAT'S EASY FOR YOU TO SAY...

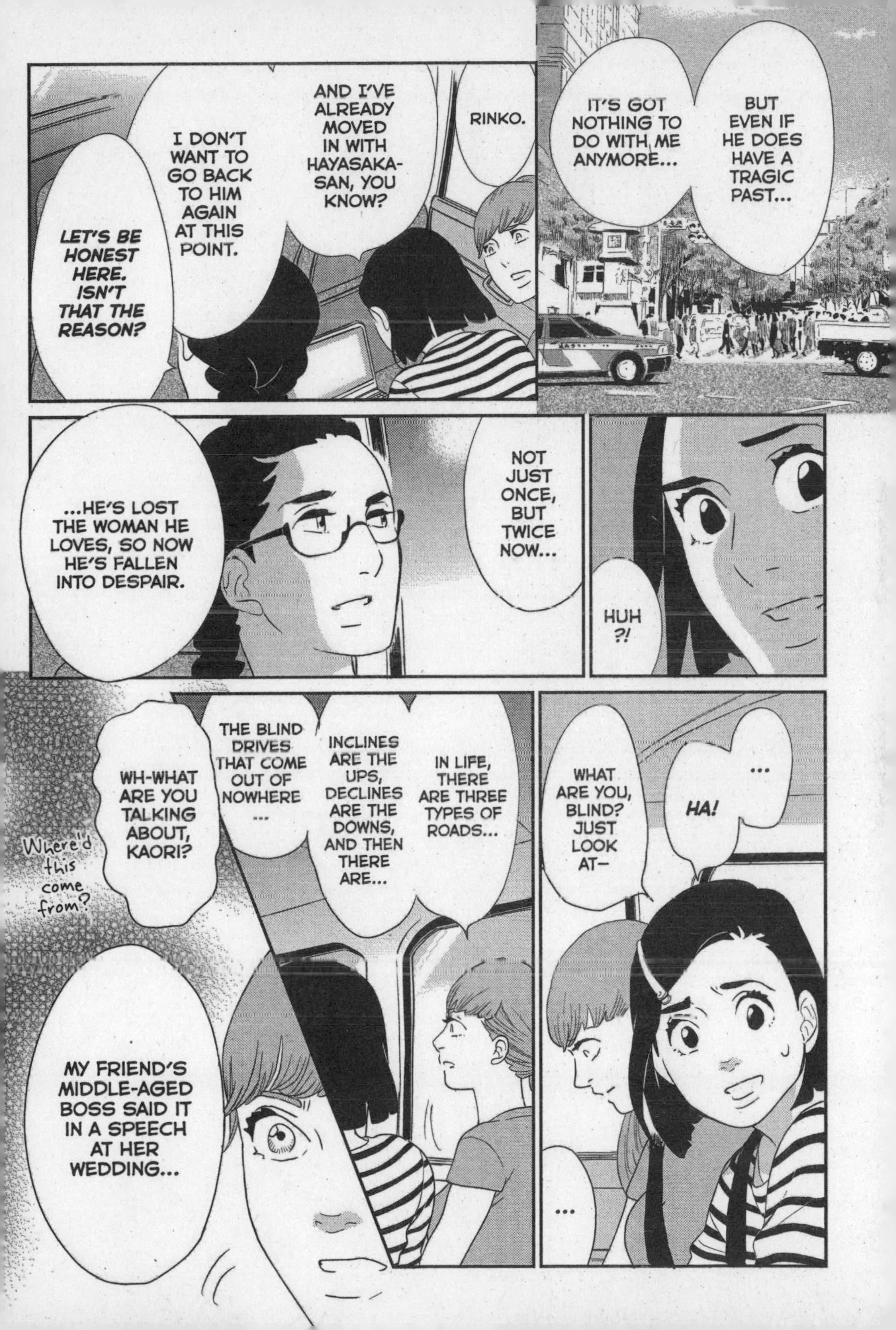
BUT EVEN IF HE DOES HAVE A TRAGIC PAST...
IT'S GOT NOTHING TO DO WITH ME ANYMORE...
RINKO.
AND I'VE ALREADY MOVED IN WITH HAYASAKA-SAN, YOU KNOW?
I DON'T WANT TO GO BACK TO HIM AGAIN AT THIS POINT.
LET'S BE HONEST HERE. ISN'T THAT THE REASON?
HUH ?!
NOT JUST ONCE, BUT TWICE NOW...
...HE'S LOST THE WOMAN HE LOVES, SO NOW HE'S FALLEN INTO DESPAIR.
...
HA!
WHAT ARE YOU, BLIND? JUST LOOK AT—
...
IN LIFE, THERE ARE THREE TYPES OF ROADS...
INCLINES ARE THE UPS, DECLINES ARE THE DOWNS, AND THEN THERE ARE...
THE BLIND DRIVES THAT COME OUT OF NOWHERE ...
WH-WHAT ARE YOU TALKING ABOUT, KAORI?
Where'd this come from?
MY FRIEND'S MIDDLE-AGED BOSS SAID IT IN A SPEECH AT HER WEDDING...

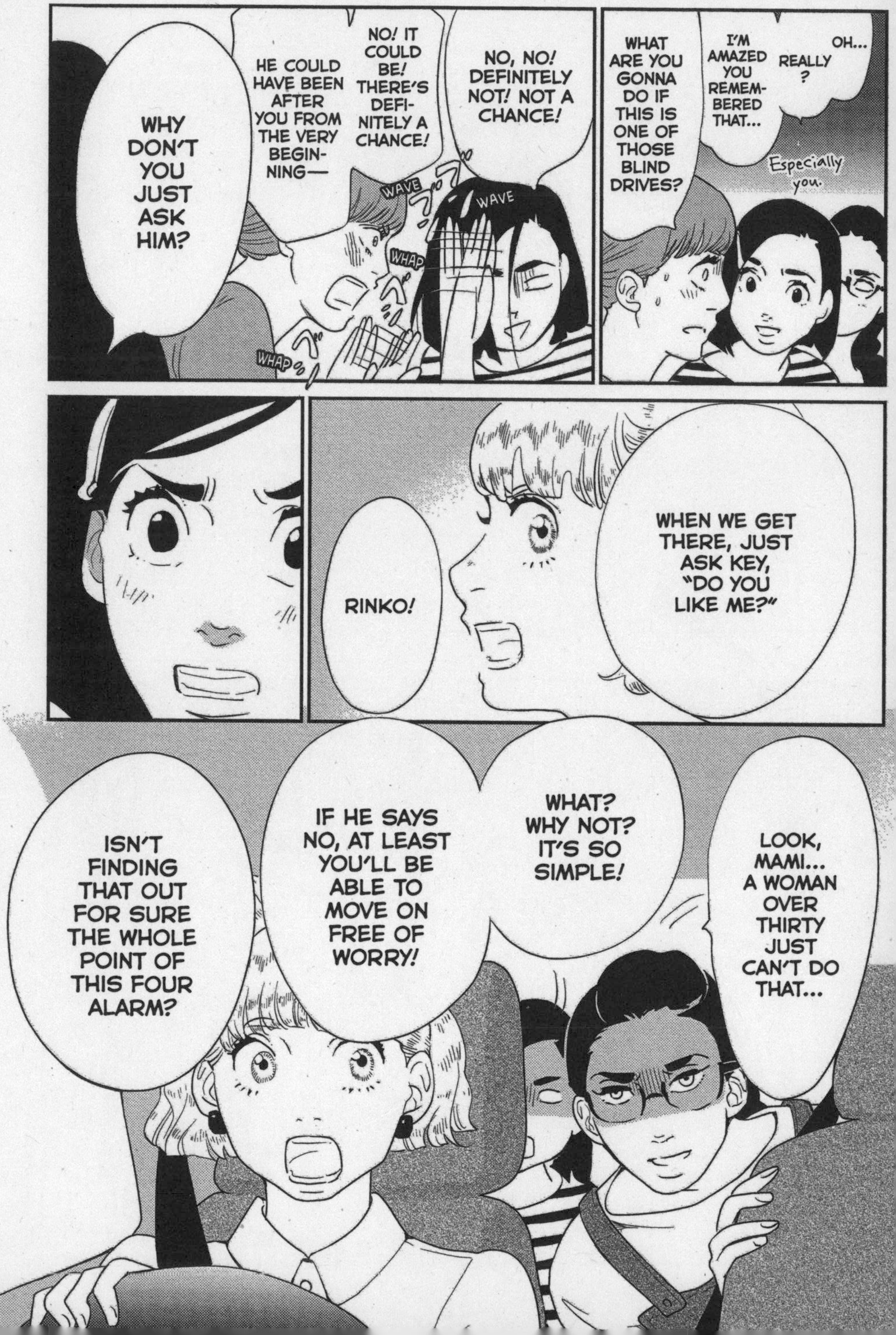
OH... REALLY?
I'M AMAZED YOU REMEMBERED THAT...
Especially you.
WHAT ARE YOU GONNA DO IF THIS IS ONE OF THOSE BLIND DRIVES?
NO, NO! DEFINITELY NOT! NOT A CHANCE!
NO! IT COULD BE! THERE'S DEFINITELY A CHANCE!
HE COULD HAVE BEEN AFTER YOU FROM THE VERY BEGINNING—
WAVE
WAVE
WHAP
WHAP
WHY DON'T YOU JUST ASK HIM?
WHEN WE GET THERE, JUST ASK KEY, "DO YOU LIKE ME?"
RINKO!
LOOK, MAMI... A WOMAN OVER THIRTY JUST CAN'T DO THAT...
WHAT? WHY NOT? IT'S SO SIMPLE!
IF HE SAYS NO, AT LEAST YOU'LL BE ABLE TO MOVE ON FREE OF WORRY!
ISN'T FINDING THAT OUT FOR SURE THE WHOLE POINT OF THIS FOUR ALARM?

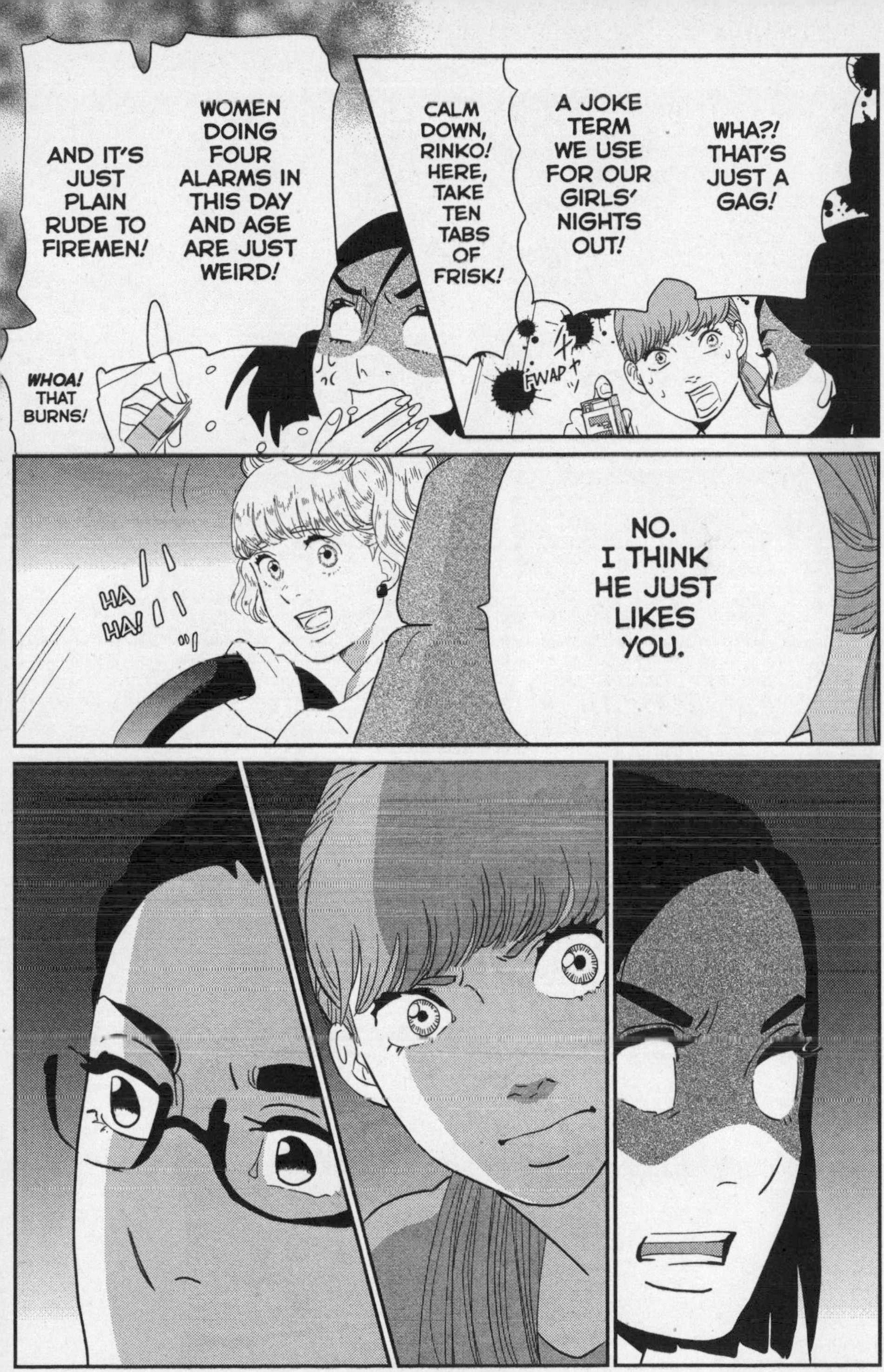
WHA?! THAT'S JUST A GAG!
A JOKE TERM WE USE FOR OUR GIRLS' NIGHTS OUT!
CALM DOWN, RINKO! HERE, TAKE TEN TABS OF FRISK!
FWAP
WOMEN DOING FOUR ALARMS IN THIS DAY AND AGE ARE JUST WEIRD!
AND IT'S JUST PLAIN RUDE TO FIREMEN!
WHOA! THAT BURNS!
NO. I THINK HE JUST LIKES YOU.
HA HA!

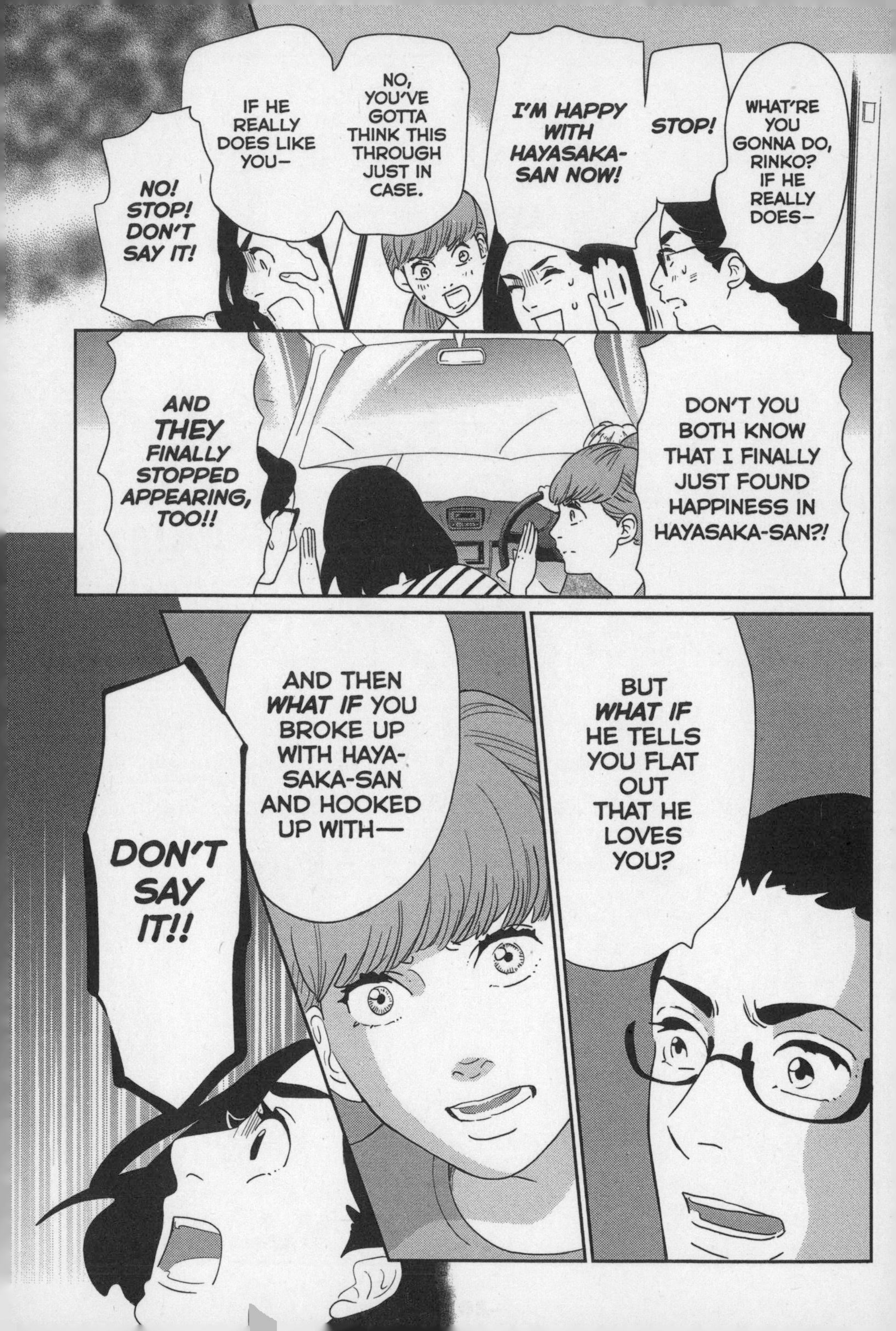
WHAT'RE YOU GONNA DO, RINKO? IF HE REALLY DOES–
STOP!
I'M HAPPY WITH HAYASAKA-SAN NOW!
NO, YOU'VE GOTTA THINK THIS THROUGH JUST IN CASE.
IF HE REALLY DOES LIKE YOU–
NO! STOP! DON'T SAY IT!
DON'T YOU BOTH KNOW THAT I FINALLY JUST FOUND HAPPINESS IN HAYASAKA-SAN?!
AND THEY FINALLY STOPPED APPEARING, TOO!!
BUT WHAT IF HE TELLS YOU FLAT OUT THAT HE LOVES YOU?
AND THEN WHAT IF YOU BROKE UP WITH HAYASAKA-SAN AND HOOKED UP WITH—
DON'T SAY IT!!

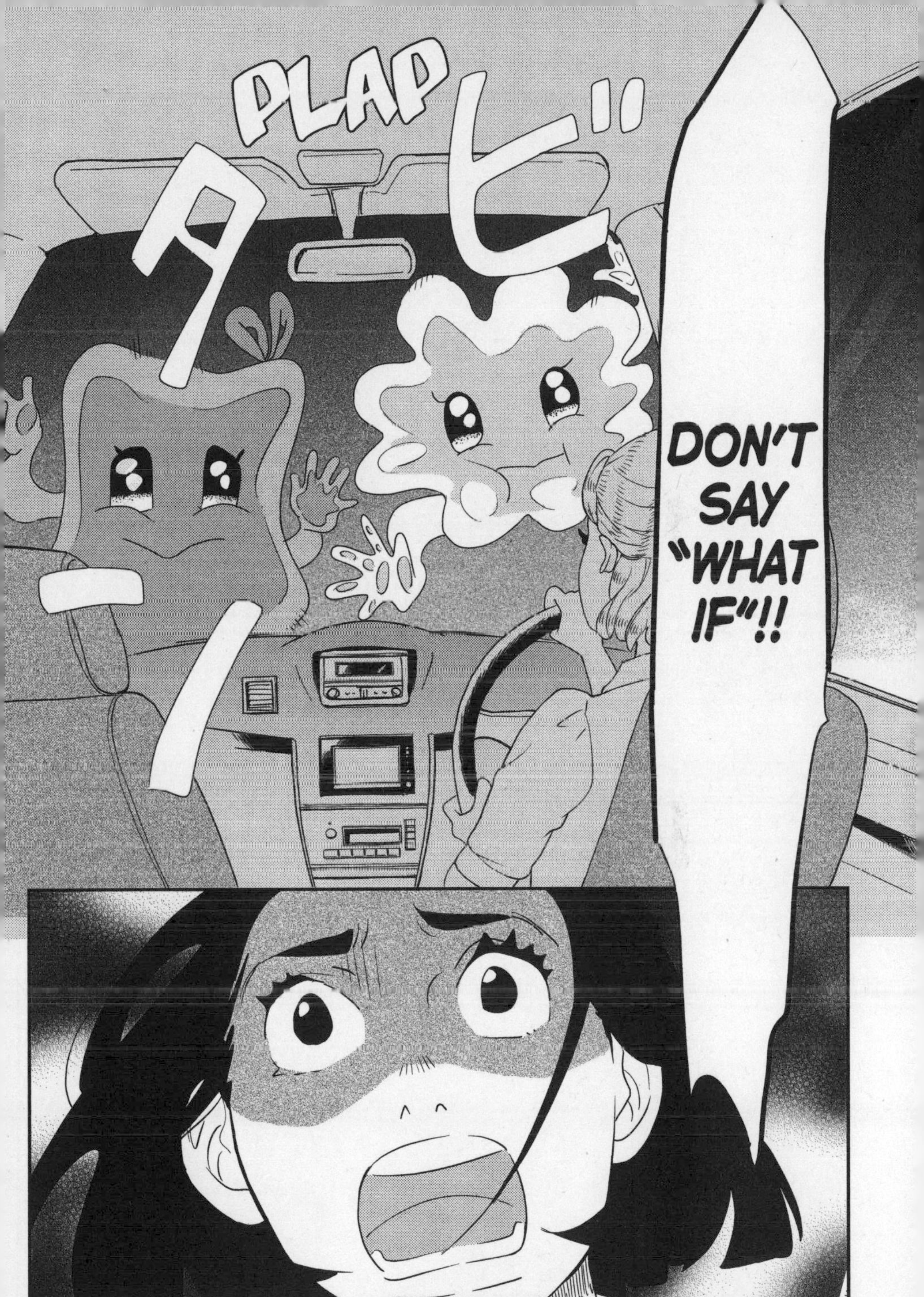
PLAP
DON'T SAY "WHAT IF"!!

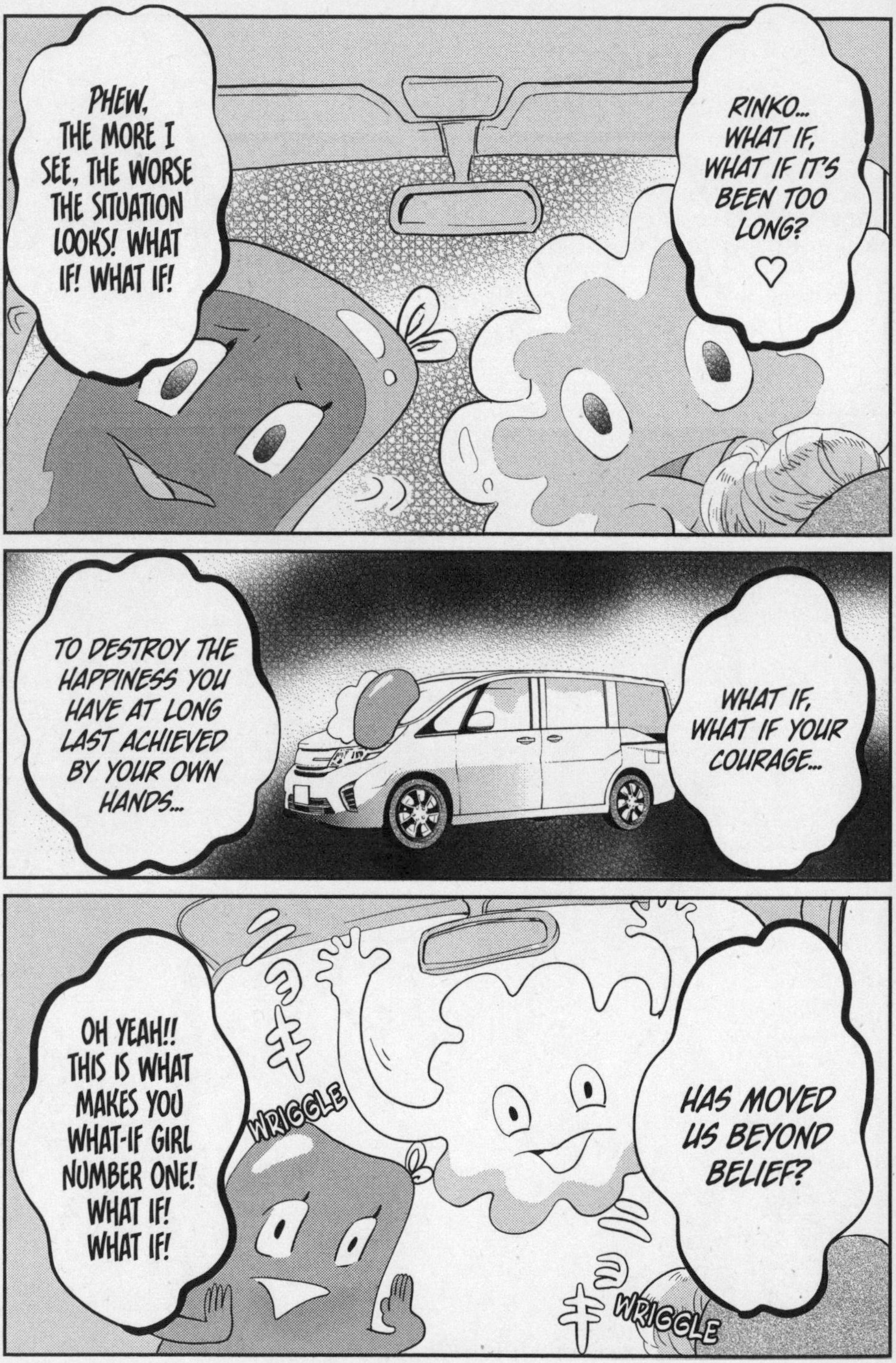
RINKO... WHAT IF, WHAT IF IT'S BEEN TOO LONG? ♡
PHEW, THE MORE I SEE, THE WORSE THE SITUATION LOOKS! WHAT IF! WHAT IF!
WHAT IF, WHAT IF YOUR COURAGE...
TO DESTROY THE HAPPINESS YOU HAVE AT LONG LAST ACHIEVED BY YOUR OWN HANDS...
HAS MOVED US BEYOND BELIEF?
WRIGGLE
WRIGGLE
OH YEAH!! THIS IS WHAT MAKES YOU WHAT-IF GIRL NUMBER ONE! WHAT IF! WHAT IF!

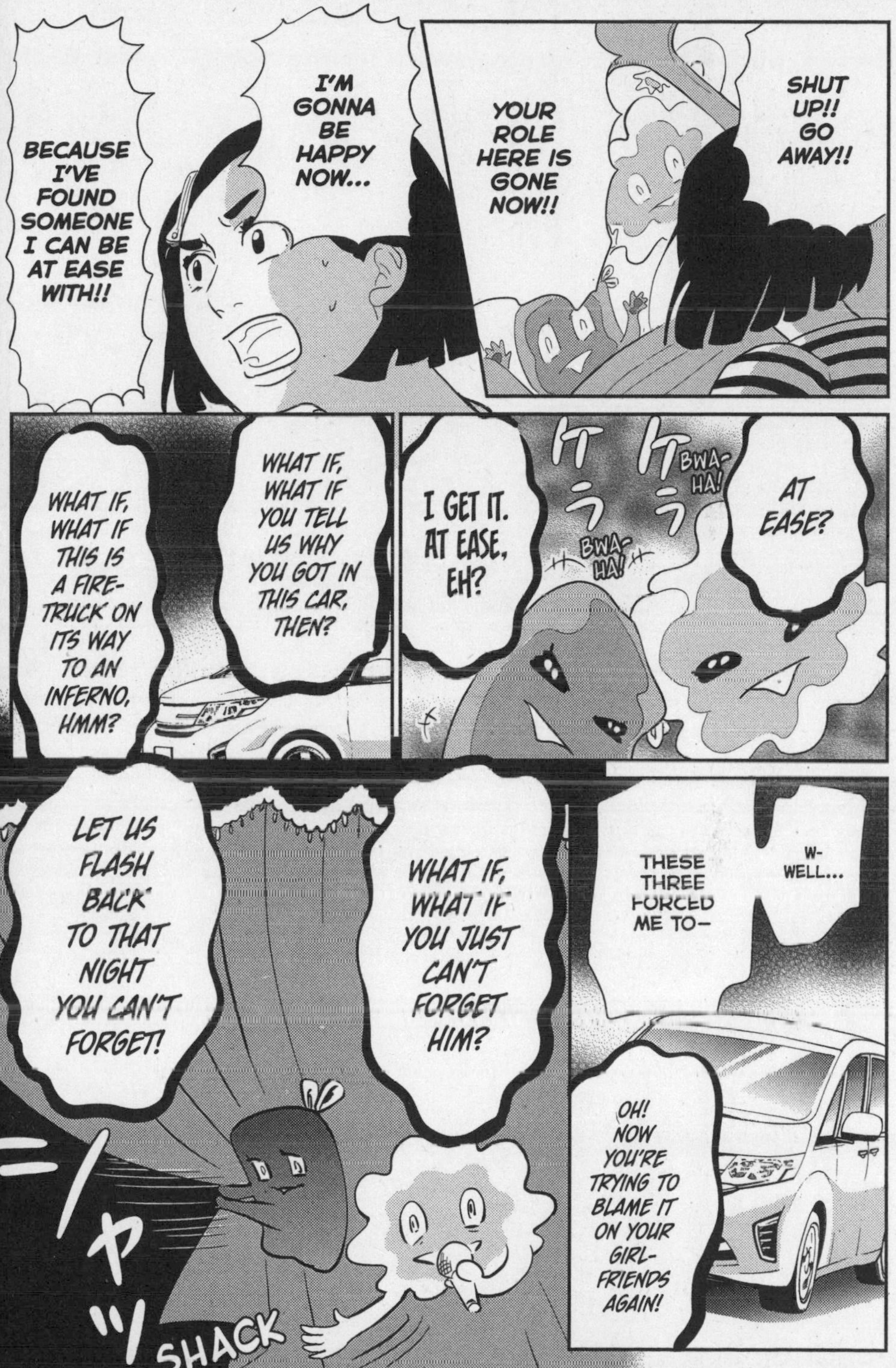
SHUT UP!! GO AWAY!!
YOUR ROLE HERE IS GONE NOW!!
I'M GONNA BE HAPPY NOW...
BECAUSE I'VE FOUND SOMEONE I CAN BE AT EASE WITH!!
AT EASE?
ケラケラ
BWA-HA!
BWA-HA!
I GET IT. AT EASE, EH?
WHAT IF, WHAT IF YOU TELL US WHY YOU GOT IN THIS CAR, THEN?
WHAT IF, WHAT IF THIS IS A FIRE-TRUCK ON ITS WAY TO AN INFERNO, HMM?
W-WELL...
THESE THREE FORCED ME TO—
OH! NOW YOU'RE TRYING TO BLAME IT ON YOUR GIRL-FRIENDS AGAIN!
WHAT IF, WHAT IF YOU JUST CAN'T FORGET HIM?
LET US FLASH BACK TO THAT NIGHT YOU CAN'T FORGET!
ニヤッ
SHACK

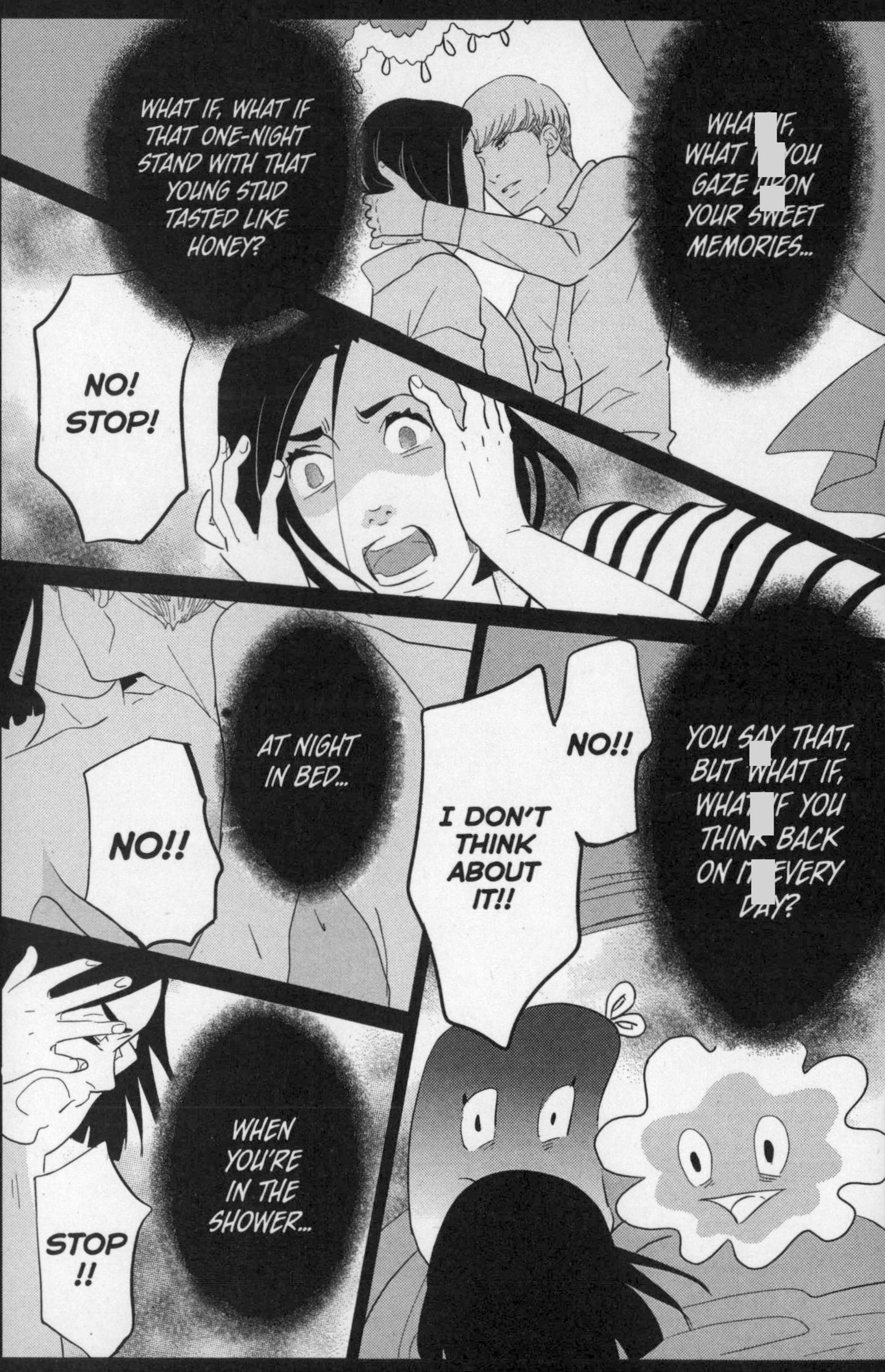
WHAT IF, WHAT IF YOU GAZE UPON YOUR SWEET MEMORIES...
WHAT IF, WHAT IF THAT ONE-NIGHT STAND WITH THAT YOUNG STUD TASTED LIKE HONEY?
NO! STOP!
YOU SAY THAT, BUT WHAT IF, WHAT IF YOU THINK BACK ON IT EVERY DAY?
NO!!
I DON'T THINK ABOUT IT!!
AT NIGHT IN BED...
NO!!
WHEN YOU'RE IN THE SHOWER...
STOP!!

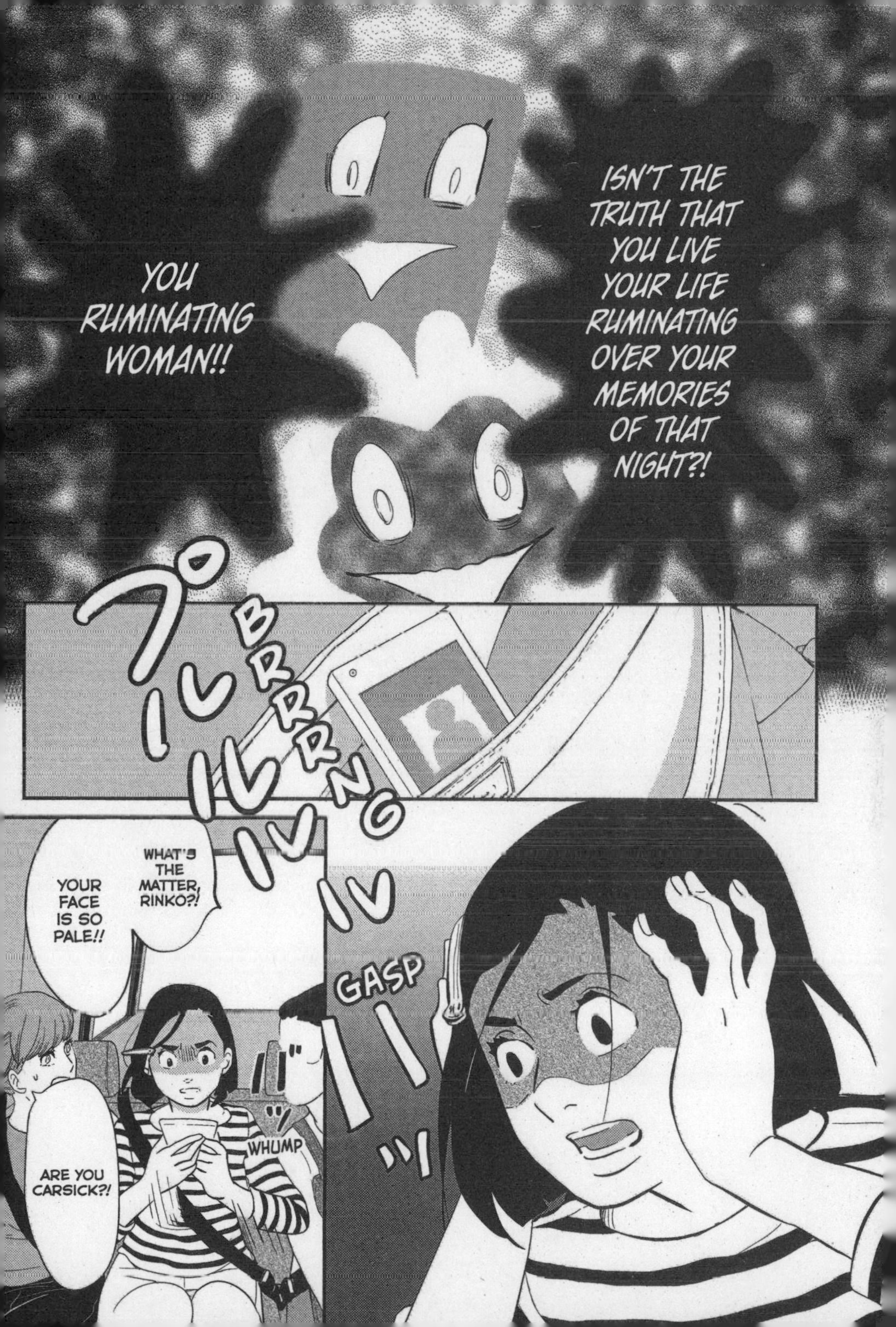
ISN'T THE TRUTH THAT YOU LIVE YOUR LIFE RUMINATING OVER YOUR MEMORIES OF THAT NIGHT?!
YOU RUMINATING WOMAN!!
BRRRRNG
GASP
WHAT'S THE MATTER, RINKO?!
YOUR FACE IS SO PALE!!
WHUMP
ARE YOU CARSICK?!

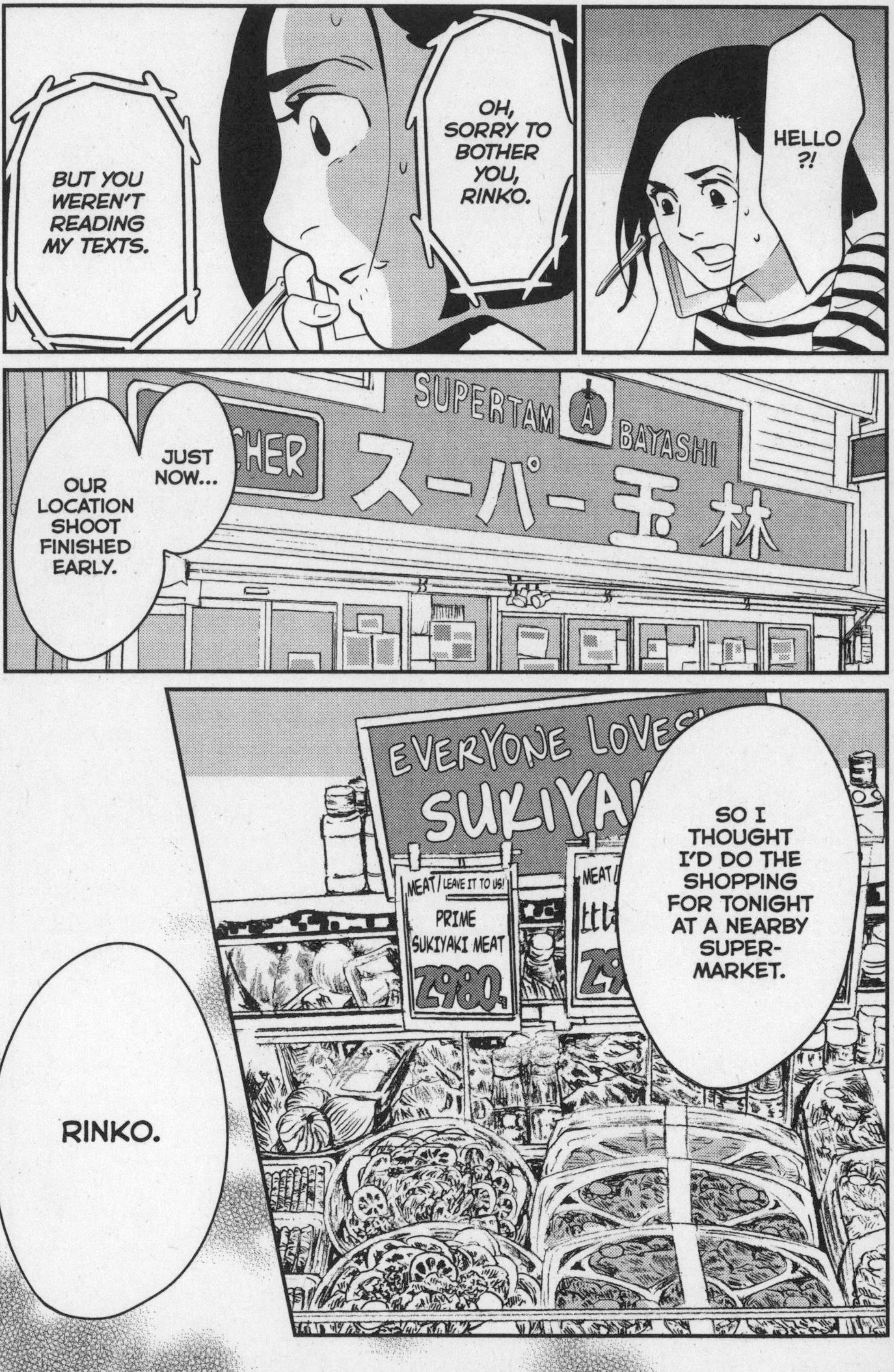
HELLO ?!
OH, SORRY TO BOTHER YOU, RINKO.
BUT YOU WEREN'T READING MY TEXTS.
SUPERTAM A BAYASHI
スーパー玉林
CHER
JUST NOW...
OUR LOCATION SHOOT FINISHED EARLY.
EVERYONE LOVES
SO I THOUGHT I'D DO THE SHOPPING FOR TONIGHT AT A NEARBY SUPER-MARKET.
MEAT / LEAVE IT TO US!
PRIME SUKIYAKI MEAT
2980
RINKO.

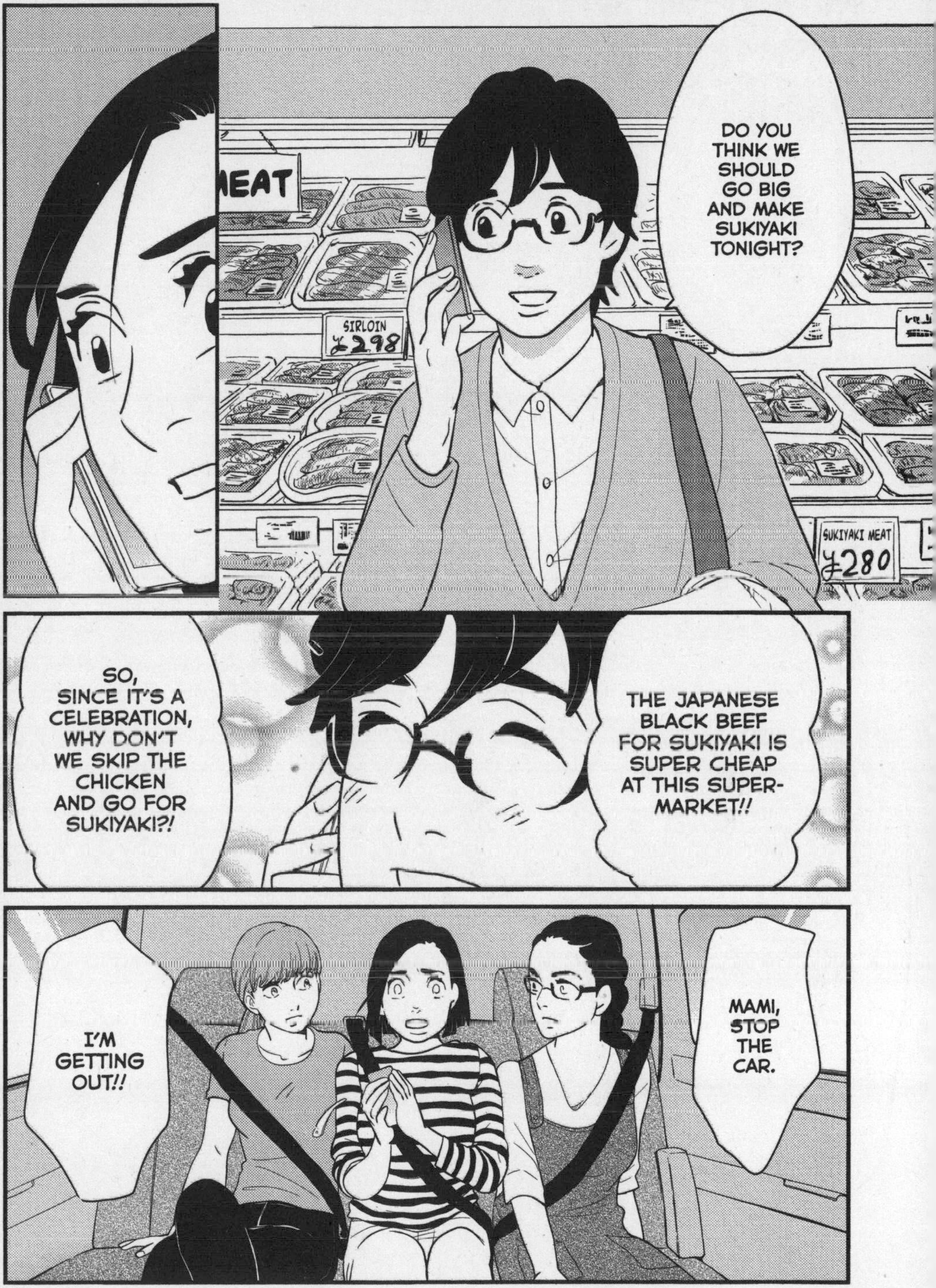
DO YOU THINK WE SHOULD GO BIG AND MAKE SUKIYAKI TONIGHT?
MEAT
SIRLOIN ¥298
SUKIYAKI MEAT ¥280
THE JAPANESE BLACK BEEF FOR SUKIYAKI IS SUPER CHEAP AT THIS SUPER-MARKET!!
SO, SINCE IT'S A CELEBRATION, WHY DON'T WE SKIP THE CHICKEN AND GO FOR SUKIYAKI?!
MAMI, STOP THE CAR.
I'M GETTING OUT!!

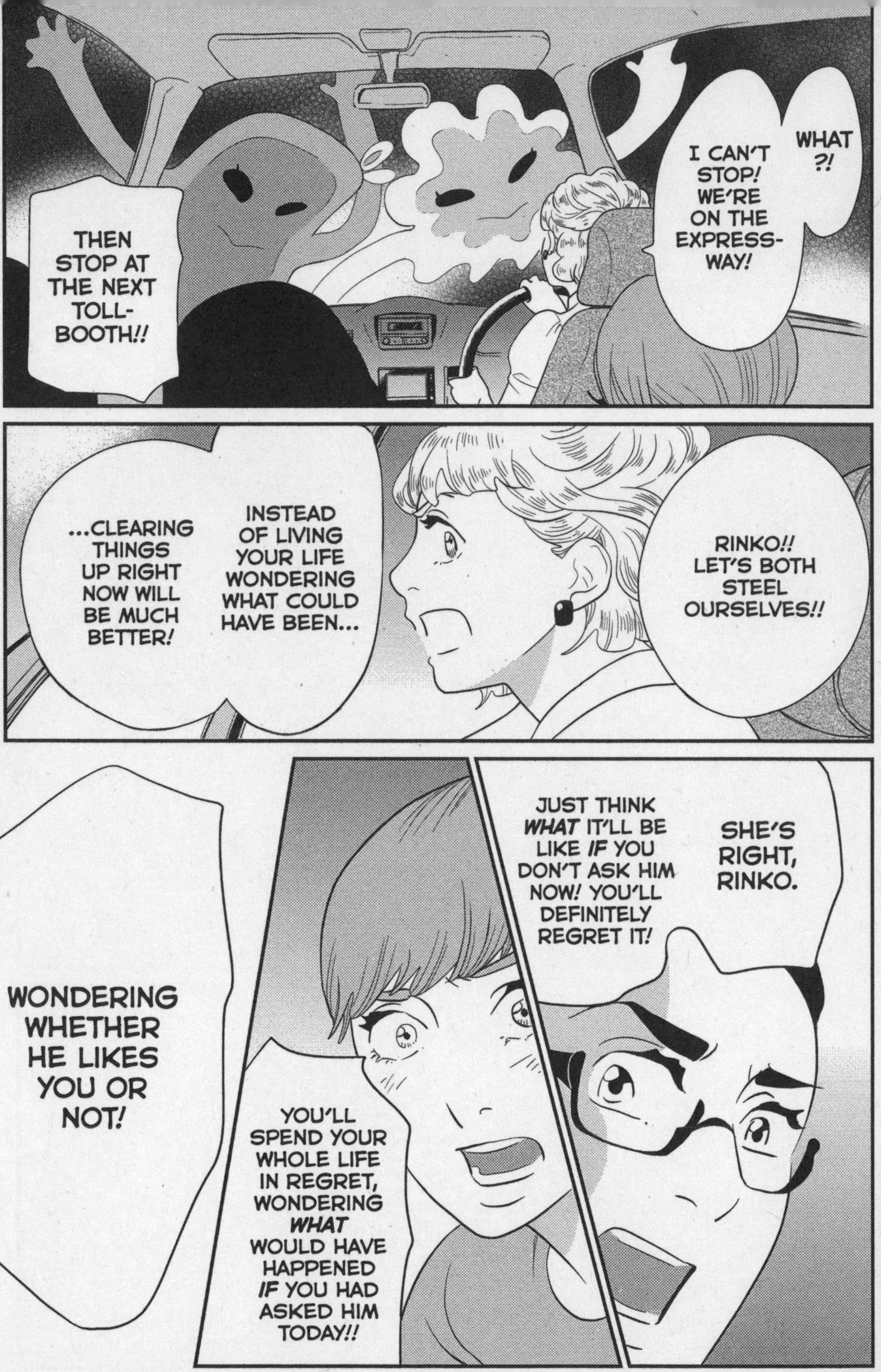
WHAT?!
I CAN'T STOP! WE'RE ON THE EXPRESSWAY!
THEN STOP AT THE NEXT TOLLBOOTH!!
RINKO!! LET'S BOTH STEEL OURSELVES!!
INSTEAD OF LIVING YOUR LIFE WONDERING WHAT COULD HAVE BEEN...
...CLEARING THINGS UP RIGHT NOW WILL BE MUCH BETTER!
SHE'S RIGHT, RINKO.
JUST THINK *WHAT* IT'LL BE LIKE *IF* YOU DON'T ASK HIM NOW! YOU'LL DEFINITELY REGRET IT!
YOU'LL SPEND YOUR WHOLE LIFE IN REGRET, WONDERING *WHAT* WOULD HAVE HAPPENED *IF* YOU HAD ASKED HIM TODAY!!
WONDERING WHETHER HE LIKES YOU OR NOT!

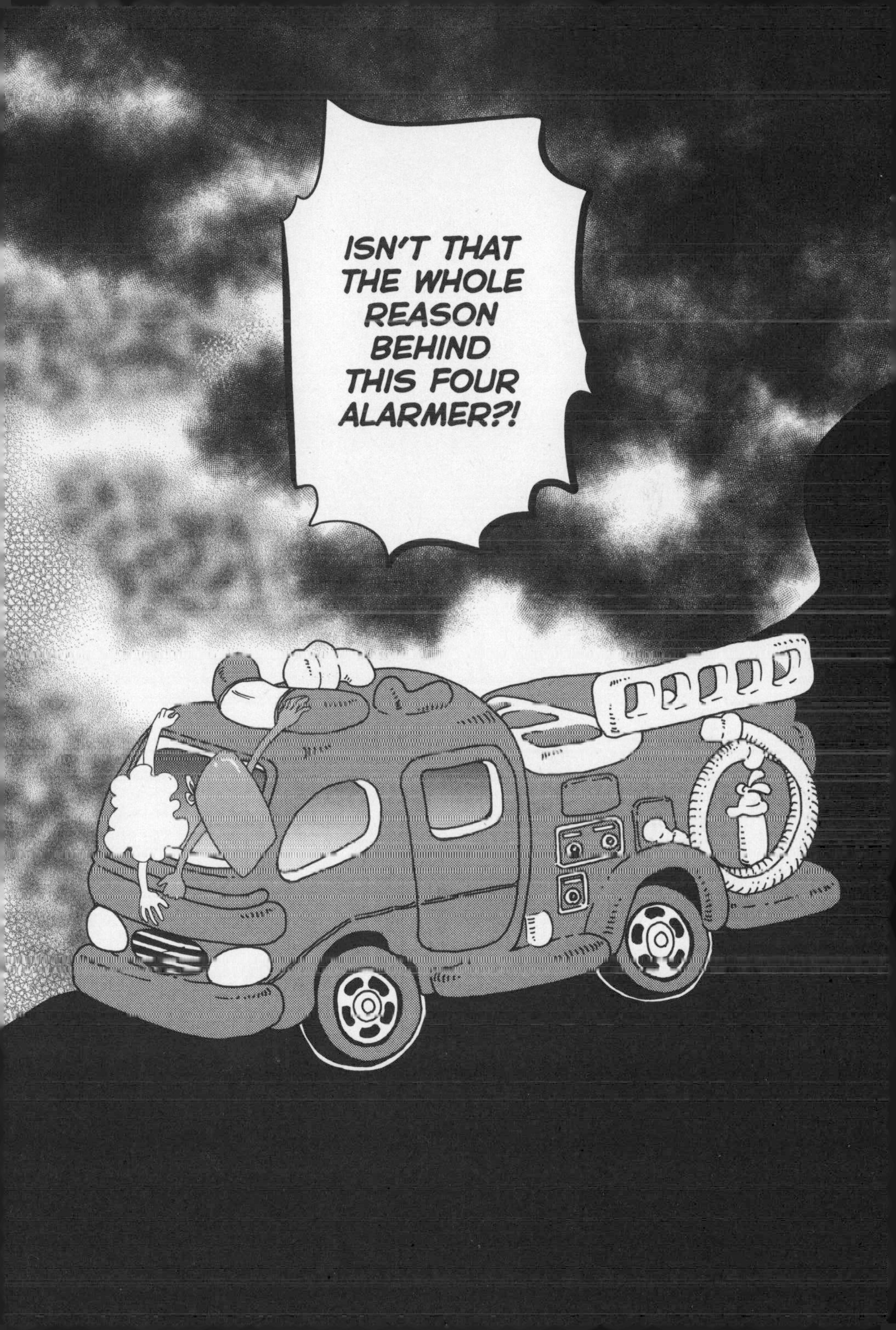
ISN'T THAT THE WHOLE REASON BEHIND THIS FOUR ALARMER?!

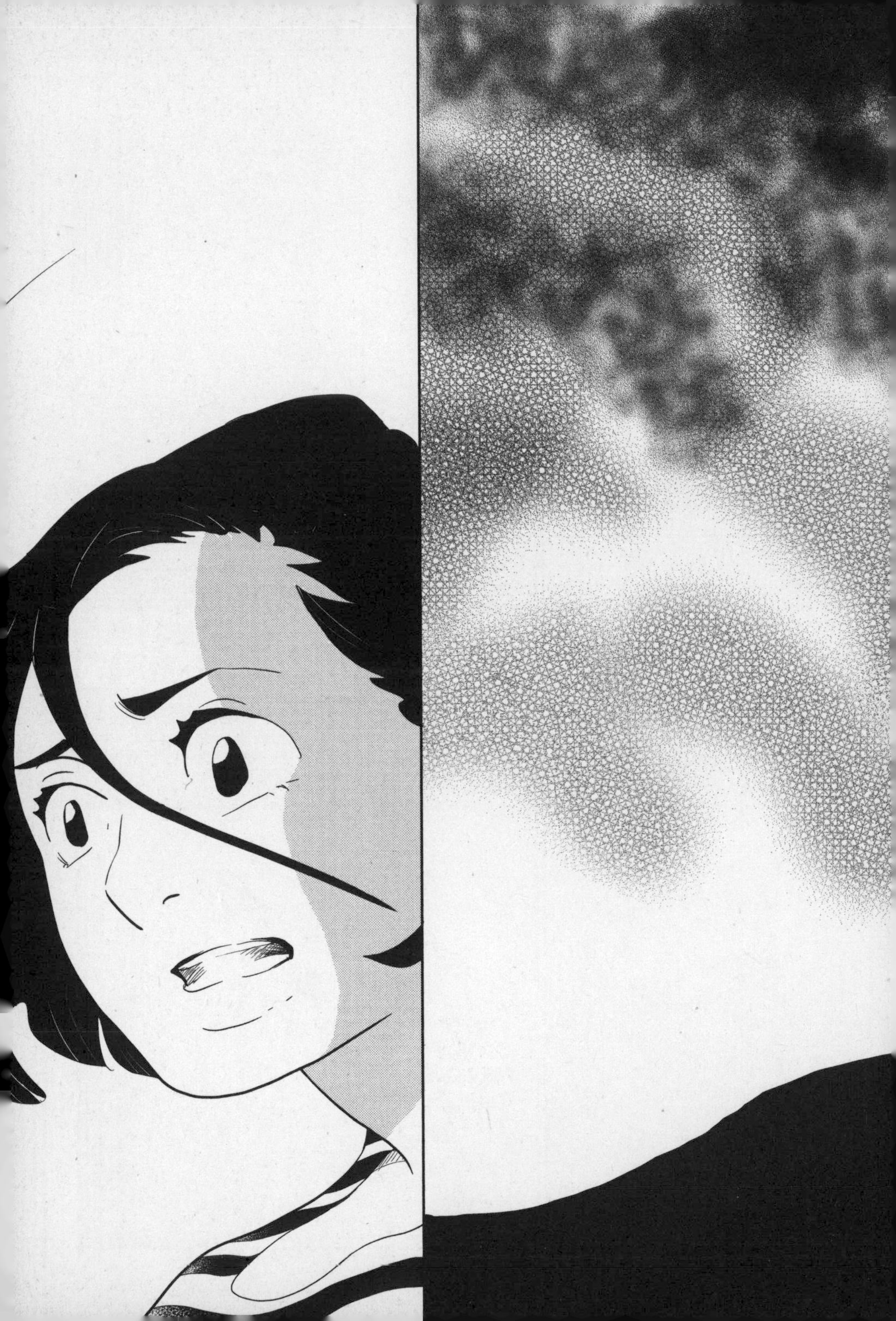

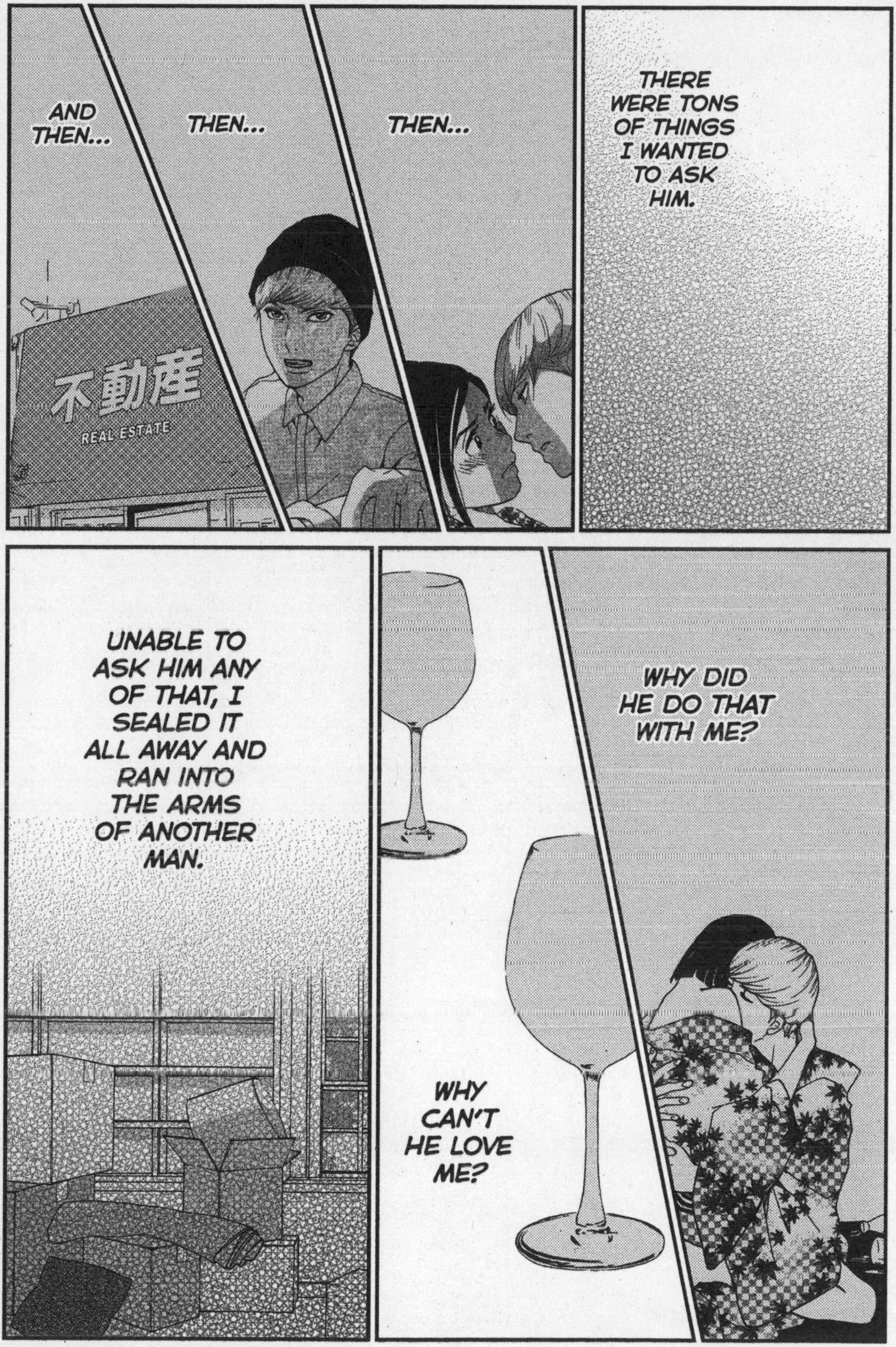
THERE WERE TONS OF THINGS I WANTED TO ASK HIM.
THEN...
THEN...
AND THEN...
不動産
REAL ESTATE
WHY DID HE DO THAT WITH ME?
WHY CAN'T HE LOVE ME?
UNABLE TO ASK HIM ANY OF THAT, I SEALED IT ALL AWAY AND RAN INTO THE ARMS OF ANOTHER MAN.

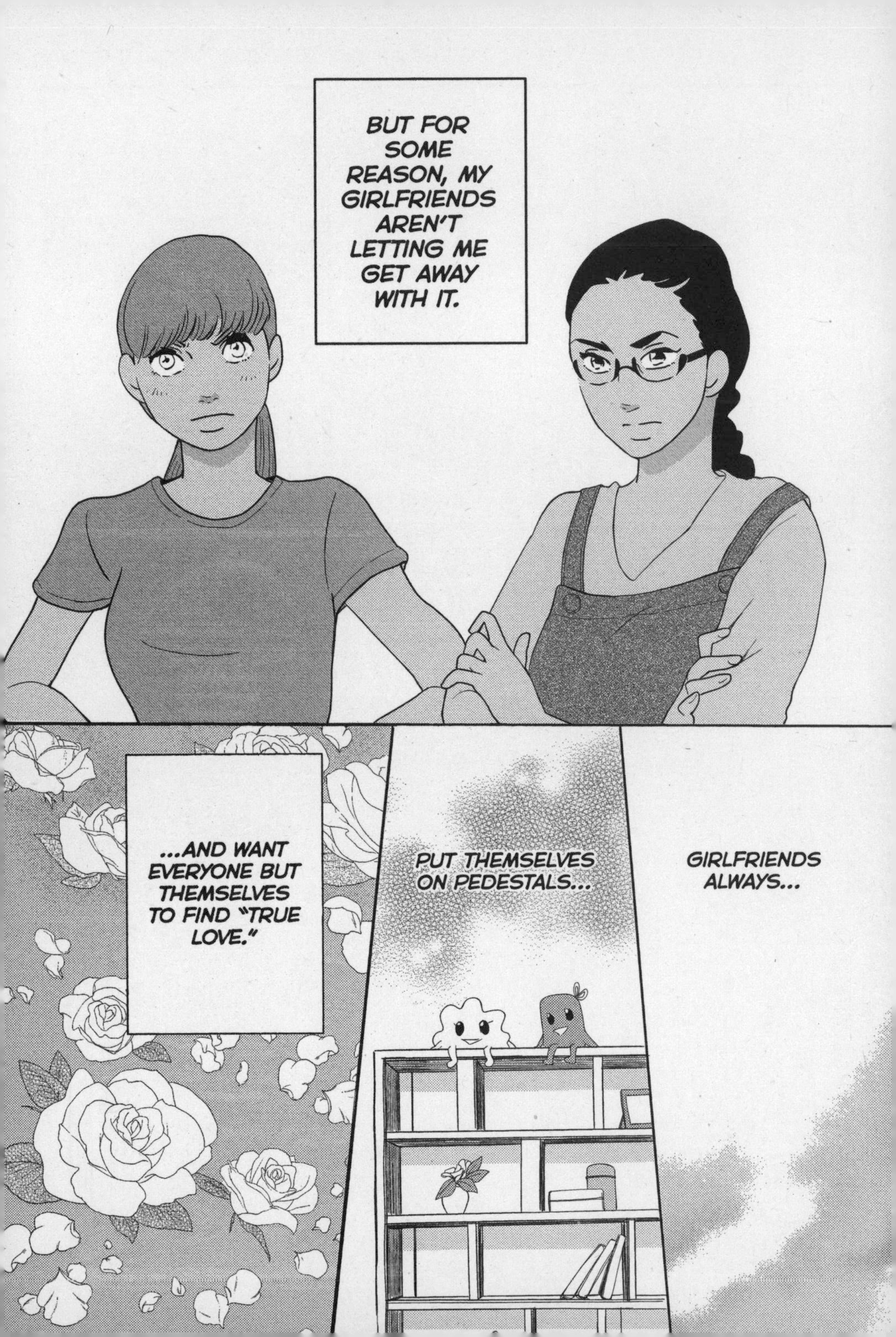
BUT FOR SOME REASON, MY GIRLFRIENDS AREN'T LETTING ME GET AWAY WITH IT.
GIRLFRIENDS ALWAYS...
PUT THEMSELVES ON PEDESTALS...
...AND WANT EVERYONE BUT THEMSELVES TO FIND "TRUE LOVE."

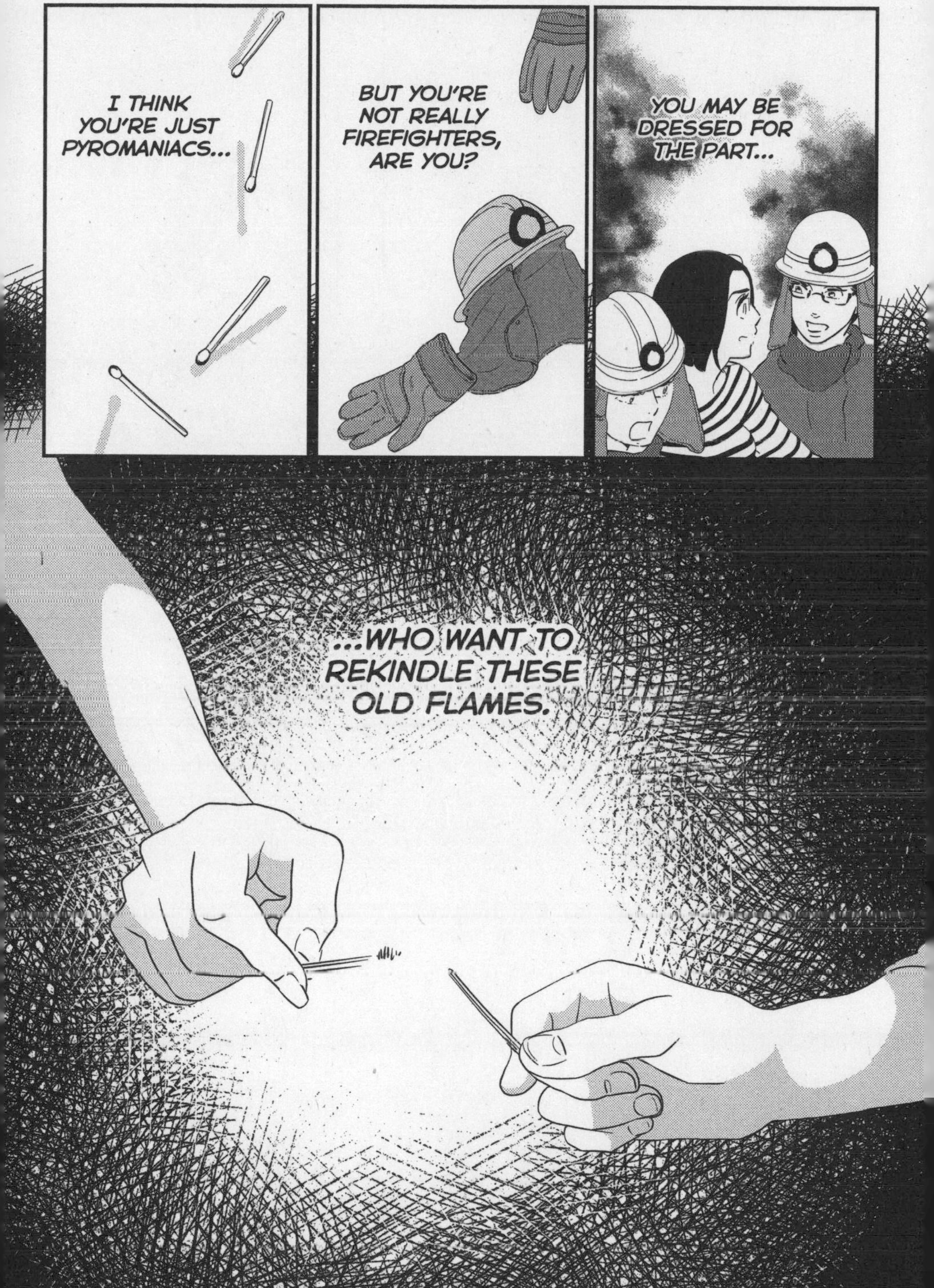
YOU MAY BE DRESSED FOR THE PART...
BUT YOU'RE NOT REALLY FIREFIGHTERS, ARE YOU?
I THINK YOU'RE JUST PYROMANIACS...
...WHO WANT TO REKINDLE THESE OLD FLAMES.

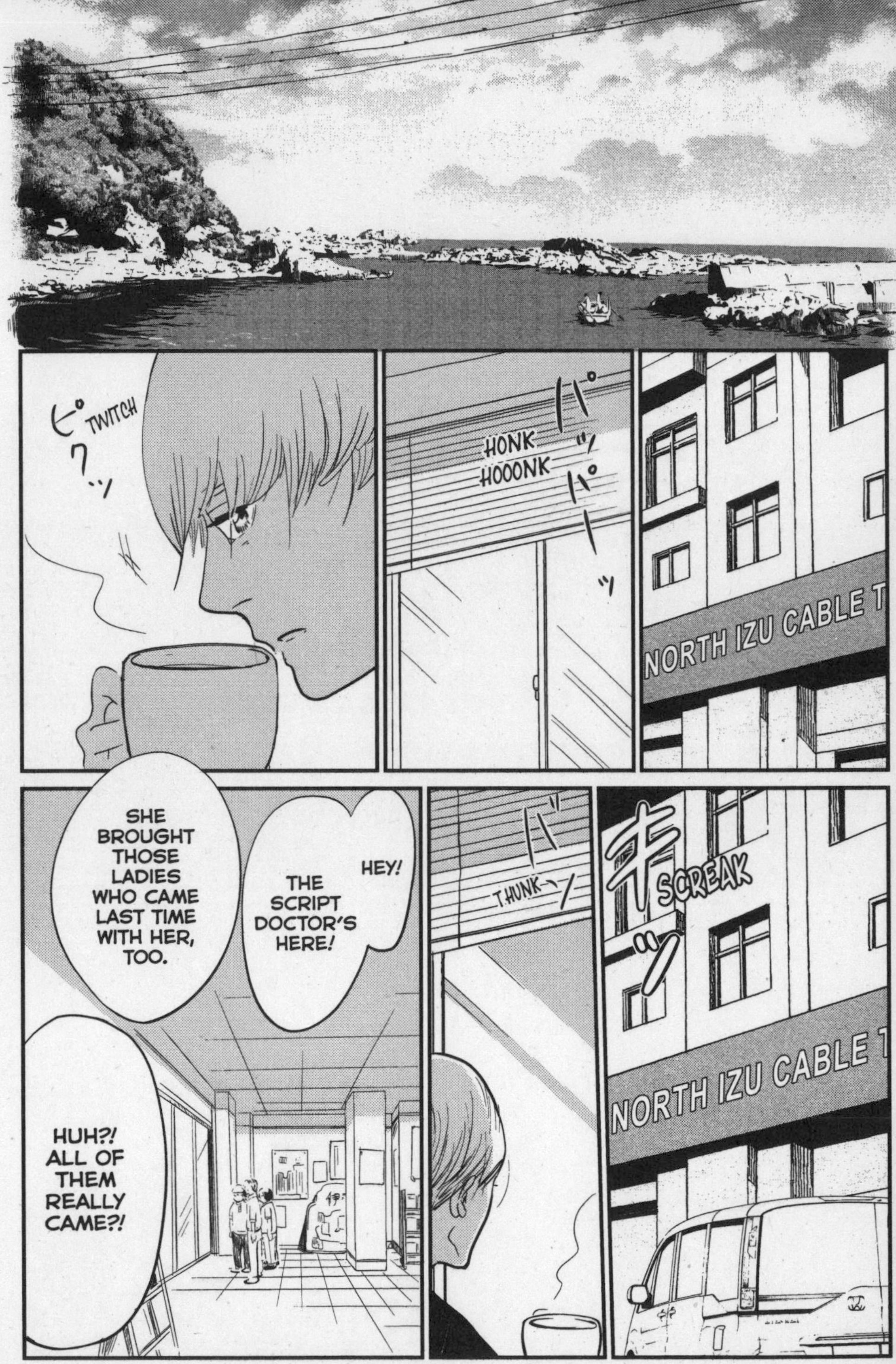
NORTH IZU CABLE T
パッパーーッ
HONK HOOONK
ピクッ
TWITCH
キーッ
SCREAK
NORTH IZU CABLE T
バン
THUNK
HEY! THE SCRIPT DOCTOR'S HERE!
SHE BROUGHT THOSE LADIES WHO CAME LAST TIME WITH HER, TOO.
HUH?! ALL OF THEM REALLY CAME?!

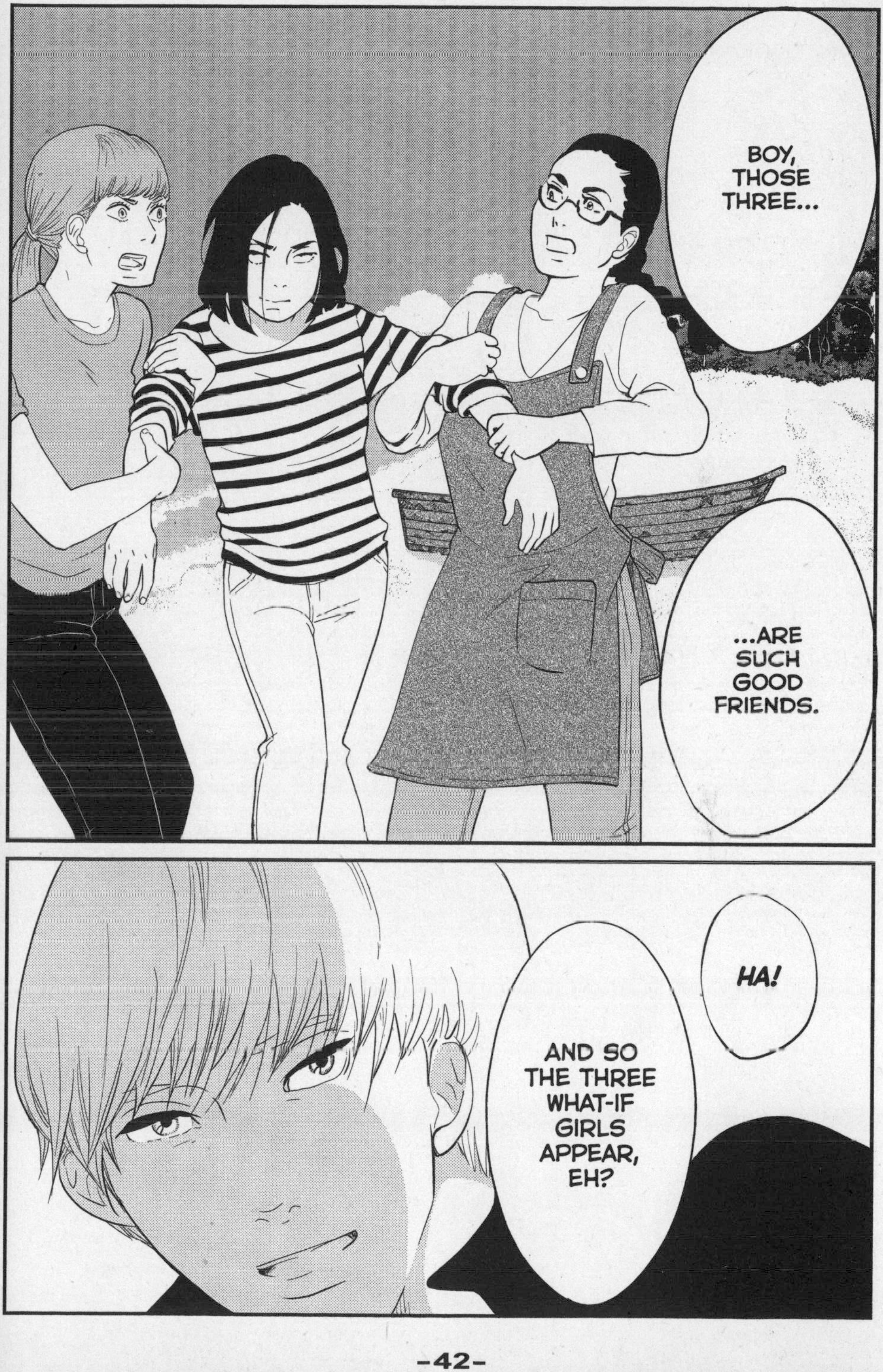
BOY, THOSE THREE...
...ARE SUCH GOOD FRIENDS.
HA!
AND SO THE THREE WHAT-IF GIRLS APPEAR, EH?

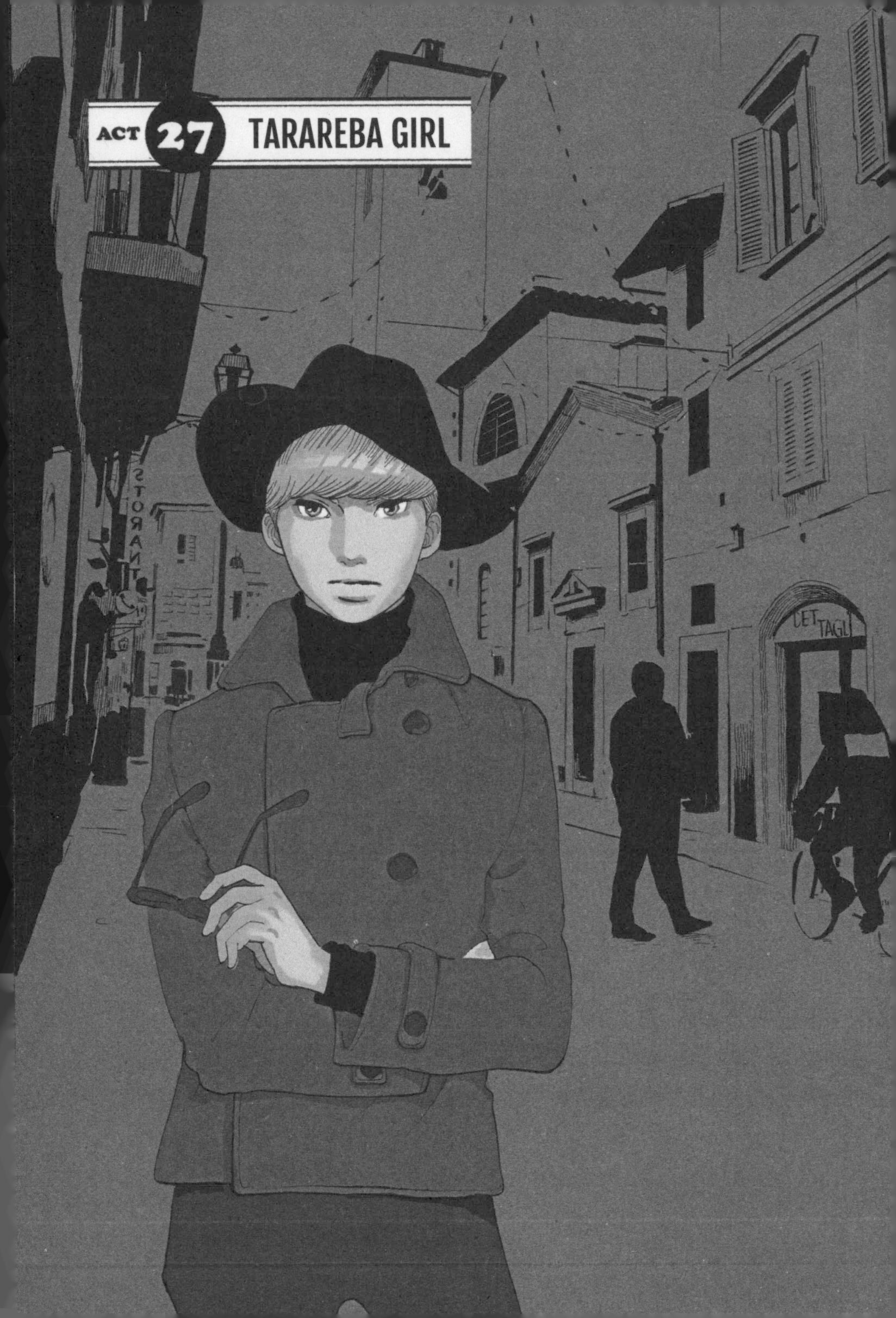
ACT 27 TARAREBA GIRL

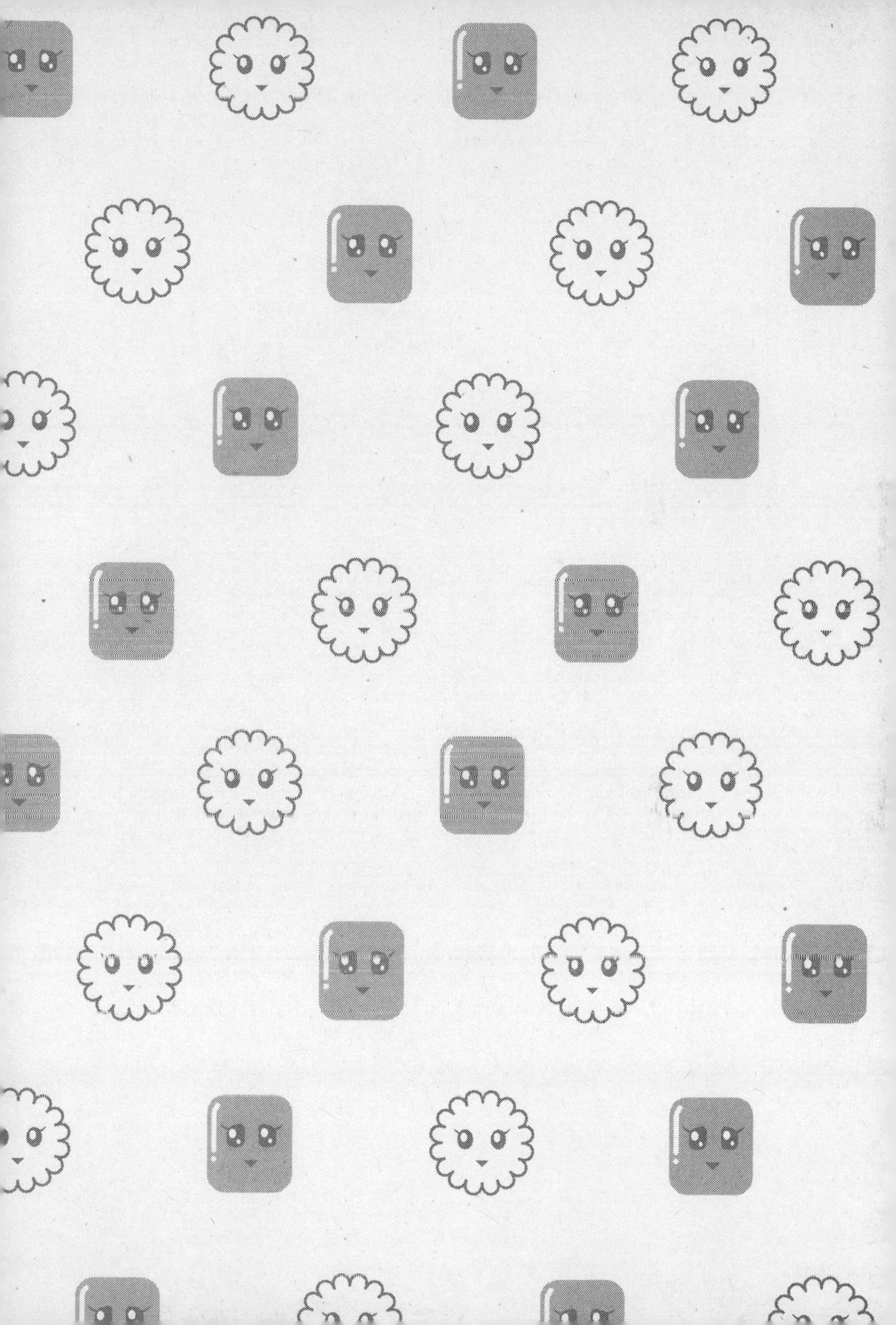

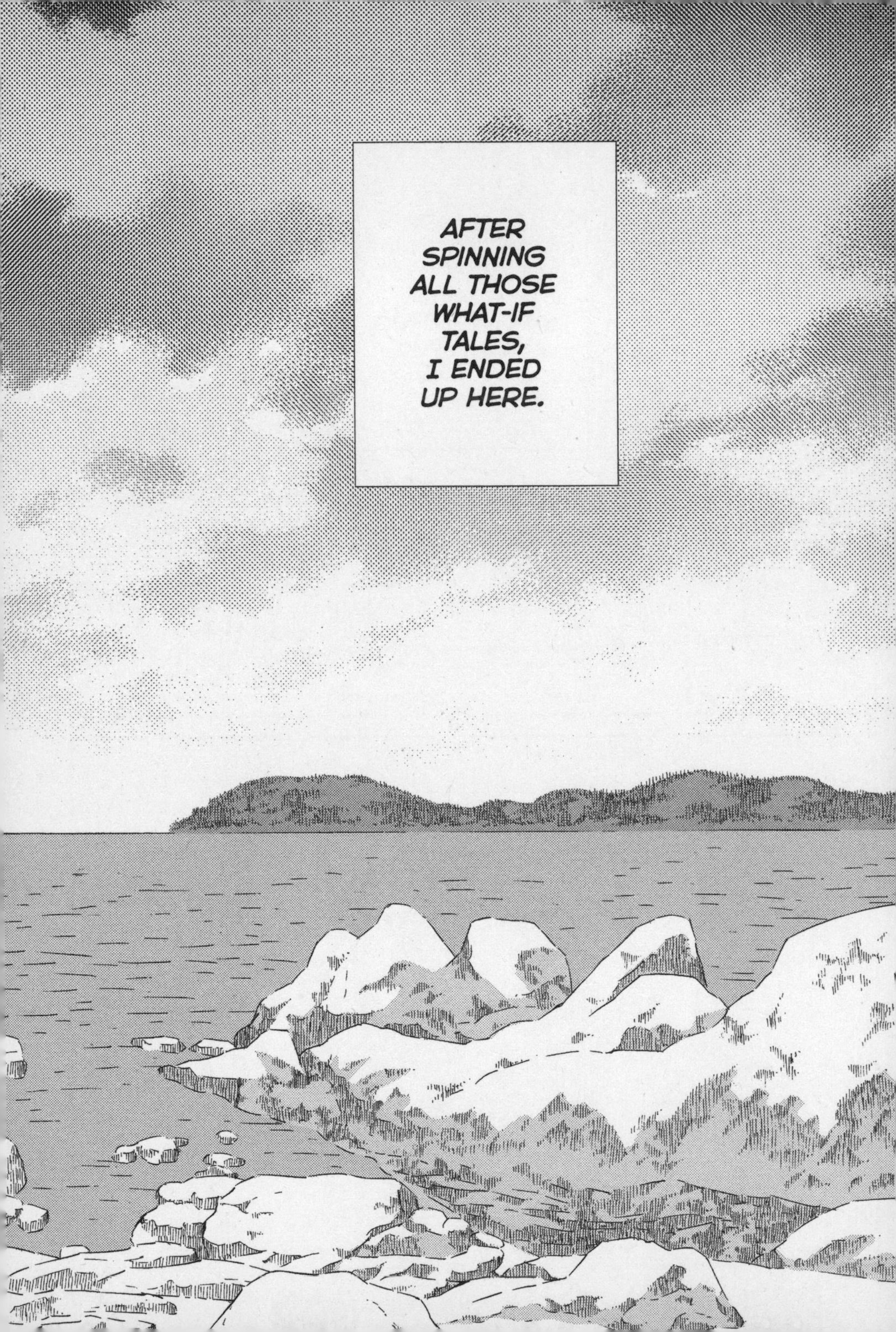
AFTER SPINNING ALL THOSE WHAT-IF TALES, I ENDED UP HERE.

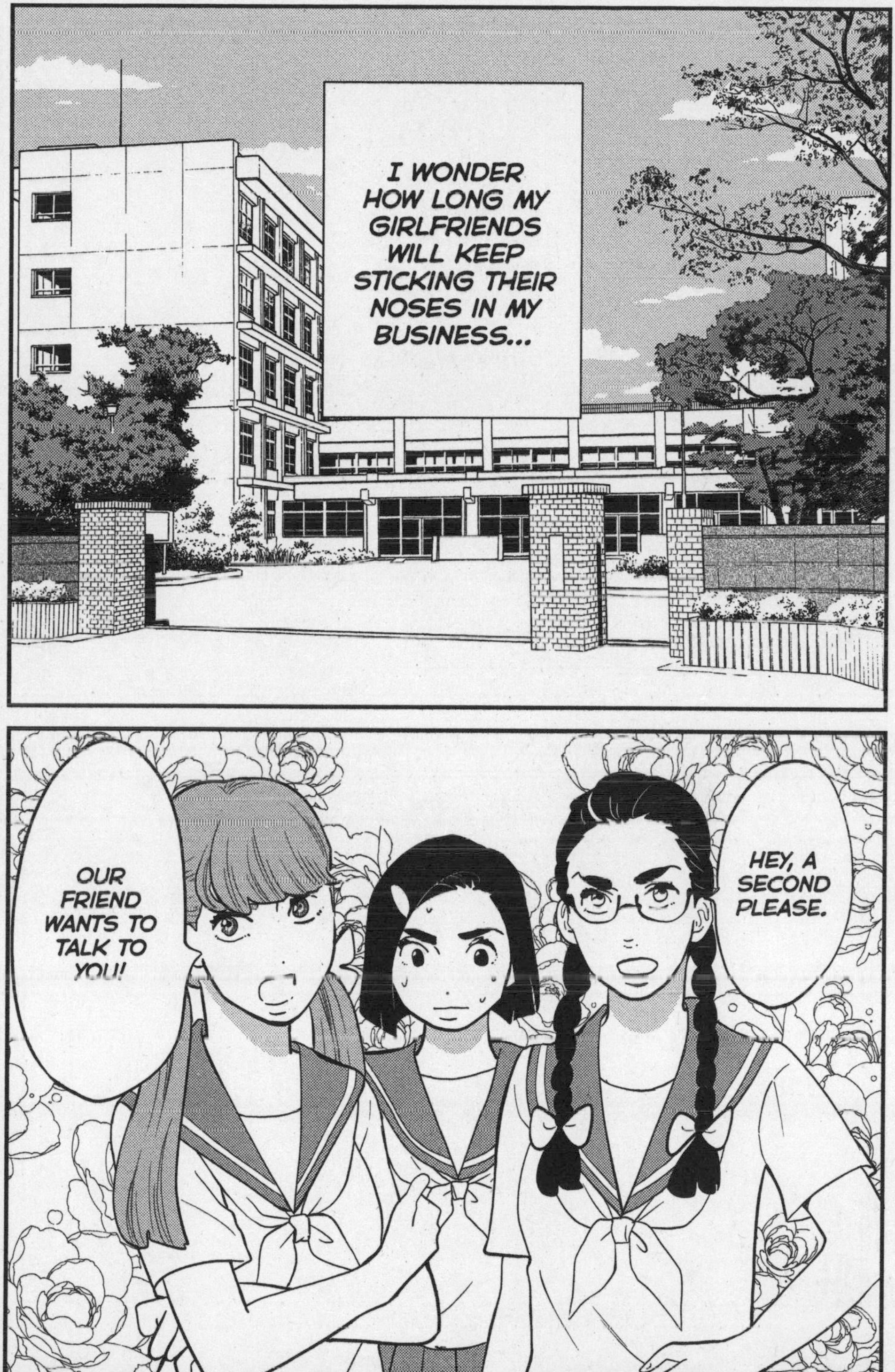
I WONDER HOW LONG MY GIRLFRIENDS WILL KEEP STICKING THEIR NOSES IN MY BUSINESS...
HEY, A SECOND PLEASE.
OUR FRIEND WANTS TO TALK TO YOU!

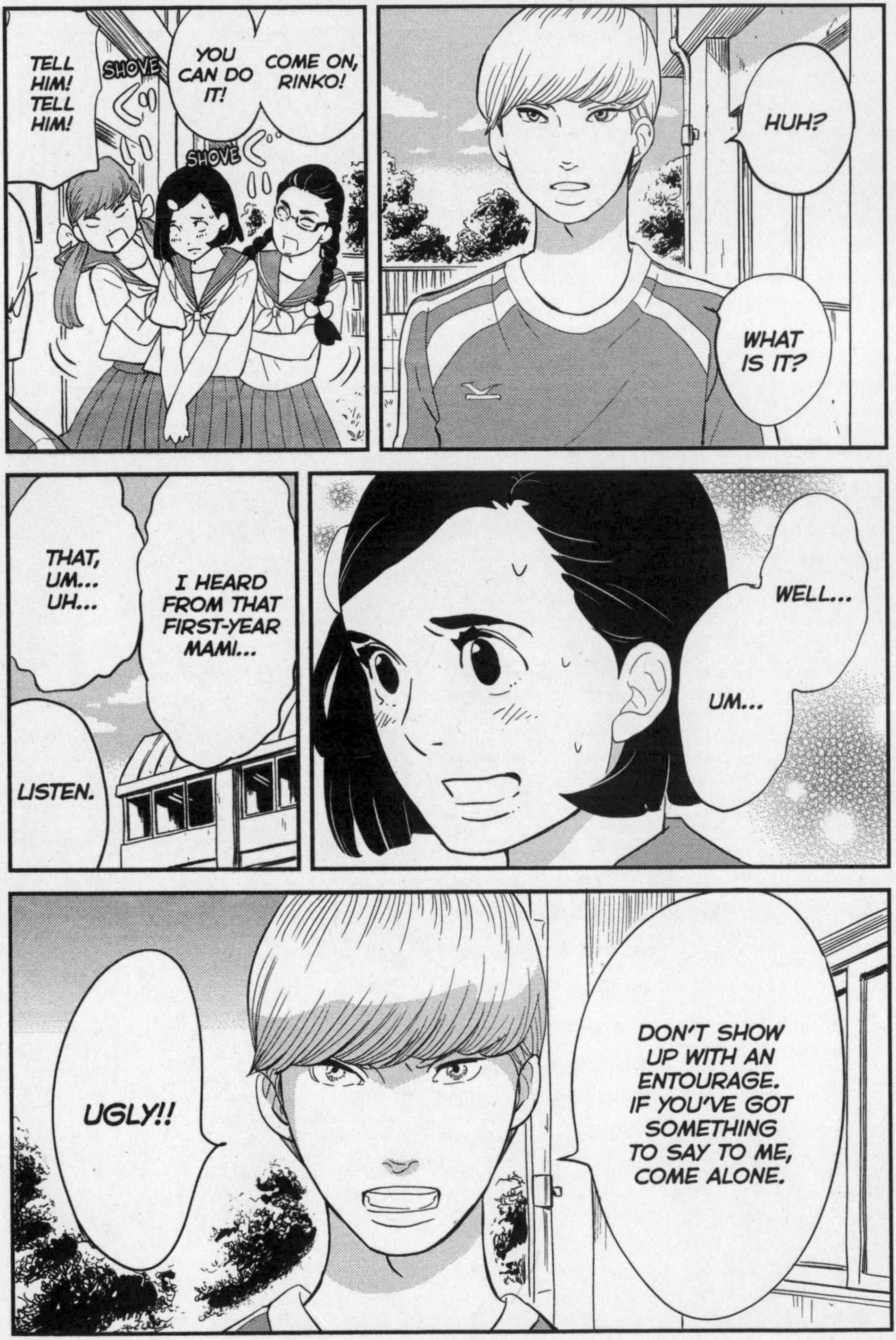
HUH?
WHAT IS IT?
COME ON, RINKO!
YOU CAN DO IT!
SHOVE
TELL HIM! TELL HIM!
SHOVE
WELL...
UM...
I HEARD FROM THAT FIRST-YEAR MAMI...
THAT, UM... UH...
LISTEN.
DON'T SHOW UP WITH AN ENTOURAGE. IF YOU'VE GOT SOMETHING TO SAY TO ME, COME ALONE.
UGLY!!

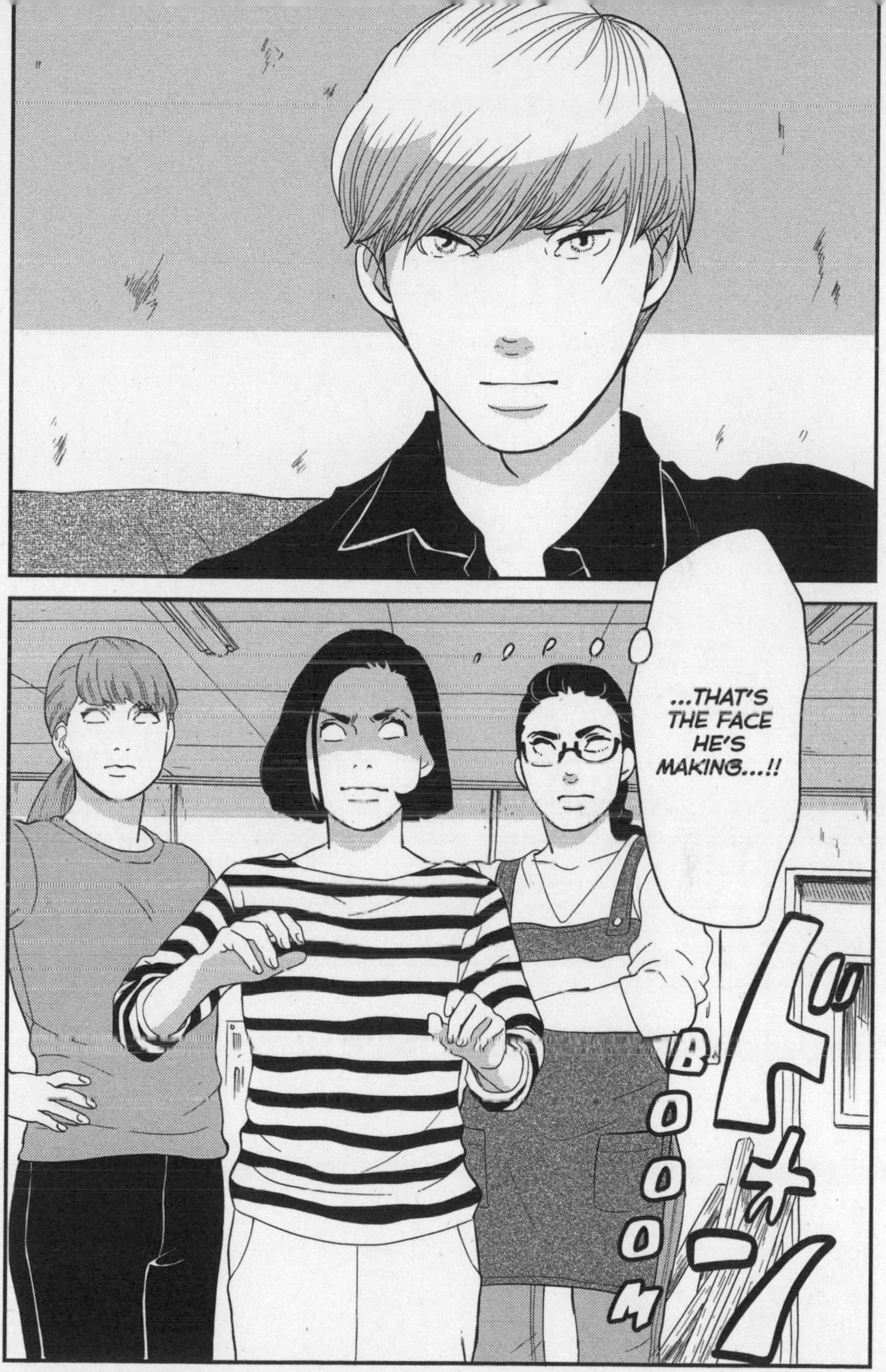
...THAT'S THE FACE HE'S MAKING...!!
BOOOOM

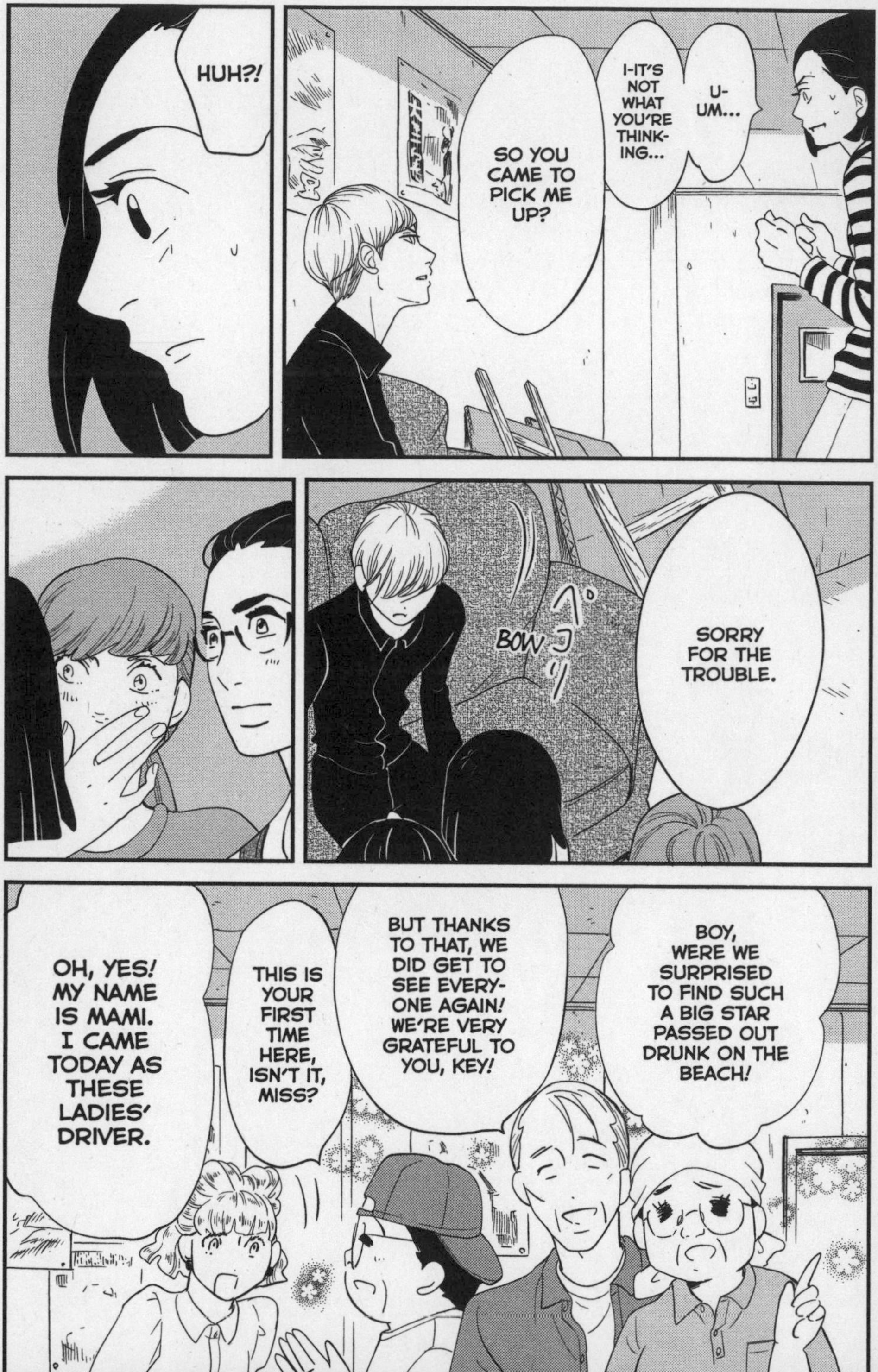
U- UM...
I-IT'S NOT WHAT YOU'RE THINKING...
SO YOU CAME TO PICK ME UP?
HUH?!
SORRY FOR THE TROUBLE.
ペコリ
BOW
BOY, WERE WE SURPRISED TO FIND SUCH A BIG STAR PASSED OUT DRUNK ON THE BEACH!
BUT THANKS TO THAT, WE DID GET TO SEE EVERY-ONE AGAIN! WE'RE VERY GRATEFUL TO YOU, KEY!
THIS IS YOUR FIRST TIME HERE, ISN'T IT, MISS?
OH, YES! MY NAME IS MAMI. I CAME TODAY AS THESE LADIES' DRIVER.

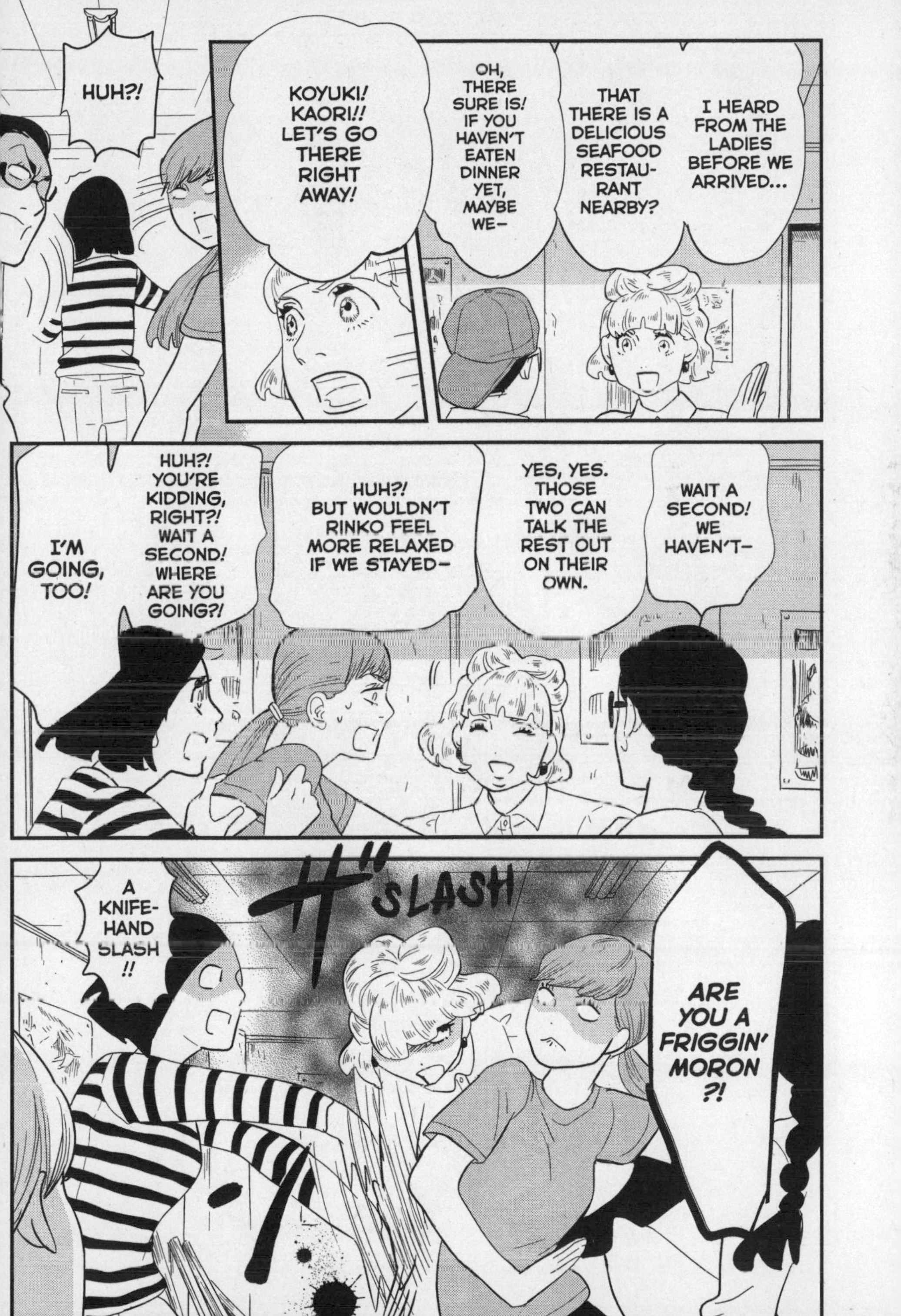
I HEARD FROM THE LADIES BEFORE WE ARRIVED...
THAT THERE IS A DELICIOUS SEAFOOD RESTAURANT NEARBY?
OH, THERE SURE IS! IF YOU HAVEN'T EATEN DINNER YET, MAYBE WE-
KOYUKI! KAORI!! LET'S GO THERE RIGHT AWAY!
HUH?!
WAIT A SECOND! WE HAVEN'T-
YES, YES. THOSE TWO CAN TALK THE REST OUT ON THEIR OWN.
HUH?! BUT WOULDN'T RINKO FEEL MORE RELAXED IF WE STAYED-
HUH?! YOU'RE KIDDING, RIGHT?! WAIT A SECOND! WHERE ARE YOU GOING?!
I'M GOING, TOO!
ARE YOU A FRIGGIN' MORON?!
SLASH
A KNIFE-HAND SLASH!!

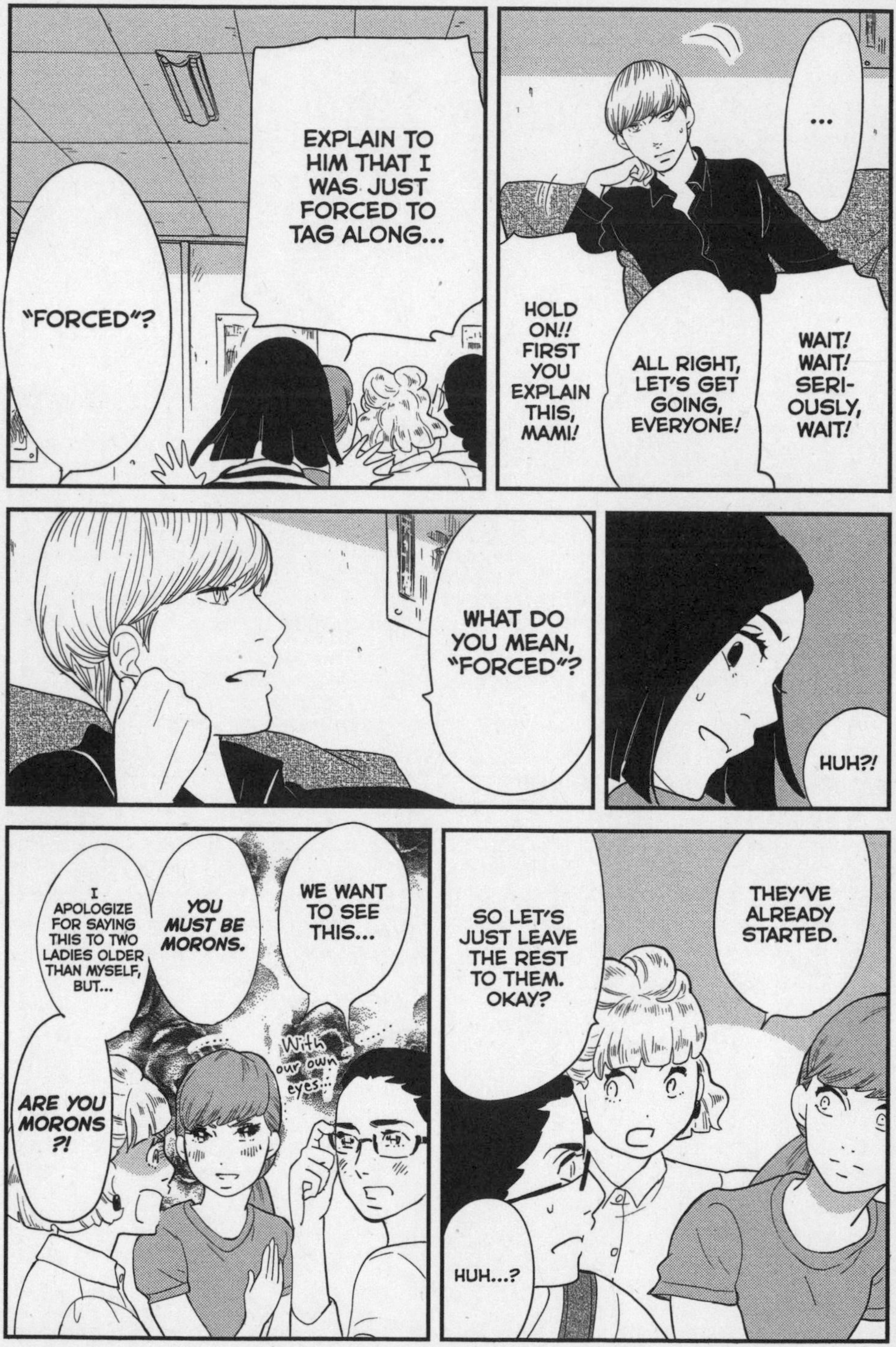
...
WAIT! WAIT! SERIOUSLY, WAIT!
ALL RIGHT, LET'S GET GOING, EVERYONE!
HOLD ON!! FIRST YOU EXPLAIN THIS, MAMI!
EXPLAIN TO HIM THAT I WAS JUST FORCED TO TAG ALONG...
"FORCED"?
HUH?!
WHAT DO YOU MEAN, "FORCED"?
THEY'VE ALREADY STARTED.
SO LET'S JUST LEAVE THE REST TO THEM. OKAY?
HUH...?
WE WANT TO SEE THIS...
With our own eyes...
YOU MUST BE MORONS.
I APOLOGIZE FOR SAYING THIS TO TWO LADIES OLDER THAN MYSELF, BUT...
ARE YOU MORONS?!

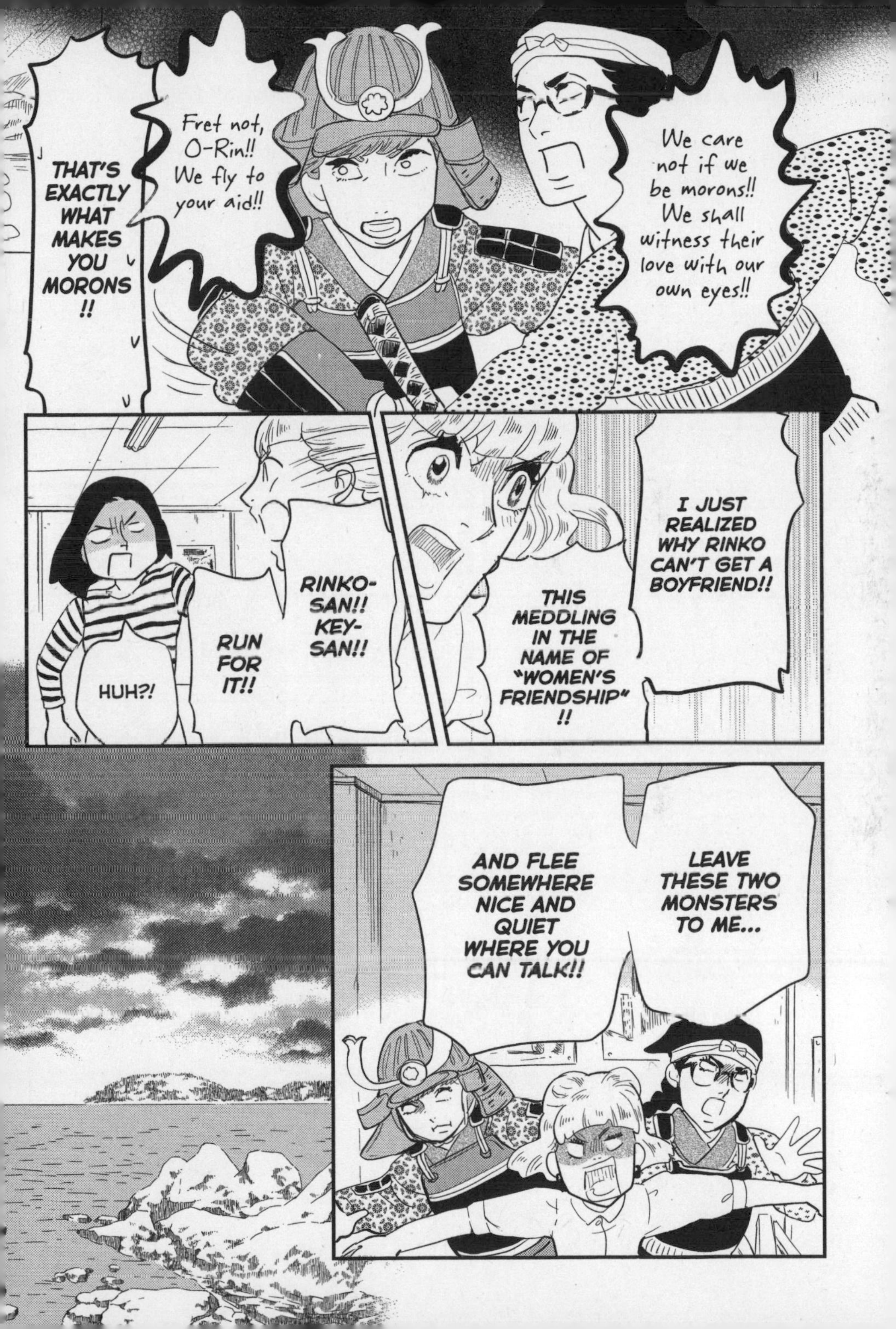
We care not if we be morons!! We shall witness their love with our own eyes!!
Fret not, O-Rin!! We fly to your aid!!
THAT'S EXACTLY WHAT MAKES YOU MORONS!!
I JUST REALIZED WHY RINKO CAN'T GET A BOYFRIEND!!
THIS MEDDLING IN THE NAME OF "WOMEN'S FRIENDSHIP"!!
RINKO-SAN!! KEY-SAN!!
RUN FOR IT!!
HUH?!
LEAVE THESE TWO MONSTERS TO ME...
AND FLEE SOMEWHERE NICE AND QUIET WHERE YOU CAN TALK!!

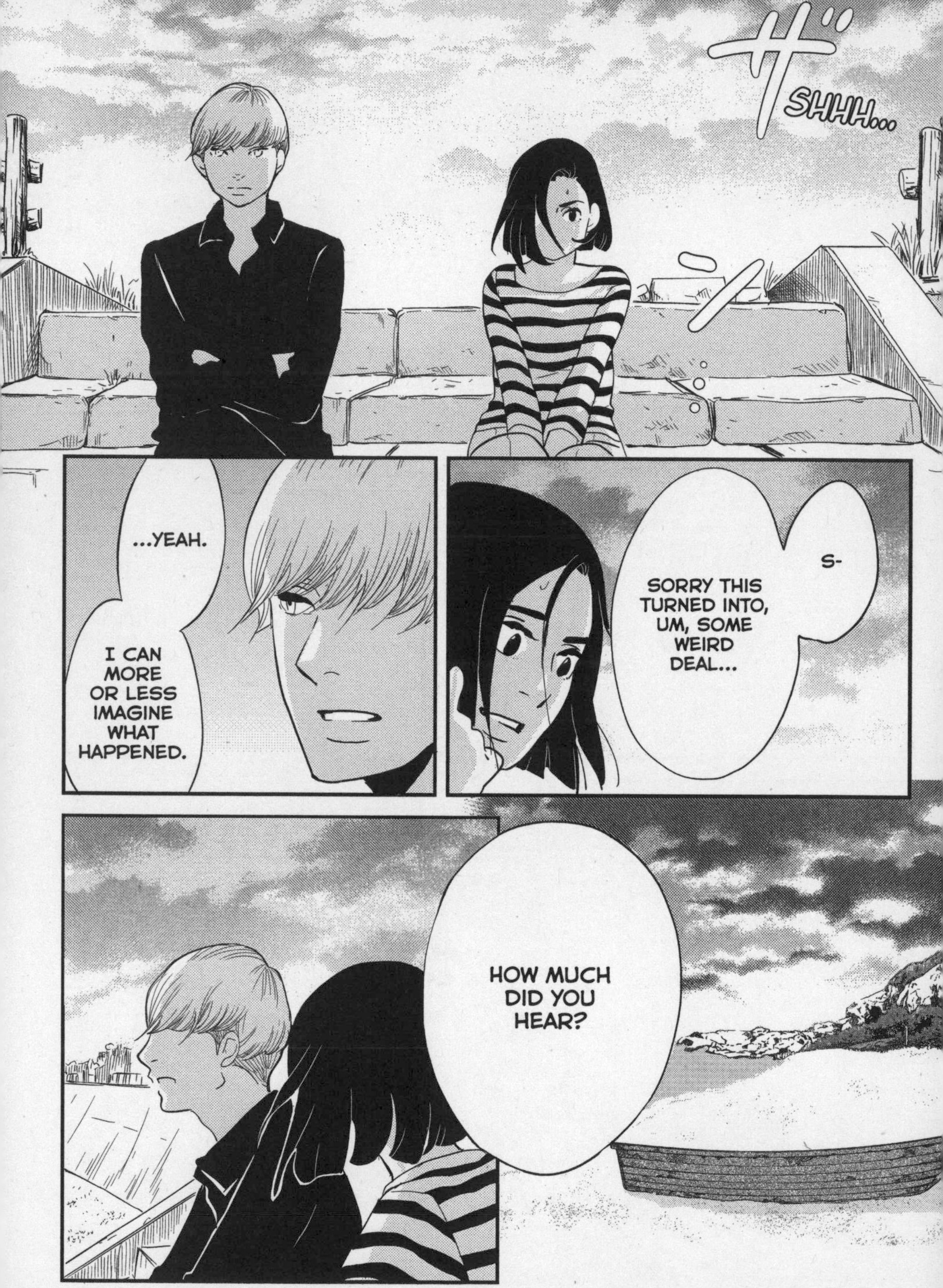
SHHH...
S-
SORRY THIS TURNED INTO, UM, SOME WEIRD DEAL...
...YEAH.
I CAN MORE OR LESS IMAGINE WHAT HAPPENED.
HOW MUCH DID YOU HEAR?

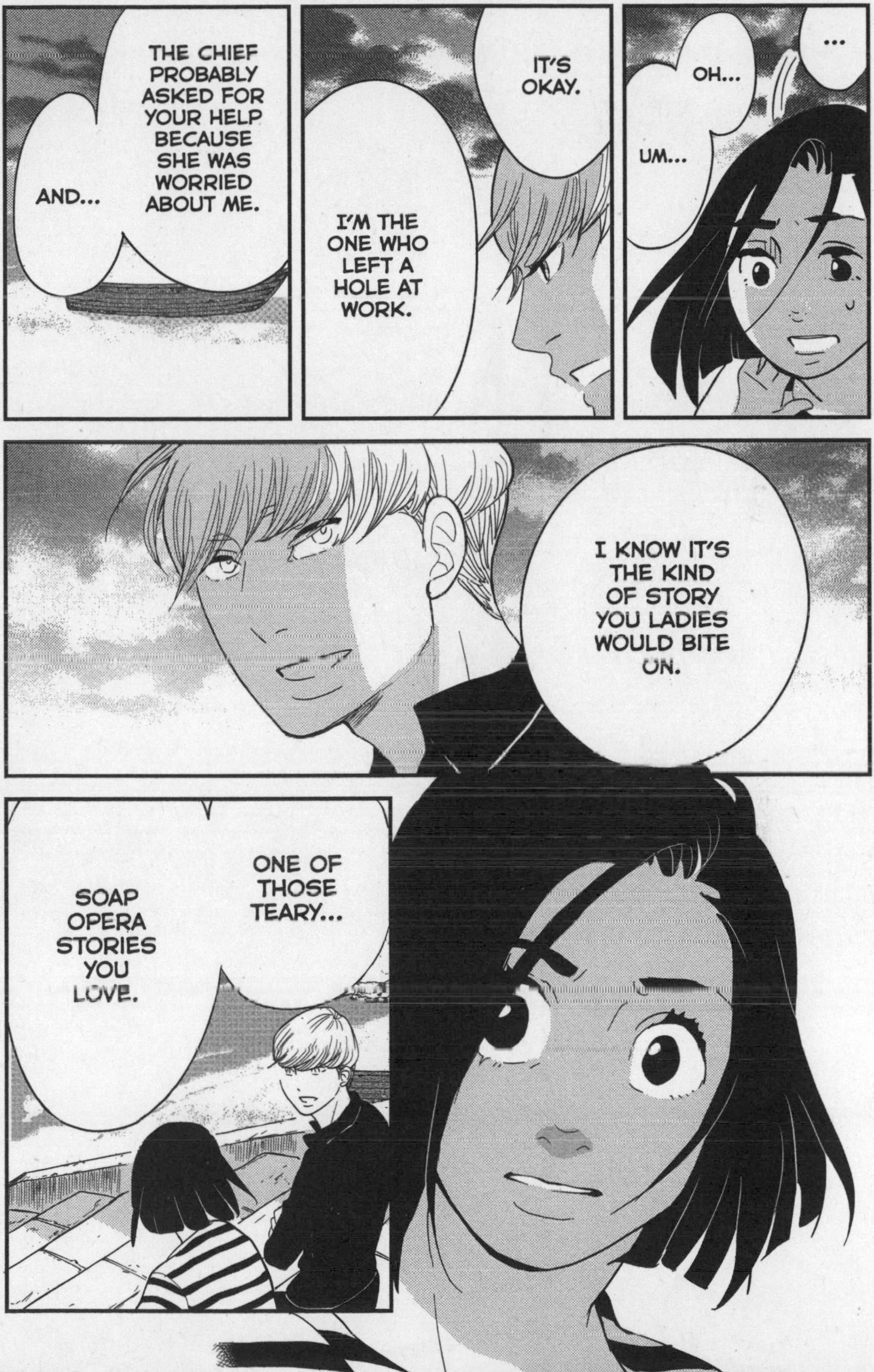
...
OH...
UM...
IT'S OKAY.
I'M THE ONE WHO LEFT A HOLE AT WORK.
THE CHIEF PROBABLY ASKED FOR YOUR HELP BECAUSE SHE WAS WORRIED ABOUT ME.
AND...
I KNOW IT'S THE KIND OF STORY YOU LADIES WOULD BITE ON.
ONE OF THOSE TEARY...
SOAP OPERA STORIES YOU LOVE.

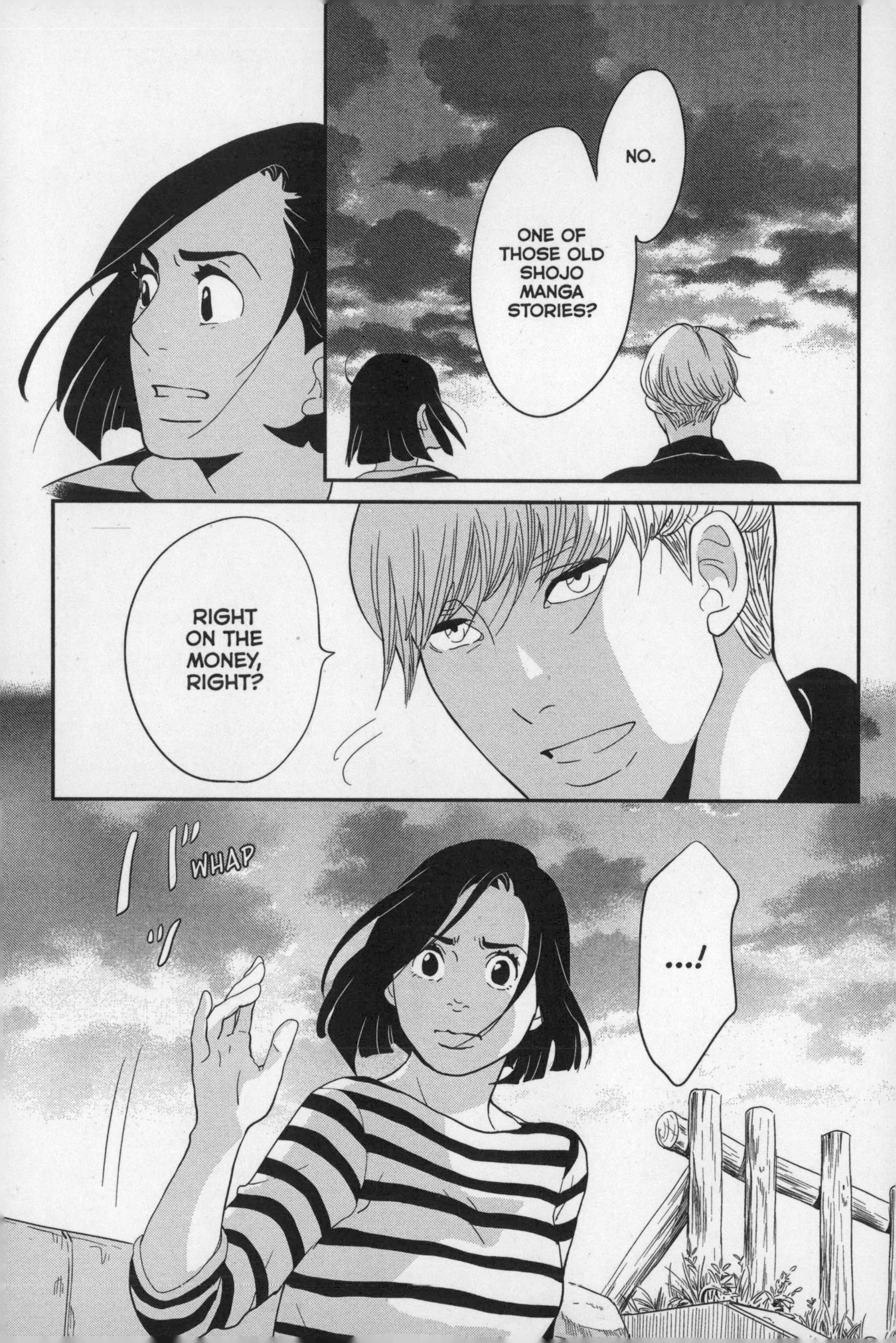
NO.
ONE OF THOSE OLD SHOJO MANGA STORIES?
RIGHT ON THE MONEY, RIGHT?
...!
WHAP

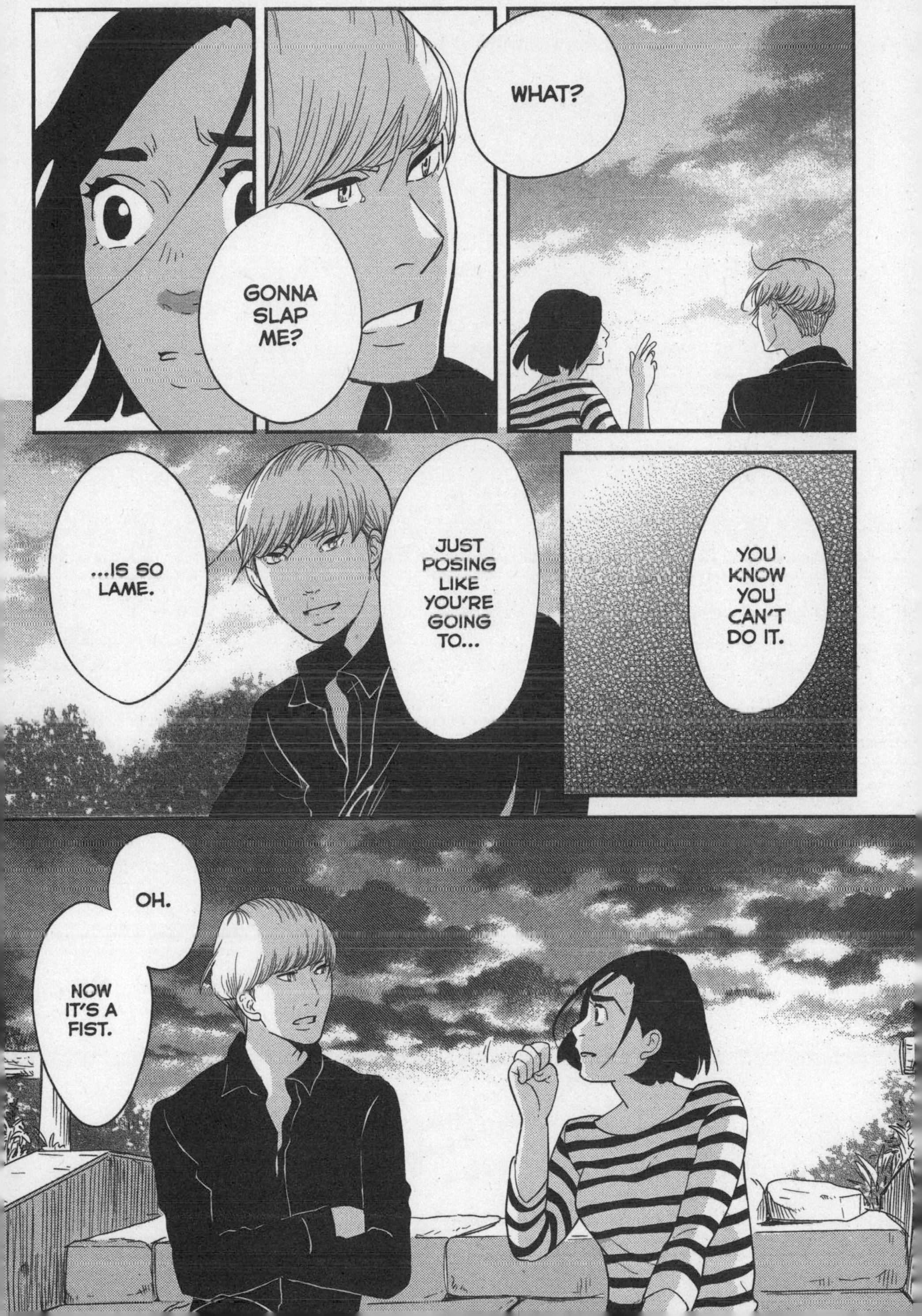
WHAT?
GONNA SLAP ME?
YOU KNOW YOU CAN'T DO IT.
JUST POSING LIKE YOU'RE GOING TO...
...IS SO LAME.
OH.
NOW IT'S A FIST.

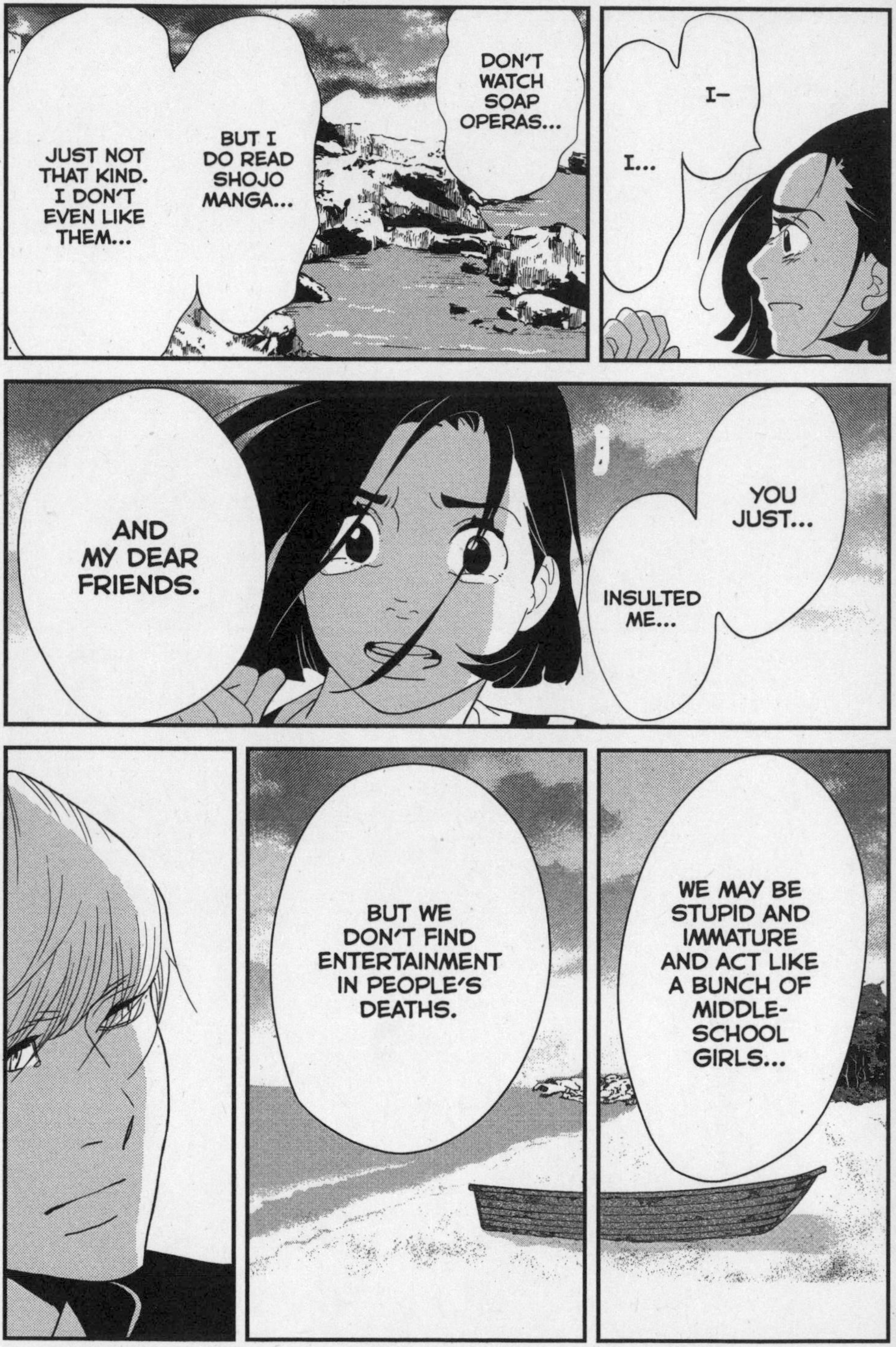
I—
I...
DON'T WATCH SOAP OPERAS...
BUT I DO READ SHOJO MANGA...
JUST NOT THAT KIND. I DON'T EVEN LIKE THEM...
YOU JUST...
INSULTED ME...
AND MY DEAR FRIENDS.
WE MAY BE STUPID AND IMMATURE AND ACT LIKE A BUNCH OF MIDDLE-SCHOOL GIRLS...
BUT WE DON'T FIND ENTERTAINMENT IN PEOPLE'S DEATHS.

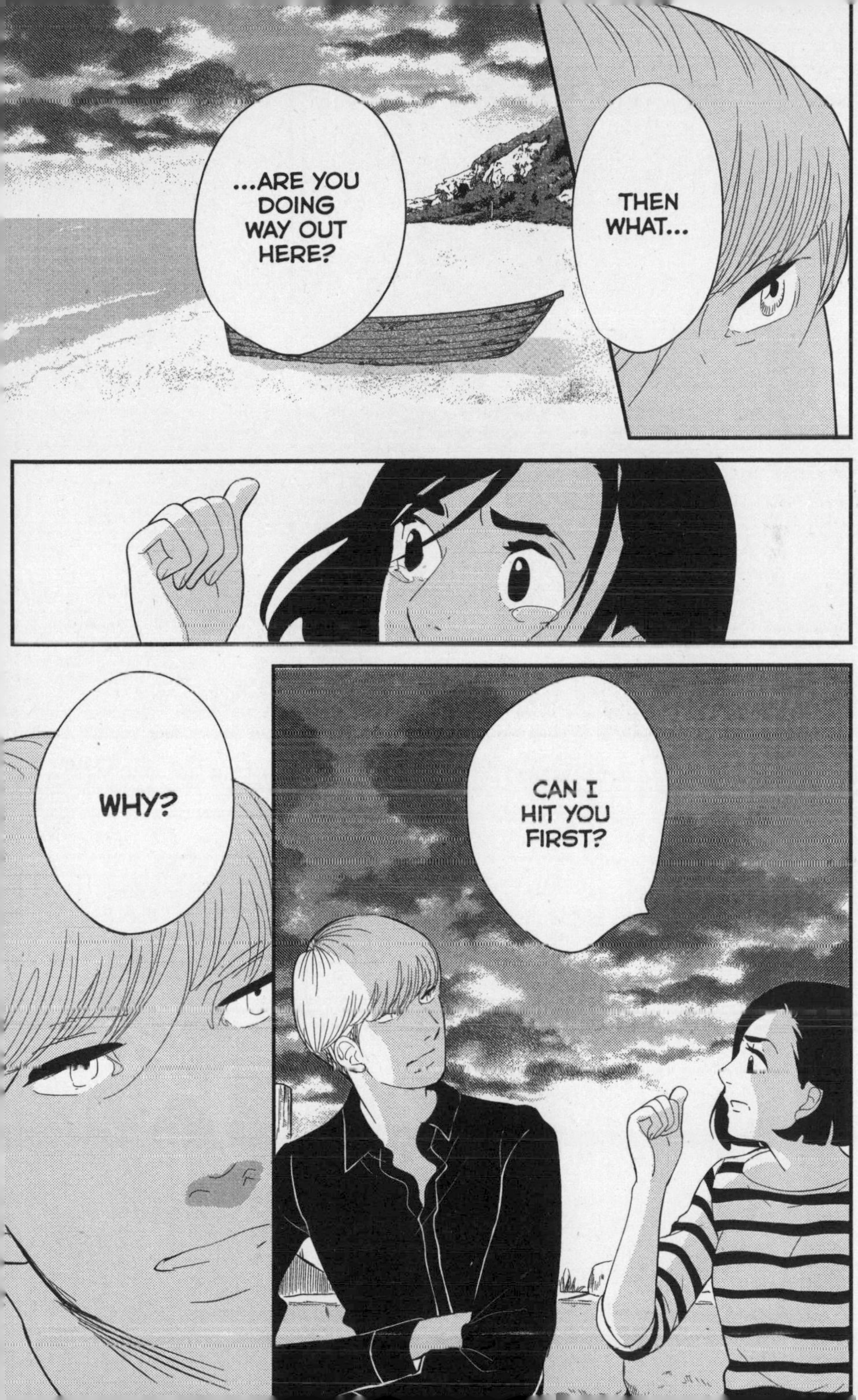
THEN WHAT...
...ARE YOU DOING WAY OUT HERE?
CAN I HIT YOU FIRST?
WHY?

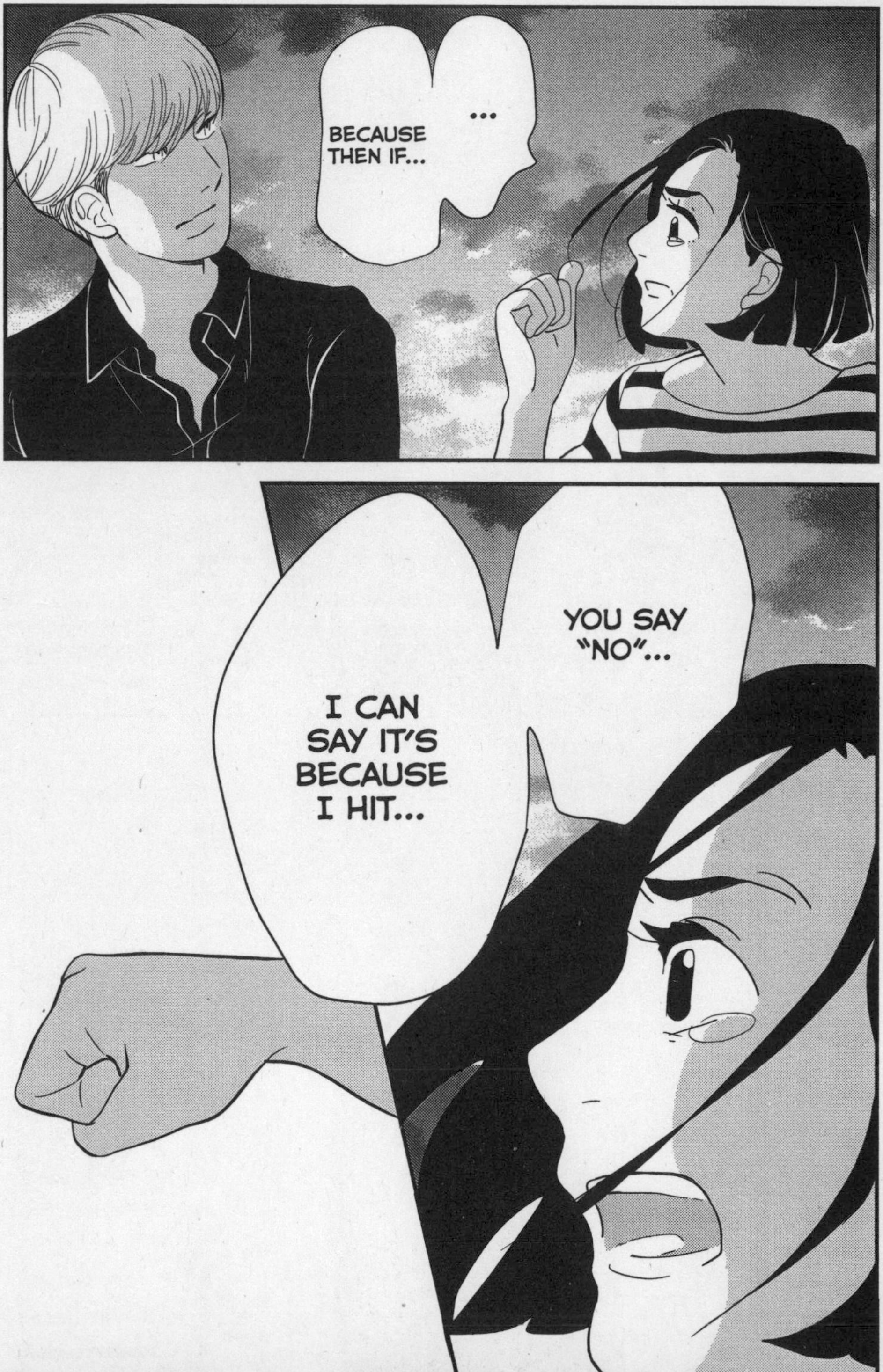
...
BECAUSE THEN IF...
YOU SAY "NO"...
I CAN SAY IT'S BECAUSE I HIT...

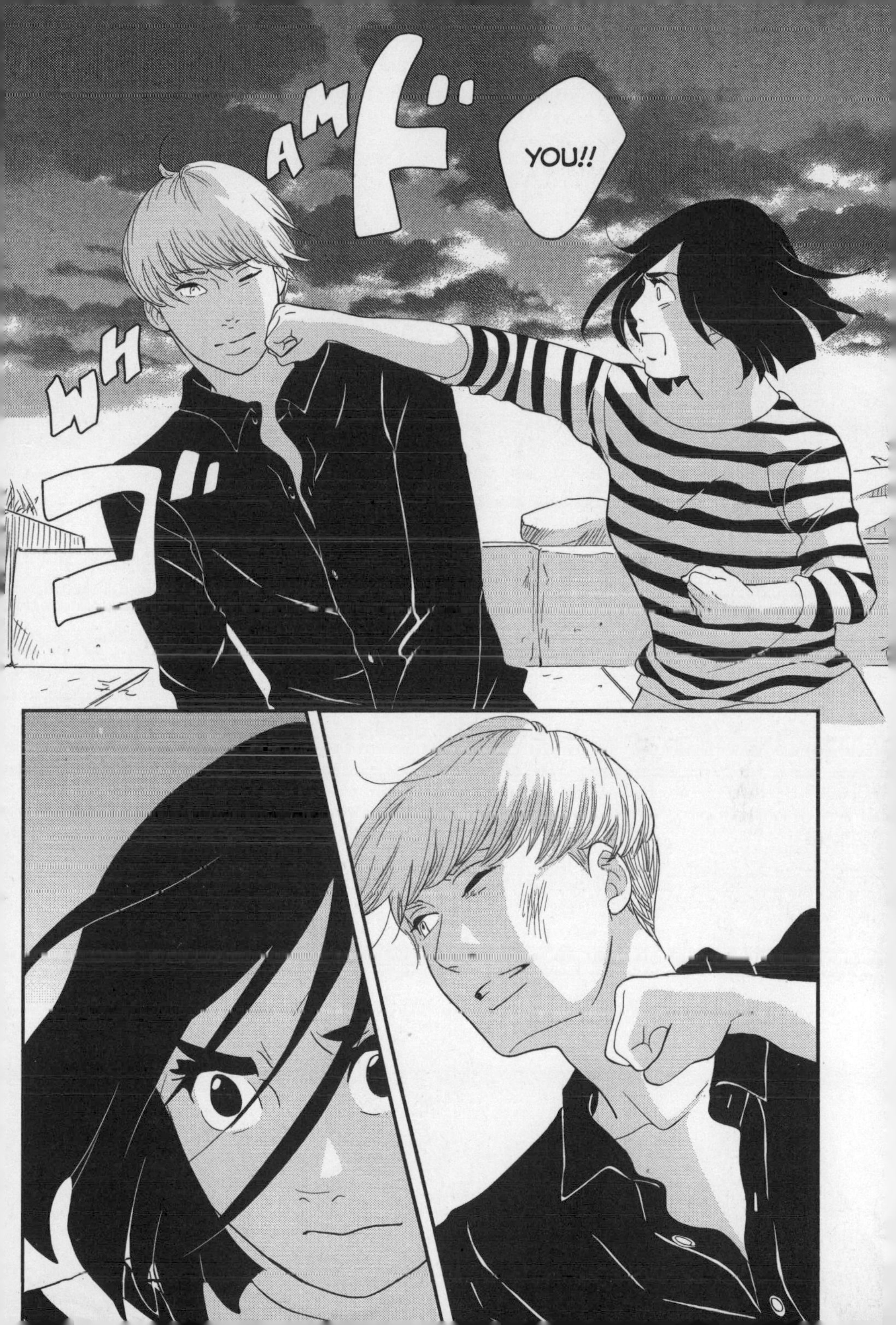
YOU!!
WHAM
ド
ゴ

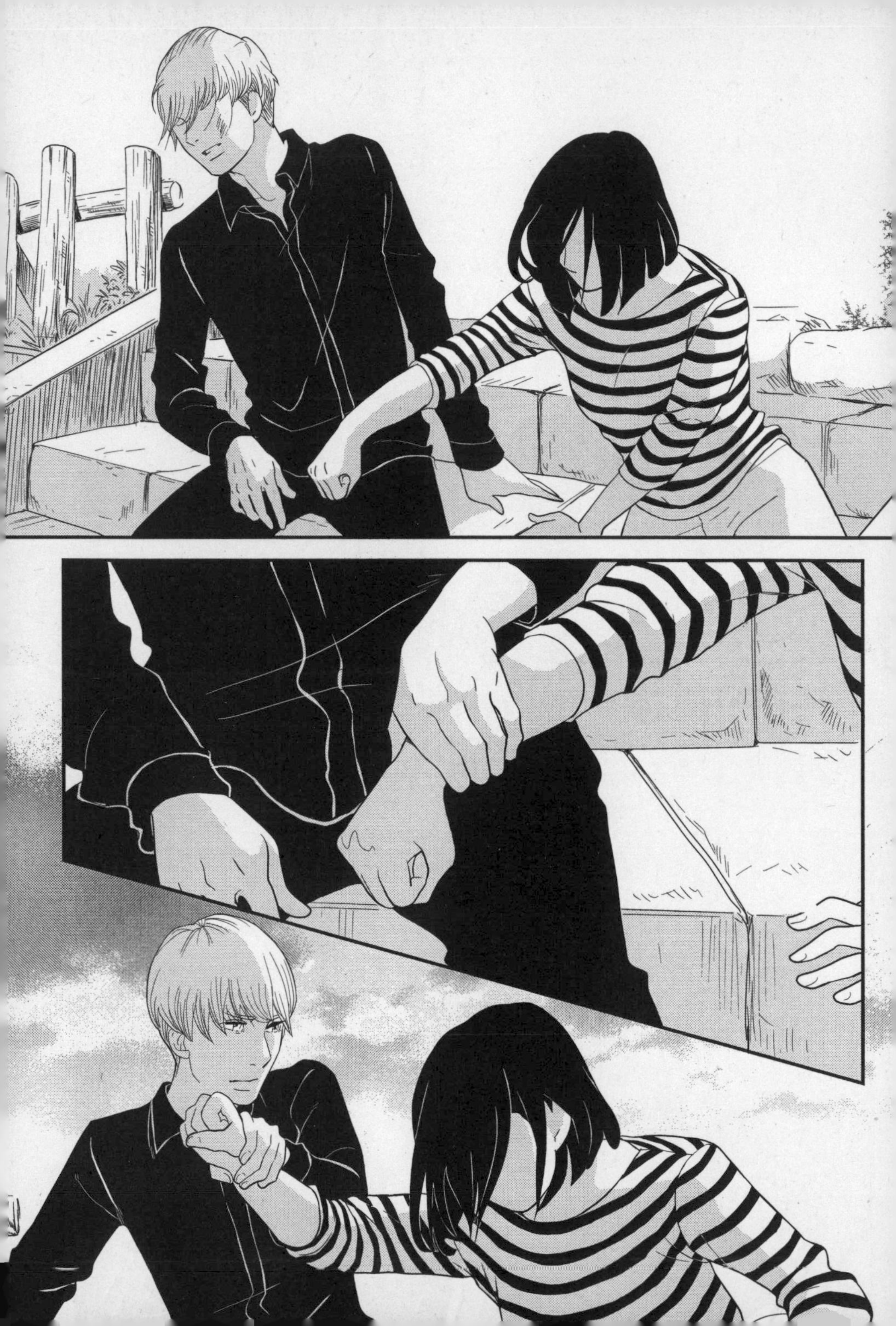

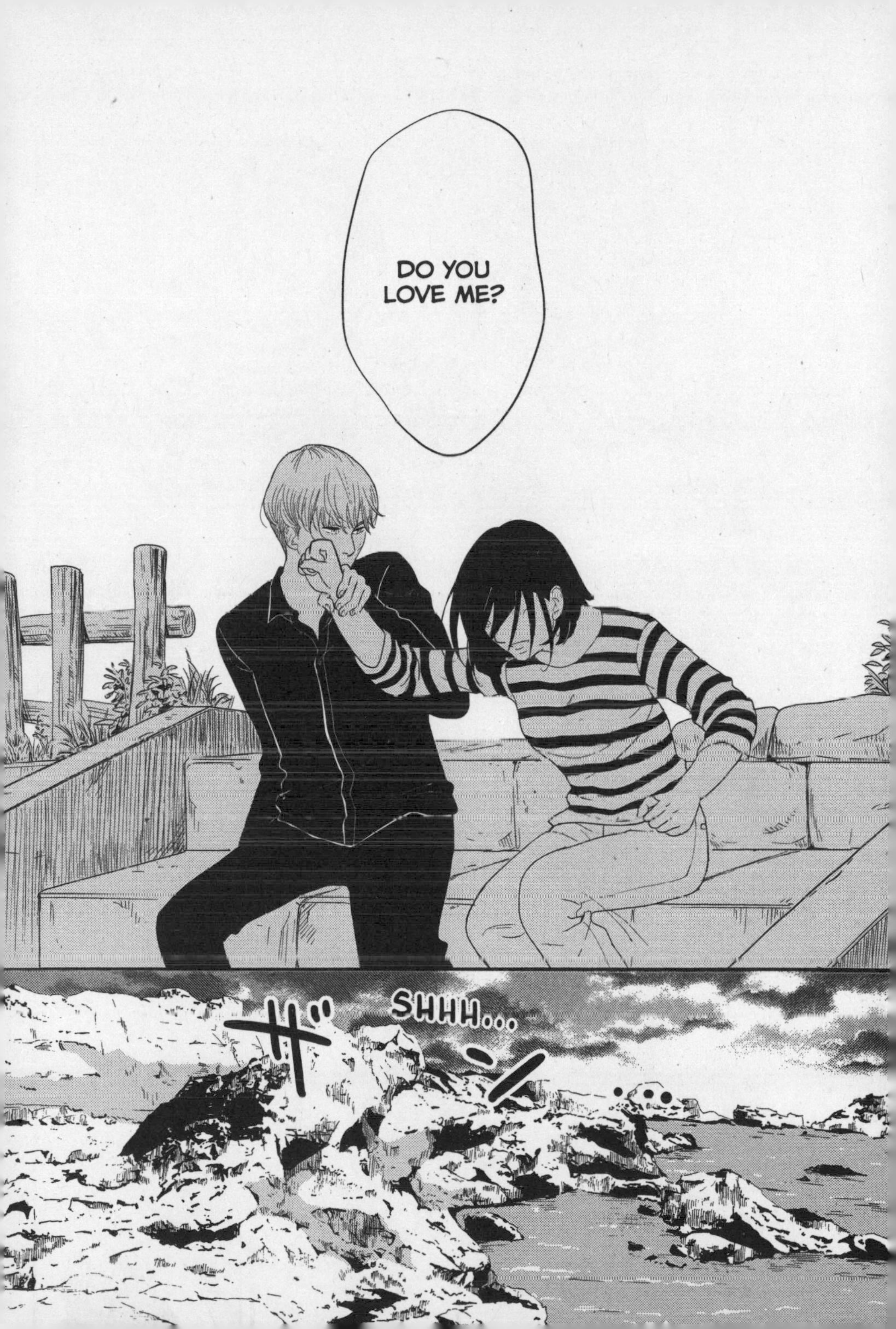
DO YOU LOVE ME?
ザー…
SHHH...

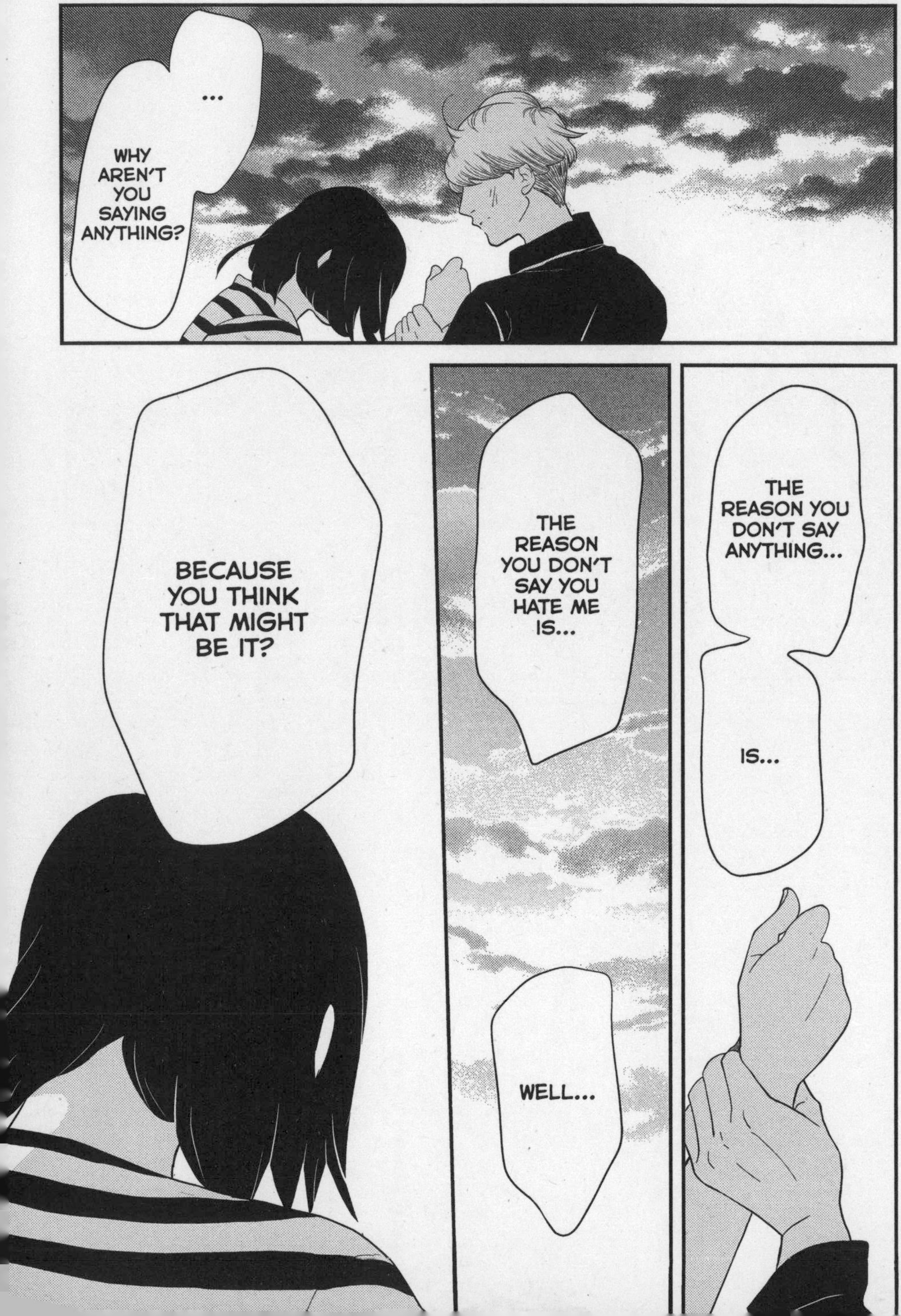
...
WHY AREN'T YOU SAYING ANYTHING?
THE REASON YOU DON'T SAY ANYTHING...
IS...
THE REASON YOU DON'T SAY YOU HATE ME IS...
WELL...
BECAUSE YOU THINK THAT MIGHT BE IT?

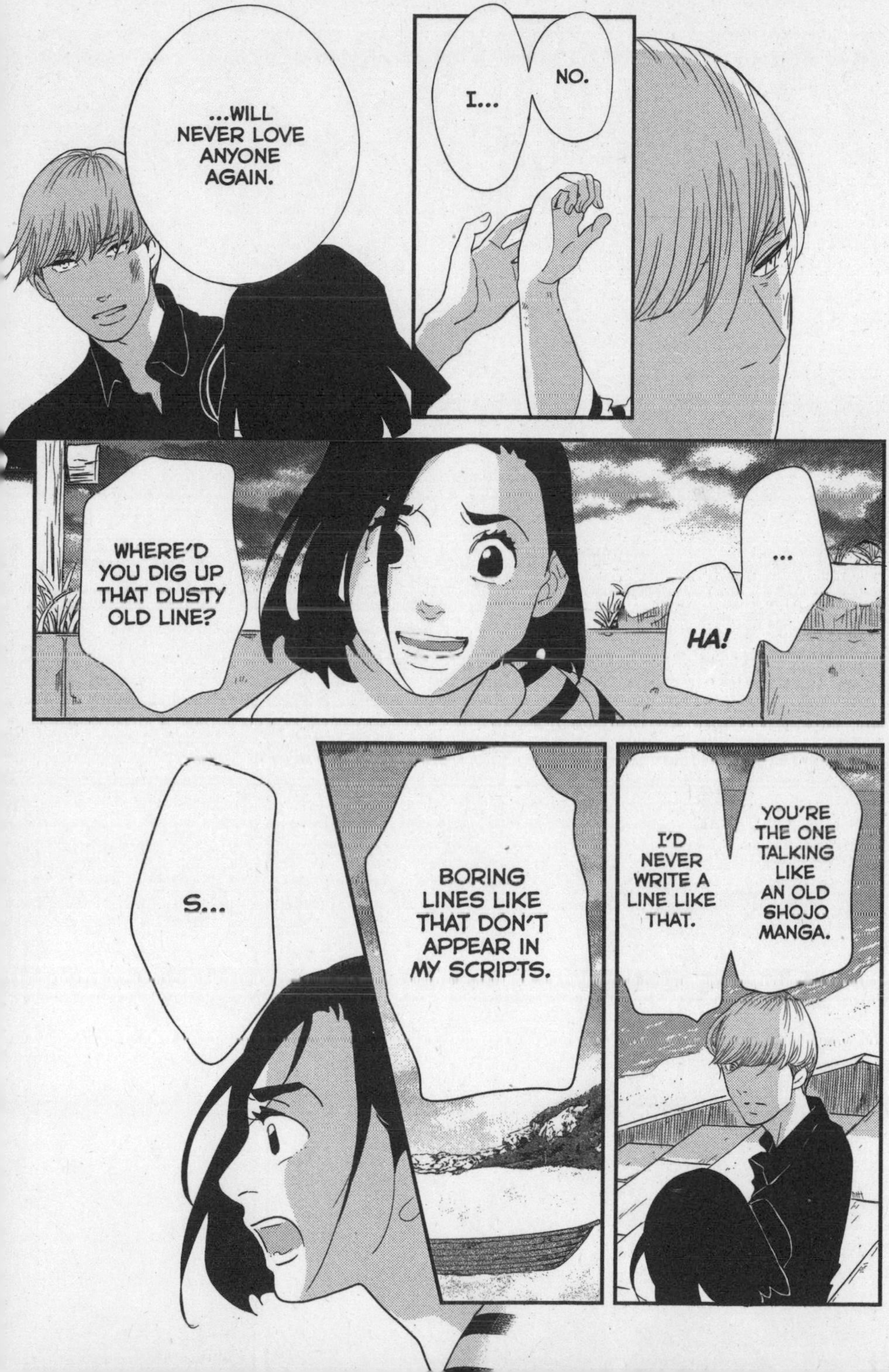
NO.
I...
...WILL NEVER LOVE ANYONE AGAIN.
... HA!
WHERE'D YOU DIG UP THAT DUSTY OLD LINE?
YOU'RE THE ONE TALKING LIKE AN OLD SHOJO MANGA.
I'D NEVER WRITE A LINE LIKE THAT.
BORING LINES LIKE THAT DON'T APPEAR IN MY SCRIPTS.
S...

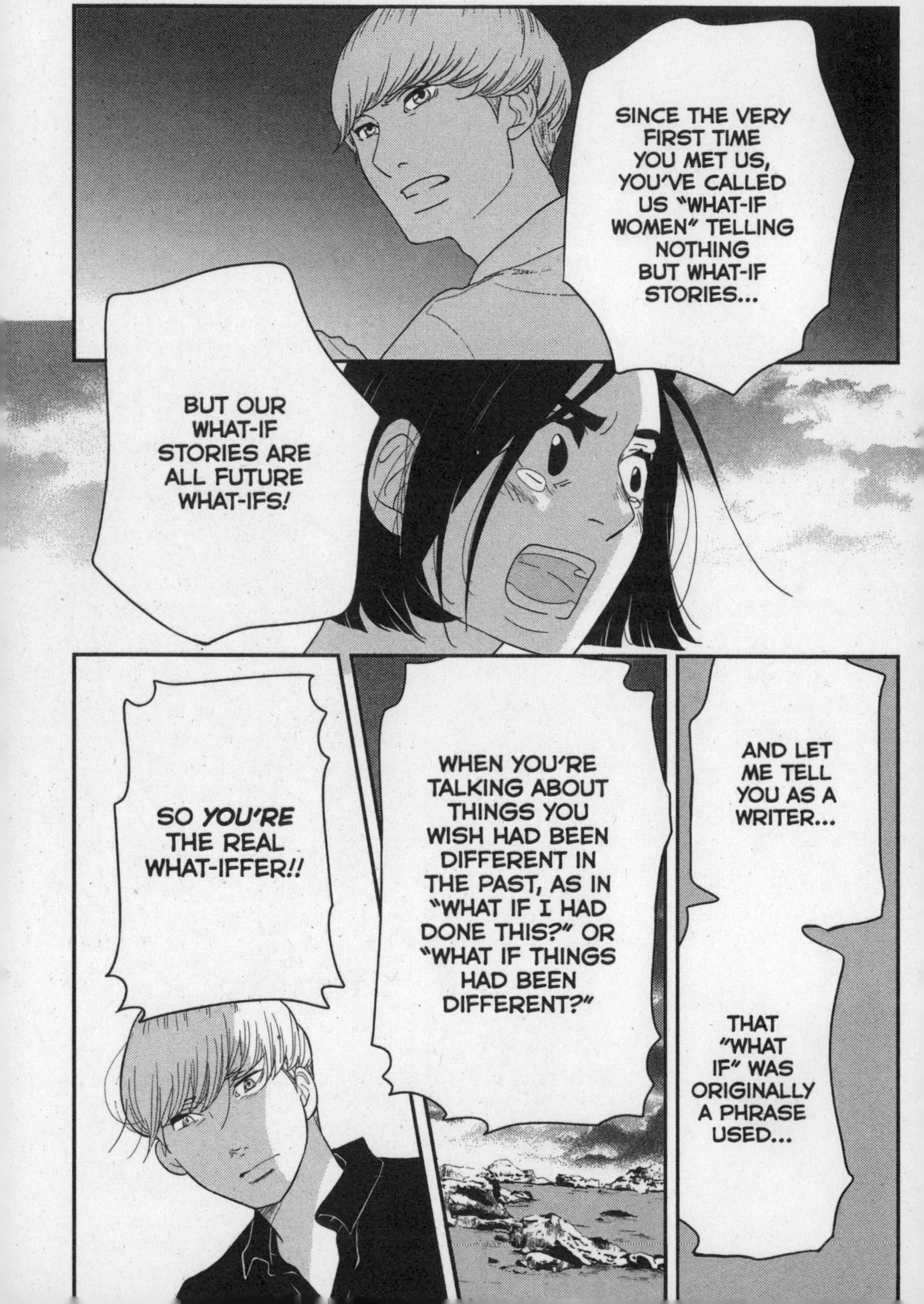
SINCE THE VERY FIRST TIME YOU MET US, YOU'VE CALLED US "WHAT-IF WOMEN" TELLING NOTHING BUT WHAT-IF STORIES...
BUT OUR WHAT-IF STORIES ARE ALL FUTURE WHAT-IFS!
AND LET ME TELL YOU AS A WRITER...
THAT "WHAT IF" WAS ORIGINALLY A PHRASE USED...
WHEN YOU'RE TALKING ABOUT THINGS YOU WISH HAD BEEN DIFFERENT IN THE PAST, AS IN "WHAT IF I HAD DONE THIS?" OR "WHAT IF THINGS HAD BEEN DIFFERENT?"
SO *YOU'RE* THE REAL WHAT-IFFER!!

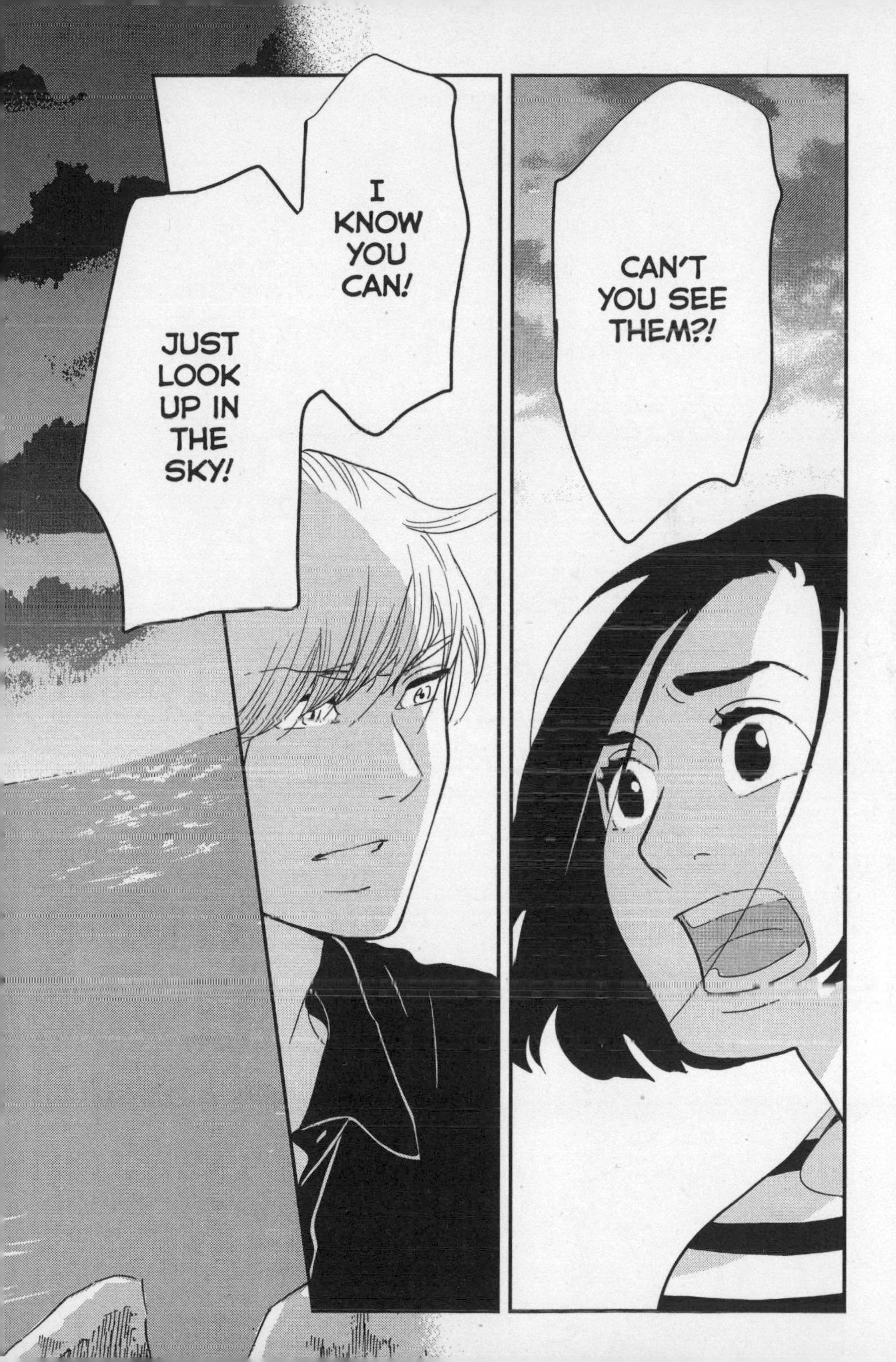
CAN'T YOU SEE THEM?!
I KNOW YOU CAN!
JUST LOOK UP IN THE SKY!

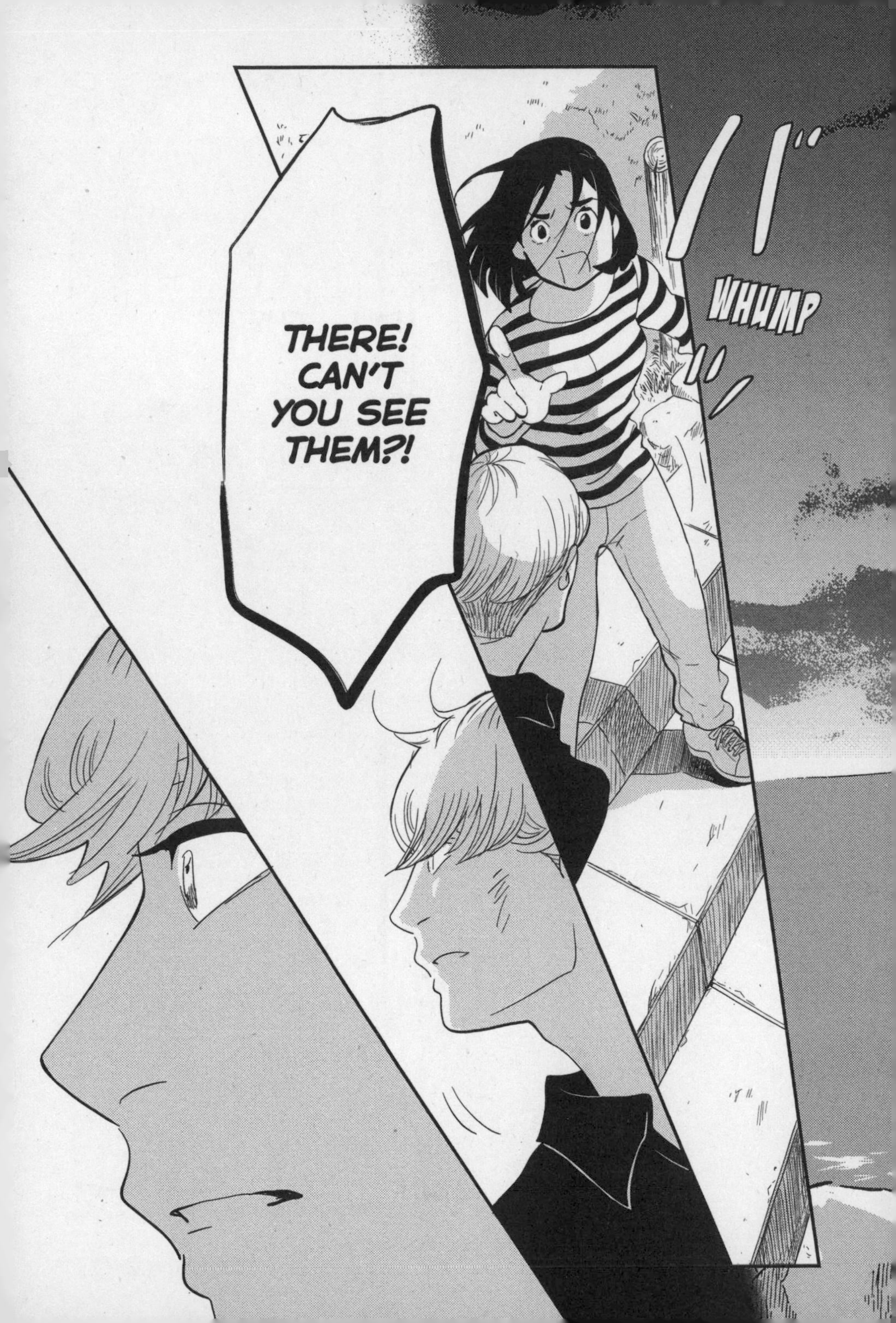
WHUMP
THERE! CAN'T YOU SEE THEM?!

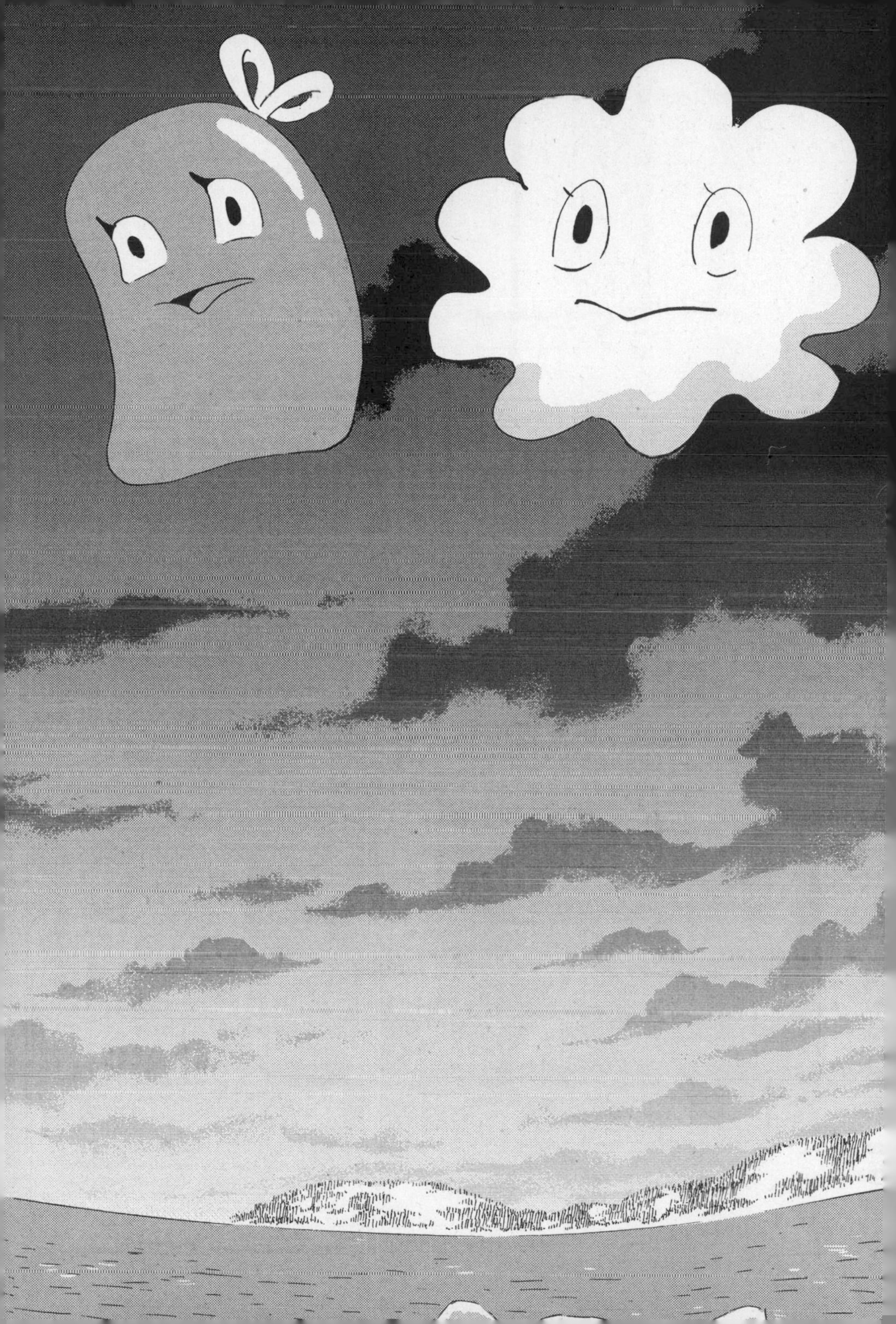

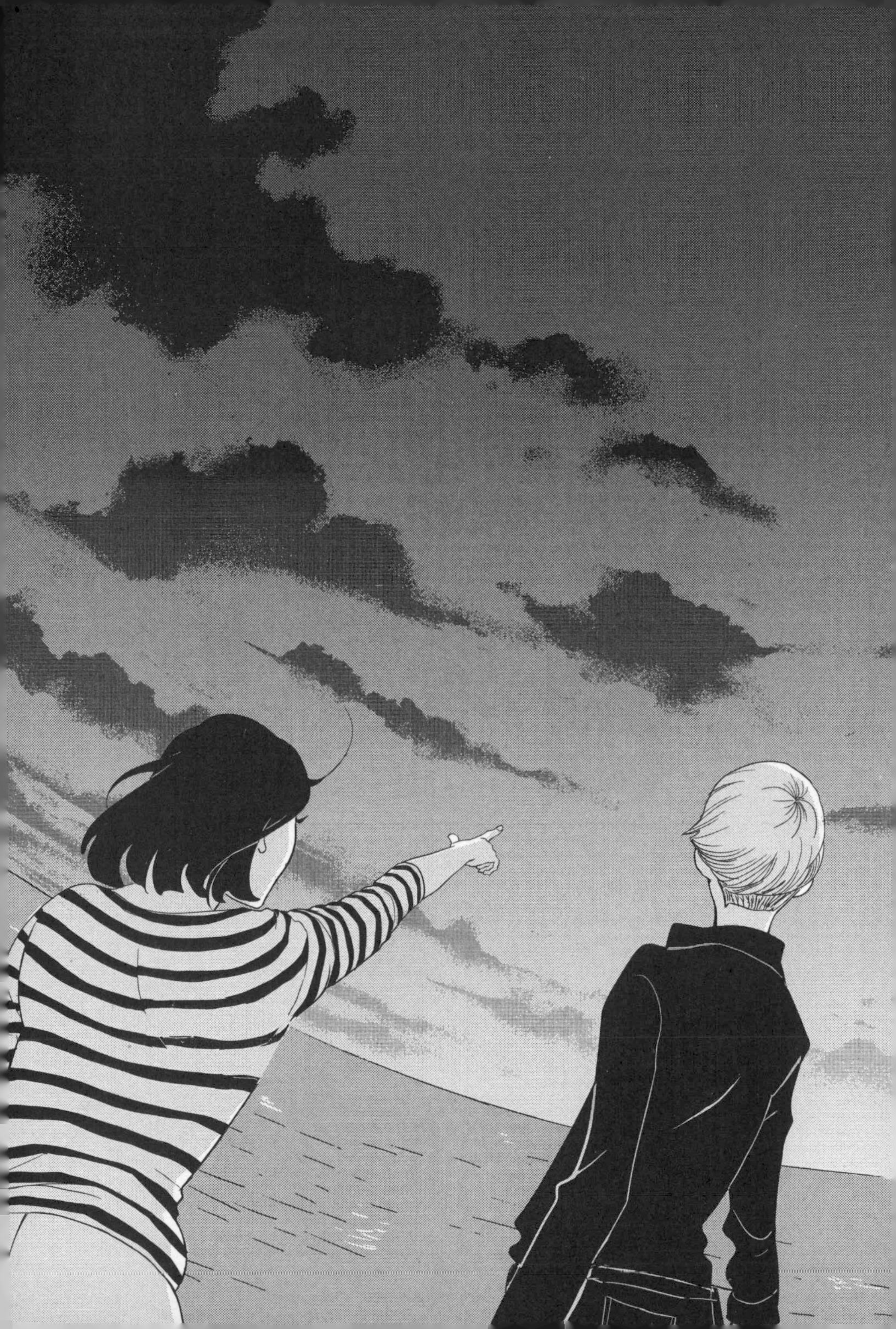

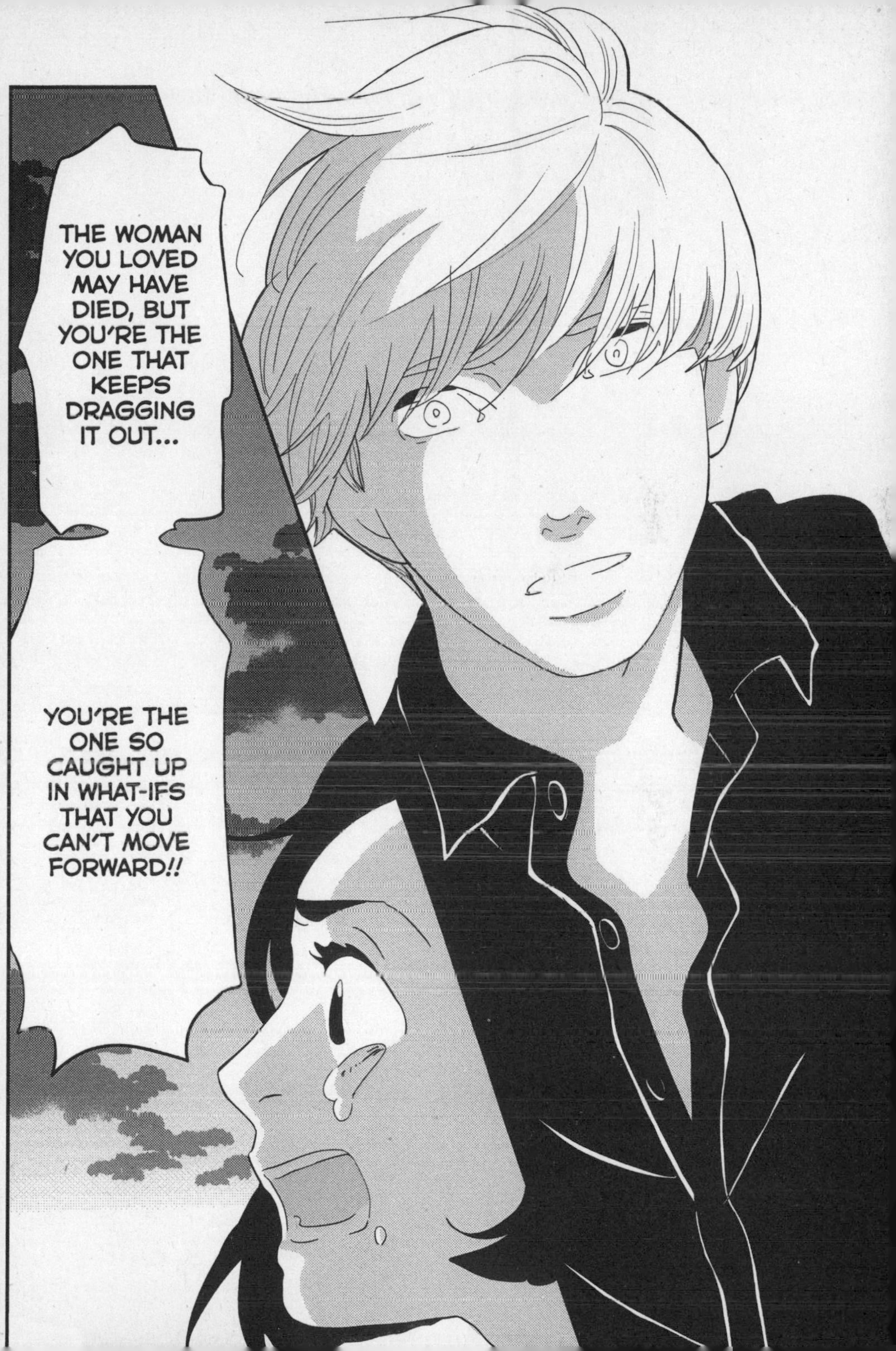
THE WOMAN YOU LOVED MAY HAVE DIED, BUT YOU'RE THE ONE THAT KEEPS DRAGGING IT OUT...
YOU'RE THE ONE SO CAUGHT UP IN WHAT-IFS THAT YOU CAN'T MOVE FORWARD!!

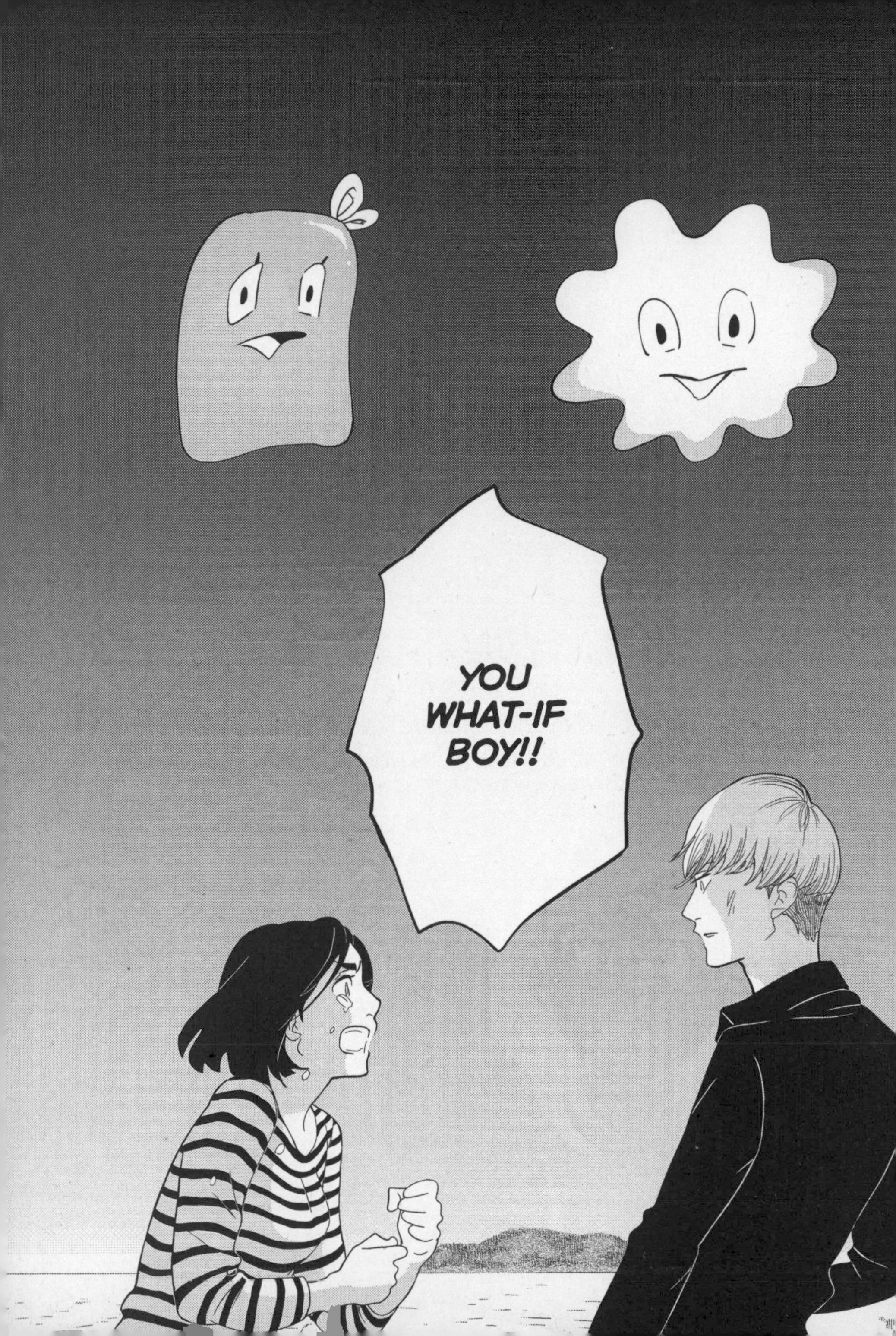
YOU WHAT-IF BOY!!

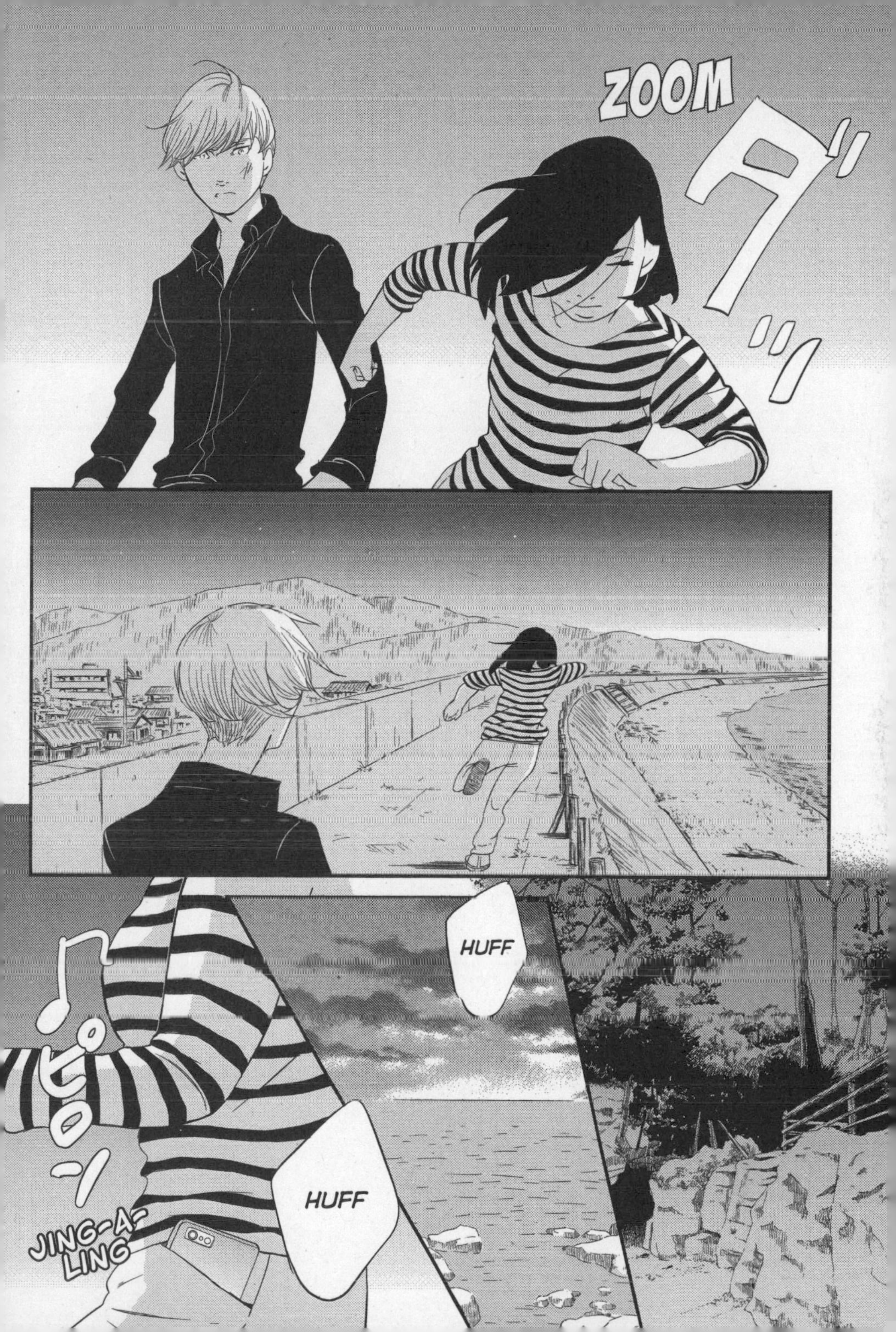
ZOOM
ダッ
HUFF
HUFF
JING-A-LING
ピローン

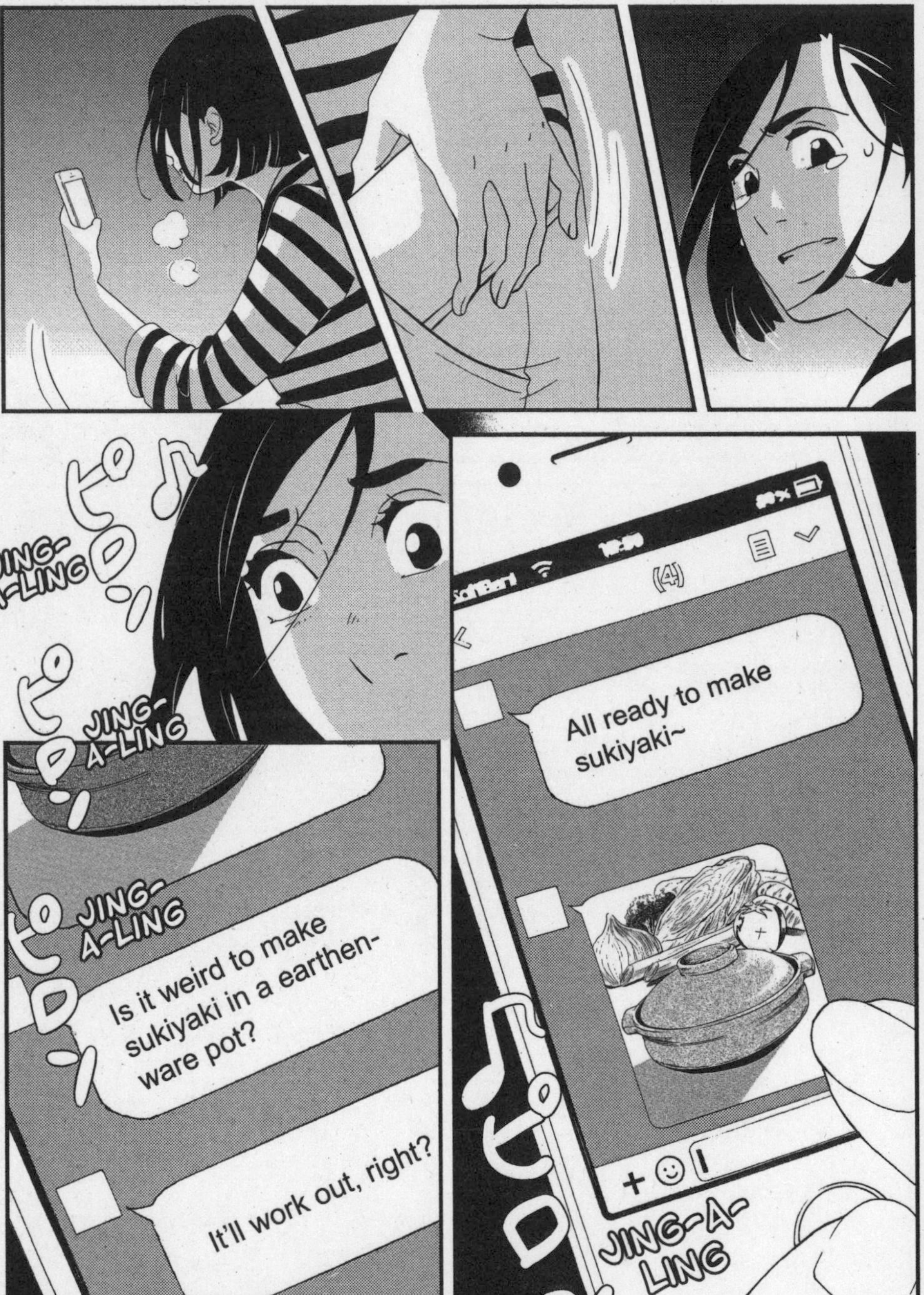
(4)
All ready to make sukiyaki~
JING-A-LING
JING-A-LING
JING-A-LING
JING-A-LING
Is it weird to make sukiyaki in a earthen-ware pot?
It'll work out, right?

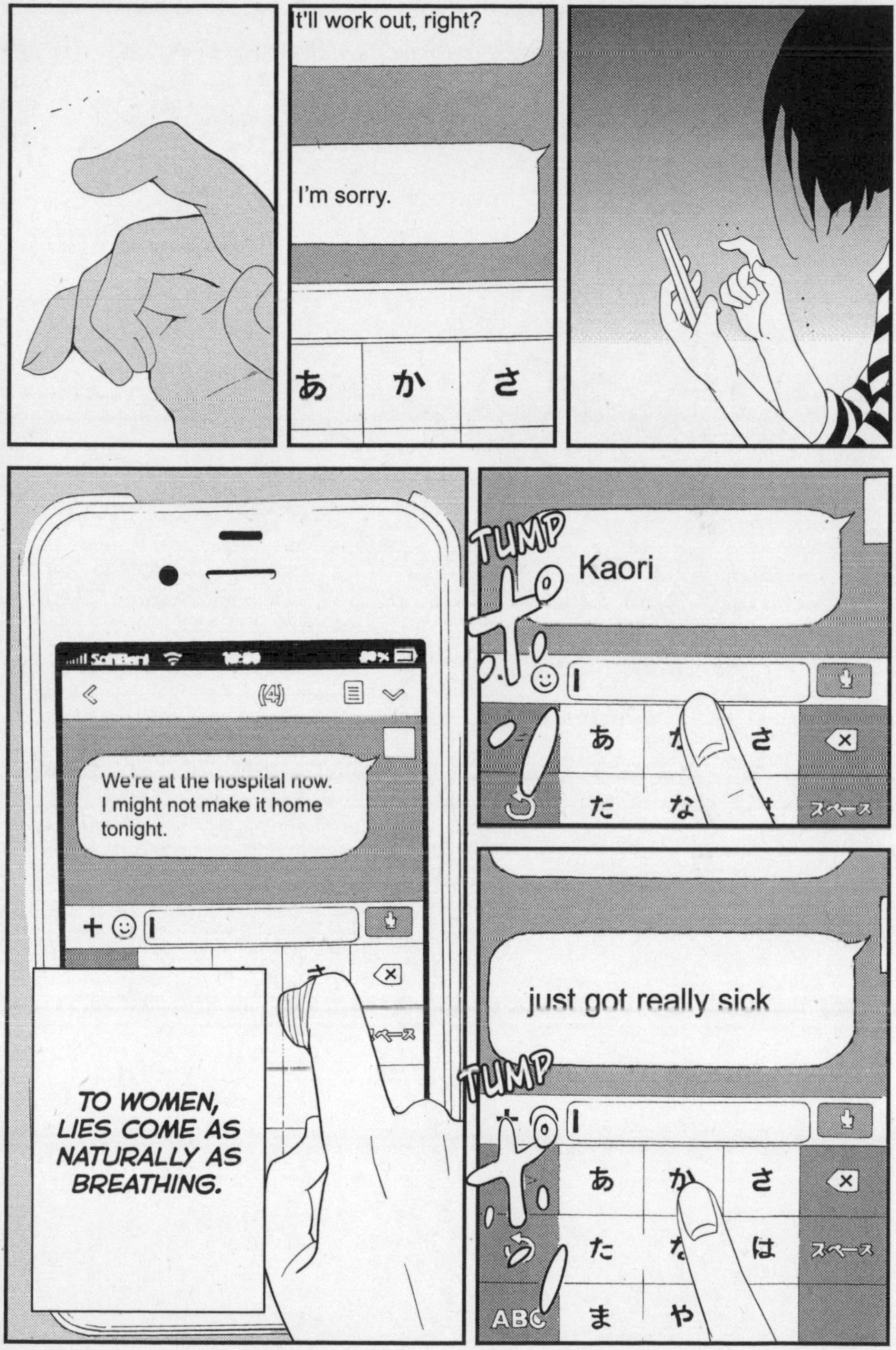

It'll work out, right?
I'm sorry.
あ か さ
TUMP
Kaori
TUMP
just got really sick
We're at the hospital now. I might not make it home tonight.
TO WOMEN, LIES COME AS NATURALLY AS BREATHING.

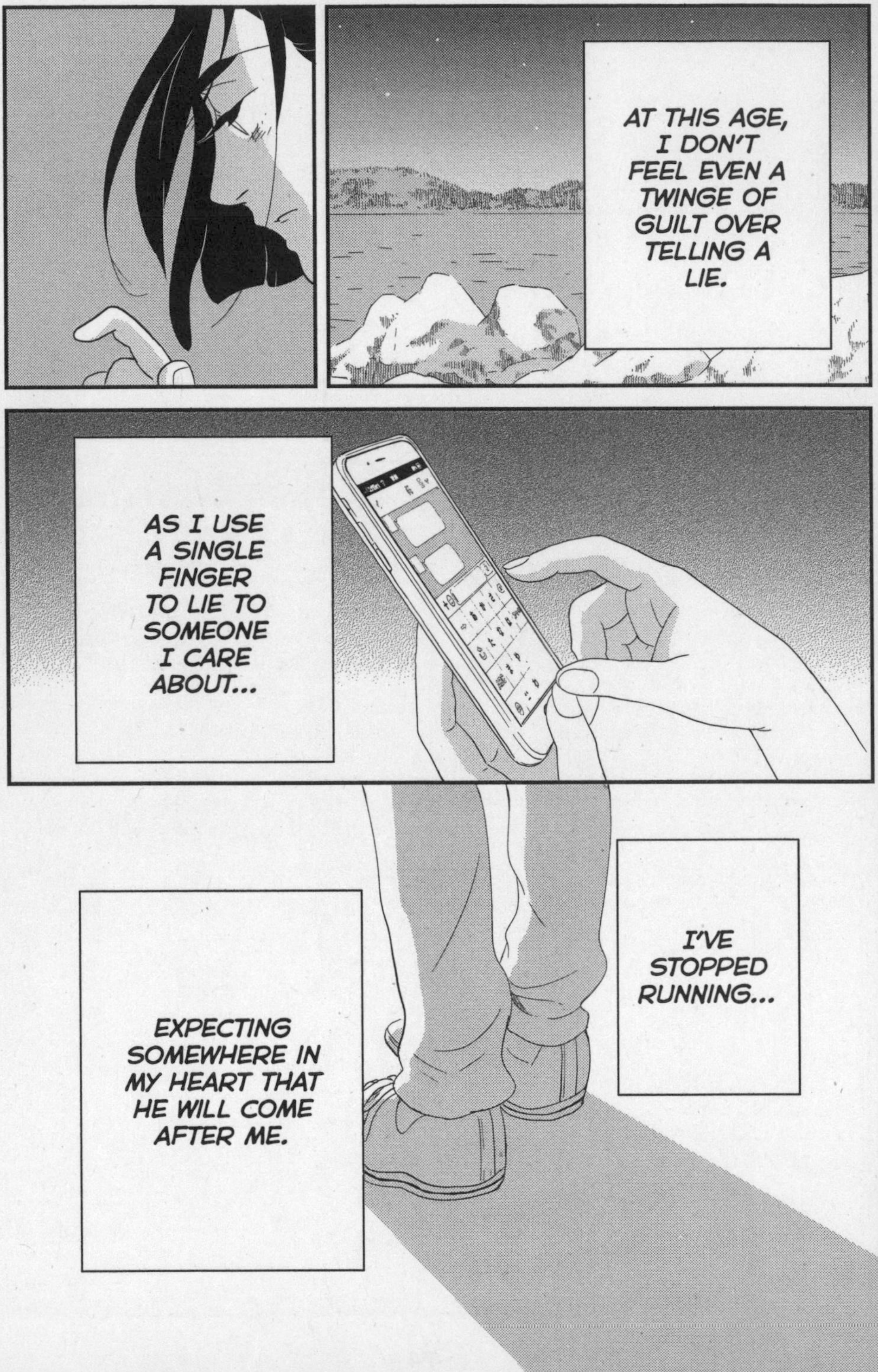
AT THIS AGE, I DON'T FEEL EVEN A TWINGE OF GUILT OVER TELLING A LIE.
AS I USE A SINGLE FINGER TO LIE TO SOMEONE I CARE ABOUT...
I'VE STOPPED RUNNING...
EXPECTING SOMEWHERE IN MY HEART THAT HE WILL COME AFTER ME.

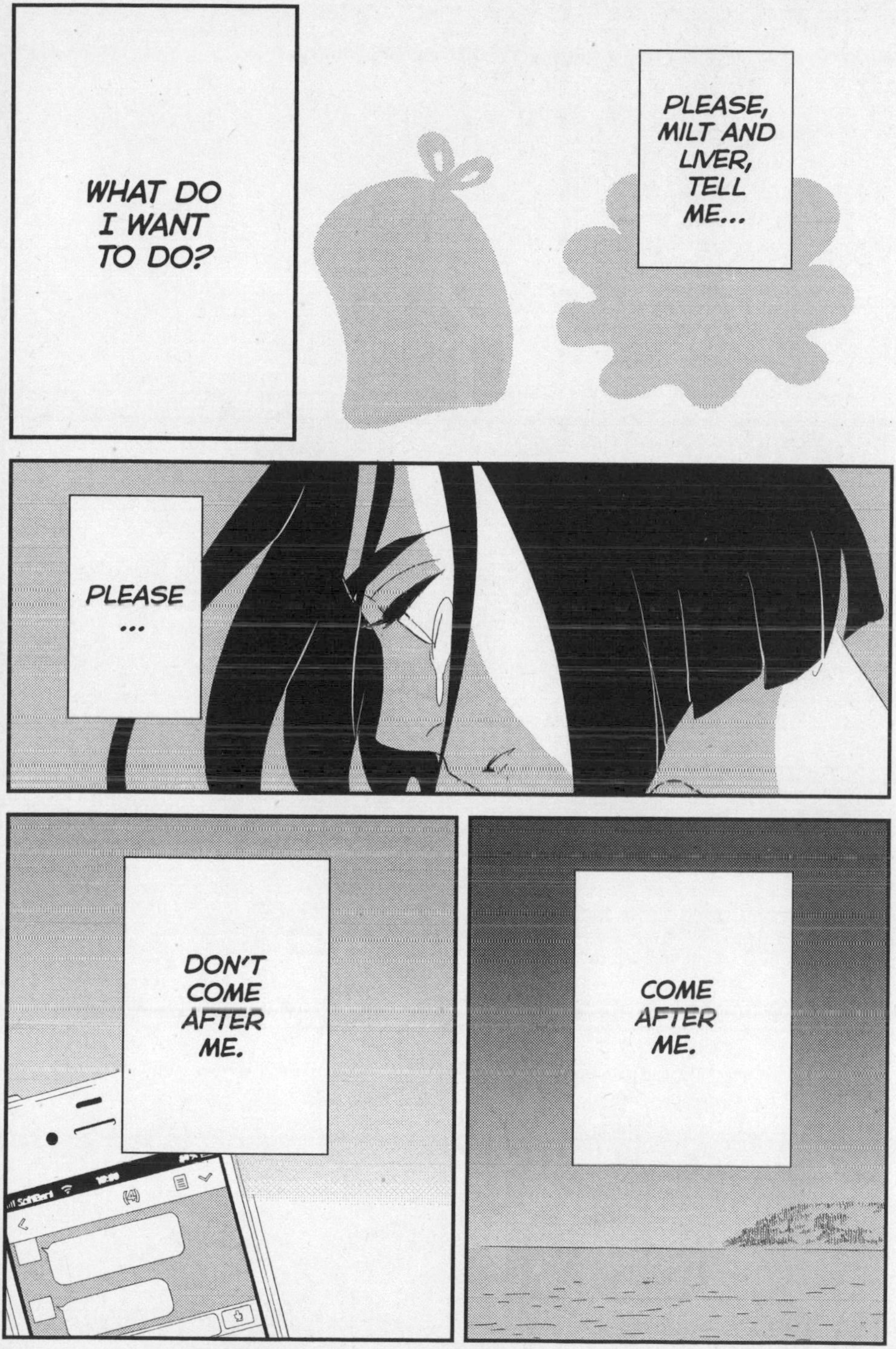
PLEASE, MILT AND LIVER, TELL ME...
WHAT DO I WANT TO DO?
PLEASE ...
COME AFTER ME.
DON'T COME AFTER ME.

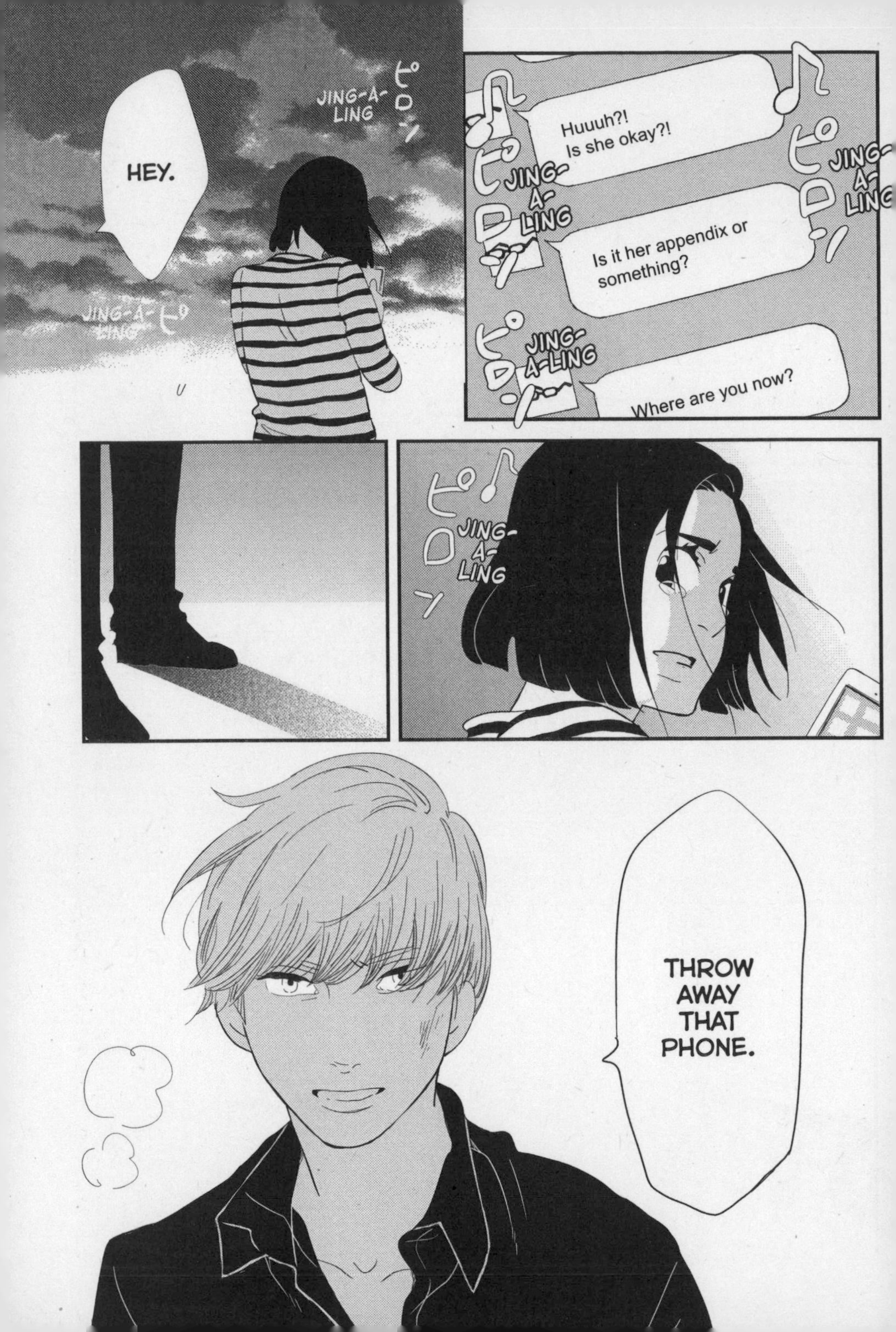
ピロン
JING-A-LING
Huuuh?!
Is she okay?!
ピロン
JING-A-LING
Is it her appendix or
something?
ピロン
JING-A-LING
Where are you now?
ピロン
JING-A-LING
HEY.
ピロン
JING-A-LING
ピロン
JING-A-LING
THROW AWAY THAT PHONE.

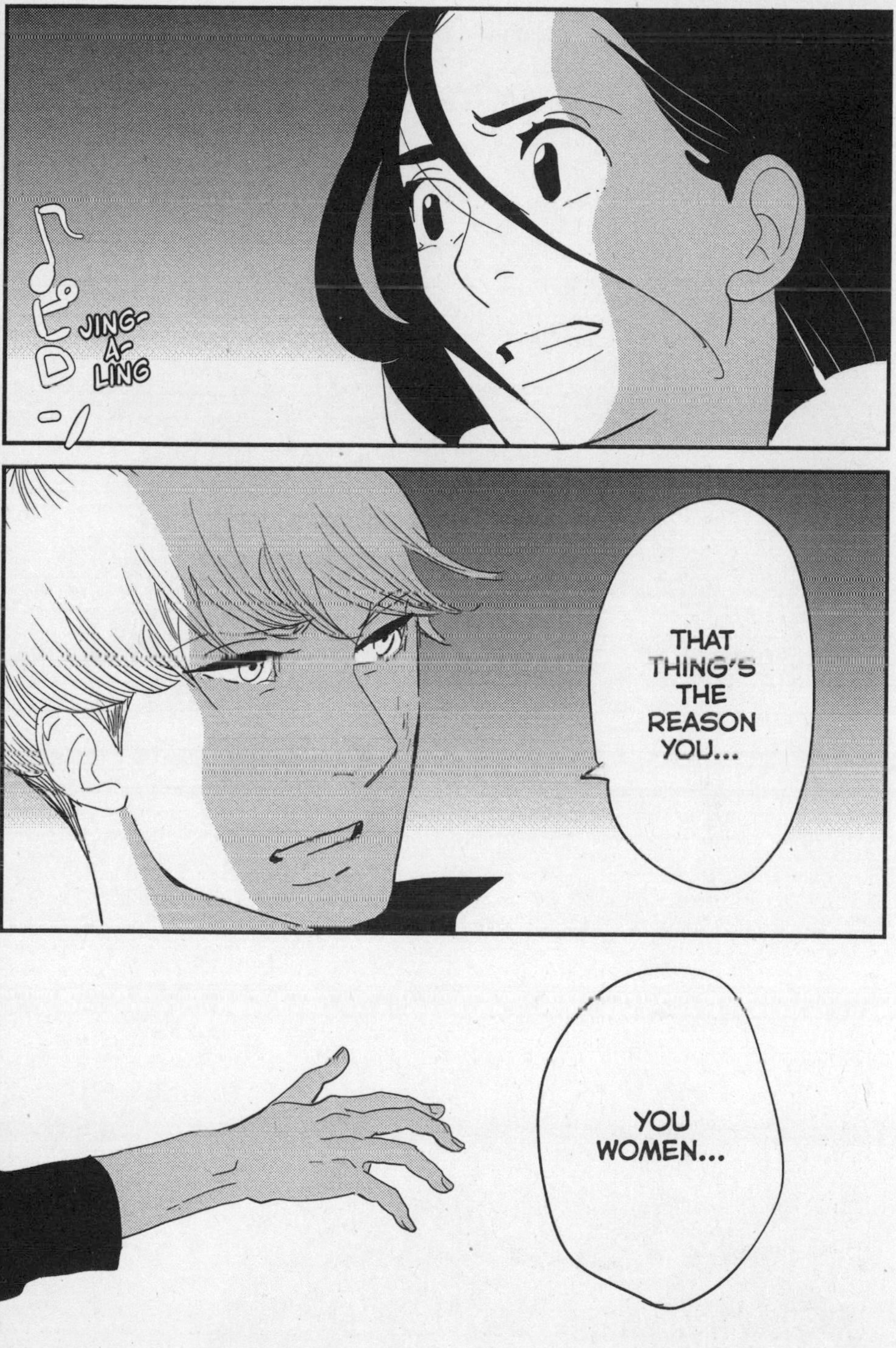
JING-A-LING
THAT THING'S THE REASON YOU...
YOU WOMEN...

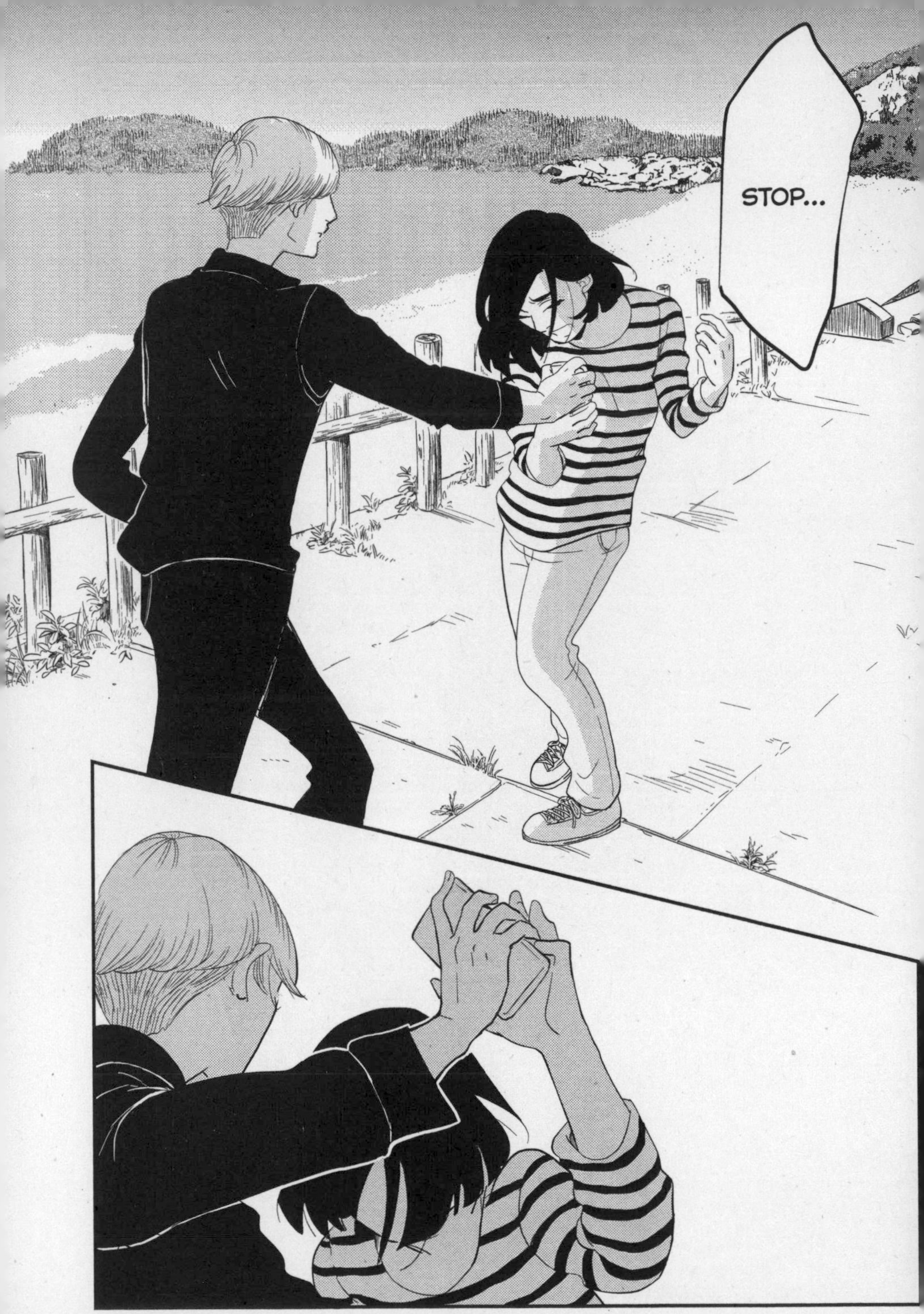
STOP...

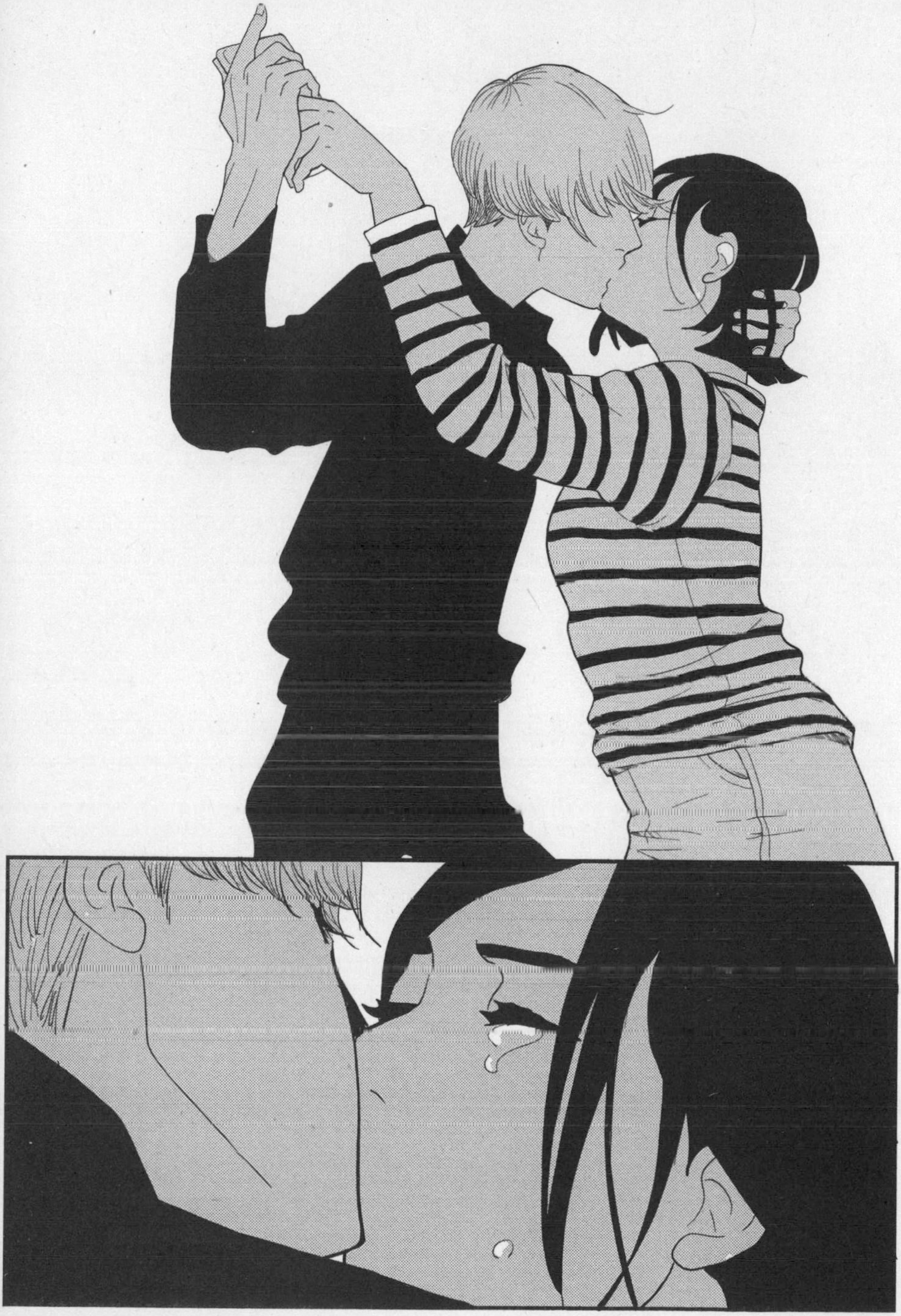

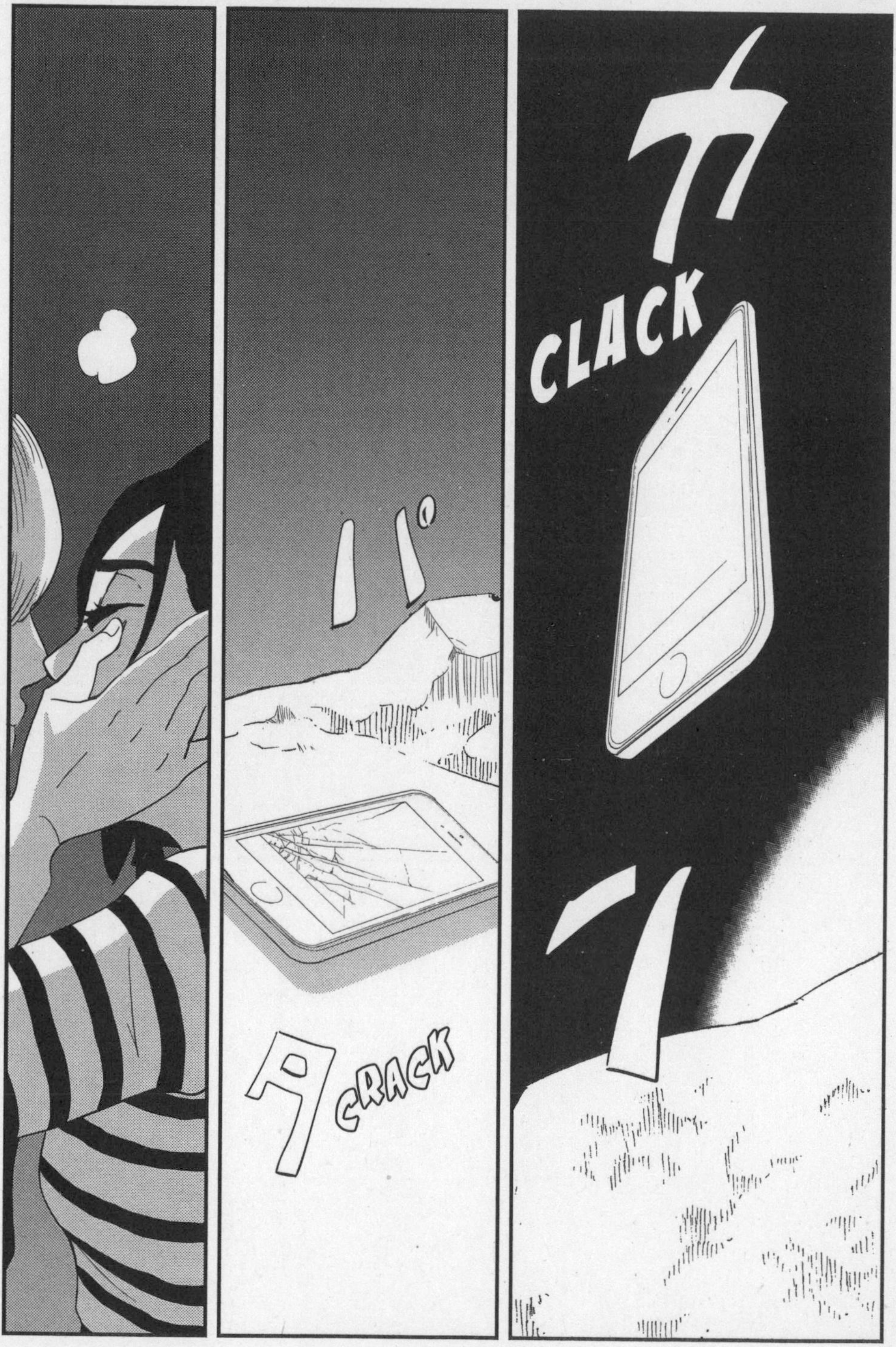
CLACK
CRACK

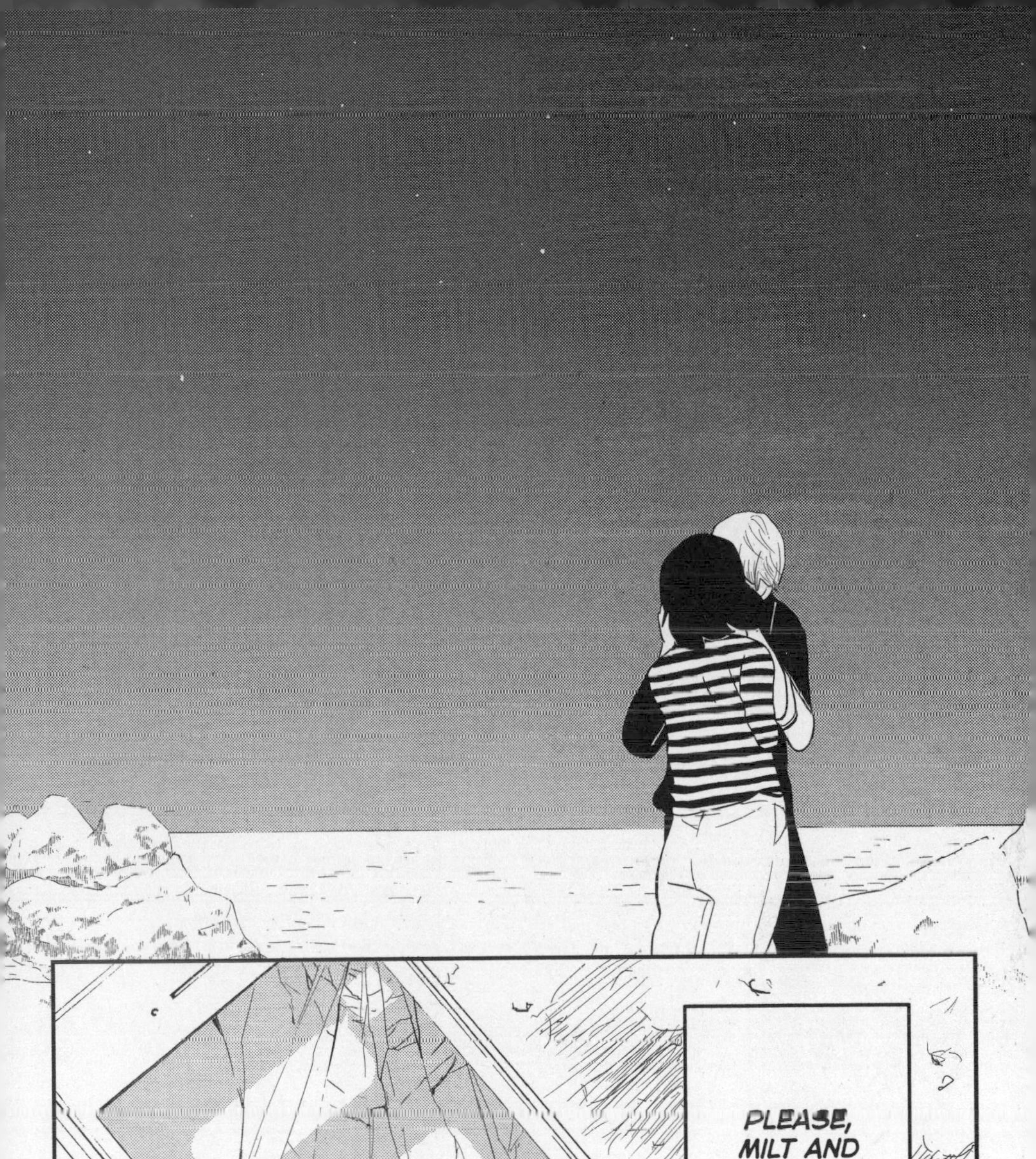

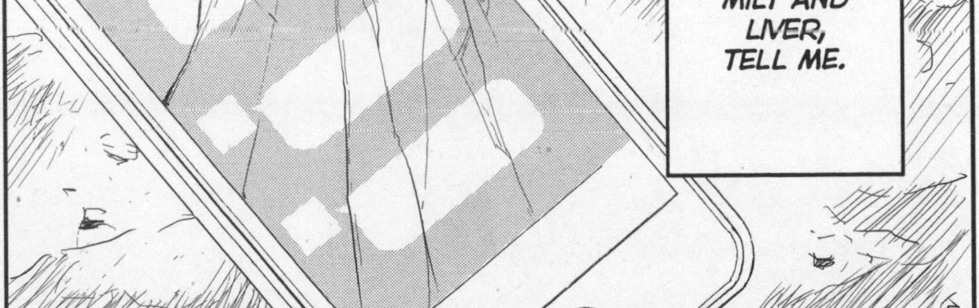
PLEASE, MILT AND LIVER, TELL ME.

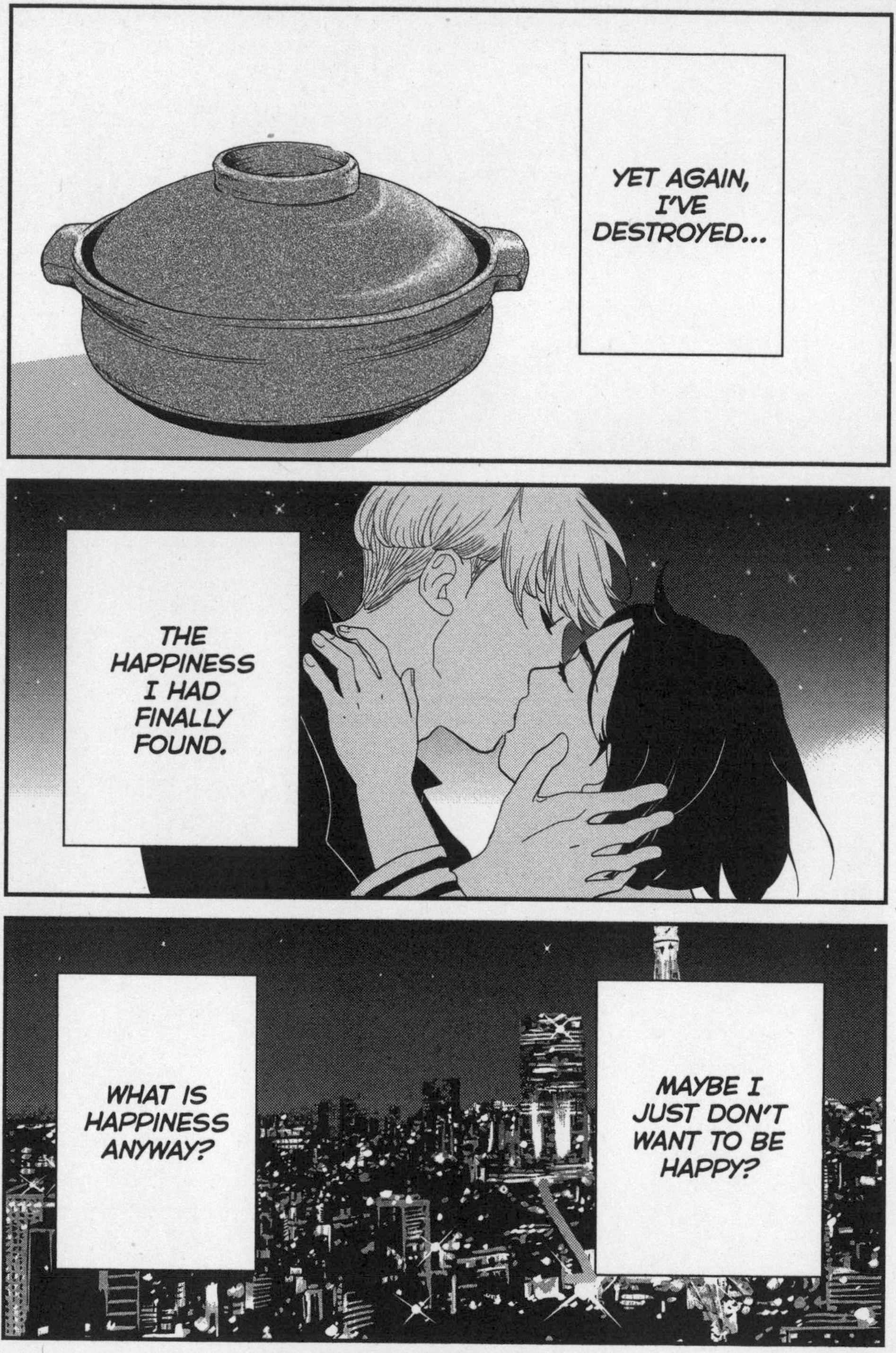
YET AGAIN, I'VE DESTROYED...
THE HAPPINESS I HAD FINALLY FOUND.
MAYBE I JUST DON'T WANT TO BE HAPPY?
WHAT IS HAPPINESS ANYWAY?

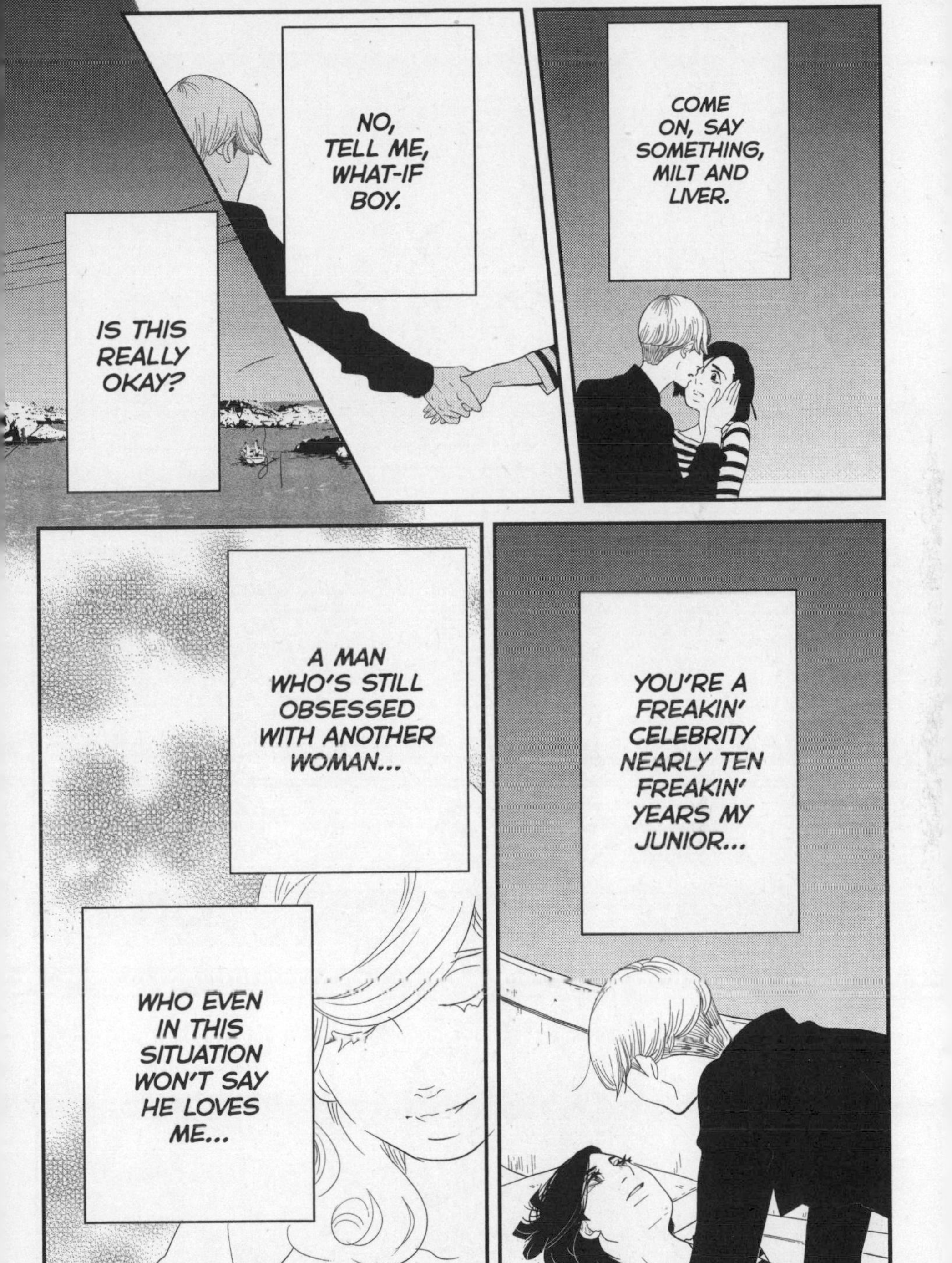
COME ON, SAY SOMETHING, MILT AND LIVER.
NO, TELL ME, WHAT-IF BOY.
IS THIS REALLY OKAY?
YOU'RE A FREAKIN' CELEBRITY NEARLY TEN FREAKIN' YEARS MY JUNIOR...
A MAN WHO'S STILL OBSESSED WITH ANOTHER WOMAN...
WHO EVEN IN THIS SITUATION WON'T SAY HE LOVES ME...

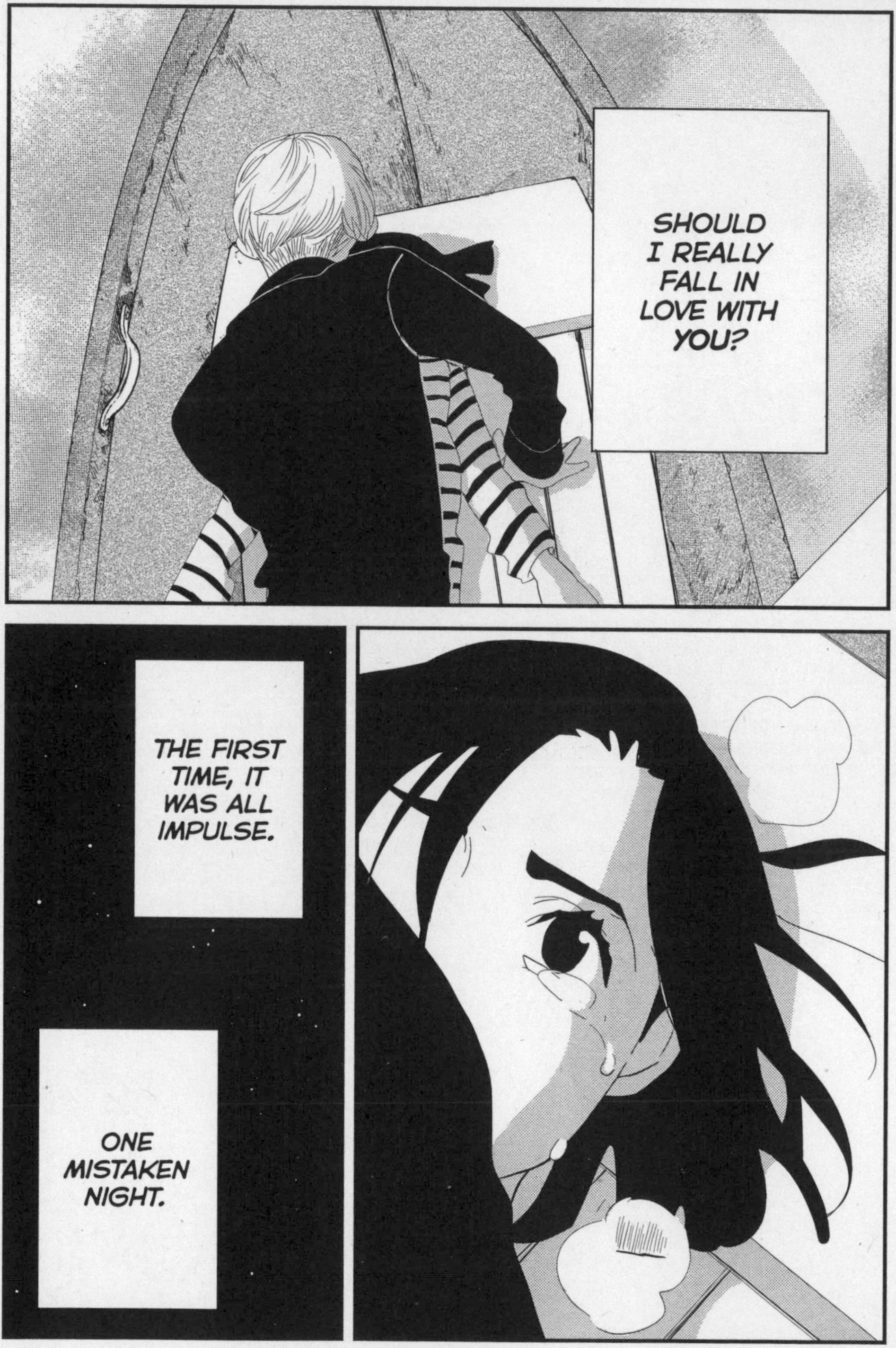
SHOULD I REALLY FALL IN LOVE WITH YOU?
THE FIRST TIME, IT WAS ALL IMPULSE.
ONE MISTAKEN NIGHT.

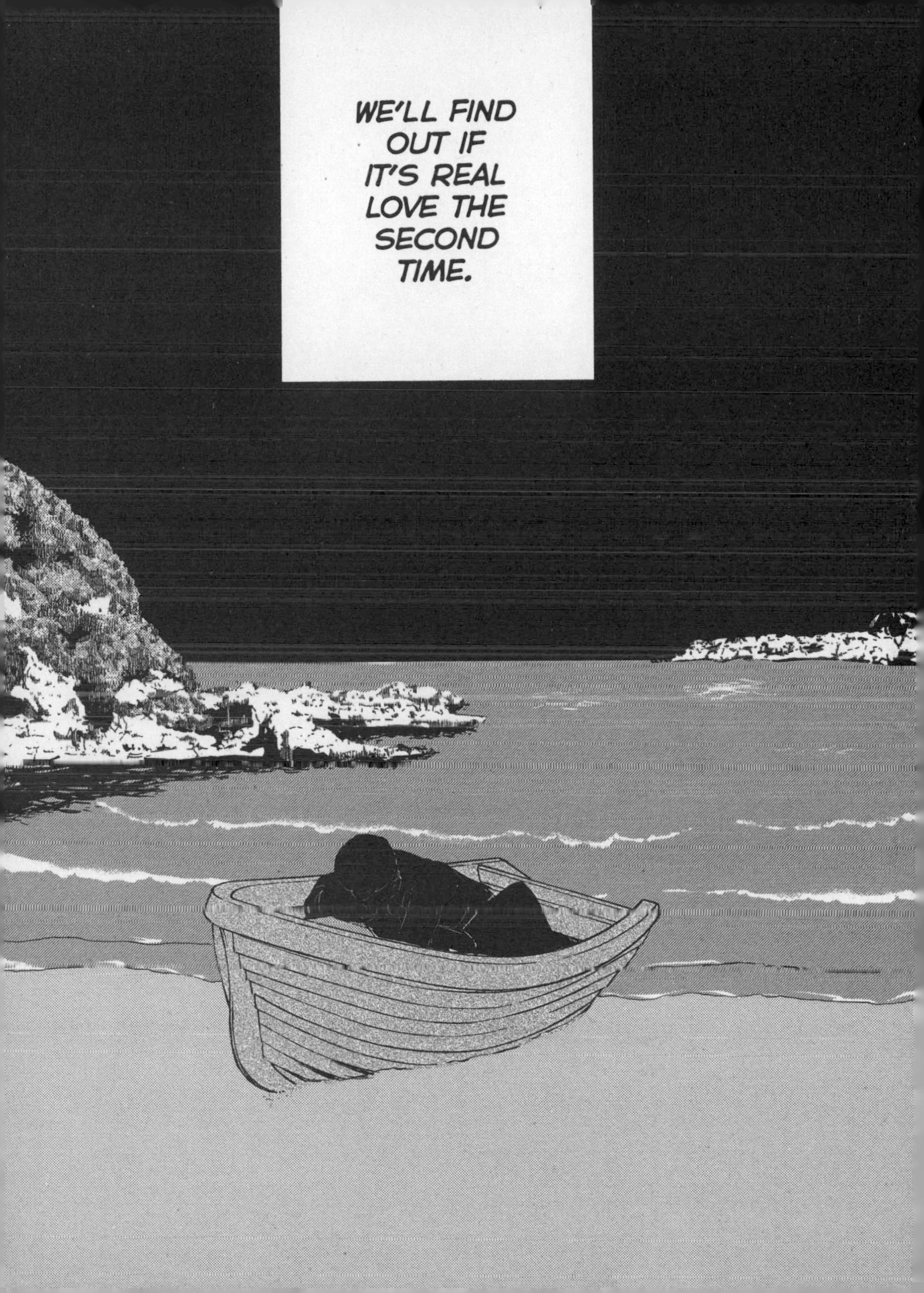
WE'LL FIND OUT IF IT'S REAL LOVE THE SECOND TIME.

ACT 0 BEFORE TARAREBA GIRLS

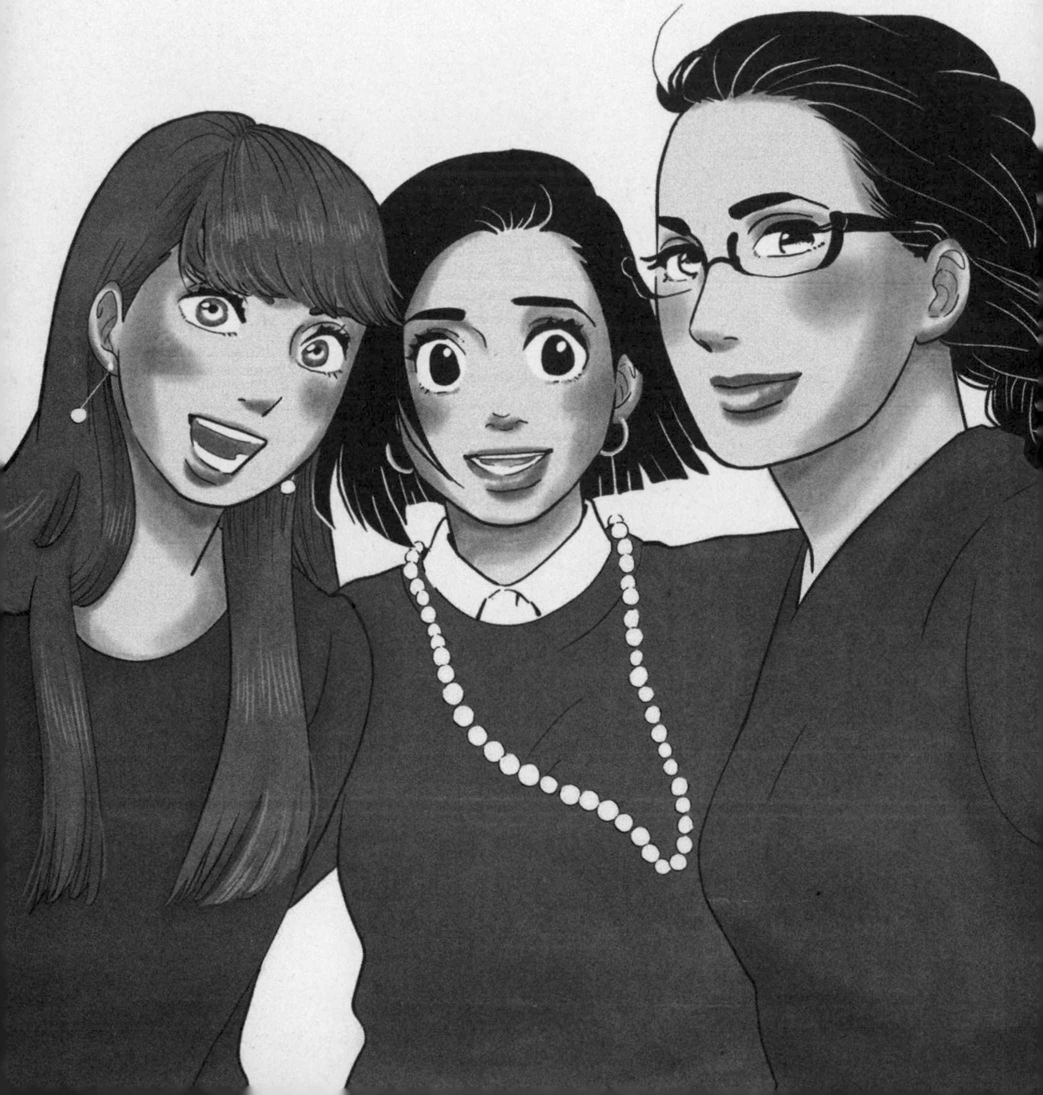

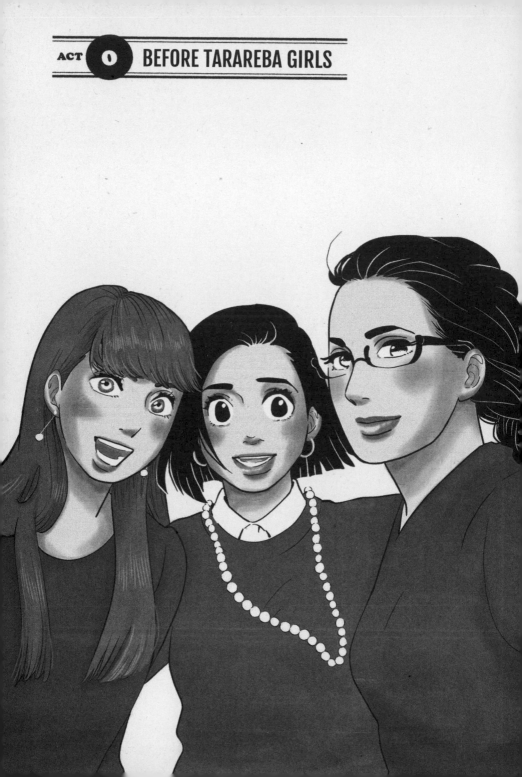

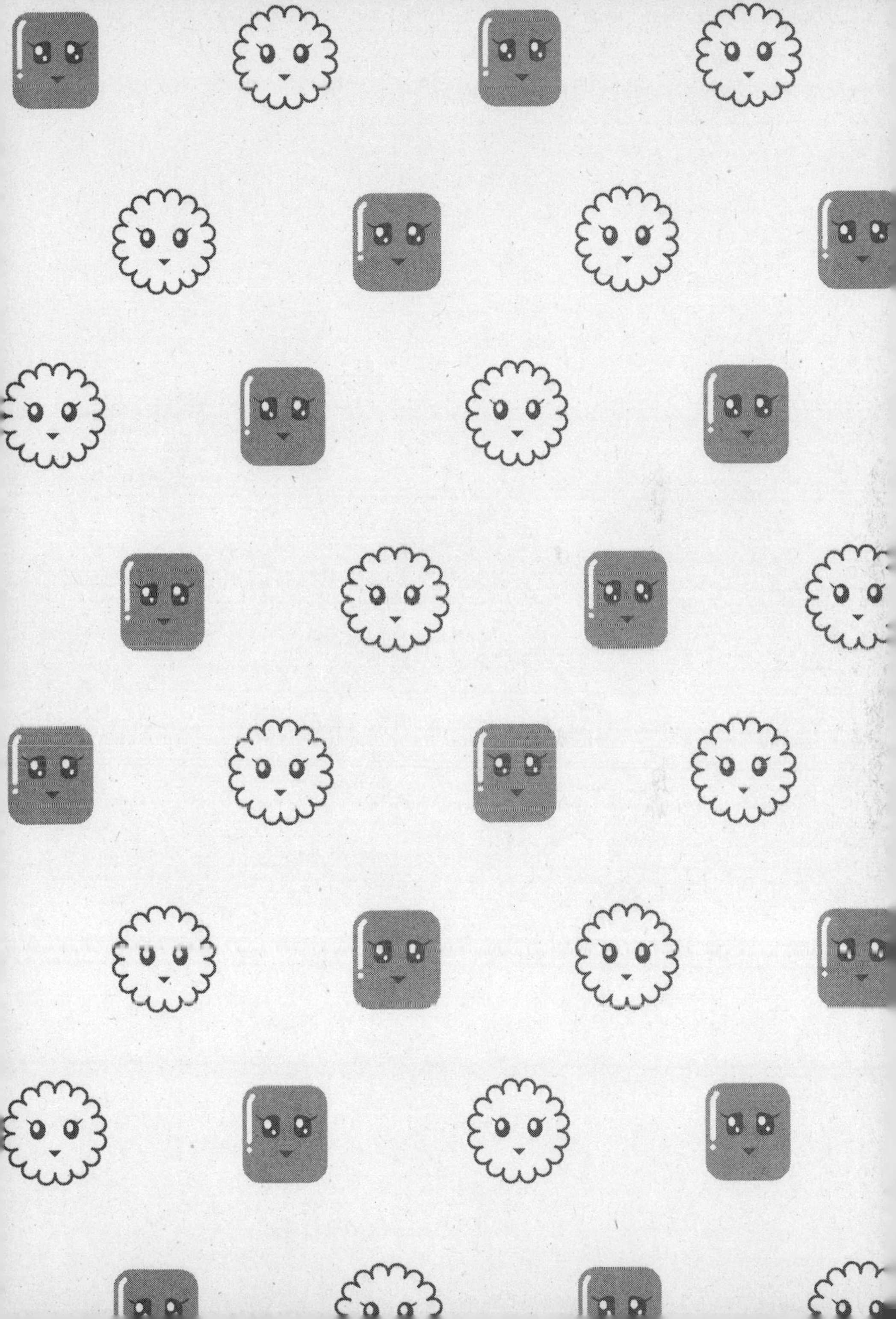

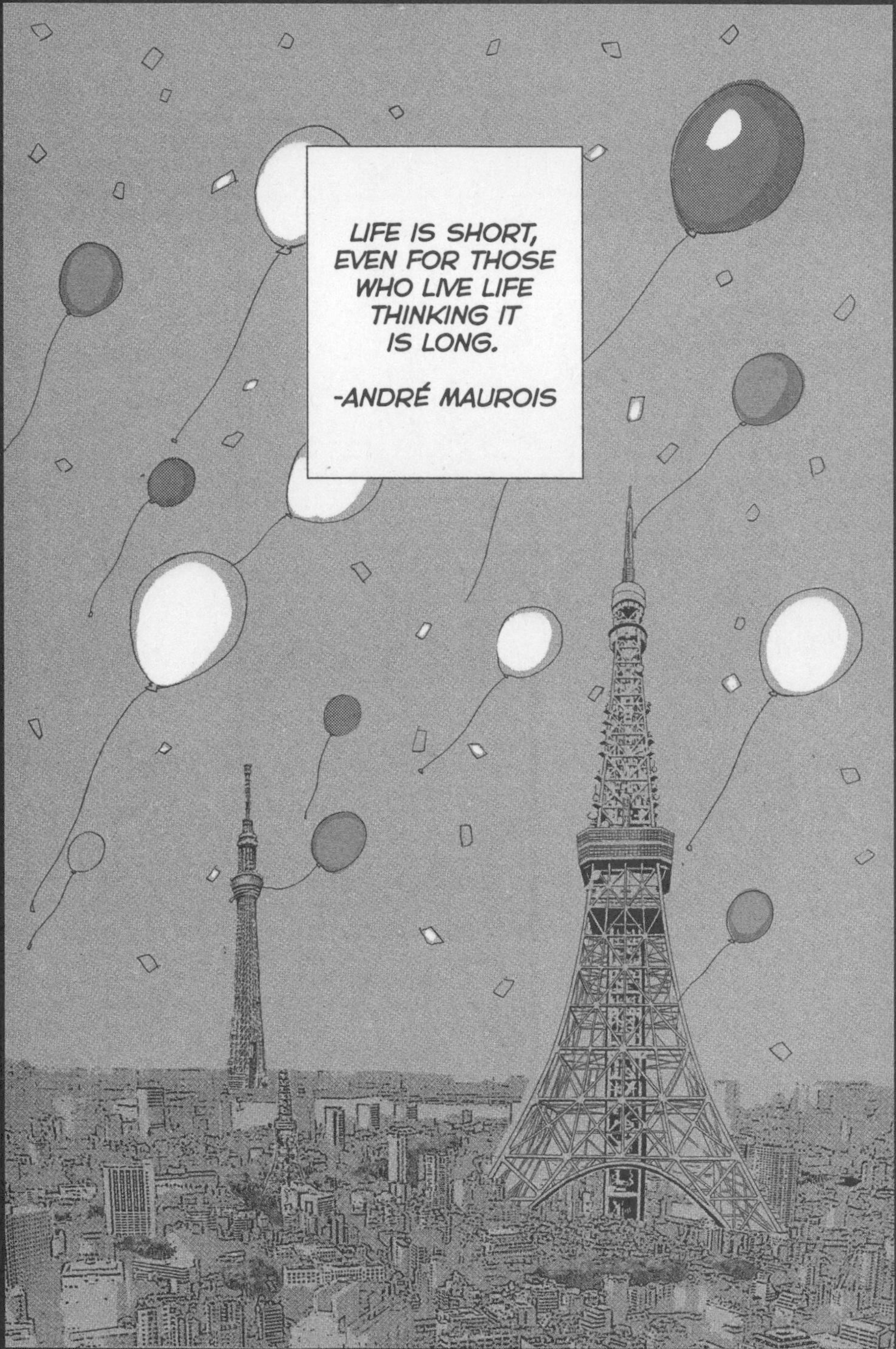
LIFE IS SHORT, EVEN FOR THOSE WHO LIVE LIFE THINKING IT IS LONG.
-ANDRÉ MAUROIS

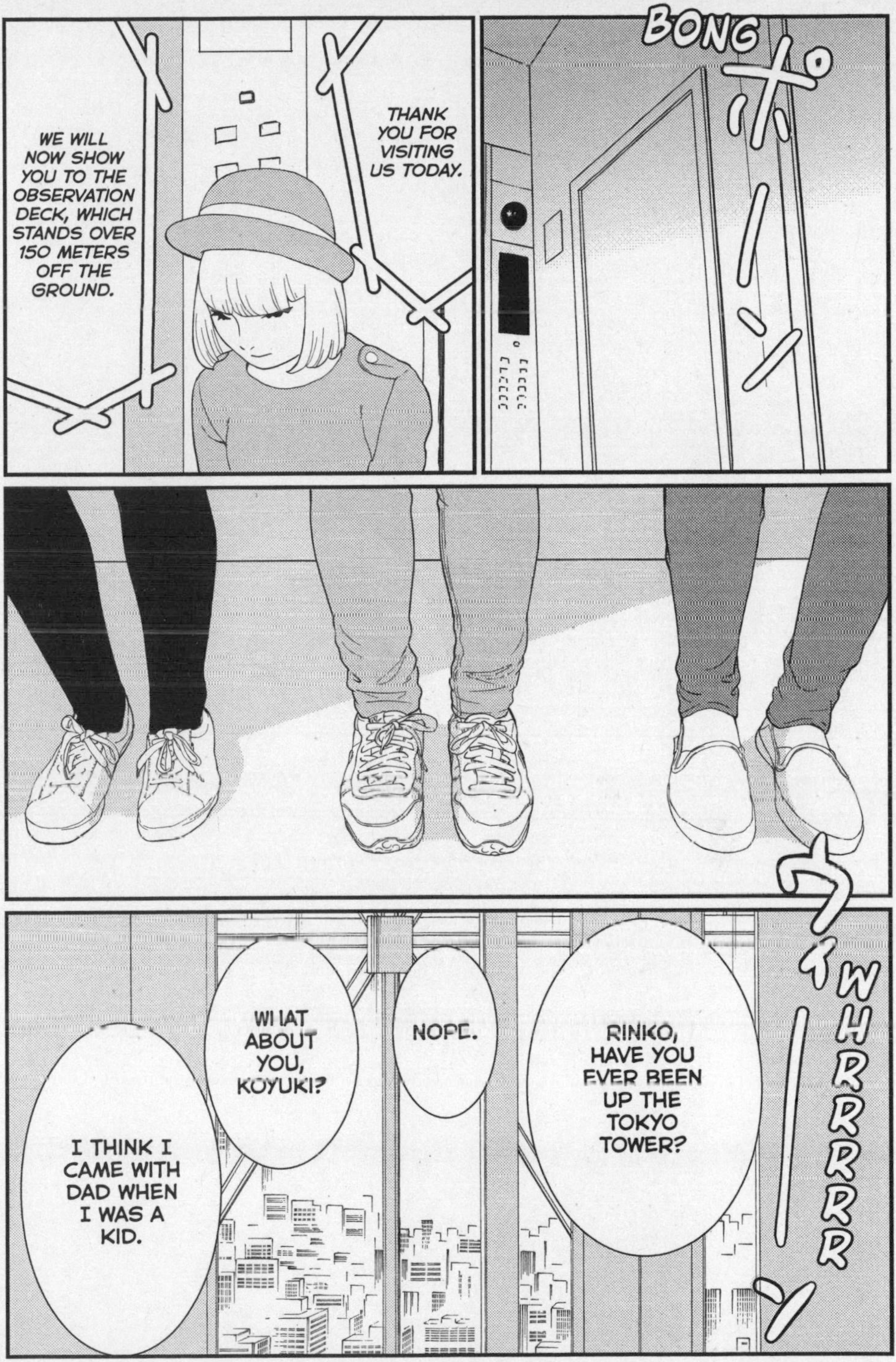
BONG
ポーン
THANK YOU FOR VISITING US TODAY.
WE WILL NOW SHOW YOU TO THE OBSERVATION DECK, WHICH STANDS OVER 150 METERS OFF THE GROUND.
ウィーン
WHRRRRR
RINKO, HAVE YOU EVER BEEN UP THE TOKYO TOWER?
NOPE.
WHAT ABOUT YOU, KOYUKI?
I THINK I CAME WITH DAD WHEN I WAS A KID.

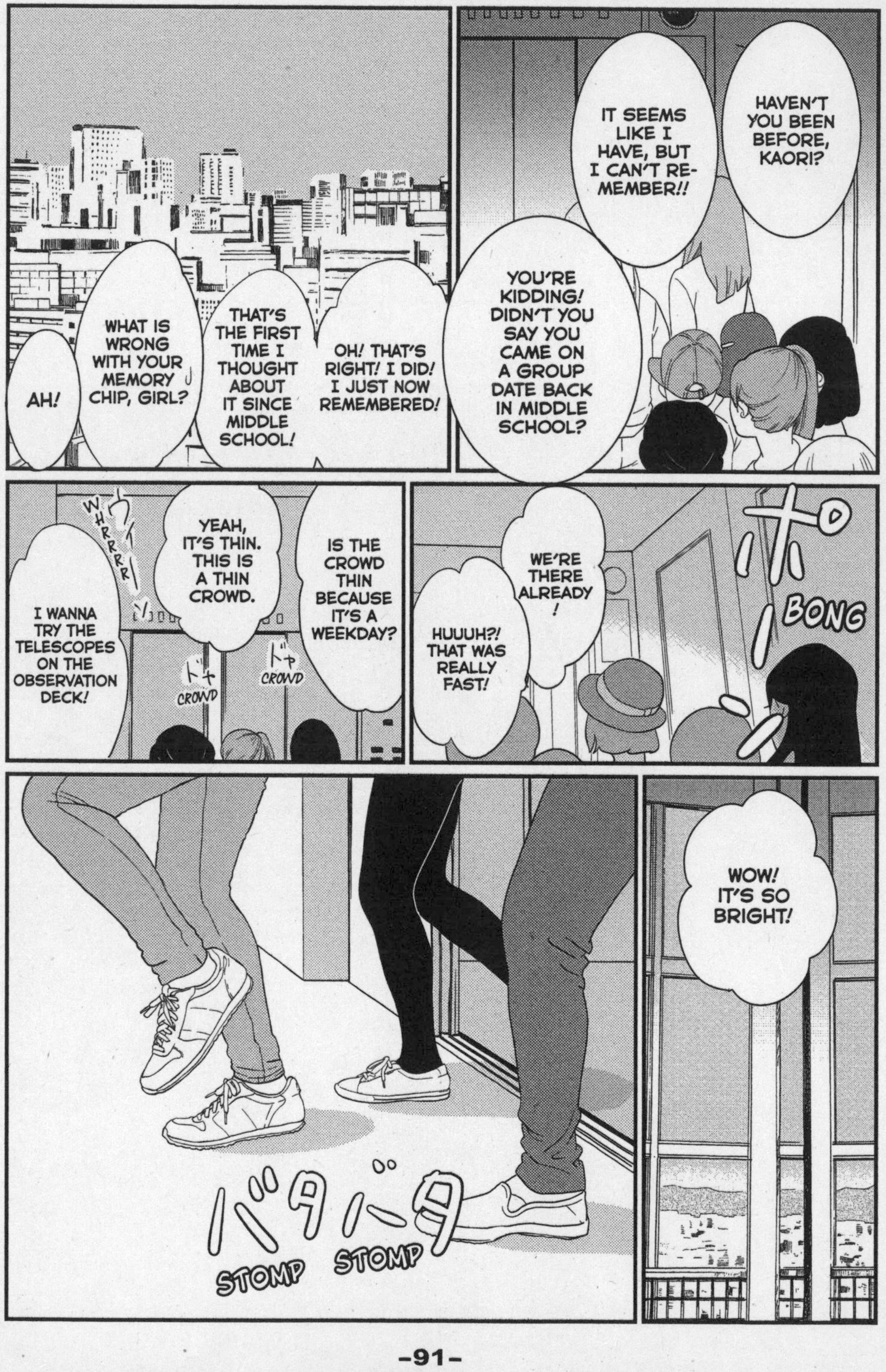
HAVEN'T YOU BEEN BEFORE, KAORI?
IT SEEMS LIKE I HAVE, BUT I CAN'T RE-MEMBER!!
YOU'RE KIDDING! DIDN'T YOU SAY YOU CAME ON A GROUP DATE BACK IN MIDDLE SCHOOL?
OH! THAT'S RIGHT! I DID! I JUST NOW REMEMBERED!
THAT'S THE FIRST TIME I THOUGHT ABOUT IT SINCE MIDDLE SCHOOL!
WHAT IS WRONG WITH YOUR MEMORY CHIP, GIRL?
AH!
ポーン
BONG
WE'RE THERE ALREADY!
HUUUH?! THAT WAS REALLY FAST!
IS THE CROWD THIN BECAUSE IT'S A WEEKDAY?
YEAH, IT'S THIN. THIS IS A THIN CROWD.
ウィーン
WHRRRR
ドヤ
CROWD
ドヤ
CROWD
I WANNA TRY THE TELESCOPES ON THE OBSERVATION DECK!
WOW! IT'S SO BRIGHT!
バタバタ
STOMP STOMP

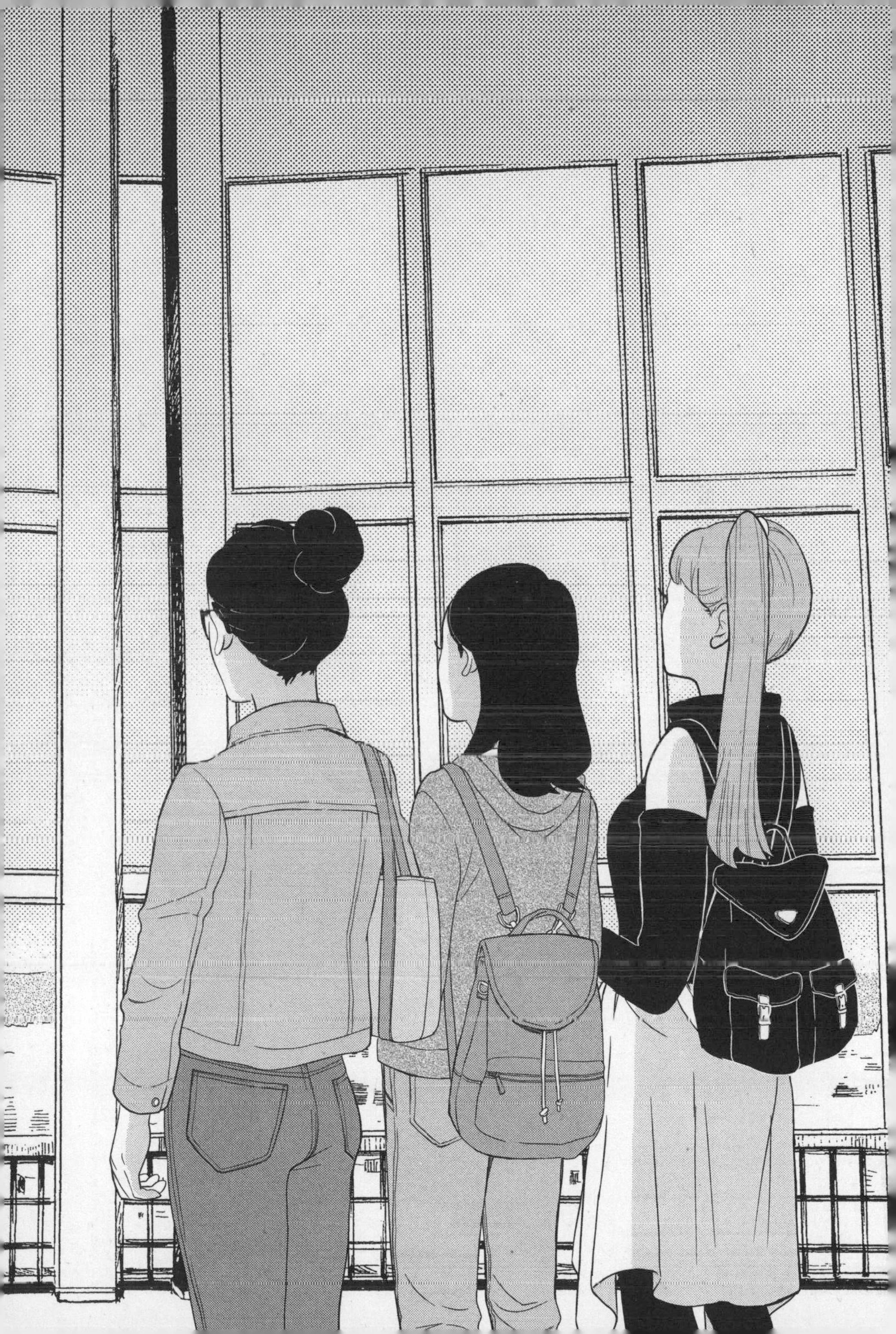

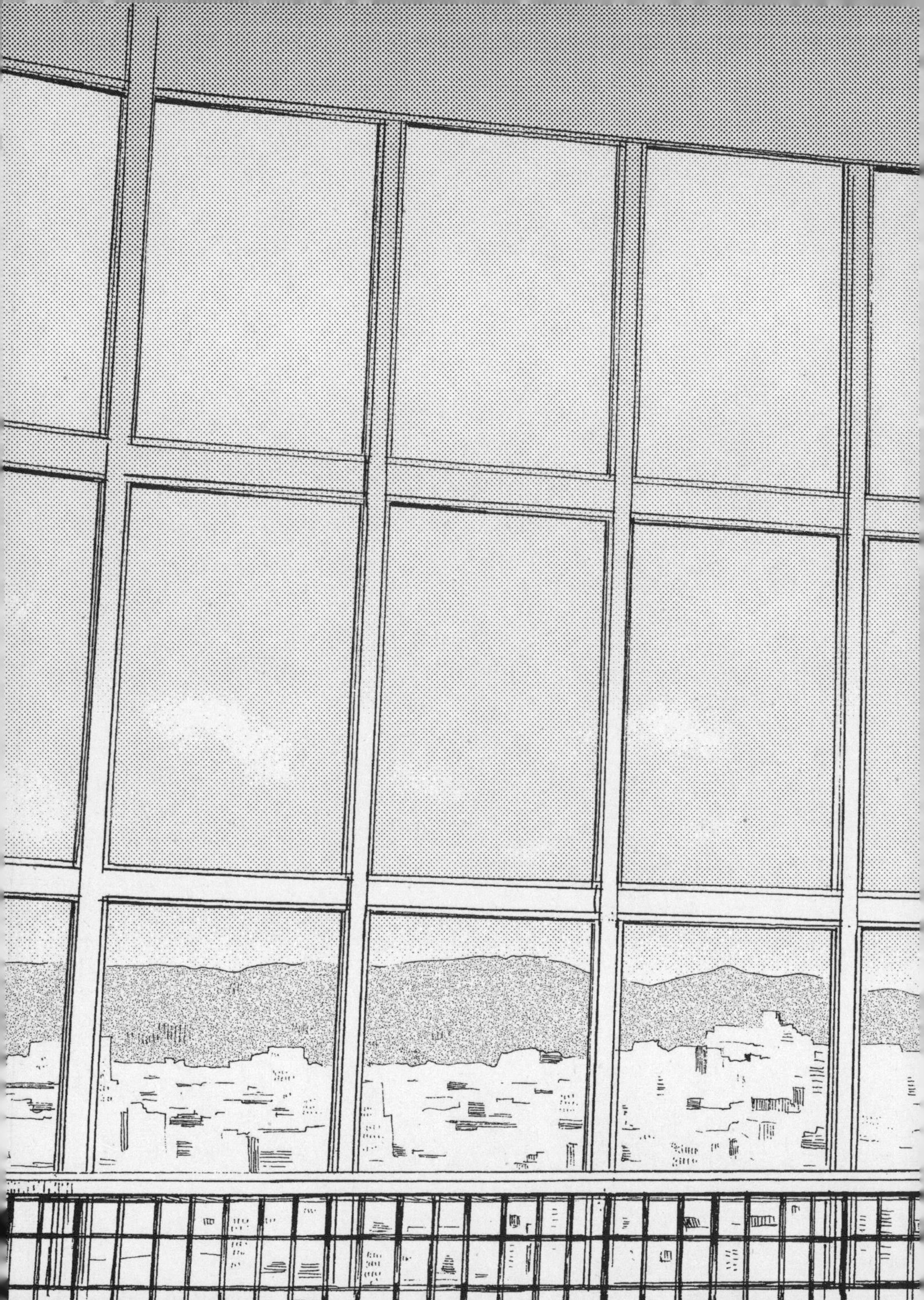

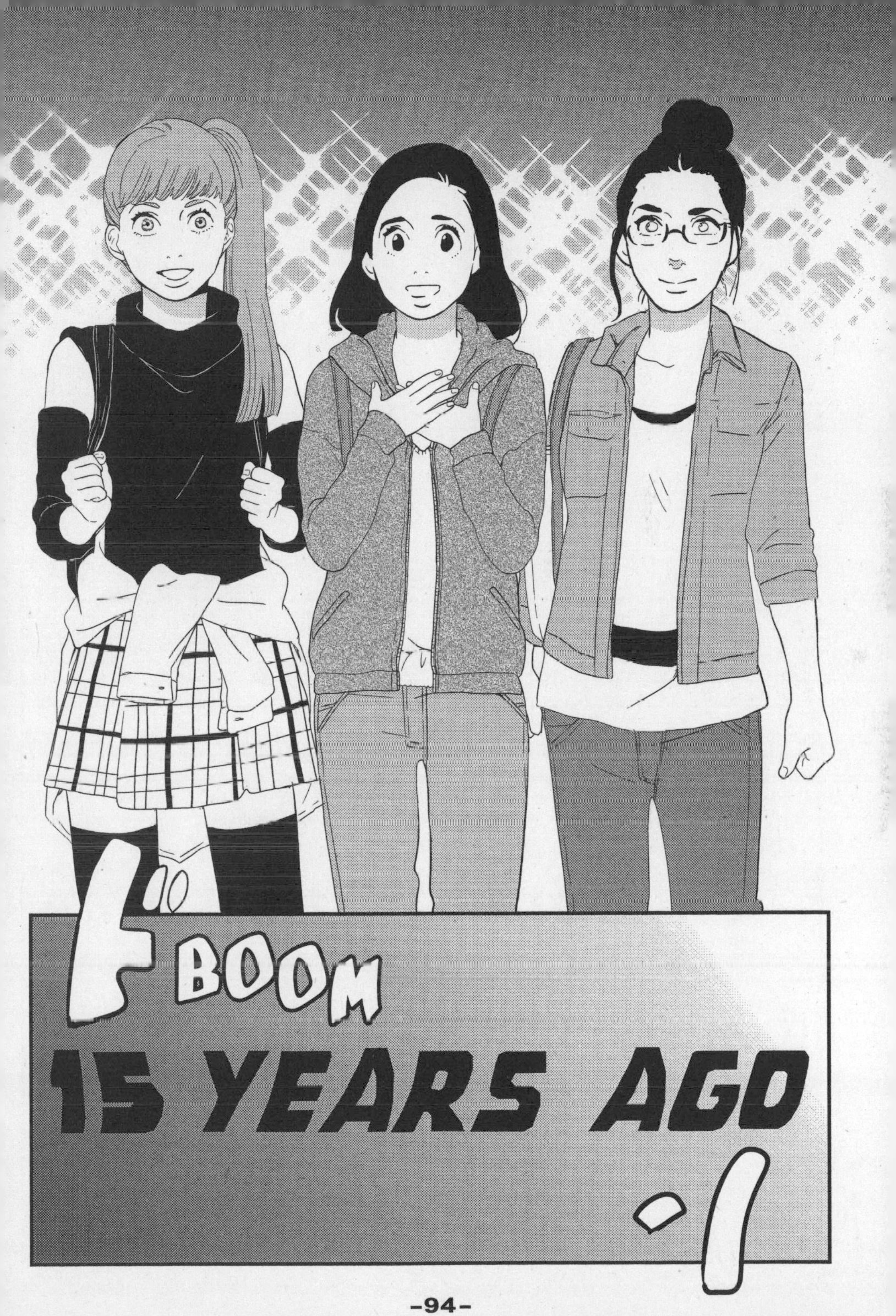
BOOM
15 YEARS AGO
-1

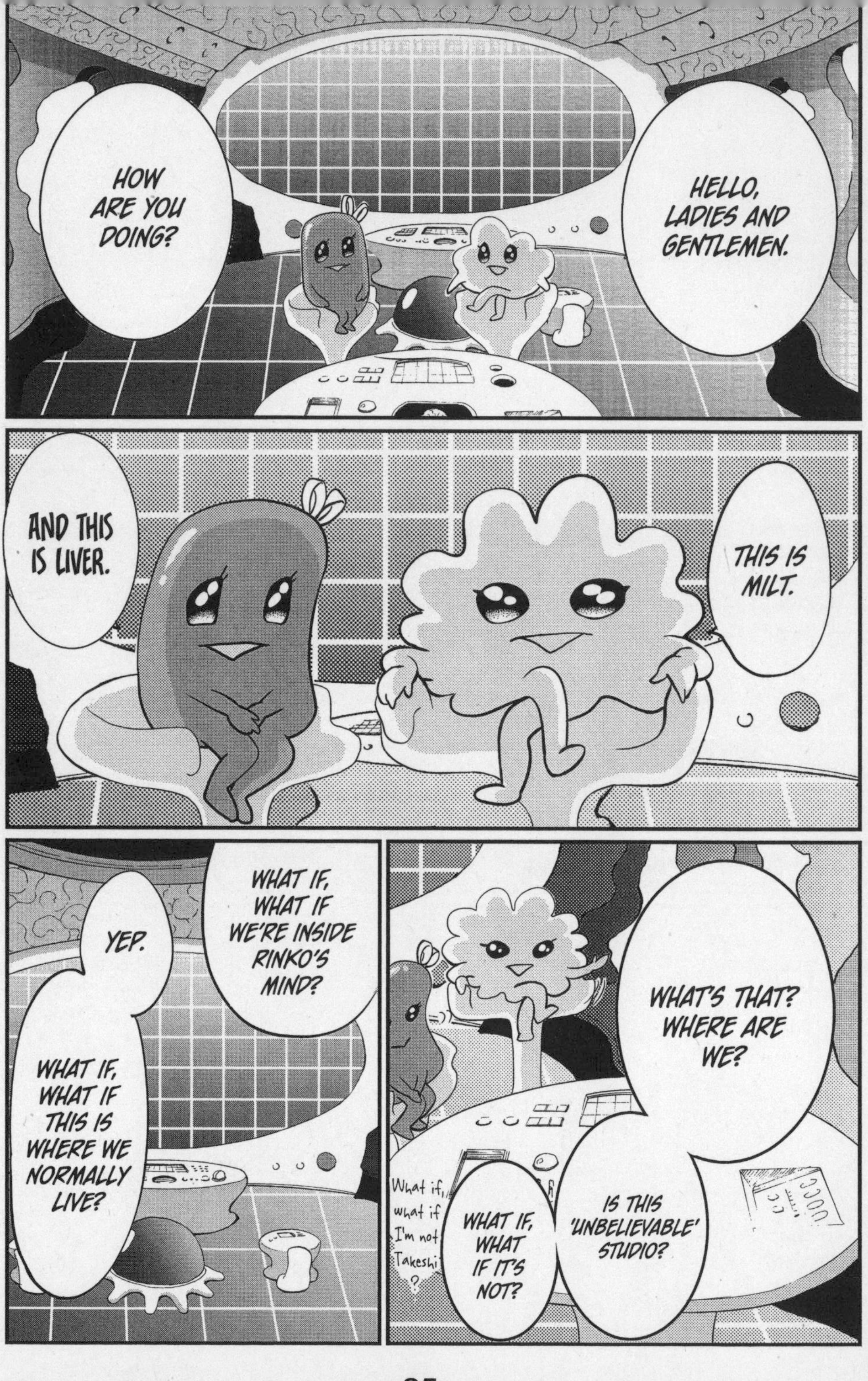
HELLO, LADIES AND GENTLEMEN.
HOW ARE YOU DOING?
THIS IS MILT.
AND THIS IS LIVER.
WHAT'S THAT? WHERE ARE WE?
IS THIS 'UNBELIEVABLE' STUDIO?
WHAT IF, WHAT IF IT'S NOT?
What if, what if I'm not Takeshi?
WHAT IF, WHAT IF WE'RE INSIDE RINKO'S MIND?
YEP.
WHAT IF, WHAT IF THIS IS WHERE WE NORMALLY LIVE?

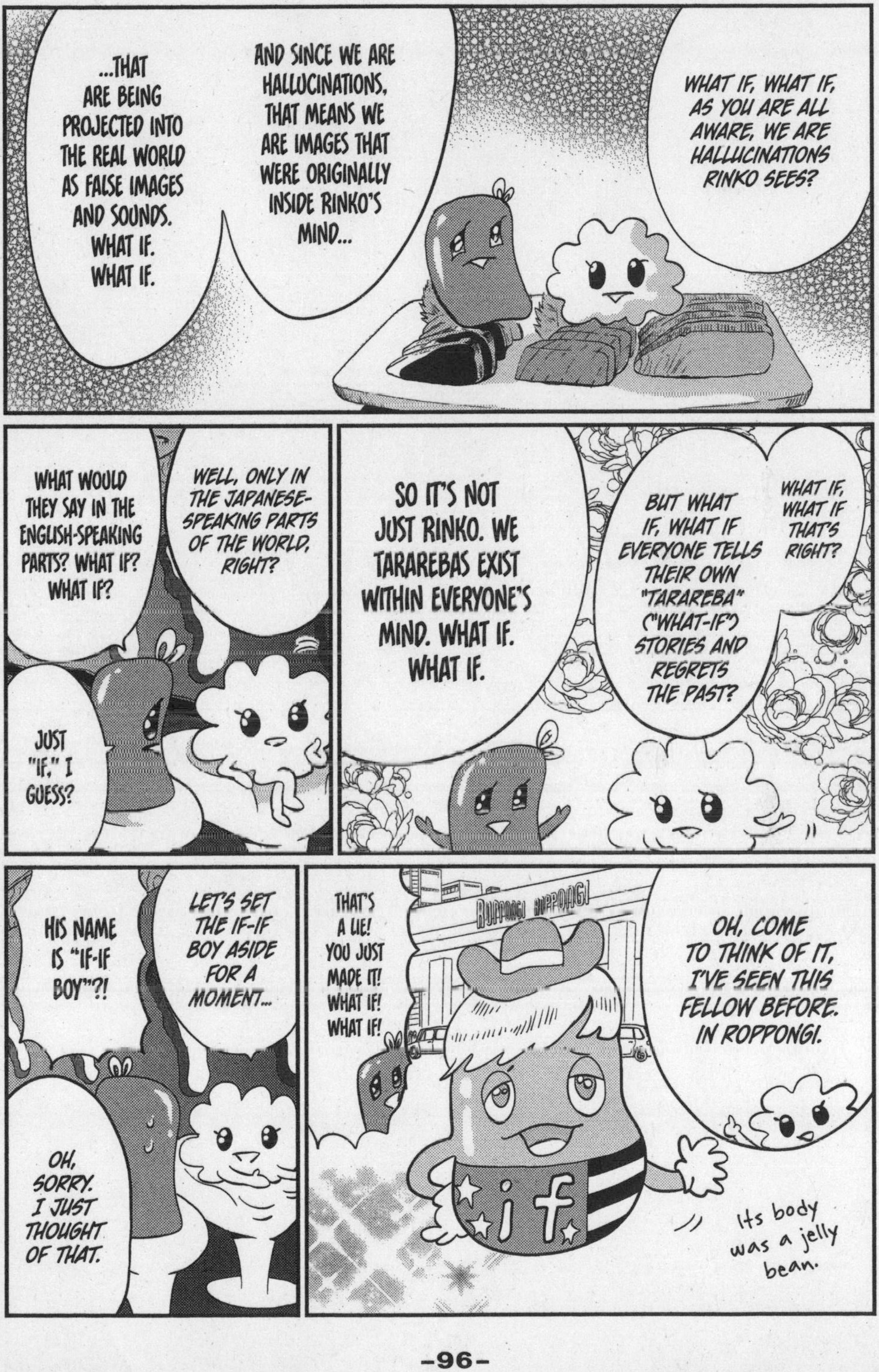
WHAT IF, WHAT IF, AS YOU ARE ALL AWARE, WE ARE HALLUCINATIONS RINKO SEES?
AND SINCE WE ARE HALLUCINATIONS, THAT MEANS WE ARE IMAGES THAT WERE ORIGINALLY INSIDE RINKO'S MIND...
...THAT ARE BEING PROJECTED INTO THE REAL WORLD AS FALSE IMAGES AND SOUNDS. WHAT IF. WHAT IF.
WHAT IF, WHAT IF THAT'S RIGHT?
BUT WHAT IF, WHAT IF EVERYONE TELLS THEIR OWN "TARAREBA" ("WHAT-IF") STORIES AND REGRETS THE PAST?
SO IT'S NOT JUST RINKO. WE TARAREBAS EXIST WITHIN EVERYONE'S MIND. WHAT IF. WHAT IF.
WELL, ONLY IN THE JAPANESE-SPEAKING PARTS OF THE WORLD, RIGHT?
WHAT WOULD THEY SAY IN THE ENGLISH-SPEAKING PARTS? WHAT IF? WHAT IF?
JUST "IF," I GUESS?
OH, COME TO THINK OF IT, I'VE SEEN THIS FELLOW BEFORE. IN ROPPONGI.
THAT'S A LIE! YOU JUST MADE IT! WHAT IF! WHAT IF!
ROPPONGI ROPPONGI
if
Its body was a jelly bean.
LET'S SET THE IF-IF BOY ASIDE FOR A MOMENT...
HIS NAME IS "IF-IF BOY"?!
OH, SORRY. I JUST THOUGHT OF THAT.

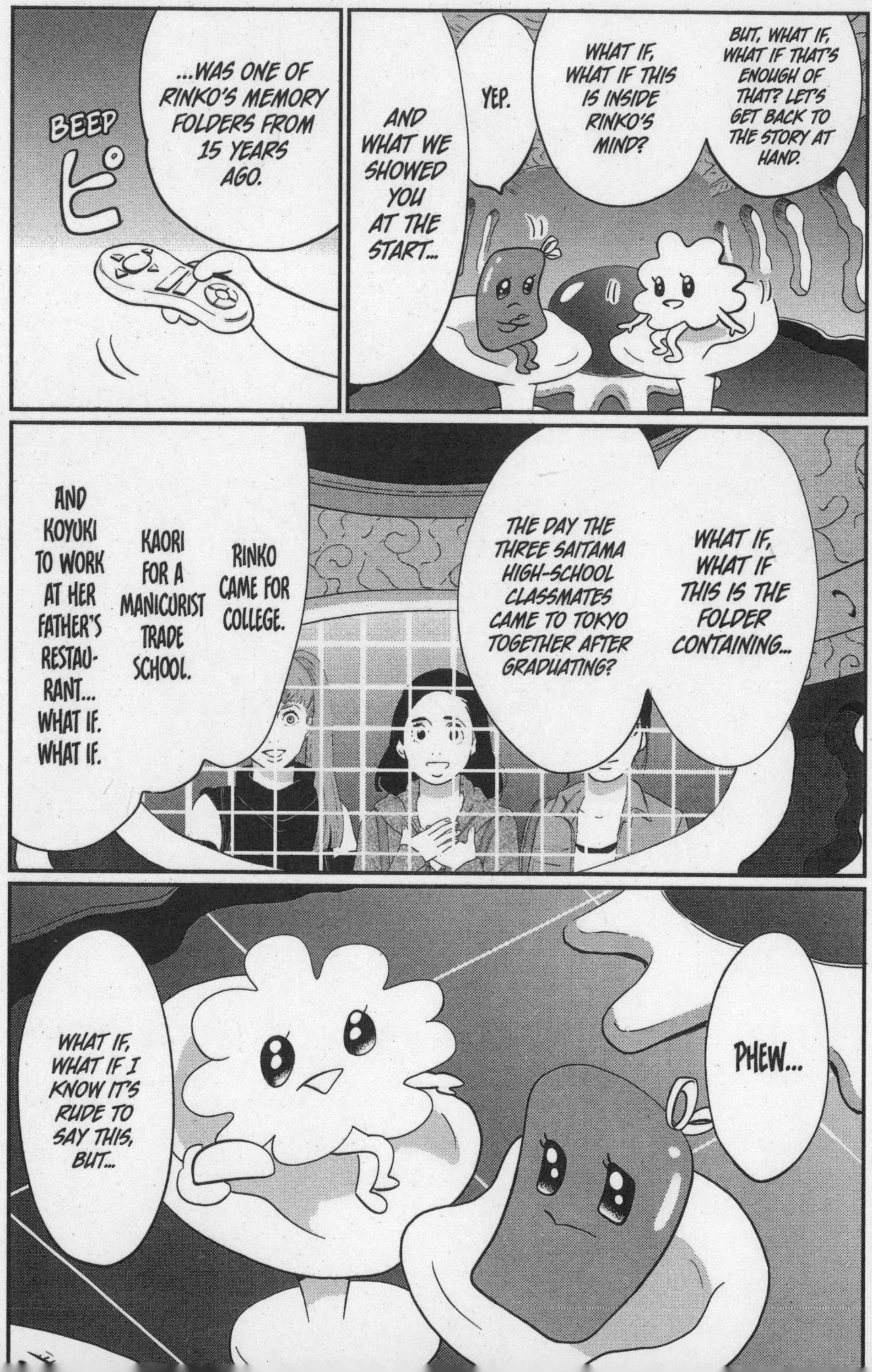
BUT, WHAT IF, WHAT IF THAT'S ENOUGH OF THAT? LET'S GET BACK TO THE STORY AT HAND.
WHAT IF, WHAT IF THIS IS INSIDE RINKO'S MIND?
YEP.
AND WHAT WE SHOWED YOU AT THE START...
...WAS ONE OF RINKO'S MEMORY FOLDERS FROM 15 YEARS AGO.
BEEP
ピ
WHAT IF, WHAT IF THIS IS THE FOLDER CONTAINING...
THE DAY THE THREE SAITAMA HIGH-SCHOOL CLASSMATES CAME TO TOKYO TOGETHER AFTER GRADUATING?
RINKO CAME FOR COLLEGE.
KAORI FOR A MANICURIST TRADE SCHOOL.
AND KOYUKI TO WORK AT HER FATHER'S RESTAU-RANT... WHAT IF. WHAT IF.
PHEW...
WHAT IF, WHAT IF I KNOW IT'S RUDE TO SAY THIS, BUT...

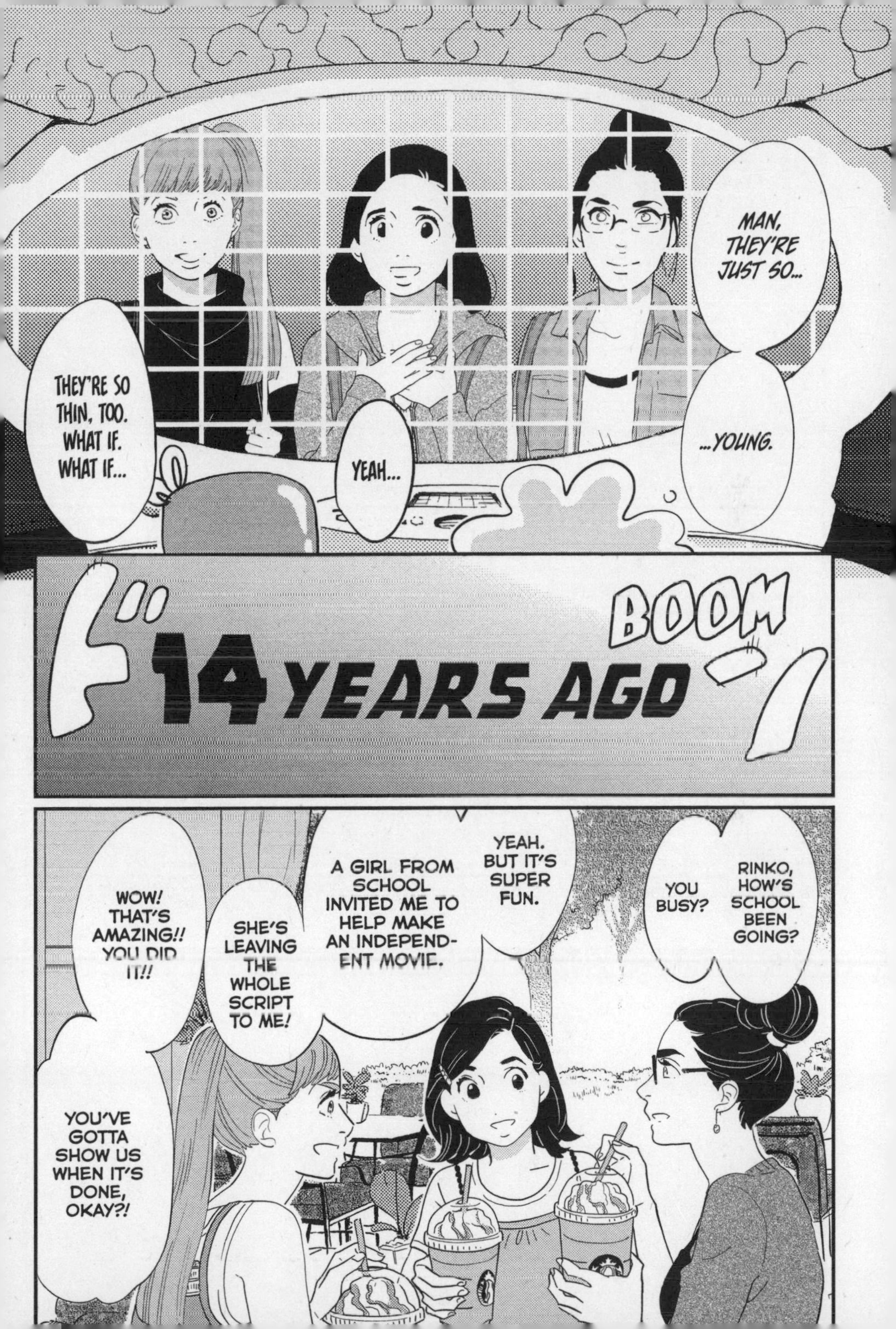
MAN, THEY'RE JUST SO...
...YOUNG.
YEAH...
THEY'RE SO THIN, TOO. WHAT IF. WHAT IF...
BOOM
14 YEARS AGO
RINKO, HOW'S SCHOOL BEEN GOING?
YOU BUSY?
YEAH. BUT IT'S SUPER FUN.
A GIRL FROM SCHOOL INVITED ME TO HELP MAKE AN INDEPEND-ENT MOVIE.
SHE'S LEAVING THE WHOLE SCRIPT TO ME!
WOW! THAT'S AMAZING!! YOU DID IT!!
YOU'VE GOTTA SHOW US WHEN IT'S DONE, OKAY?!

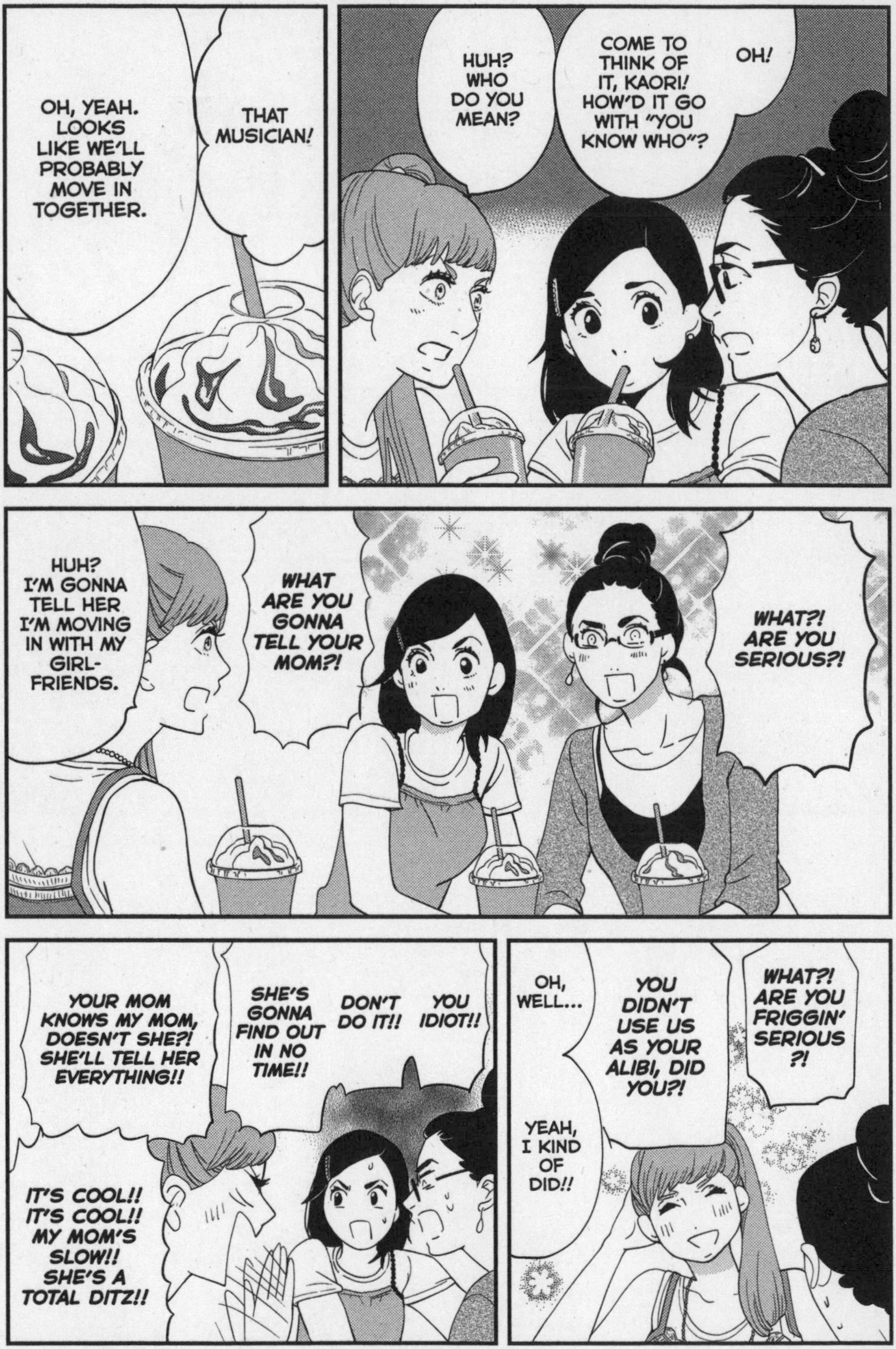
OH!
COME TO THINK OF IT, KAORI! HOW'D IT GO WITH "YOU KNOW WHO"?
HUH? WHO DO YOU MEAN?
THAT MUSICIAN!
OH, YEAH. LOOKS LIKE WE'LL PROBABLY MOVE IN TOGETHER.
WHAT?! ARE YOU SERIOUS?!
WHAT ARE YOU GONNA TELL YOUR MOM?!
HUH? I'M GONNA TELL HER I'M MOVING IN WITH MY GIRL-FRIENDS.
WHAT?! ARE YOU FRIGGIN' SERIOUS ?!
YOU DIDN'T USE US AS YOUR ALIBI, DID YOU?!
OH, WELL...
YEAH, I KIND OF DID!!
YOU IDIOT!!
DON'T DO IT!!
SHE'S GONNA FIND OUT IN NO TIME!!
YOUR MOM KNOWS MY MOM, DOESN'T SHE?! SHE'LL TELL HER EVERYTHING!!
IT'S COOL!! IT'S COOL!! MY MOM'S SLOW!! SHE'S A TOTAL DITZ!!

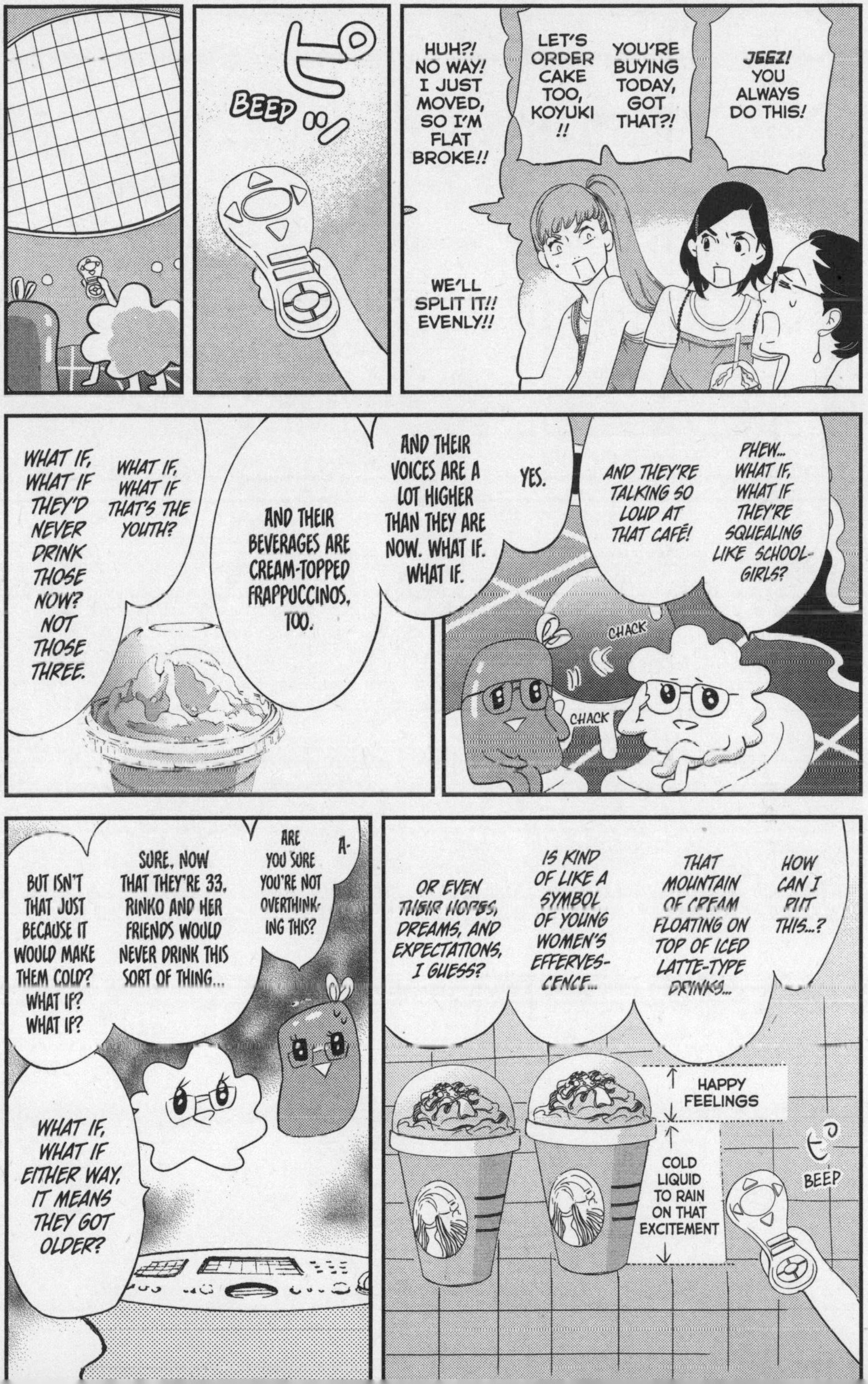
JEEZ! YOU ALWAYS DO THIS!
YOU'RE BUYING TODAY, GOT THAT?!
LET'S ORDER CAKE TOO, KOYUKI!!
HUH?! NO WAY! I JUST MOVED, SO I'M FLAT BROKE!!
WE'LL SPLIT IT!! EVENLY!!
BEEP
PHEW... WHAT IF, WHAT IF THEY'RE SQUEALING LIKE SCHOOL-GIRLS?
AND THEY'RE TALKING SO LOUD AT THAT CAFÉ!
YES.
AND THEIR VOICES ARE A LOT HIGHER THAN THEY ARE NOW. WHAT IF. WHAT IF.
CHACK
CHACK
AND THEIR BEVERAGES ARE CREAM-TOPPED FRAPPUCCINOS, TOO.
WHAT IF, WHAT IF THAT'S THE YOUTH?
WHAT IF, WHAT IF THEY'D NEVER DRINK THOSE NOW? NOT THOSE THREE.
HOW CAN I PUT THIS...?
THAT MOUNTAIN OF CREAM FLOATING ON TOP OF ICED LATTE-TYPE DRINKS...
IS KIND OF LIKE A SYMBOL OF YOUNG WOMEN'S EFFERVESCENCE...
OR EVEN THEIR HOPES, DREAMS, AND EXPECTATIONS, I GUESS?
HAPPY FEELINGS
COLD LIQUID TO RAIN ON THAT EXCITEMENT
BEEP
A-
ARE YOU SURE YOU'RE NOT OVERTHINKING THIS?
SURE, NOW THAT THEY'RE 33, RINKO AND HER FRIENDS WOULD NEVER DRINK THIS SORT OF THING...
BUT ISN'T THAT JUST BECAUSE IT WOULD MAKE THEM COLD? WHAT IF? WHAT IF?
WHAT IF, WHAT IF EITHER WAY, IT MEANS THEY GOT OLDER?

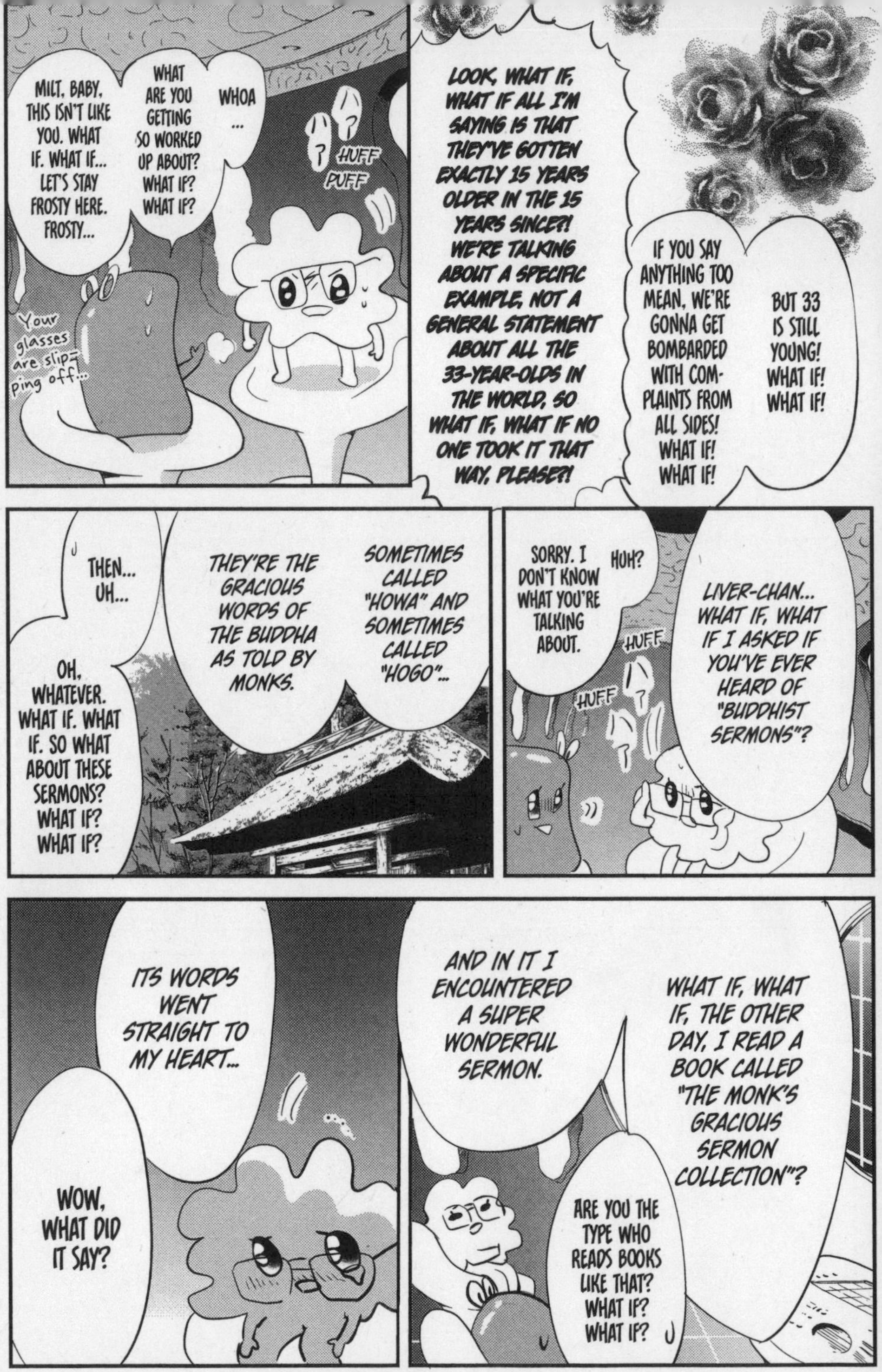
BUT 33 IS STILL YOUNG! WHAT IF! WHAT IF!
LOOK, WHAT IF, WHAT IF ALL I'M SAYING IS THAT THEY'VE GOTTEN EXACTLY 15 YEARS OLDER IN THE 15 YEARS SINCE?! WE'RE TALKING ABOUT A SPECIFIC EXAMPLE, NOT A GENERAL STATEMENT ABOUT ALL THE 33-YEAR-OLDS IN THE WORLD, SO WHAT IF, WHAT IF NO ONE TOOK IT THAT WAY, PLEASE?!
IF YOU SAY ANYTHING TOO MEAN, WE'RE GONNA GET BOMBARDED WITH COM-PLAINTS FROM ALL SIDES! WHAT IF! WHAT IF!
WHOA ...
HUFF
PUFF
WHAT ARE YOU GETTING SO WORKED UP ABOUT? WHAT IF? WHAT IF?
MILT, BABY, THIS ISN'T LIKE YOU. WHAT IF. WHAT IF... LET'S STAY FROSTY HERE. FROSTY...
Your glasses are slip-ping off!...
LIVER-CHAN... WHAT IF, WHAT IF I ASKED IF YOU'VE EVER HEARD OF "BUDDHIST SERMONS"?
HUH?
SORRY. I DON'T KNOW WHAT YOU'RE TALKING ABOUT.
HUFF
HUFF
SOMETIMES CALLED "HOWA" AND SOMETIMES CALLED "HOGO"...
THEY'RE THE GRACIOUS WORDS OF THE BUDDHA AS TOLD BY MONKS.
THEN... UH...
OH, WHATEVER. WHAT IF. WHAT IF. SO WHAT ABOUT THESE SERMONS? WHAT IF? WHAT IF?
WHAT IF, WHAT IF, THE OTHER DAY, I READ A BOOK CALLED "THE MONK'S GRACIOUS SERMON COLLECTION"?
AND IN IT I ENCOUNTERED A SUPER WONDERFUL SERMON.
ARE YOU THE TYPE WHO READS BOOKS LIKE THAT? WHAT IF? WHAT IF?
ITS WORDS WENT STRAIGHT TO MY HEART...
WOW, WHAT DID IT SAY?

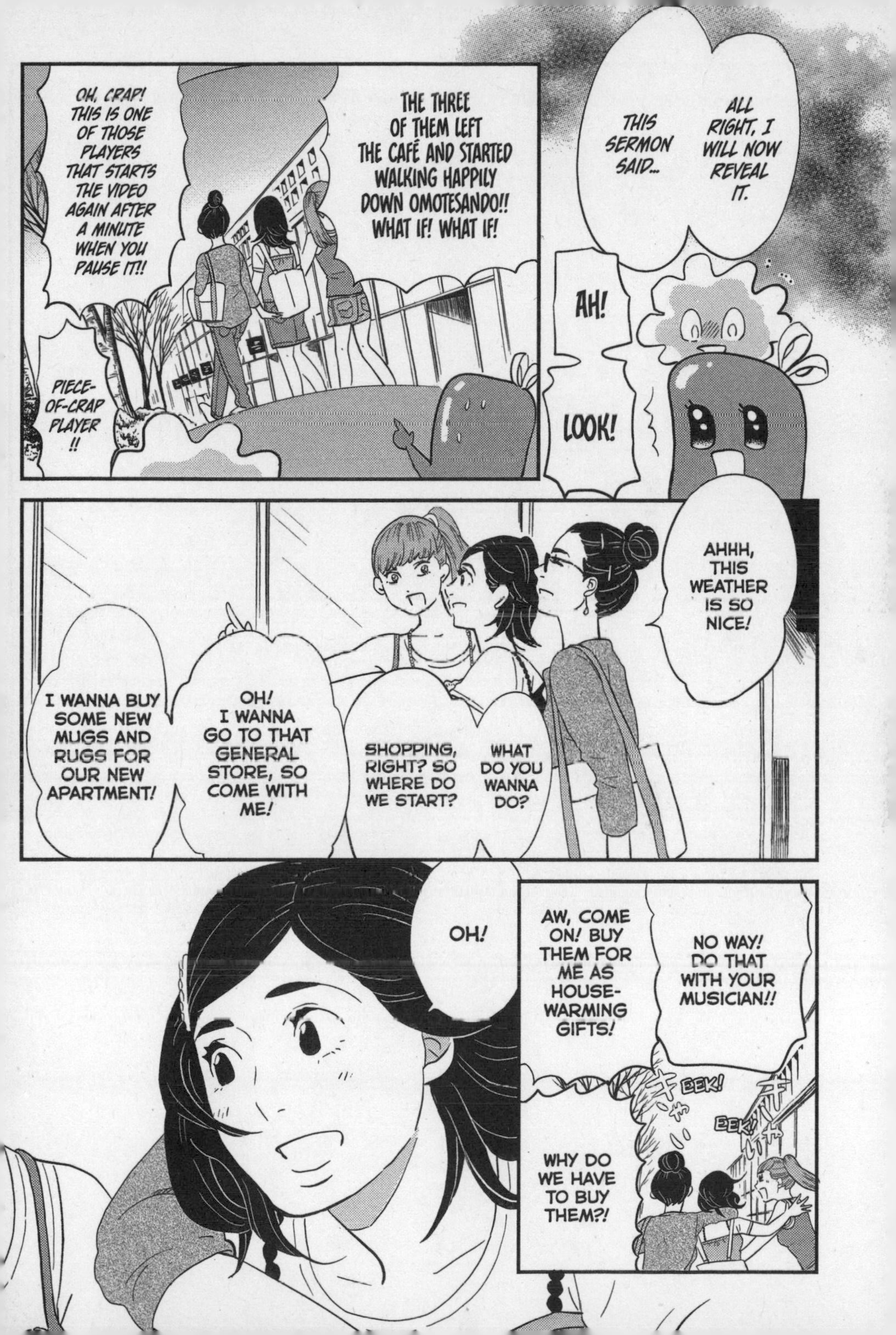
ALL RIGHT, I WILL NOW REVEAL IT.
THIS SERMON SAID...
AH!
LOOK!
THE THREE OF THEM LEFT THE CAFÉ AND STARTED WALKING HAPPILY DOWN OMOTESANDO!! WHAT IF! WHAT IF!
OH, CRAP! THIS IS ONE OF THOSE PLAYERS THAT STARTS THE VIDEO AGAIN AFTER A MINUTE WHEN YOU PAUSE IT!!
PIECE-OF-CRAP PLAYER !!
AHHH, THIS WEATHER IS SO NICE!
WHAT DO YOU WANNA DO?
SHOPPING, RIGHT? SO WHERE DO WE START?
OH! I WANNA GO TO THAT GENERAL STORE, SO COME WITH ME!
I WANNA BUY SOME NEW MUGS AND RUGS FOR OUR NEW APARTMENT!
NO WAY! DO THAT WITH YOUR MUSICIAN!!
AW, COME ON! BUY THEM FOR ME AS HOUSE-WARMING GIFTS!
EEK!
EEK!
WHY DO WE HAVE TO BUY THEM?!
OH!

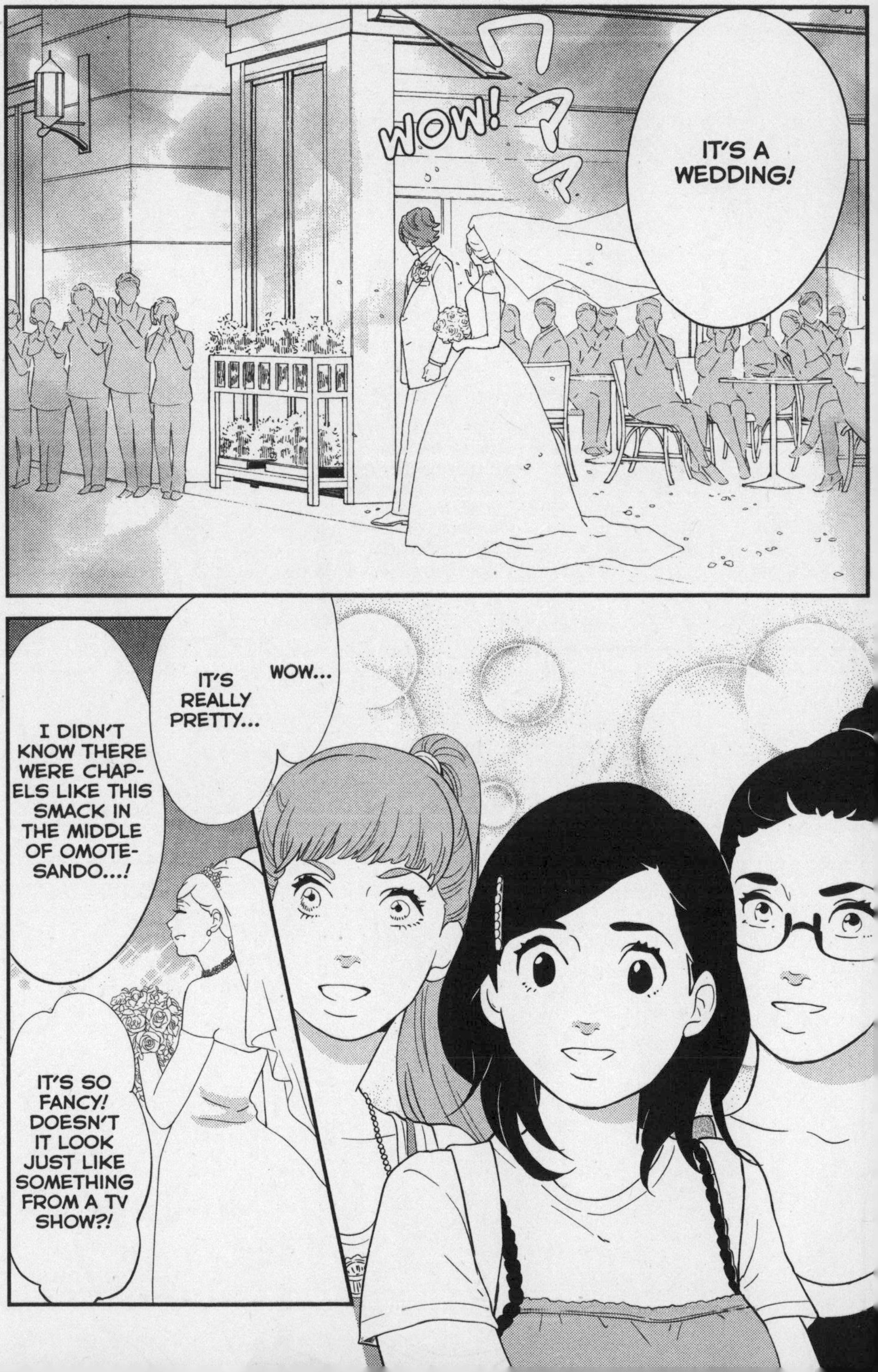
WOW!
ワアア
IT'S A WEDDING!
WOW...
IT'S REALLY PRETTY...
I DIDN'T KNOW THERE WERE CHAPELS LIKE THIS SMACK IN THE MIDDLE OF OMOTESANDO...!
IT'S SO FANCY! DOESN'T IT LOOK JUST LIKE SOMETHING FROM A TV SHOW?!

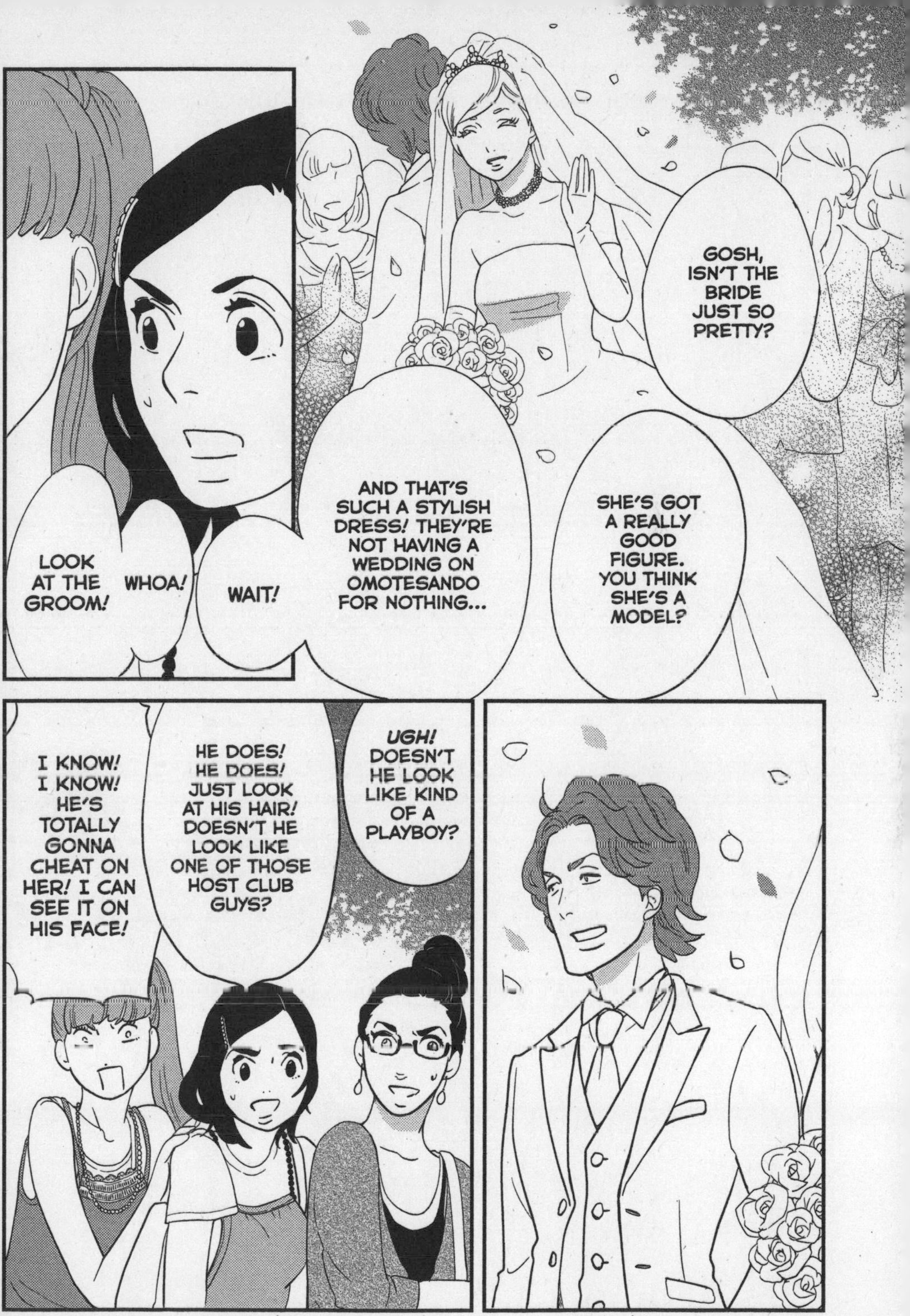
GOSH, ISN'T THE BRIDE JUST SO PRETTY?
SHE'S GOT A REALLY GOOD FIGURE. YOU THINK SHE'S A MODEL?
AND THAT'S SUCH A STYLISH DRESS! THEY'RE NOT HAVING A WEDDING ON OMOTESANDO FOR NOTHING...
WAIT!
WHOA!
LOOK AT THE GROOM!
UGH! DOESN'T HE LOOK LIKE KIND OF A PLAYBOY?
HE DOES! HE DOES! JUST LOOK AT HIS HAIR! DOESN'T HE LOOK LIKE ONE OF THOSE HOST CLUB GUYS?
I KNOW! I KNOW! HE'S TOTALLY GONNA CHEAT ON HER! I CAN SEE IT ON HIS FACE!

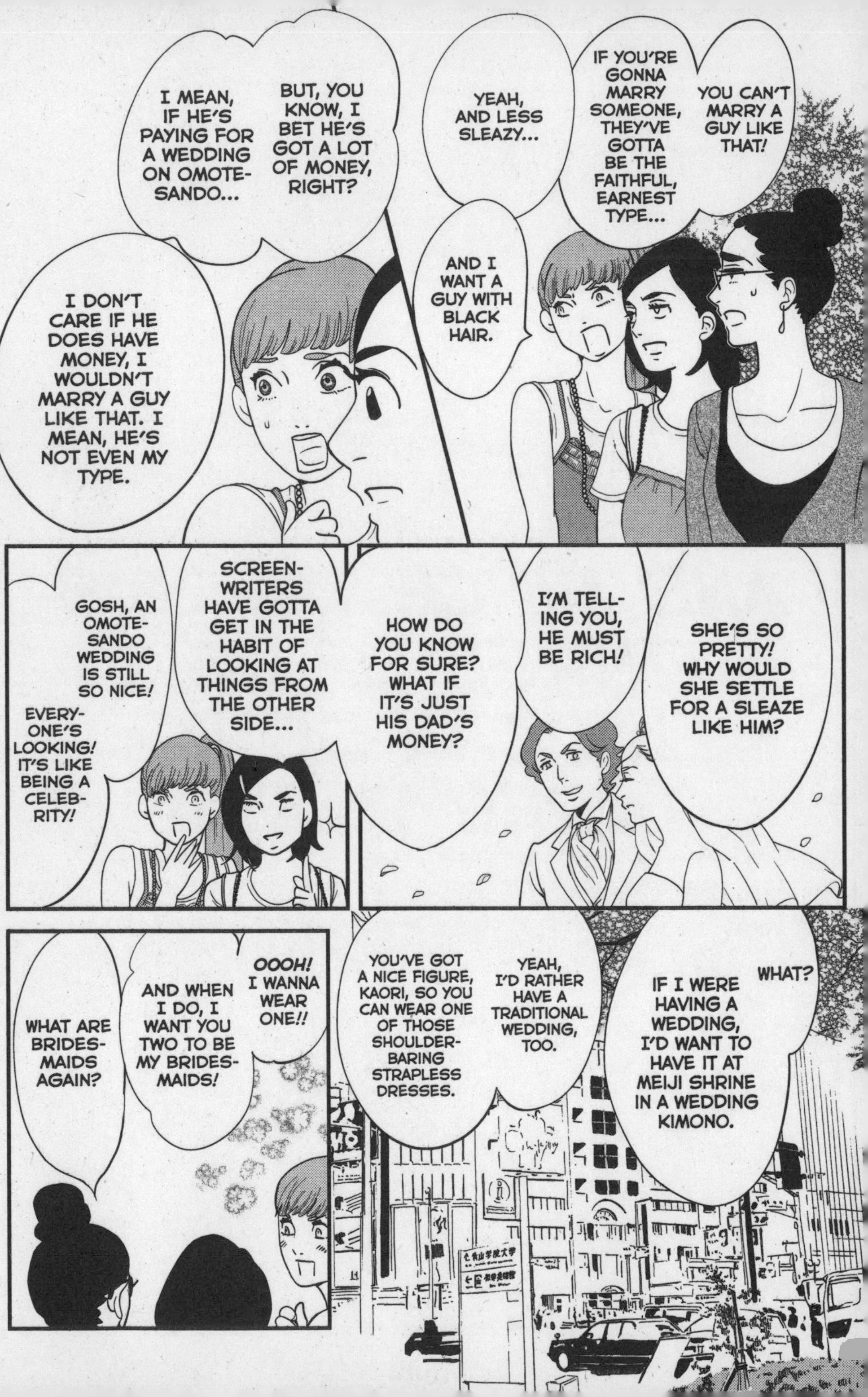
YOU CAN'T MARRY A GUY LIKE THAT!
IF YOU'RE GONNA MARRY SOMEONE, THEY'VE GOTTA BE THE FAITHFUL, EARNEST TYPE...
YEAH, AND LESS SLEAZY...
AND I WANT A GUY WITH BLACK HAIR.
BUT, YOU KNOW, I BET HE'S GOT A LOT OF MONEY, RIGHT?
I MEAN, IF HE'S PAYING FOR A WEDDING ON OMOTE-SANDO...
I DON'T CARE IF HE DOES HAVE MONEY, I WOULDN'T MARRY A GUY LIKE THAT. I MEAN, HE'S NOT EVEN MY TYPE.
SHE'S SO PRETTY! WHY WOULD SHE SETTLE FOR A SLEAZE LIKE HIM?
I'M TELL-ING YOU, HE MUST BE RICH!
HOW DO YOU KNOW FOR SURE? WHAT IF IT'S JUST HIS DAD'S MONEY?
SCREEN-WRITERS HAVE GOTTA GET IN THE HABIT OF LOOKING AT THINGS FROM THE OTHER SIDE...
GOSH, AN OMOTE-SANDO WEDDING IS STILL SO NICE!
EVERY-ONE'S LOOKING! IT'S LIKE BEING A CELEB-RITY!
WHAT?
IF I WERE HAVING A WEDDING, I'D WANT TO HAVE IT AT MEIJI SHRINE IN A WEDDING KIMONO.
YEAH, I'D RATHER HAVE A TRADITIONAL WEDDING, TOO.
YOU'VE GOT A NICE FIGURE, KAORI, SO YOU CAN WEAR ONE OF THOSE SHOULDER-BARING STRAPLESS DRESSES.
OOOH! I WANNA WEAR ONE!!
AND WHEN I DO, I WANT YOU TWO TO BE MY BRIDES-MAIDS!
WHAT ARE BRIDES-MAIDS AGAIN?

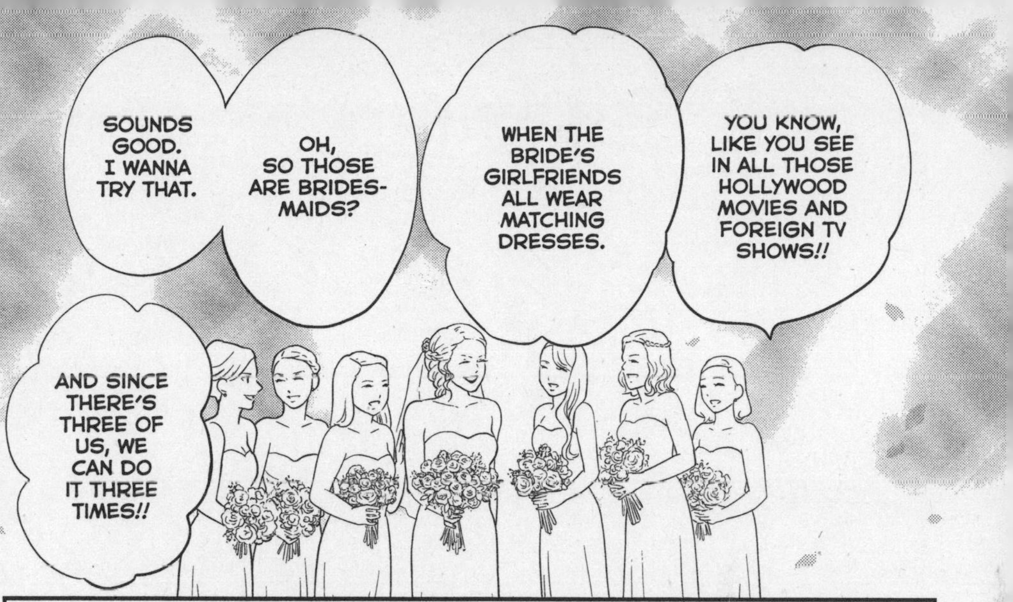
YOU KNOW, LIKE YOU SEE IN ALL THOSE HOLLYWOOD MOVIES AND FOREIGN TV SHOWS!!
WHEN THE BRIDE'S GIRLFRIENDS ALL WEAR MATCHING DRESSES.
OH, SO THOSE ARE BRIDES-MAIDS?
SOUNDS GOOD. I WANNA TRY THAT.
AND SINCE THERE'S THREE OF US, WE CAN DO IT THREE TIMES!!

AND SINCE THERE'S THREE OF US, WE CAN DO IT THREE TIMES!!

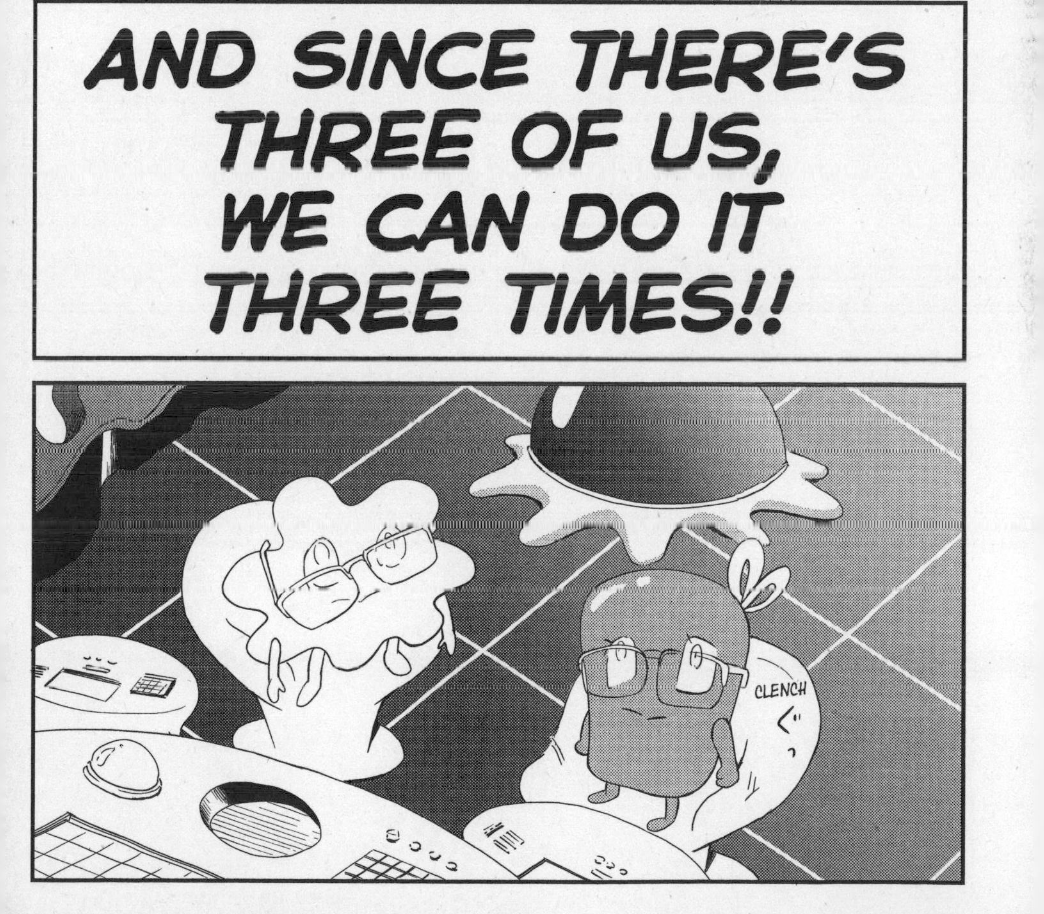
CLENCH

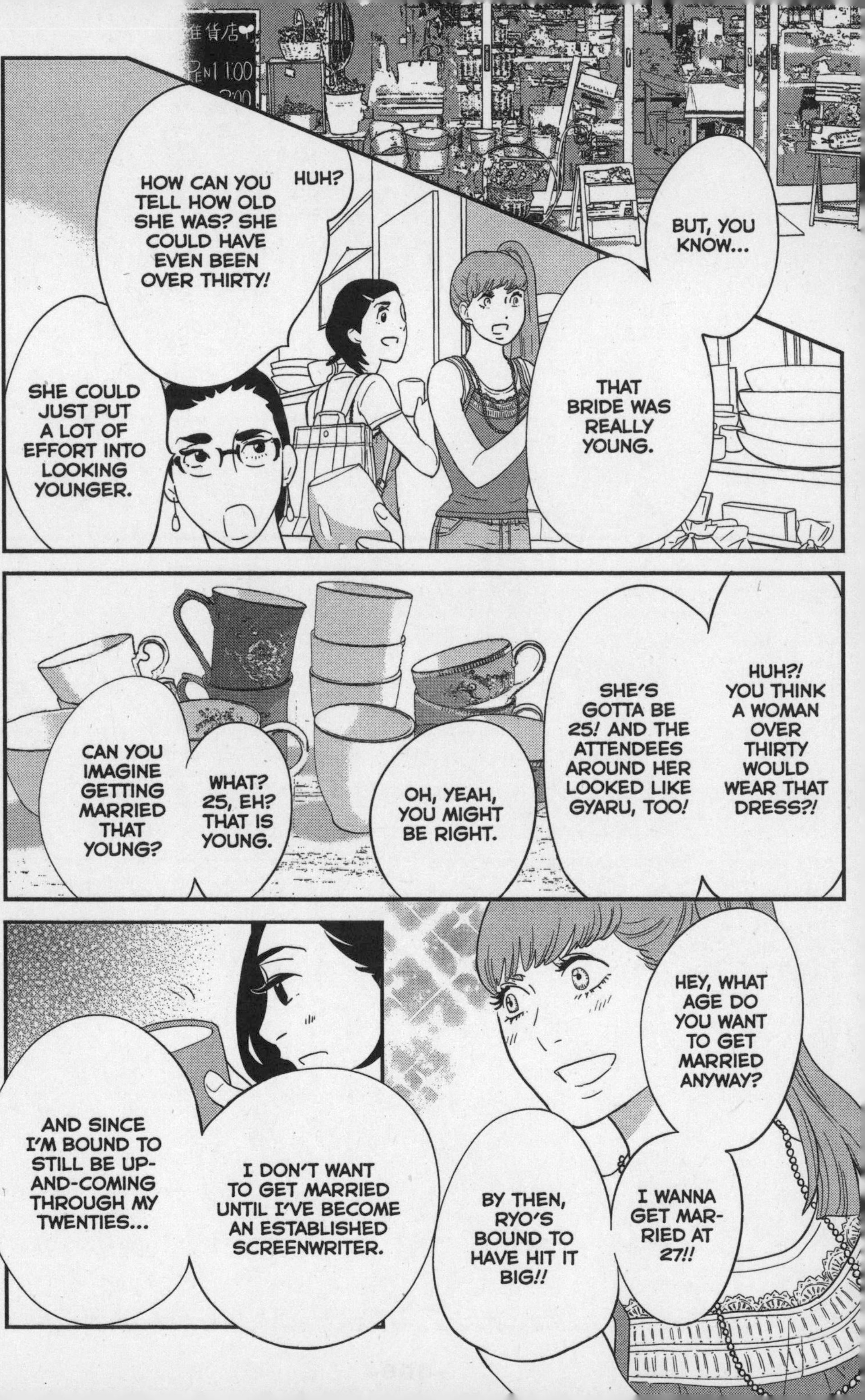
BUT, YOU KNOW...
THAT BRIDE WAS REALLY YOUNG.
HUH?
HOW CAN YOU TELL HOW OLD SHE WAS? SHE COULD HAVE EVEN BEEN OVER THIRTY!
SHE COULD JUST PUT A LOT OF EFFORT INTO LOOKING YOUNGER.
HUH?! YOU THINK A WOMAN OVER THIRTY WOULD WEAR THAT DRESS?!
SHE'S GOTTA BE 25! AND THE ATTENDEES AROUND HER LOOKED LIKE GYARU, TOO!
OH, YEAH, YOU MIGHT BE RIGHT.
WHAT? 25, EH? THAT IS YOUNG.
CAN YOU IMAGINE GETTING MARRIED THAT YOUNG?
HEY, WHAT AGE DO YOU WANT TO GET MARRIED ANYWAY?
I WANNA GET MARRIED AT 27!!
BY THEN, RYO'S BOUND TO HAVE HIT IT BIG!!
I DON'T WANT TO GET MARRIED UNTIL I'VE BECOME AN ESTABLISHED SCREENWRITER.
AND SINCE I'M BOUND TO STILL BE UP-AND-COMING THROUGH MY TWENTIES...

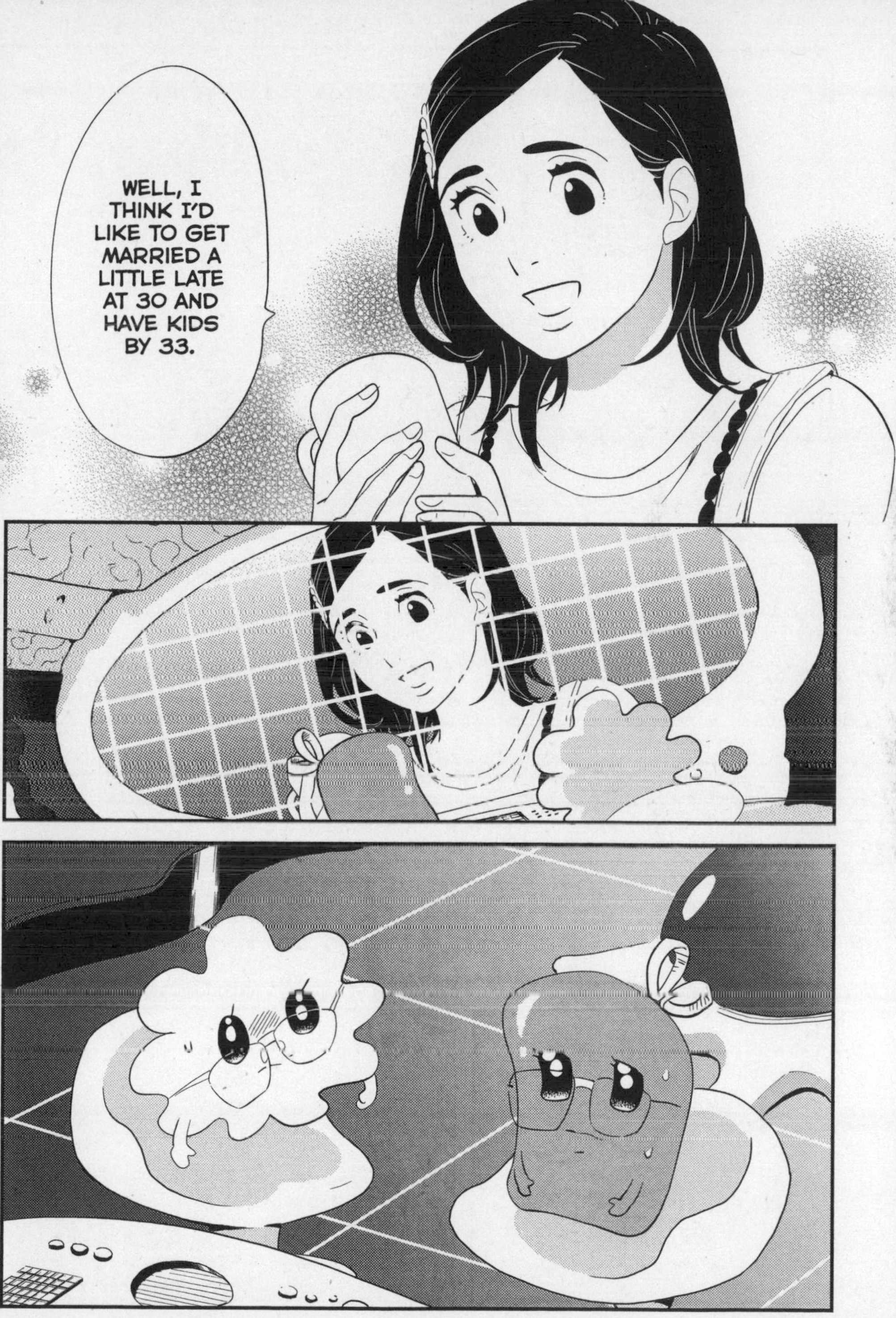
WELL, I THINK I'D LIKE TO GET MARRIED A LITTLE LATE AT 30 AND HAVE KIDS BY 33.

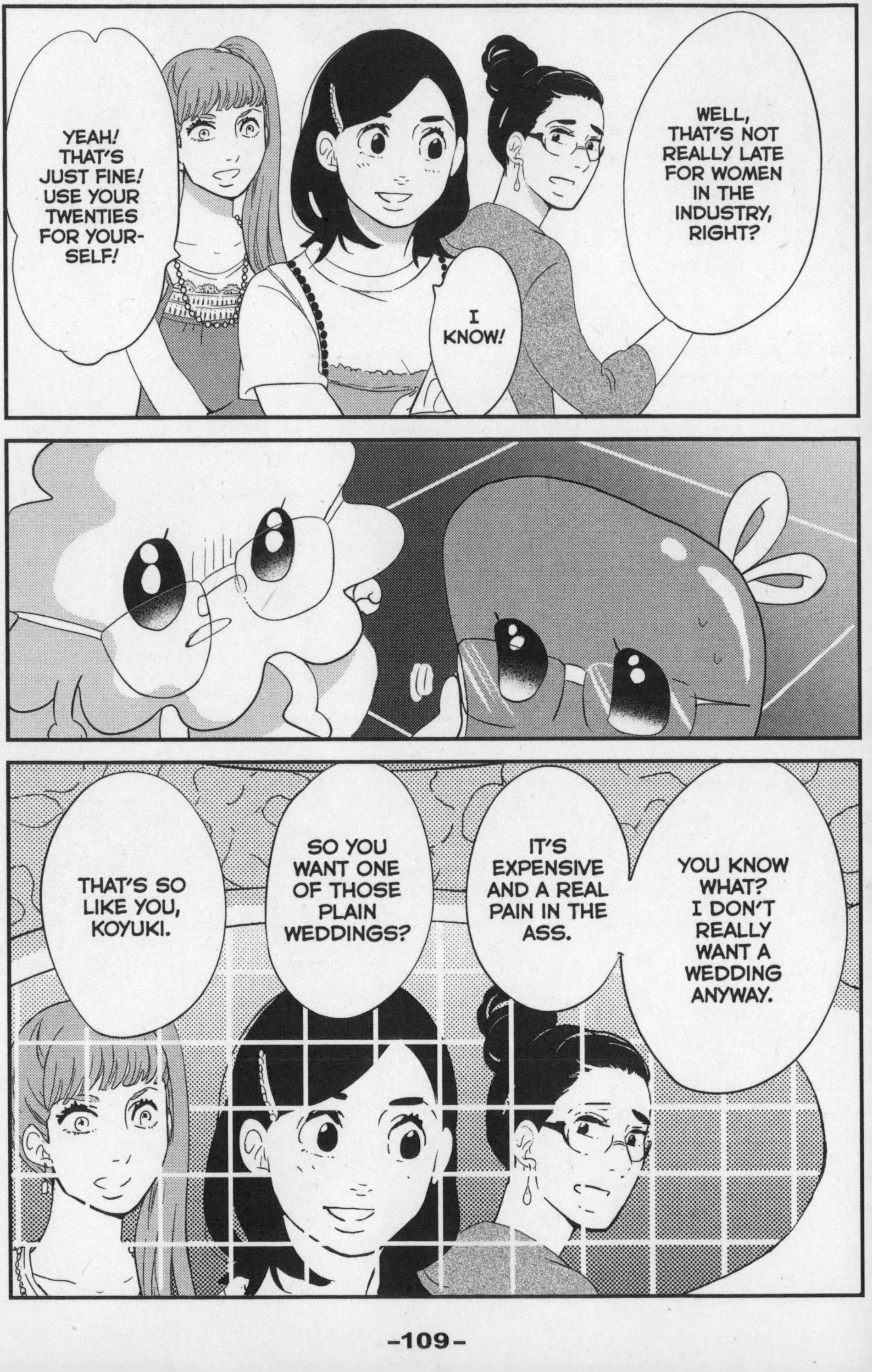
WELL, THAT'S NOT REALLY LATE FOR WOMEN IN THE INDUSTRY, RIGHT?
I KNOW!
YEAH! THAT'S JUST FINE! USE YOUR TWENTIES FOR YOUR-SELF!
YOU KNOW WHAT? I DON'T REALLY WANT A WEDDING ANYWAY.
IT'S EXPENSIVE AND A REAL PAIN IN THE ASS.
SO YOU WANT ONE OF THOSE PLAIN WEDDINGS?
THAT'S SO LIKE YOU, KOYUKI.

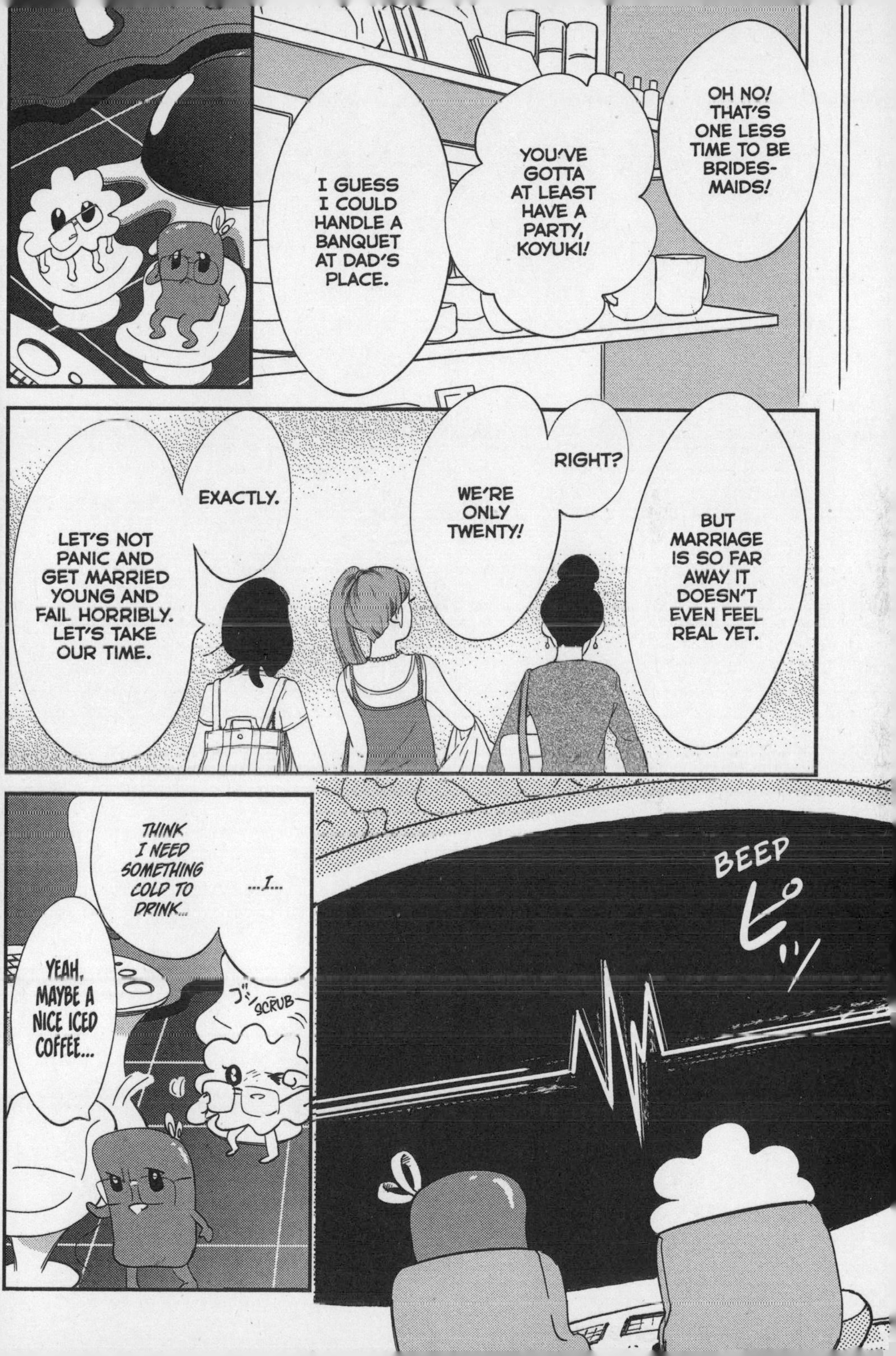
OH NO! THAT'S ONE LESS TIME TO BE BRIDES-MAIDS!
YOU'VE GOTTA AT LEAST HAVE A PARTY, KOYUKI!
I GUESS I COULD HANDLE A BANQUET AT DAD'S PLACE.
BUT MARRIAGE IS SO FAR AWAY IT DOESN'T EVEN FEEL REAL YET.
RIGHT?
WE'RE ONLY TWENTY!
EXACTLY.
LET'S NOT PANIC AND GET MARRIED YOUNG AND FAIL HORRIBLY. LET'S TAKE OUR TIME.
BEEP
ピッ
...I...
THINK I NEED SOMETHING COLD TO DRINK...
ゴシ SCRUB
YEAH, MAYBE A NICE ICED COFFEE...

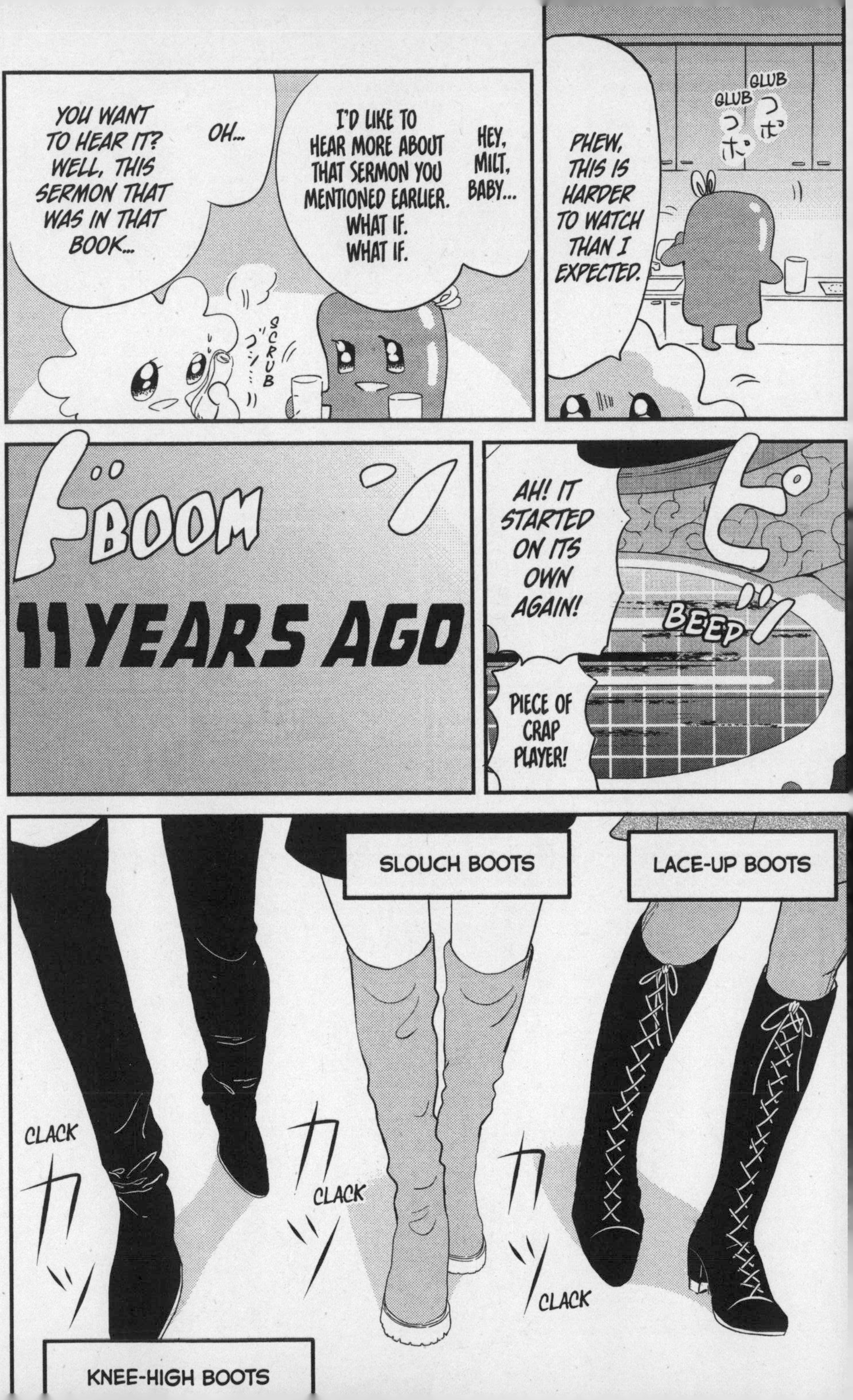
GLUB
GLUB
PHEW, THIS IS HARDER TO WATCH THAN I EXPECTED.
HEY, MILT, BABY...
I'D LIKE TO HEAR MORE ABOUT THAT SERMON YOU MENTIONED EARLIER. WHAT IF. WHAT IF.
OH...
YOU WANT TO HEAR IT? WELL, THIS SERMON THAT WAS IN THAT BOOK...
SCRUB
AH! IT STARTED ON ITS OWN AGAIN!
BEEP
PIECE OF CRAP PLAYER!
BOOM
11 YEARS AGO
LACE-UP BOOTS
SLOUCH BOOTS
CLACK
CLACK
CLACK
KNEE-HIGH BOOTS

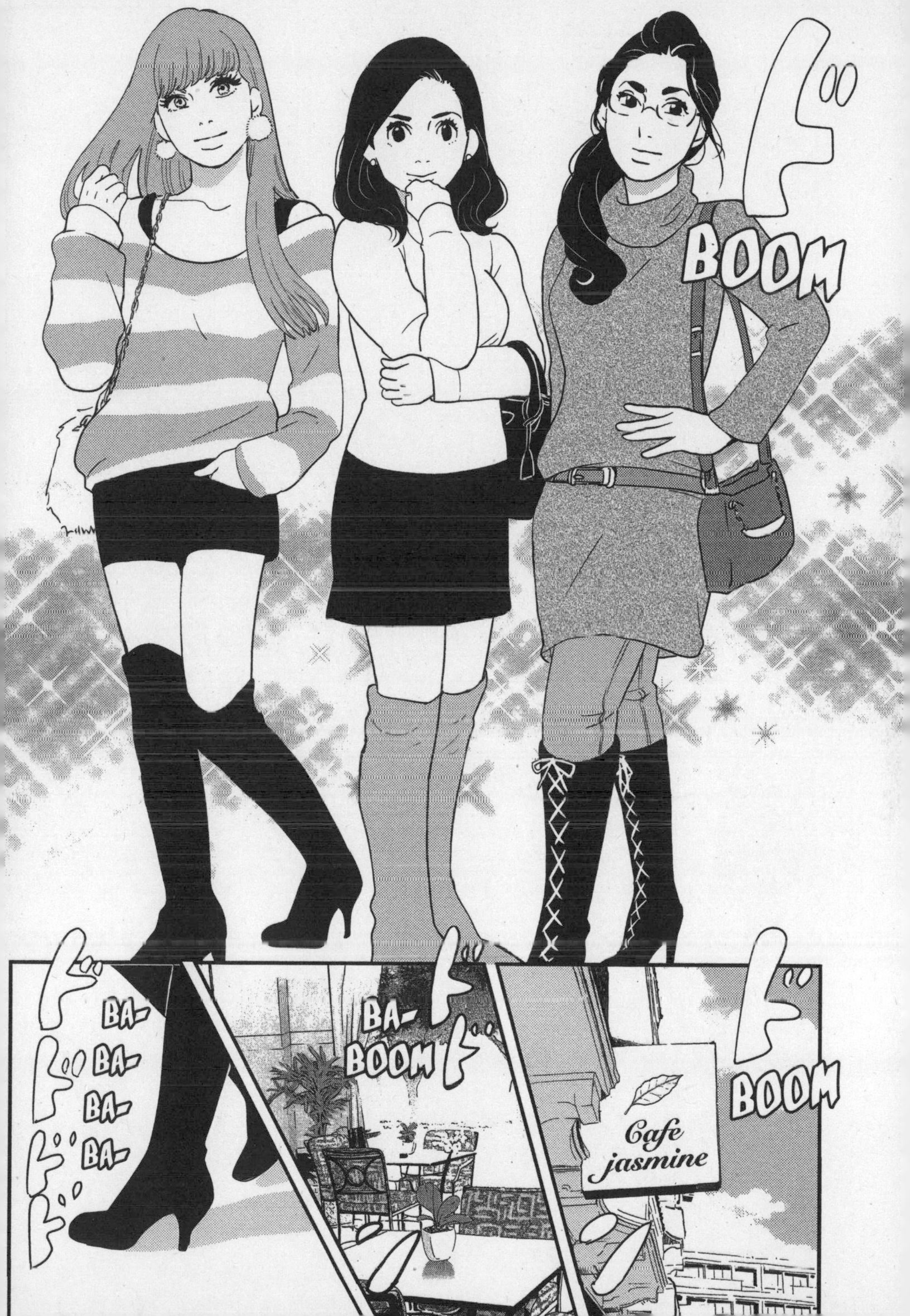
ド
BOOM
ド
BOOM
Cafe jasmine
BA-BOOM
ド ド
ドドドド
BA- BA- BA- BA-

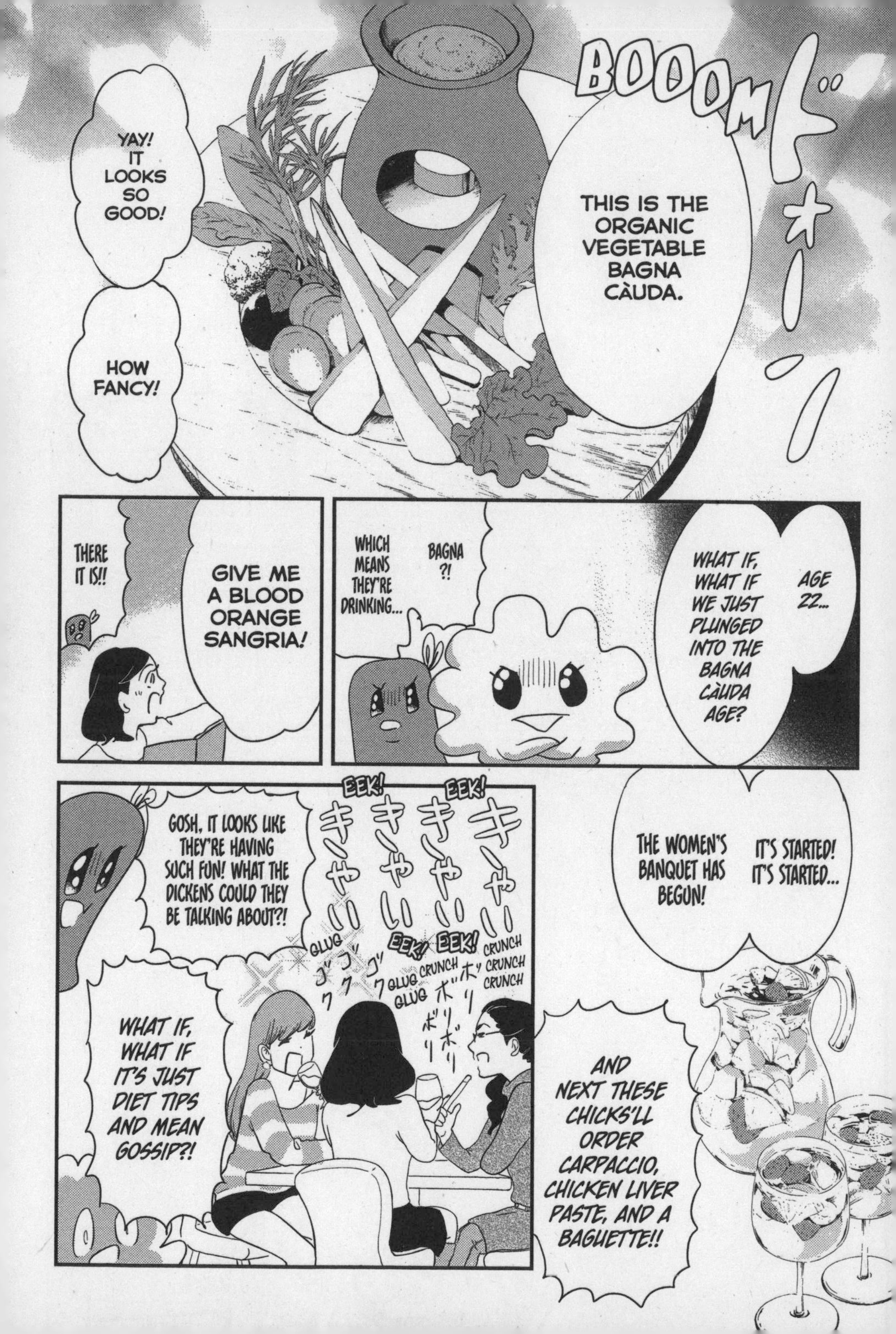
BOOOM
THIS IS THE ORGANIC VEGETABLE BAGNA CÀUDA.
YAY! IT LOOKS SO GOOD!
HOW FANCY!
AGE 22...
WHAT IF, WHAT IF WE JUST PLUNGED INTO THE BAGNA CÀUDA AGE?
BAGNA ?!
WHICH MEANS THEY'RE DRINKING...
GIVE ME A BLOOD ORANGE SANGRIA!
THERE IT IS!!
IT'S STARTED! IT'S STARTED...
THE WOMEN'S BANQUET HAS BEGUN!
AND NEXT THESE CHICKS'LL ORDER CARPACCIO, CHICKEN LIVER PASTE, AND A BAGUETTE!!
EEK! EEK!
GOSH, IT LOOKS LIKE THEY'RE HAVING SUCH FUN! WHAT THE DICKENS COULD THEY BE TALKING ABOUT?!
EEK! EEK!
CRUNCH CRUNCH CRUNCH
GLUG CRUNCH
GLUG GLUG
WHAT IF, WHAT IF IT'S JUST DIET TIPS AND MEAN GOSSIP?!

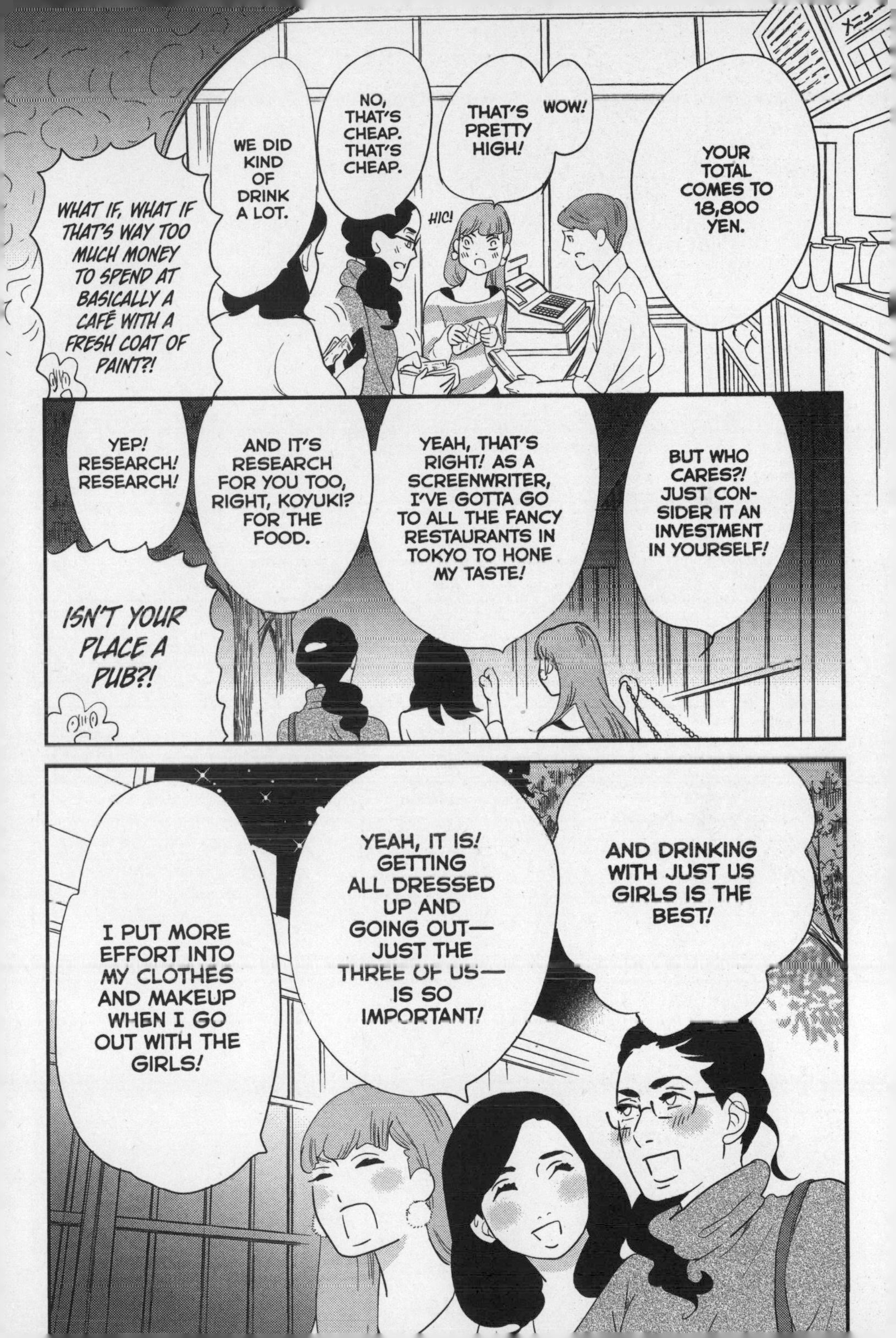
YOUR TOTAL COMES TO 18,800 YEN.
WOW!
THAT'S PRETTY HIGH!
HIC!
NO, THAT'S CHEAP. THAT'S CHEAP.
WE DID KIND OF DRINK A LOT.
WHAT IF, WHAT IF THAT'S WAY TOO MUCH MONEY TO SPEND AT BASICALLY A CAFÉ WITH A FRESH COAT OF PAINT?!
BUT WHO CARES?! JUST CON-SIDER IT AN INVESTMENT IN YOURSELF!
YEAH, THAT'S RIGHT! AS A SCREENWRITER, I'VE GOTTA GO TO ALL THE FANCY RESTAURANTS IN TOKYO TO HONE MY TASTE!
AND IT'S RESEARCH FOR YOU TOO, RIGHT, KOYUKI? FOR THE FOOD.
YEP! RESEARCH! RESEARCH!
ISN'T YOUR PLACE A PUB?!
AND DRINKING WITH JUST US GIRLS IS THE BEST!
YEAH, IT IS! GETTING ALL DRESSED UP AND GOING OUT—JUST THE THREE OF US—IS SO IMPORTANT!
I PUT MORE EFFORT INTO MY CLOTHES AND MAKEUP WHEN I GO OUT WITH THE GIRLS!

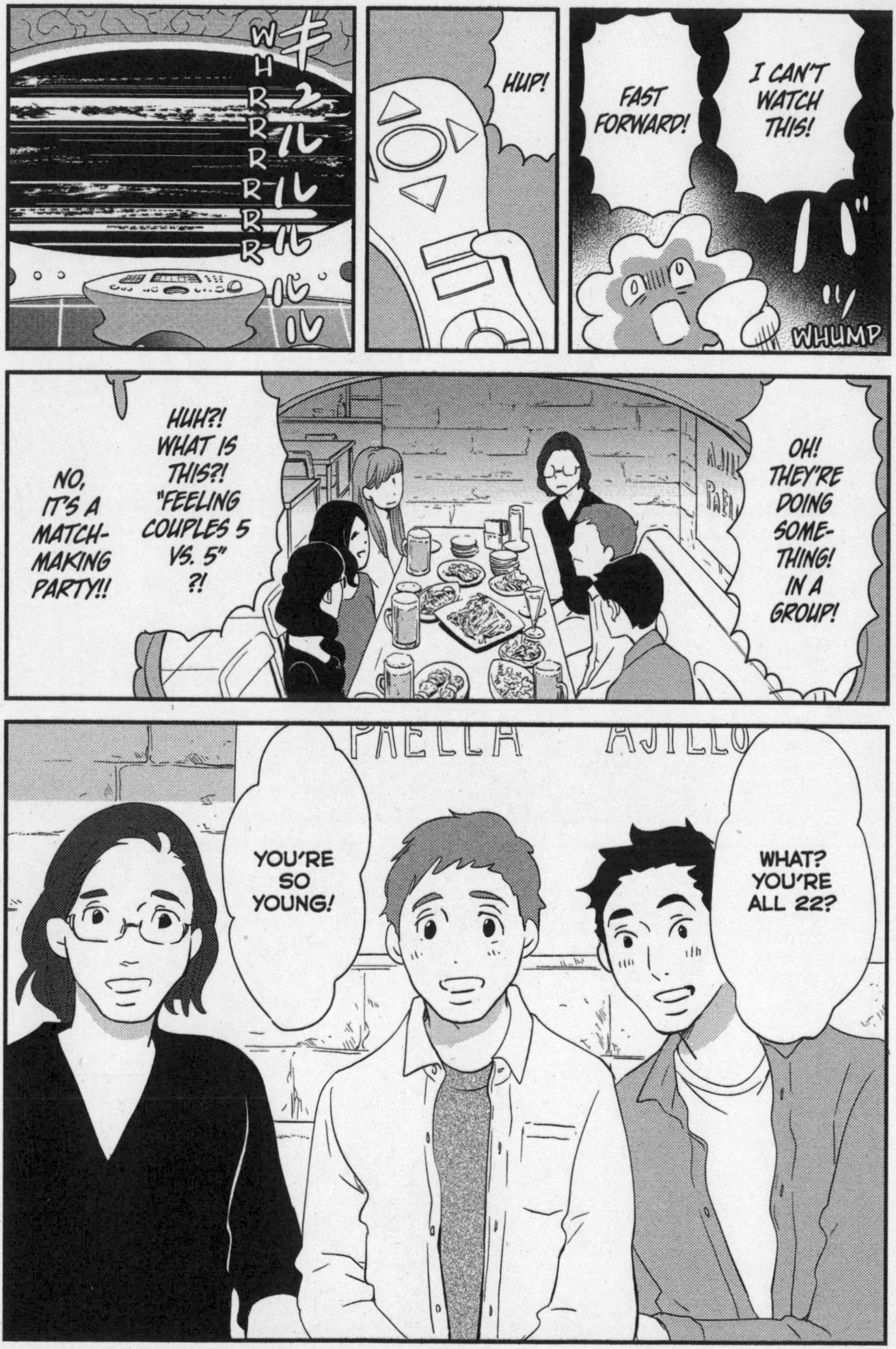
I CAN'T WATCH THIS!
FAST FORWARD!
WHUMP
HUP!
WHRRRRRR
OH! THEY'RE DOING SOMETHING! IN A GROUP!
HUH?! WHAT IS THIS?! "FEELING COUPLES 5 VS. 5" ?!
NO, IT'S A MATCH-MAKING PARTY!!
PAELLA AJILLO
WHAT? YOU'RE ALL 22?
YOU'RE SO YOUNG!

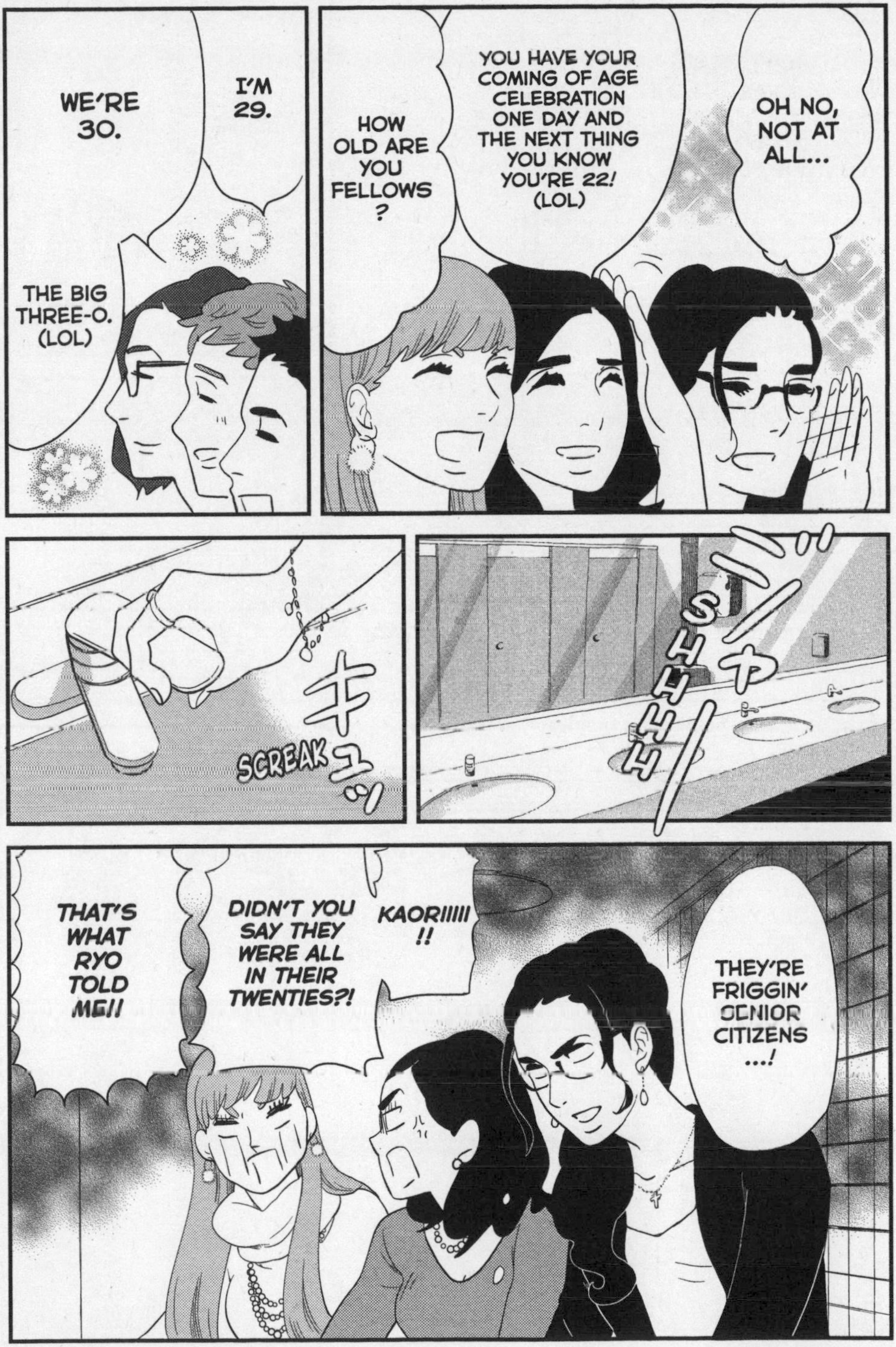
OH NO, NOT AT ALL...
YOU HAVE YOUR COMING OF AGE CELEBRATION ONE DAY AND THE NEXT THING YOU KNOW YOU'RE 22! (LOL)
HOW OLD ARE YOU FELLOWS?
I'M 29.
WE'RE 30.
THE BIG THREE-O. (LOL)
SHHHH
SCREAK
THEY'RE FRIGGIN' SENIOR CITIZENS...!
KAORIIIII!!
DIDN'T YOU SAY THEY WERE ALL IN THEIR TWENTIES?!
THAT'S WHAT RYO TOLD ME!!

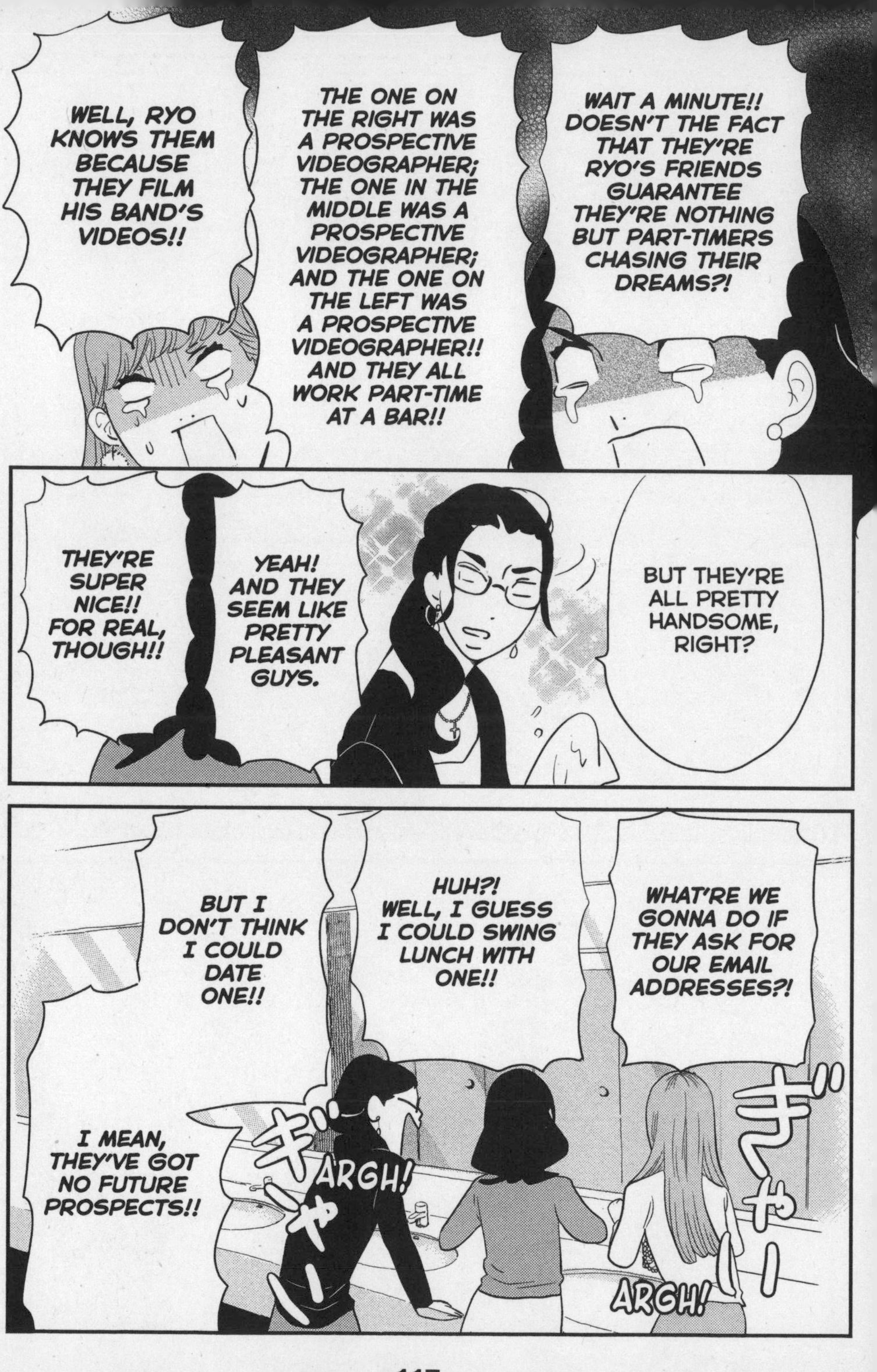

WAIT A MINUTE!! DOESN'T THE FACT THAT THEY'RE RYO'S FRIENDS GUARANTEE THEY'RE NOTHING BUT PART-TIMERS CHASING THEIR DREAMS?!
THE ONE ON THE RIGHT WAS A PROSPECTIVE VIDEOGRAPHER; THE ONE IN THE MIDDLE WAS A PROSPECTIVE VIDEOGRAPHER; AND THE ONE ON THE LEFT WAS A PROSPECTIVE VIDEOGRAPHER!! AND THEY ALL WORK PART-TIME AT A BAR!!
WELL, RYO KNOWS THEM BECAUSE THEY FILM HIS BAND'S VIDEOS!!
BUT THEY'RE ALL PRETTY HANDSOME, RIGHT?
YEAH! AND THEY SEEM LIKE PRETTY PLEASANT GUYS.
THEY'RE SUPER NICE!! FOR REAL, THOUGH!!
WHAT'RE WE GONNA DO IF THEY ASK FOR OUR EMAIL ADDRESSES?!
HUH?! WELL, I GUESS I COULD SWING LUNCH WITH ONE!!
BUT I DON'T THINK I COULD DATE ONE!!
I MEAN, THEY'VE GOT NO FUTURE PROSPECTS!!
ぎゃー
ARGH!
ギャー
ARGH!

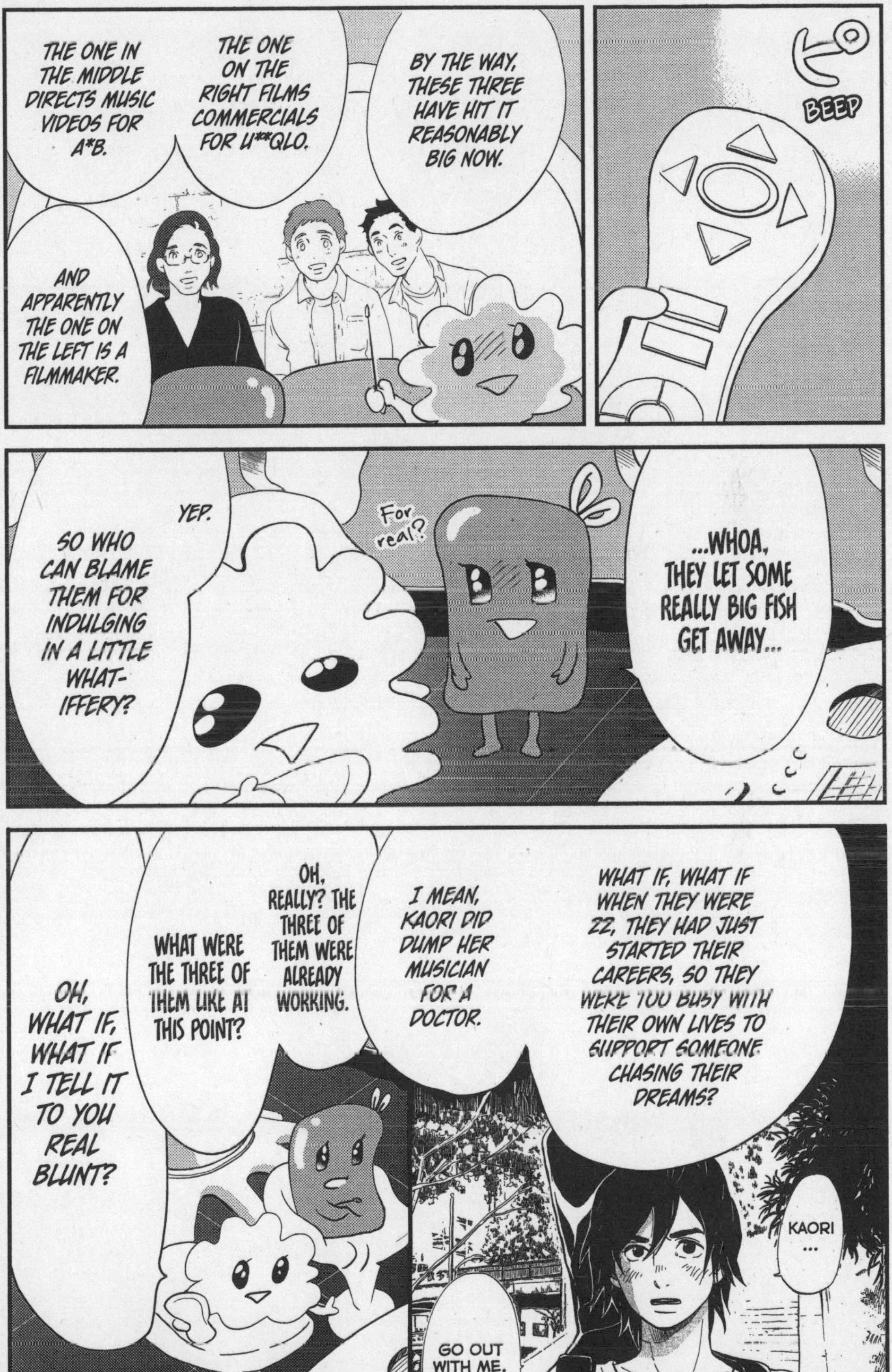
ピ
BEEP
BY THE WAY, THESE THREE HAVE HIT IT REASONABLY BIG NOW.
THE ONE ON THE RIGHT FILMS COMMERCIALS FOR U**QLO.
THE ONE IN THE MIDDLE DIRECTS MUSIC VIDEOS FOR A*B.
AND APPARENTLY THE ONE ON THE LEFT IS A FILMMAKER.
...WHOA, THEY LET SOME REALLY BIG FISH GET AWAY...
For real?
YEP.
SO WHO CAN BLAME THEM FOR INDULGING IN A LITTLE WHAT-IFFERY?
WHAT IF, WHAT IF WHEN THEY WERE 22, THEY HAD JUST STARTED THEIR CAREERS, SO THEY WERE TOO BUSY WITH THEIR OWN LIVES TO SUPPORT SOMEONE CHASING THEIR DREAMS?
I MEAN, KAORI DID DUMP HER MUSICIAN FOR A DOCTOR.
OH, REALLY? THE THREE OF THEM WERE ALREADY WORKING.
WHAT WERE THE THREE OF THEM LIKE AT THIS POINT?
OH, WHAT IF, WHAT IF I TELL IT TO YOU REAL BLUNT?
KAORI ...
GO OUT WITH ME.

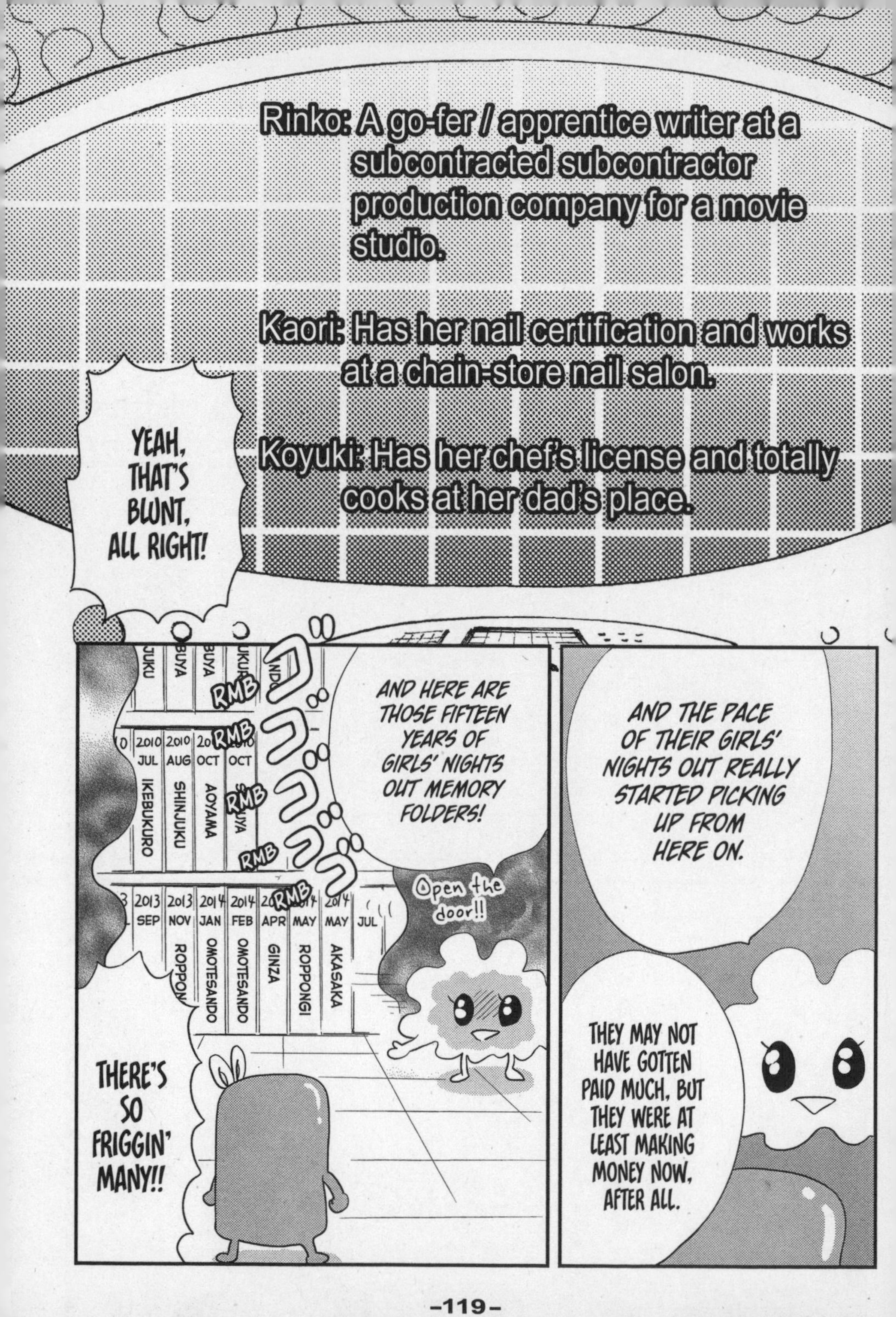
Rinko: A go-fer / apprentice writer at a subcontracted subcontractor production company for a movie studio.
Kaori: Has her nail certification and works at a chain-store nail salon.
Koyuki: Has her chef's license and totally cooks at her dad's place.
YEAH, THAT'S BLUNT, ALL RIGHT!
AND THE PACE OF THEIR GIRLS' NIGHTS OUT REALLY STARTED PICKING UP FROM HERE ON.
THEY MAY NOT HAVE GOTTEN PAID MUCH, BUT THEY WERE AT LEAST MAKING MONEY NOW, AFTER ALL.
AND HERE ARE THOSE FIFTEEN YEARS OF GIRLS' NIGHTS OUT MEMORY FOLDERS!
RMB
RMB
RMB
RMB
RMB
Open the door!!
THERE'S SO FRIGGIN' MANY!!

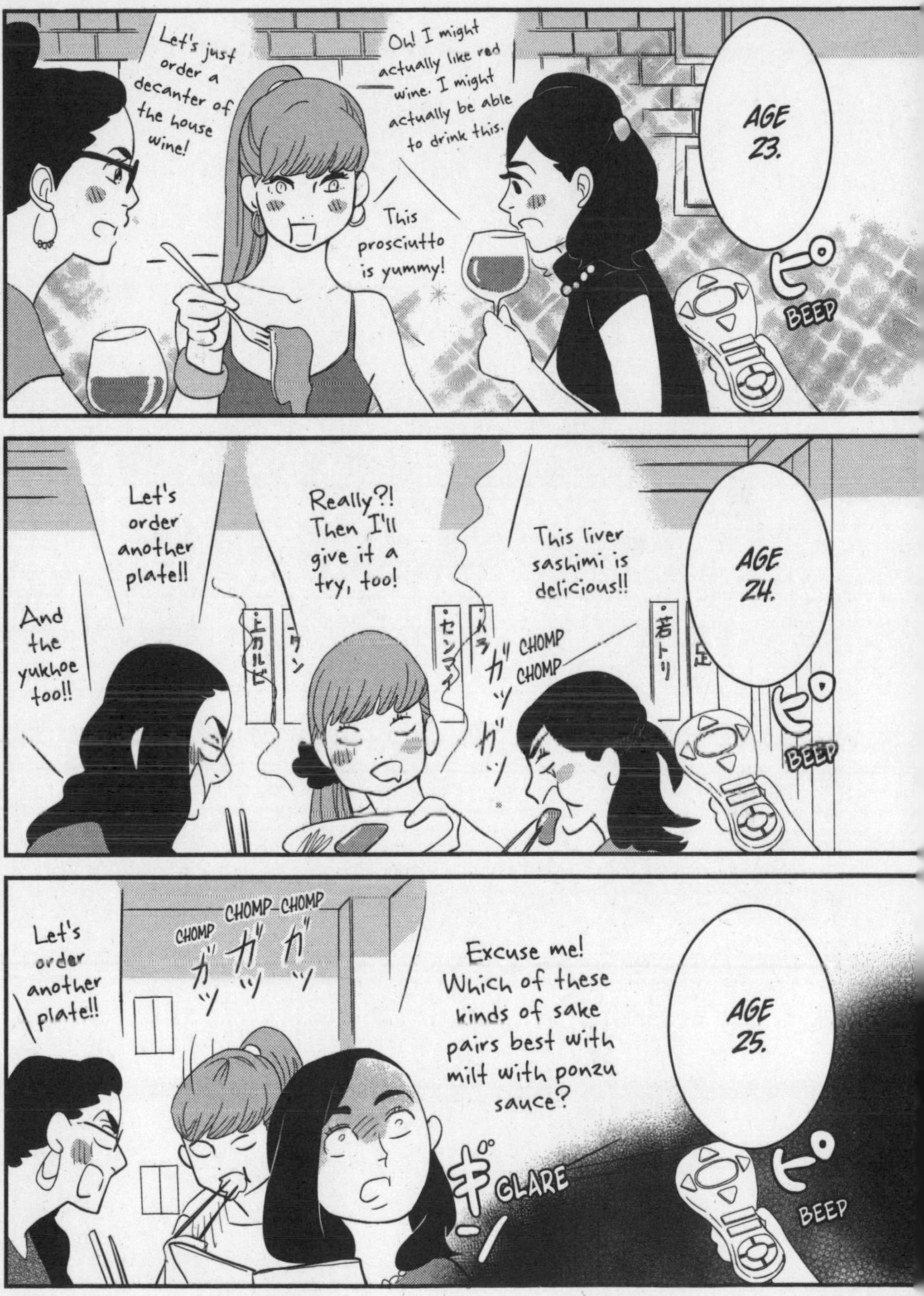
AGE 23.
ピ
BEEP
Oh! I might actually like red wine. I might actually be able to drink this.
This prosciutto is yummy!
Let's just order a decanter of the house wine!
AGE 24.
ピ
BEEP
若トリ
This liver sashimi is delicious!!
ガツガツ
CHOMP CHOMP
センマイ
Really?! Then I'll give it a try, too!
上カルビ
Let's order another plate!!
And the yukhoe too!!
AGE 25.
ピ
BEEP
ギー
GLARE
Excuse me! Which of these kinds of sake pairs best with milt with ponzu sauce?
ガッガッガッ
CHOMP-CHOMP
CHOMP
Let's order another plate!!

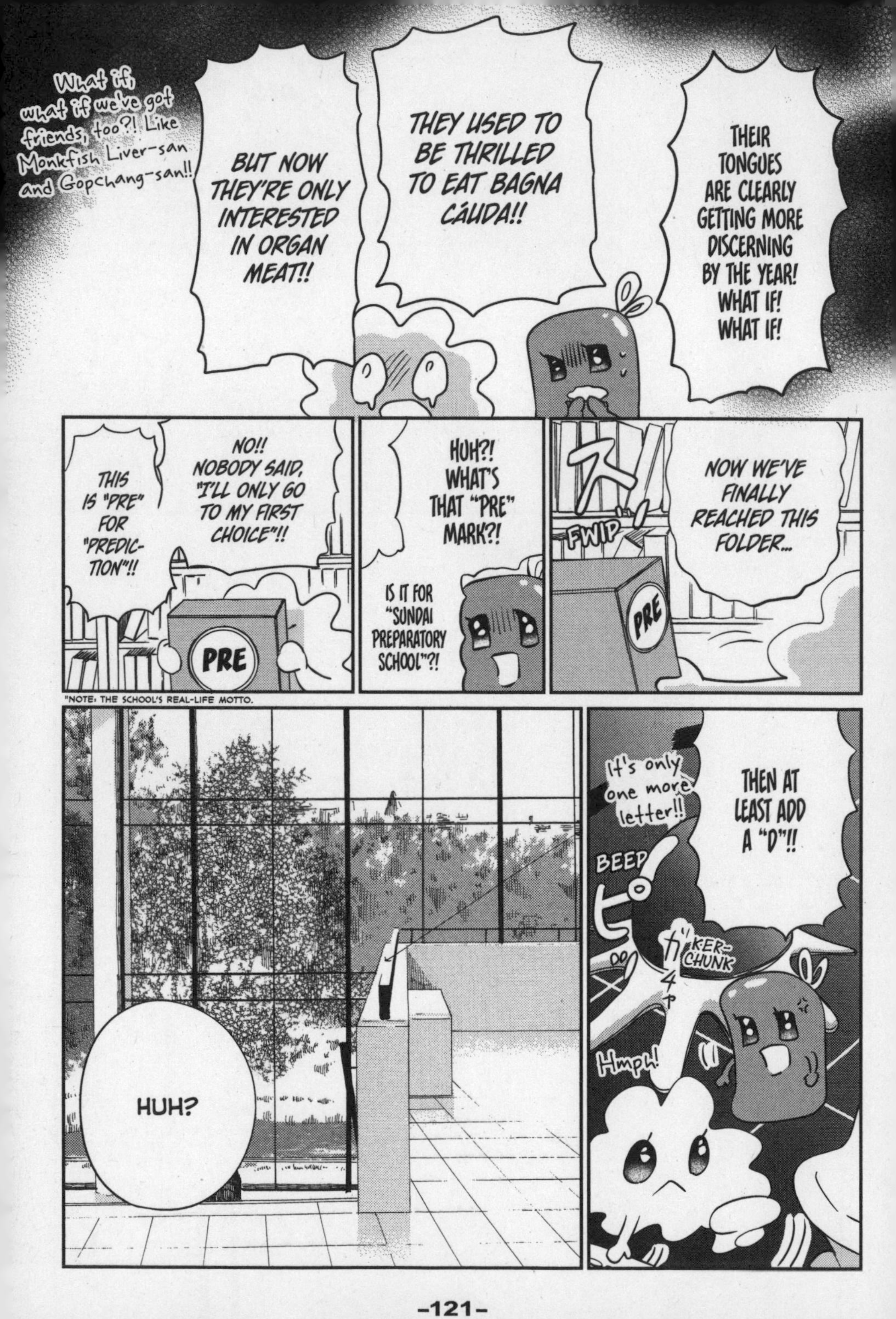
THEIR TONGUES ARE CLEARLY GETTING MORE DISCERNING BY THE YEAR! WHAT IF! WHAT IF!
THEY USED TO BE THRILLED TO EAT BAGNA CÁUDA!!
BUT NOW THEY'RE ONLY INTERESTED IN ORGAN MEAT!!
What if, what if we've got friends, too?! Like Monkfish Liver-san and Gopchang-san!!
FWIP
NOW WE'VE FINALLY REACHED THIS FOLDER...
PRE
HUH?! WHAT'S THAT "PRE" MARK?!
IS IT FOR "SUNDAI PREPARATORY SCHOOL"?!
NO!! NOBODY SAID, "I'LL ONLY GO TO MY FIRST CHOICE"!!
THIS IS "PRE" FOR "PREDICTION"!!
PRE
THEN AT LEAST ADD A "D"!!
It's only one more letter!!
BEEP
KER-CHUNK
Hmph!
HUH?
*NOTE: THE SCHOOL'S REAL-LIFE MOTTO.

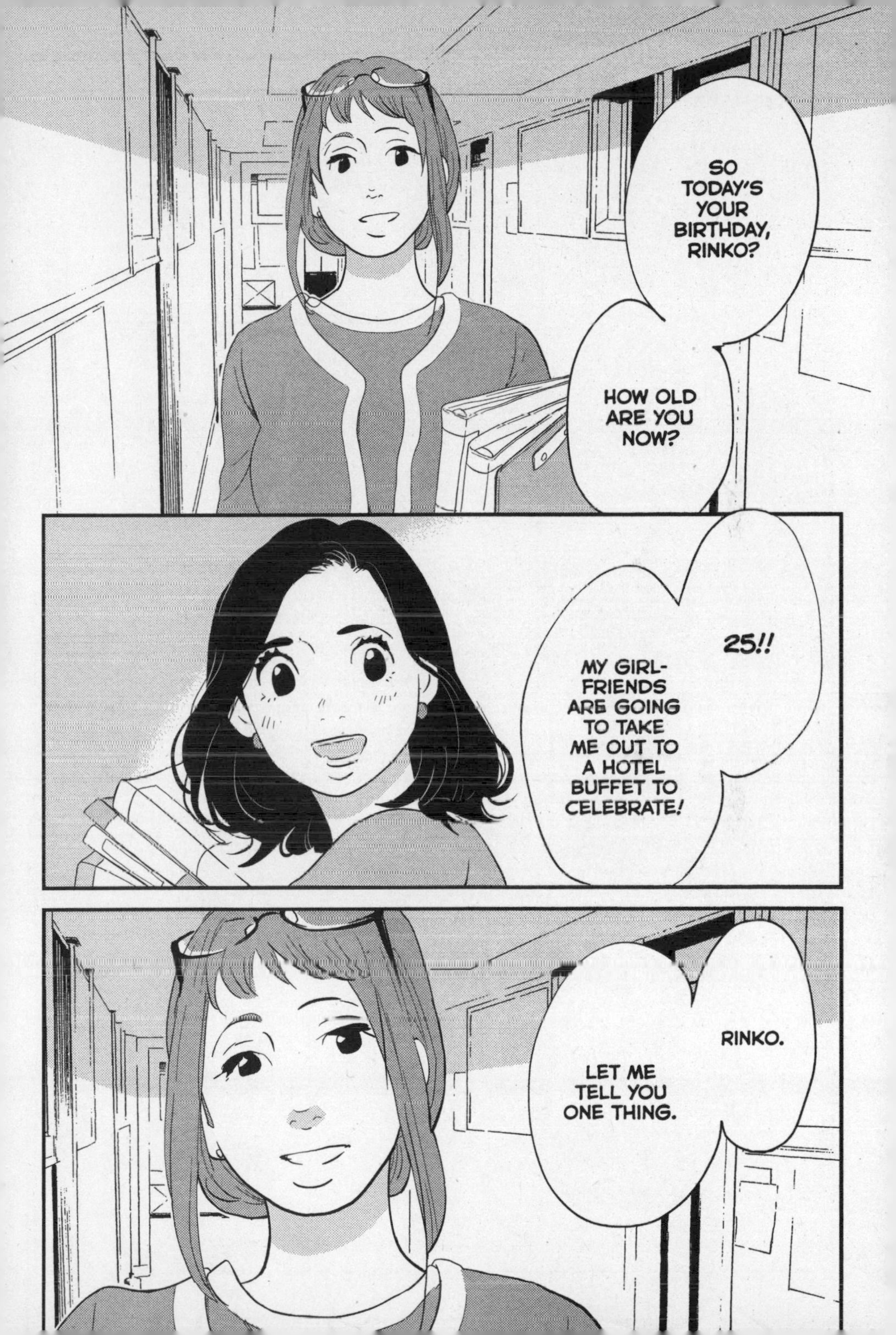
SO TODAY'S YOUR BIRTHDAY, RINKO?
HOW OLD ARE YOU NOW?
25!!
MY GIRL-FRIENDS ARE GOING TO TAKE ME OUT TO A HOTEL BUFFET TO CELEBRATE!
RINKO.
LET ME TELL YOU ONE THING.

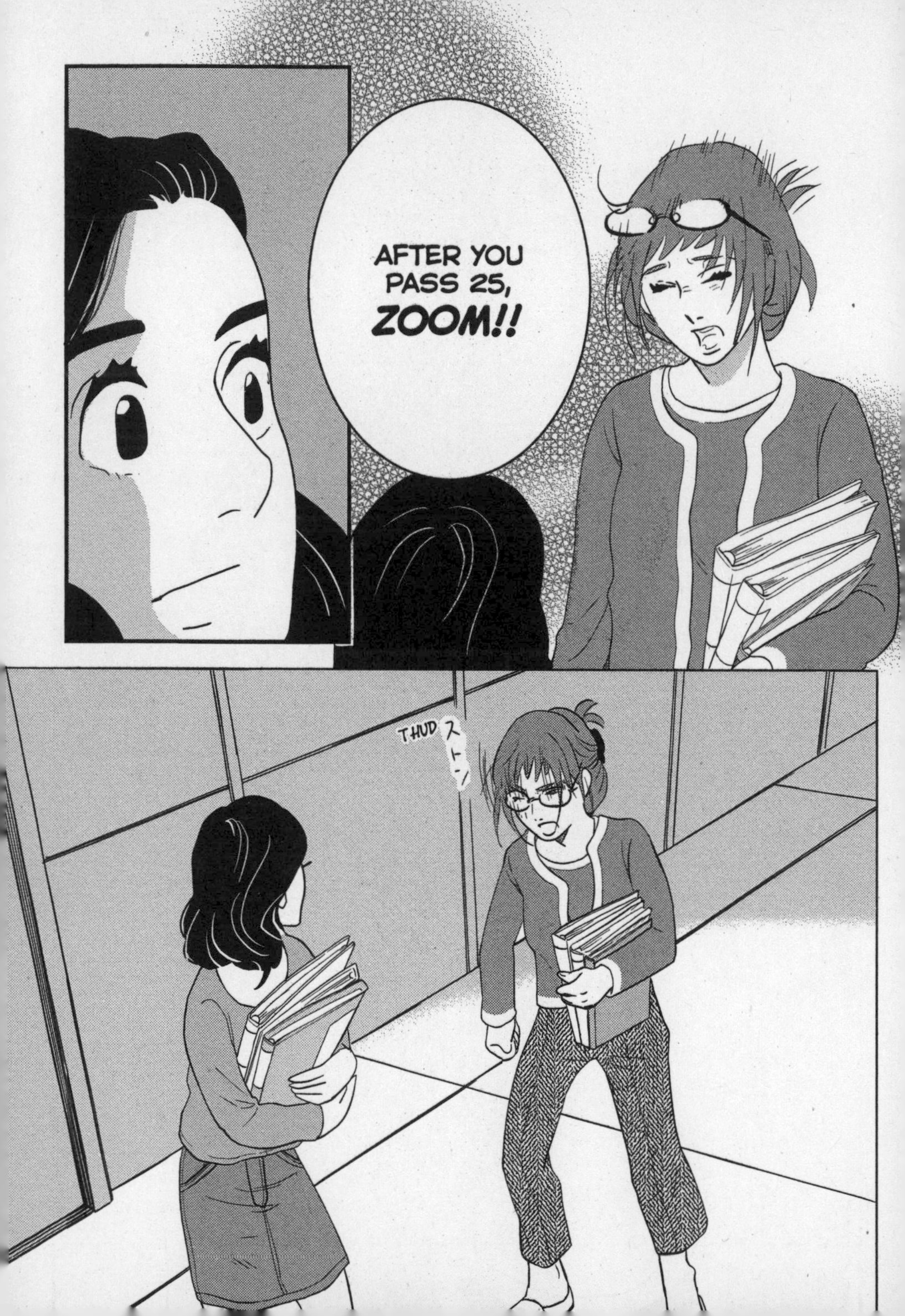
AFTER YOU PASS 25, ZOOM!!
THUD
ストン

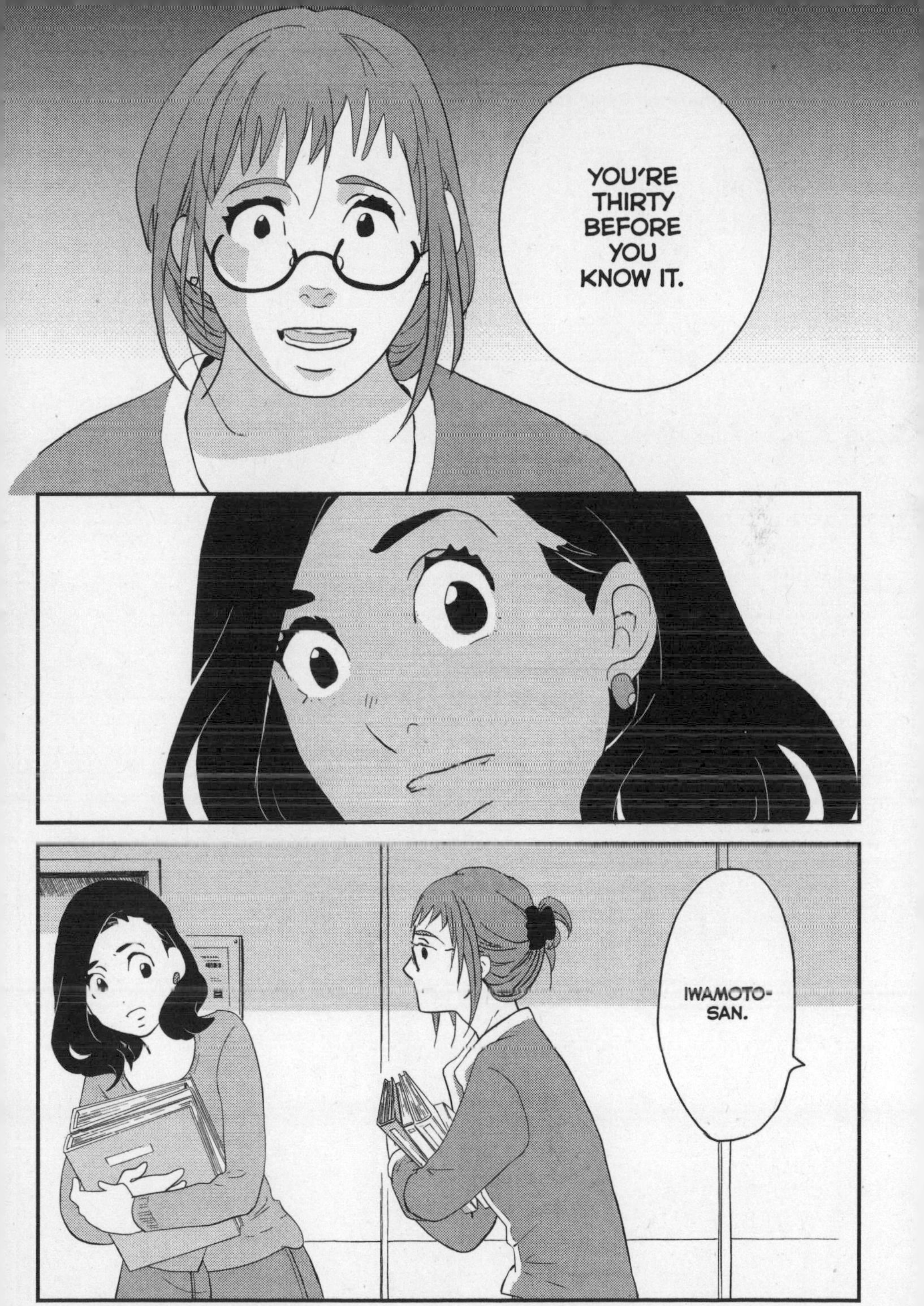
YOU'RE THIRTY BEFORE YOU KNOW IT.
IWAMOTO-SAN.

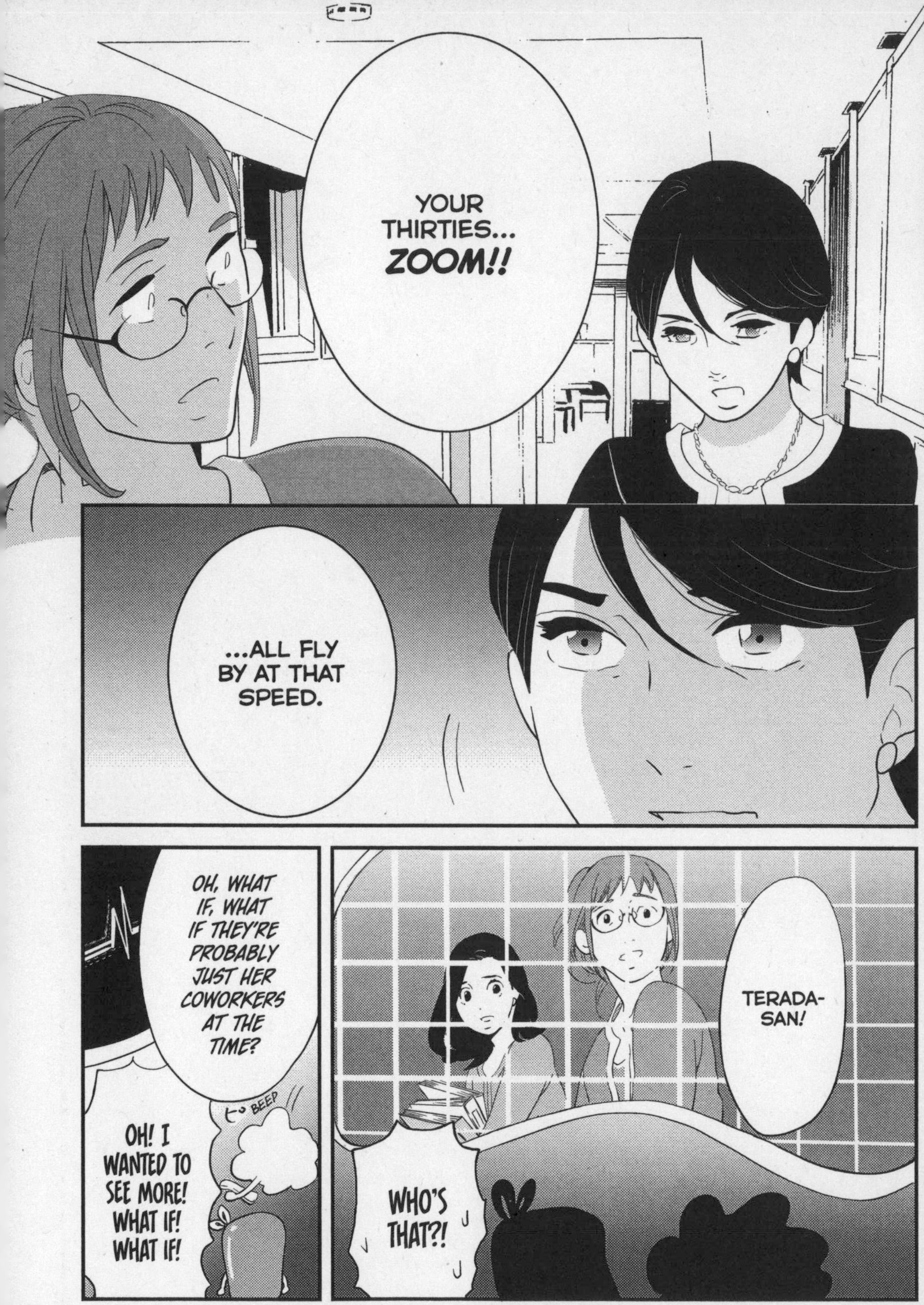
YOUR THIRTIES... ZOOM!!
...ALL FLY BY AT THAT SPEED.
TERADA-SAN!
WHO'S THAT?!
OH, WHAT IF, WHAT IF THEY'RE PROBABLY JUST HER COWORKERS AT THE TIME?
ピ BEEP
OH! I WANTED TO SEE MORE! WHAT IF! WHAT IF!

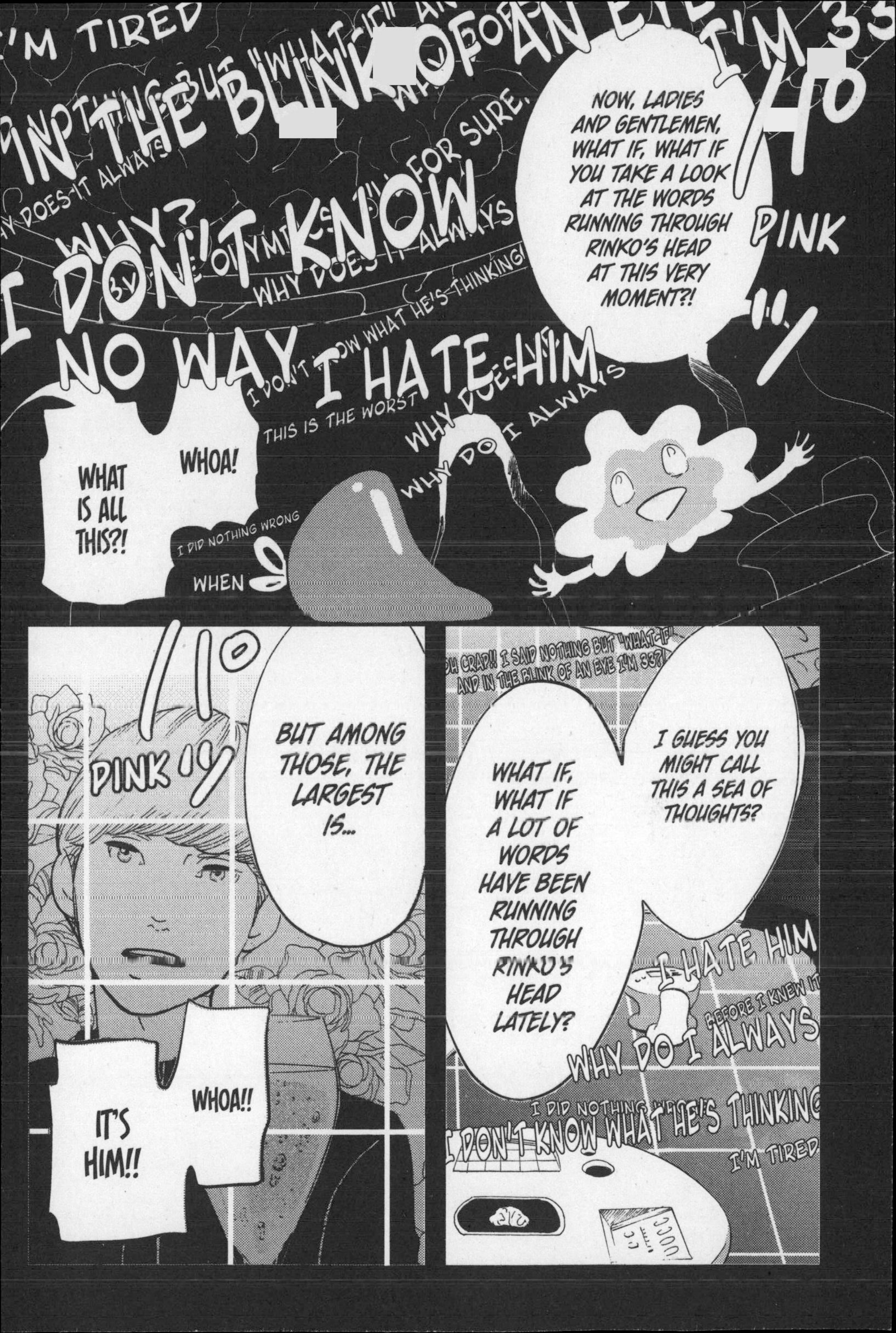
I'M 33
NOW, LADIES AND GENTLEMEN, WHAT IF, WHAT IF YOU TAKE A LOOK AT THE WORDS RUNNING THROUGH RINKO'S HEAD AT THIS VERY MOMENT?!
PINK
IN THE BLINK OF AN EYE
I'M TIRED
FOR SURE.
WHY DOES IT ALWAYS
WHY?
I DON'T KNOW
WHY DOES IT ALWAYS
NO WAY
I HATE HIM
THIS IS THE WORST
WHY DO I ALWAYS
WHOA!
WHAT IS ALL THIS?!
I DID NOTHING WRONG
WHEN
CRAP!! I SAID NOTHING BUT "WHAT IF" AND IN THE BLINK OF AN EYE I'M 33?!
I GUESS YOU MIGHT CALL THIS A SEA OF THOUGHTS?
WHAT IF, WHAT IF A LOT OF WORDS HAVE BEEN RUNNING THROUGH RINKO'S HEAD LATELY?
I HATE HIM
BEFORE I KNEW IT
WHY DO I ALWAYS
I DID NOTHING
I DON'T KNOW WHAT HE'S THINKING
I'M TIRED
BUT AMONG THOSE, THE LARGEST IS...
PINK
WHOA!!
IT'S HIM!!

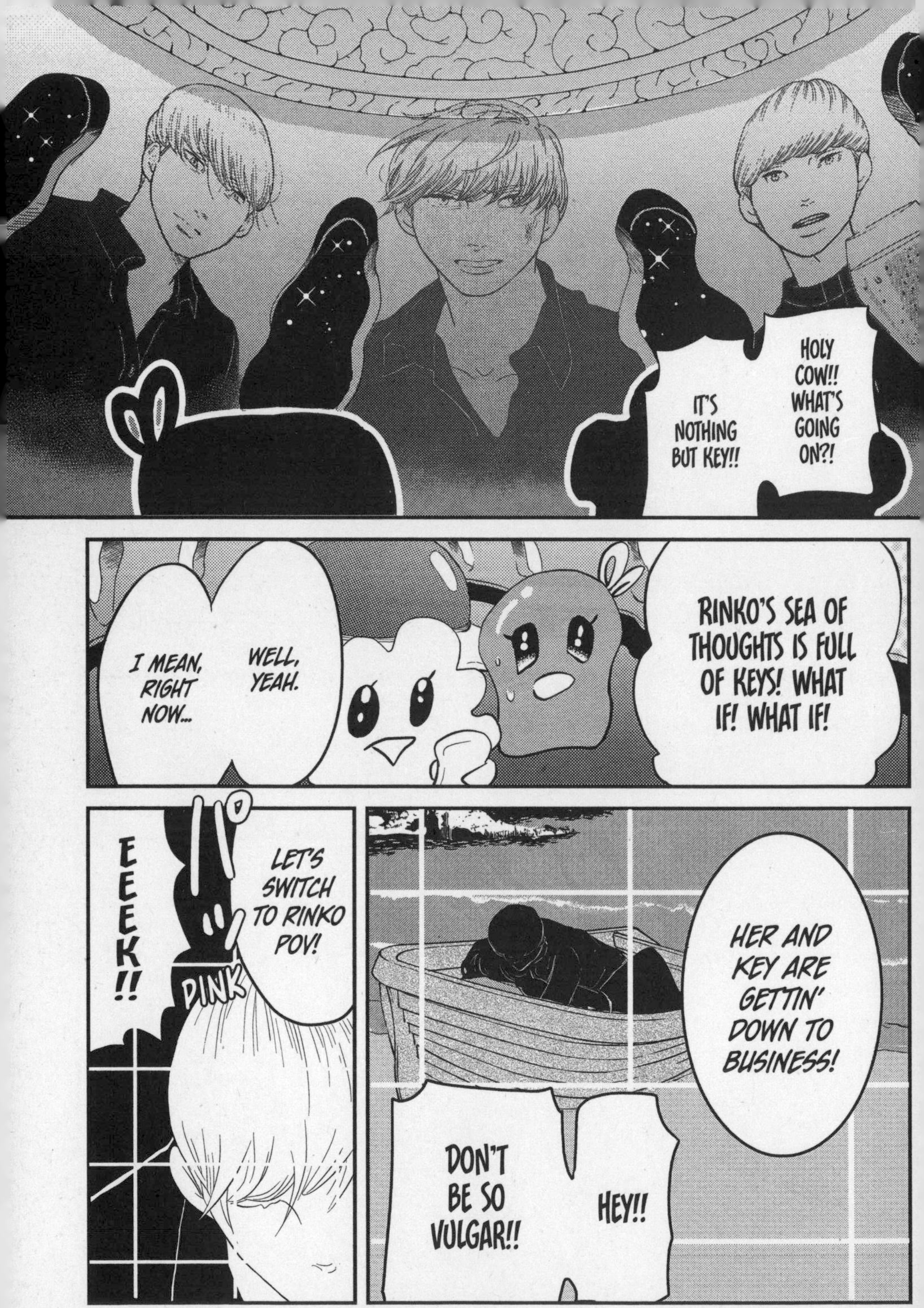
HOLY COW!! WHAT'S GOING ON?!
IT'S NOTHING BUT KEY!!
RINKO'S SEA OF THOUGHTS IS FULL OF KEYS! WHAT IF! WHAT IF!
WELL, YEAH.
I MEAN, RIGHT NOW...
HER AND KEY ARE GETTIN' DOWN TO BUSINESS!
HEY!!
DON'T BE SO VULGAR!!
LET'S SWITCH TO RINKO POV!
DINK
EEEK!!

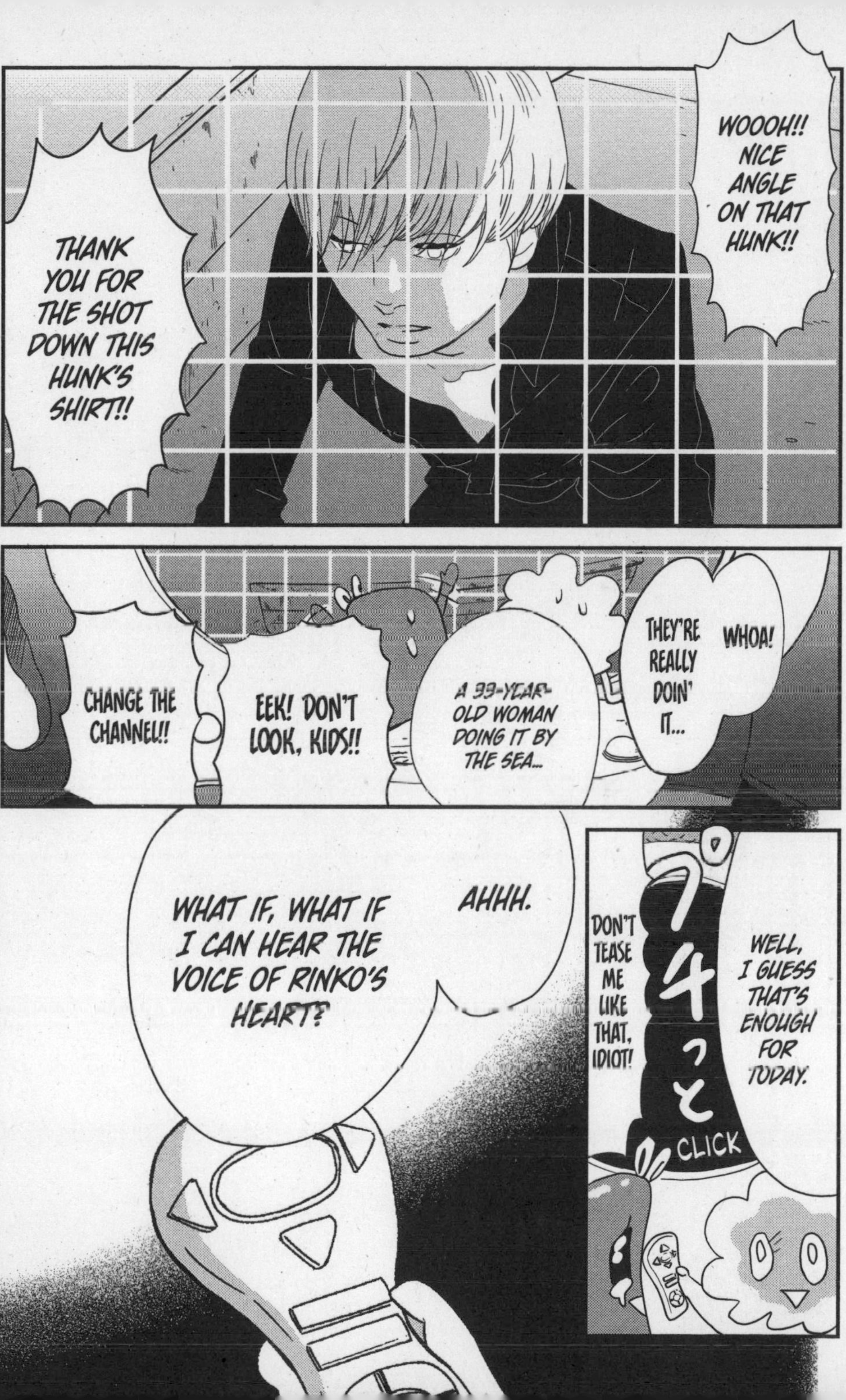
WOOOH!! NICE ANGLE ON THAT HUNK!!
THANK YOU FOR THE SHOT DOWN THIS HUNK'S SHIRT!!
WHOA!
THEY'RE REALLY DOIN' IT...
A 33-YEAR-OLD WOMAN DOING IT BY THE SEA...
EEK! DON'T LOOK, KIDS!!
CHANGE THE CHANNEL!!
WELL, I GUESS THAT'S ENOUGH FOR TODAY.
プチっと
CLICK
DON'T TEASE ME LIKE THAT, IDIOT!
AHHH.
WHAT IF, WHAT IF I CAN HEAR THE VOICE OF RINKO'S HEART?

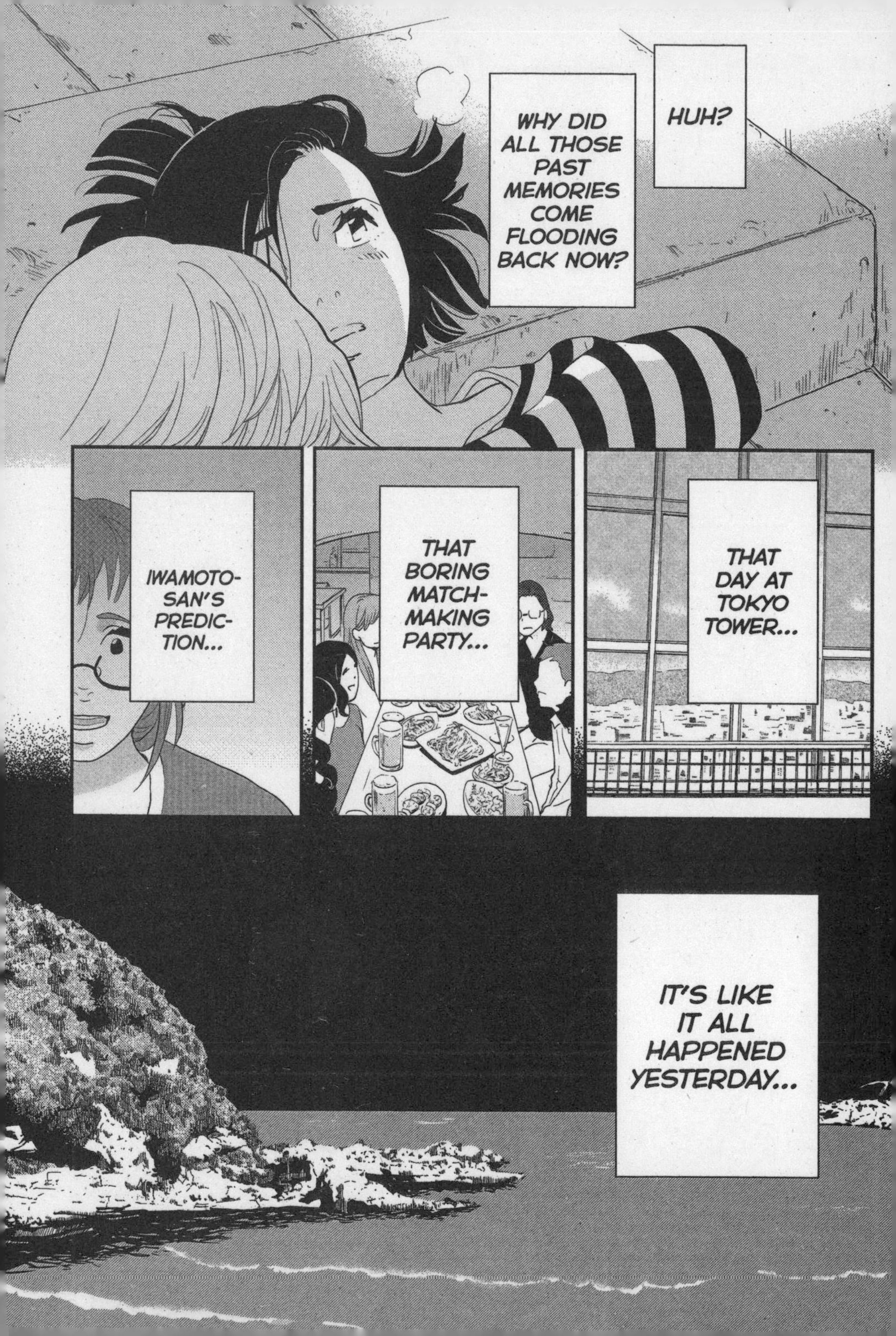
HUH?
WHY DID ALL THOSE PAST MEMORIES COME FLOODING BACK NOW?
THAT DAY AT TOKYO TOWER...
THAT BORING MATCH-MAKING PARTY...
IWAMOTO-SAN'S PREDIC-TION...
IT'S LIKE IT ALL HAPPENED YESTERDAY...

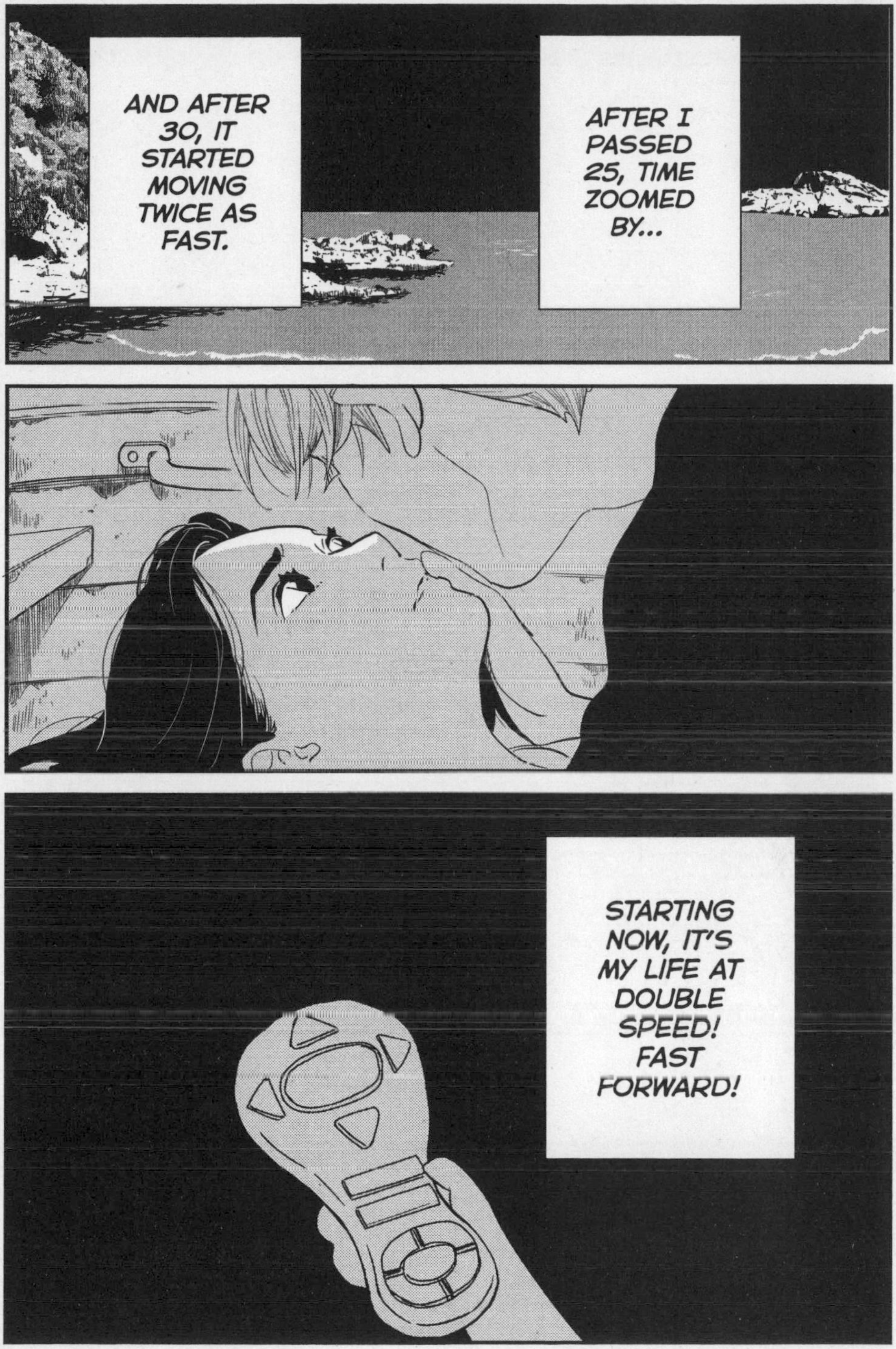
AFTER I PASSED 25, TIME ZOOMED BY...
AND AFTER 30, IT STARTED MOVING TWICE AS FAST.
STARTING NOW, IT'S MY LIFE AT DOUBLE SPEED! FAST FORWARD!

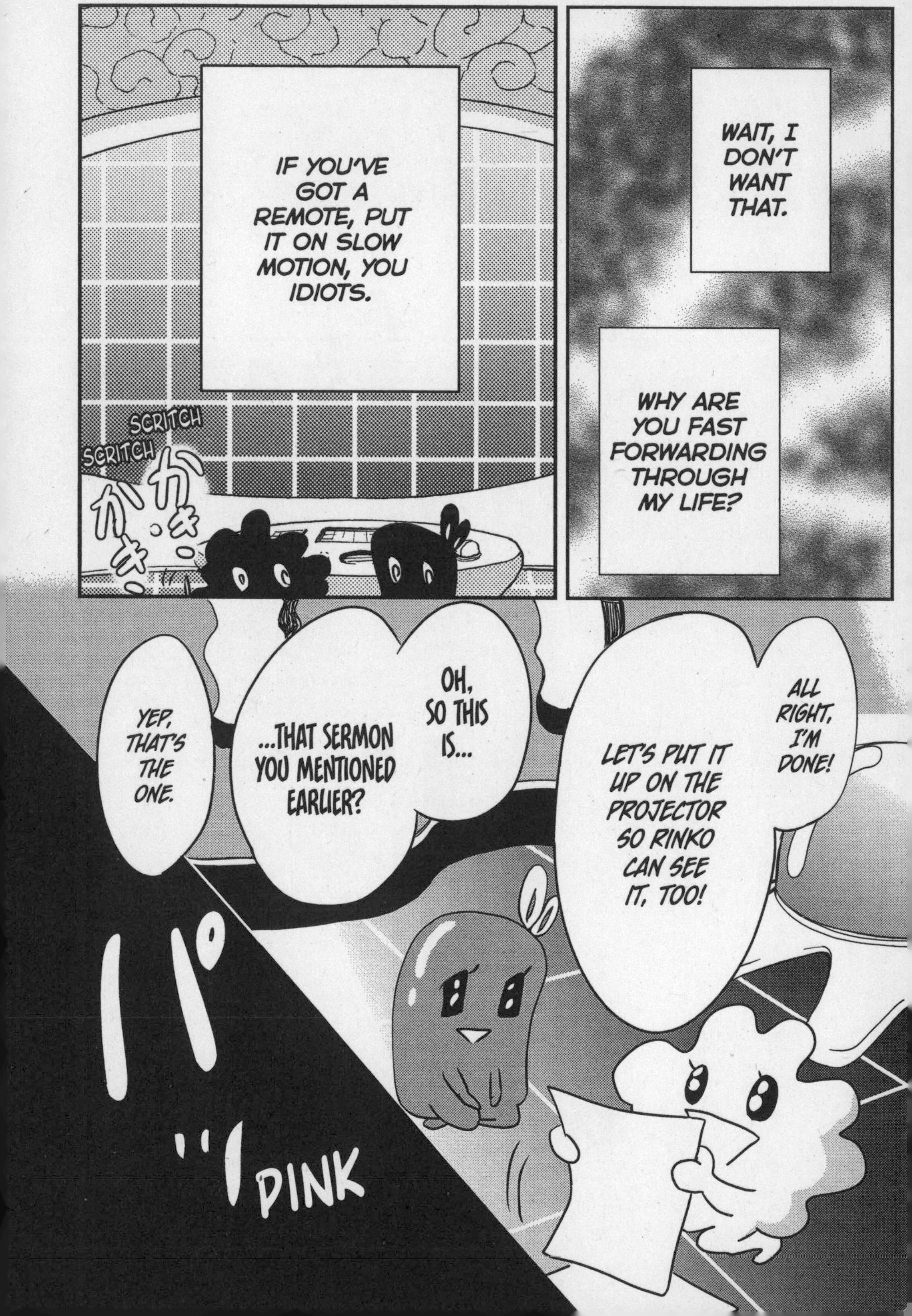
WAIT, I DON'T WANT THAT.
WHY ARE YOU FAST FORWARDING THROUGH MY LIFE?
IF YOU'VE GOT A REMOTE, PUT IT ON SLOW MOTION, YOU IDIOTS.
SCRITCH
SCRITCH
かき
かき
ALL RIGHT, I'M DONE!
LET'S PUT IT UP ON THE PROJECTOR SO RINKO CAN SEE IT, TOO!
OH, SO THIS IS...
...THAT SERMON YOU MENTIONED EARLIER?
YEP, THAT'S THE ONE.
DINK

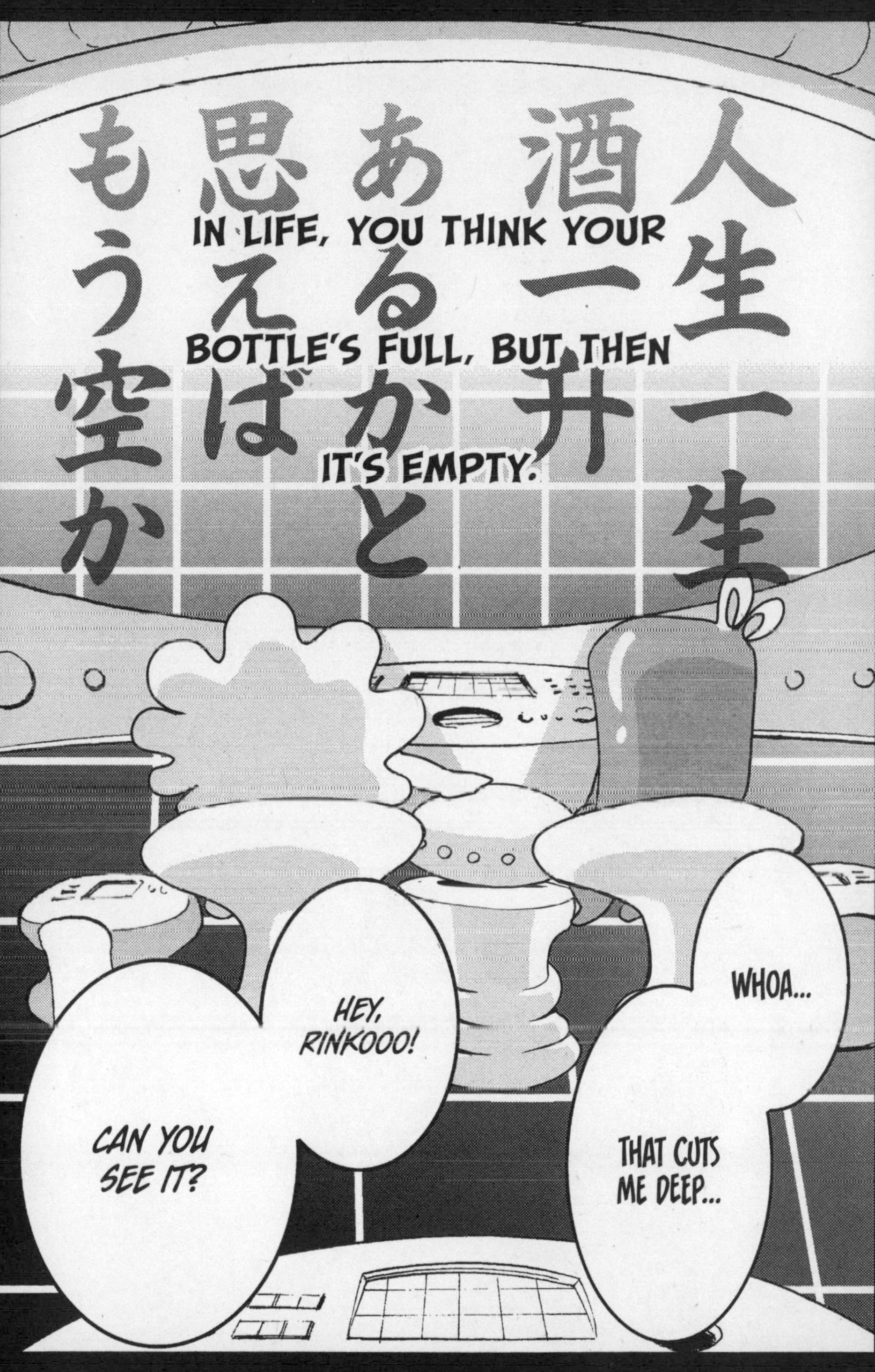
人生一生
酒一升
あるかと
思えば
もう空か
IN LIFE, YOU THINK YOUR BOTTLE'S FULL, BUT THEN IT'S EMPTY.
WHOA...
THAT CUTS ME DEEP...
HEY, RINKOOO!
CAN YOU SEE IT?

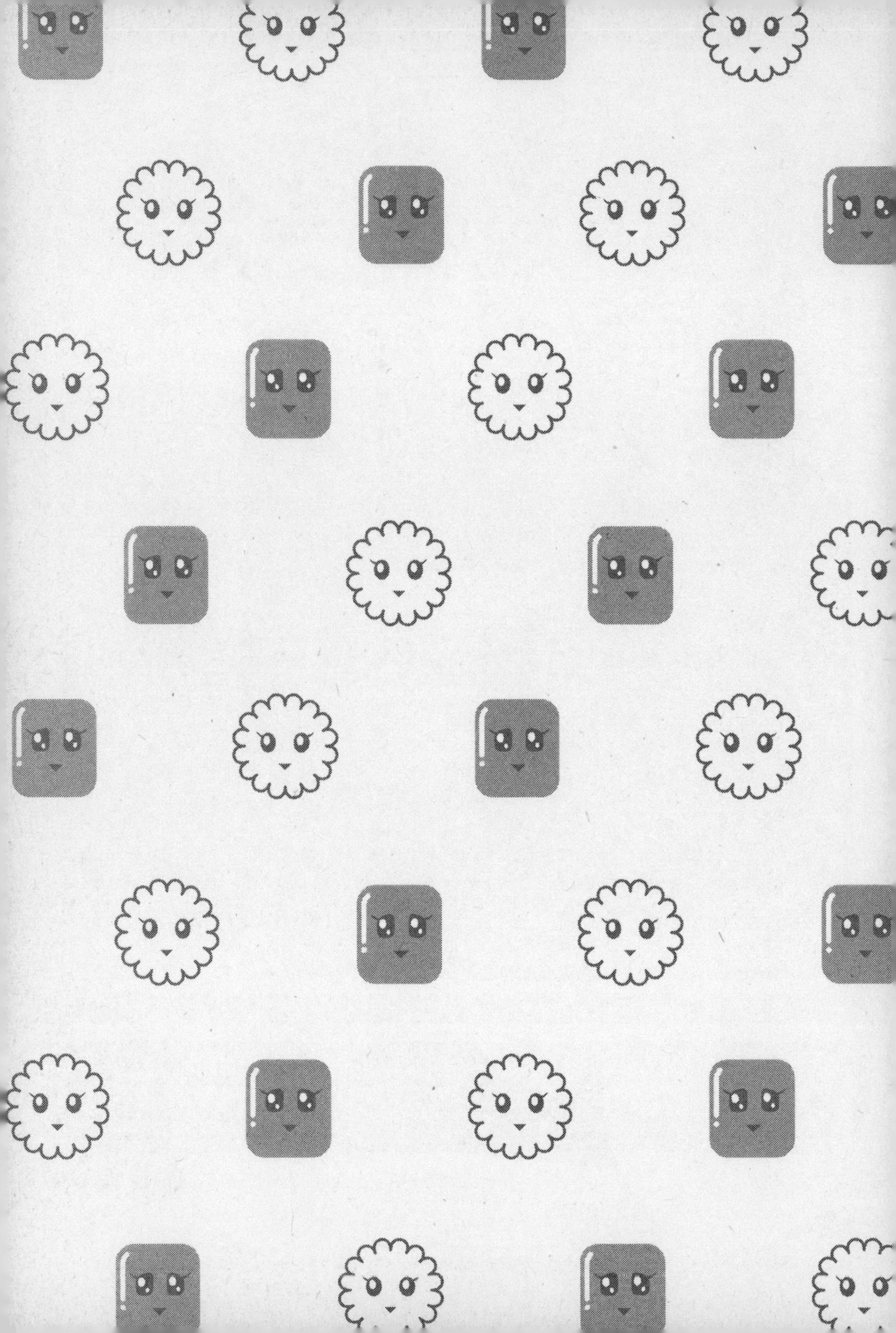

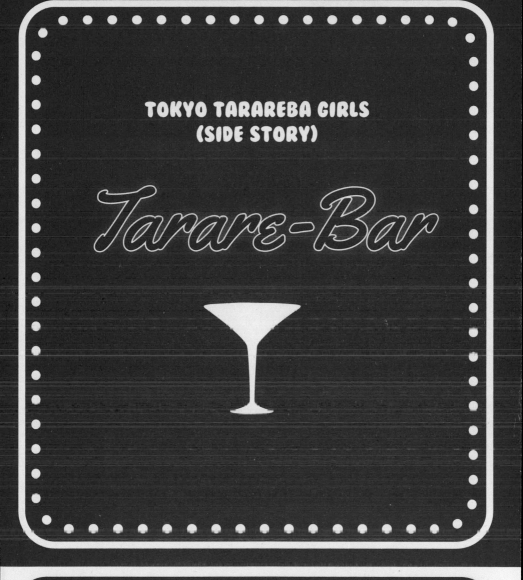

TOKYO TARAREBA GIRLS
(SIDE STORY)

Tarare-Bar

IN THE FOLLOWING SIDE STORY, "TARARE-BAR," WE PUBLISH PROBLEMS SUBMITTED BY READERS FROM ACROSS THE COUNTRY.

★ NIGHT 15 ★

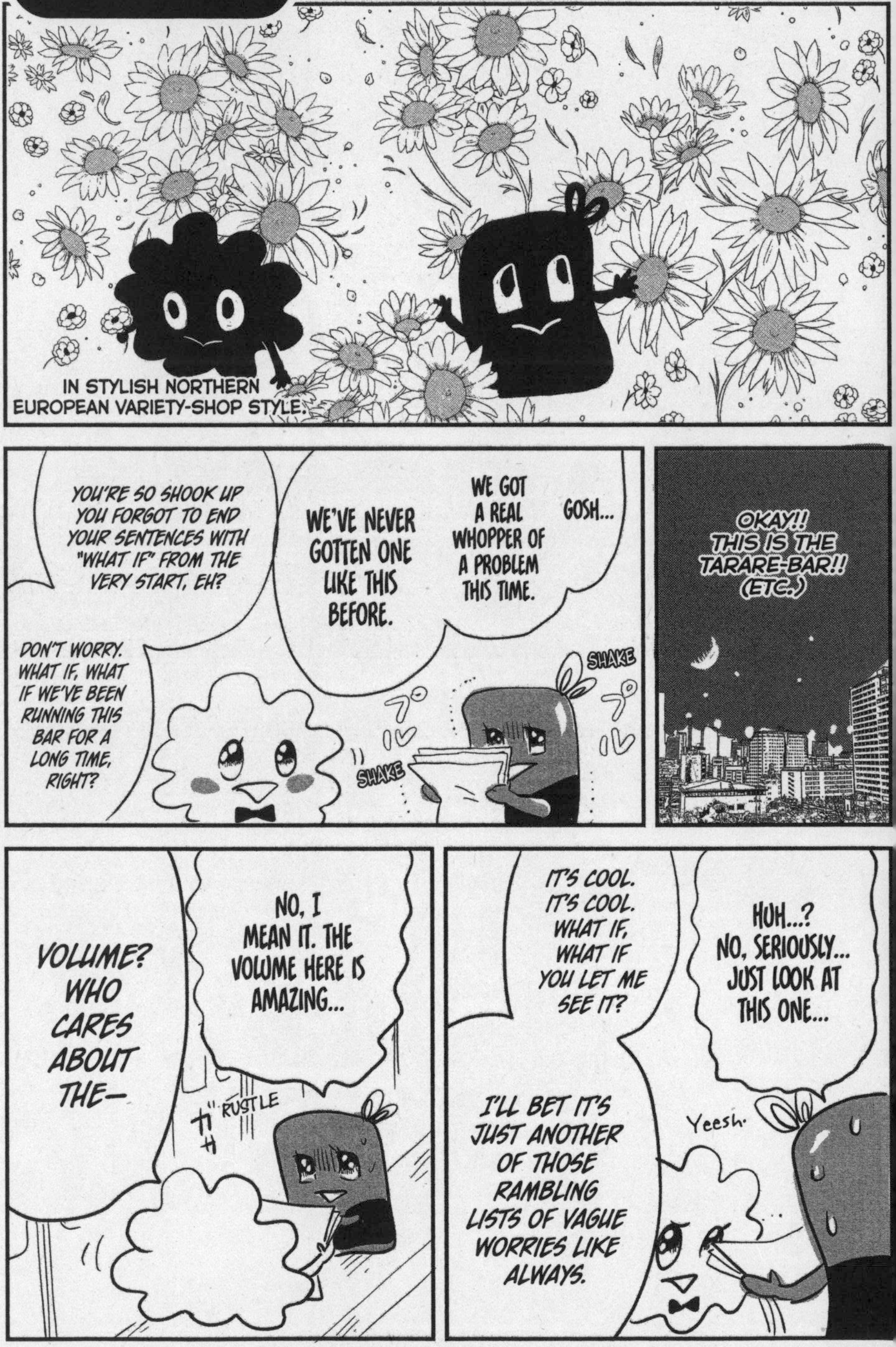
IN STYLISH NORTHERN EUROPEAN VARIETY-SHOP STYLE.
OKAY!! THIS IS THE TARARE-BAR!! (ETC.)
GOSH...
WE GOT A REAL WHOPPER OF A PROBLEM THIS TIME.
SHAKE
WE'VE NEVER GOTTEN ONE LIKE THIS BEFORE.
YOU'RE SO SHOOK UP YOU FORGOT TO END YOUR SENTENCES WITH "WHAT IF" FROM THE VERY START, EH?
DON'T WORRY. WHAT IF, WHAT IF WE'VE BEEN RUNNING THIS BAR FOR A LONG TIME, RIGHT?
SHAKE
HUH...? NO, SERIOUSLY... JUST LOOK AT THIS ONE...
IT'S COOL. IT'S COOL. WHAT IF, WHAT IF YOU LET ME SEE IT?
Yeesh.
I'LL BET IT'S JUST ANOTHER OF THOSE RAMBLING LISTS OF VAGUE WORRIES LIKE ALWAYS.
NO, I MEAN IT. THE VOLUME HERE IS AMAZING...
VOLUME? WHO CARES ABOUT THE—
RUSTLE

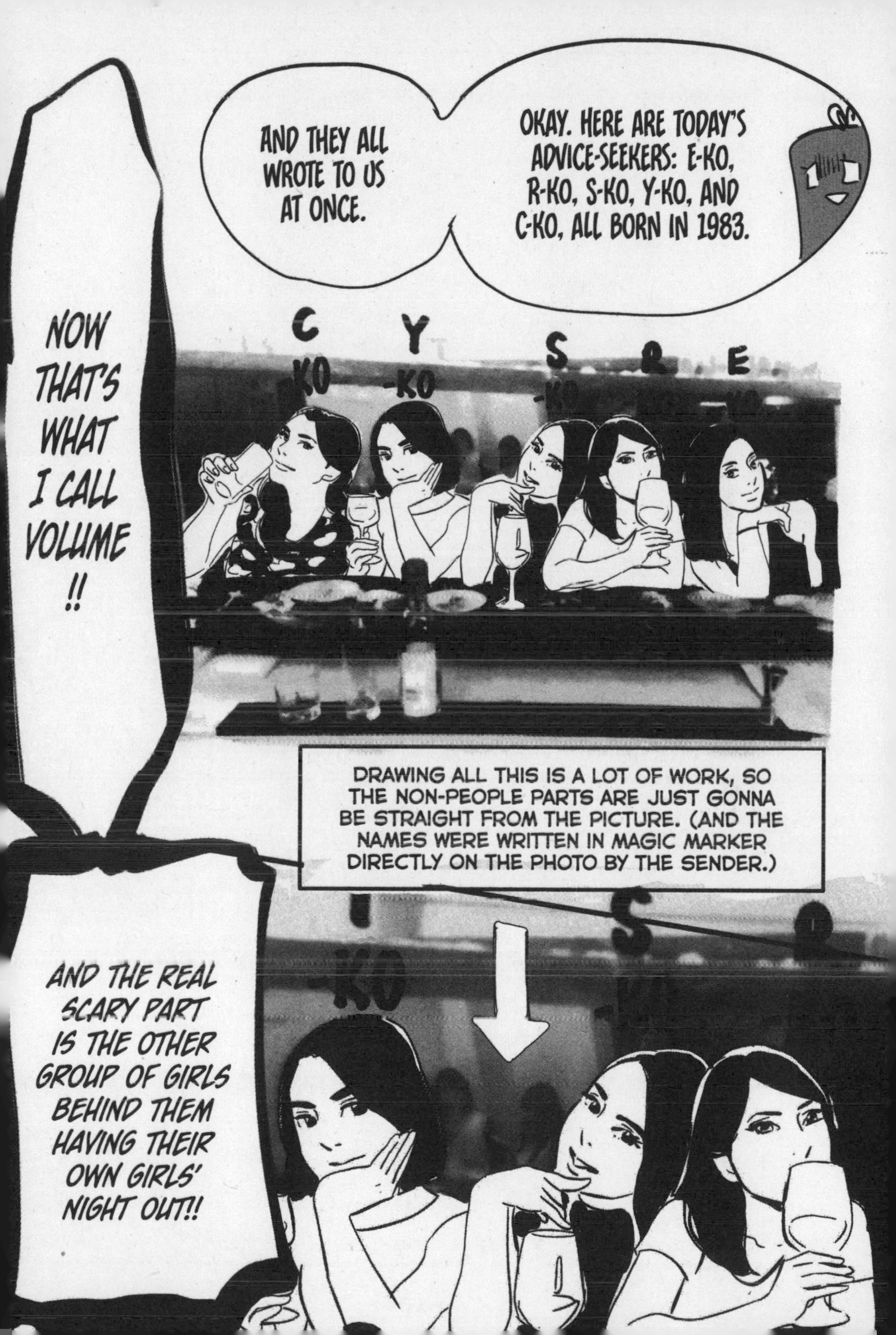
OKAY. HERE ARE TODAY'S ADVICE-SEEKERS: E-KO, R-KO, S-KO, Y-KO, AND C-KO, ALL BORN IN 1983.
AND THEY ALL WROTE TO US AT ONCE.
NOW THAT'S WHAT I CALL VOLUME !!
DRAWING ALL THIS IS A LOT OF WORK, SO THE NON-PEOPLE PARTS ARE JUST GONNA BE STRAIGHT FROM THE PICTURE. (AND THE NAMES WERE WRITTEN IN MAGIC MARKER DIRECTLY ON THE PHOTO BY THE SENDER.)
AND THE REAL SCARY PART IS THE OTHER GROUP OF GIRLS BEHIND THEM HAVING THEIR OWN GIRLS' NIGHT OUT!!

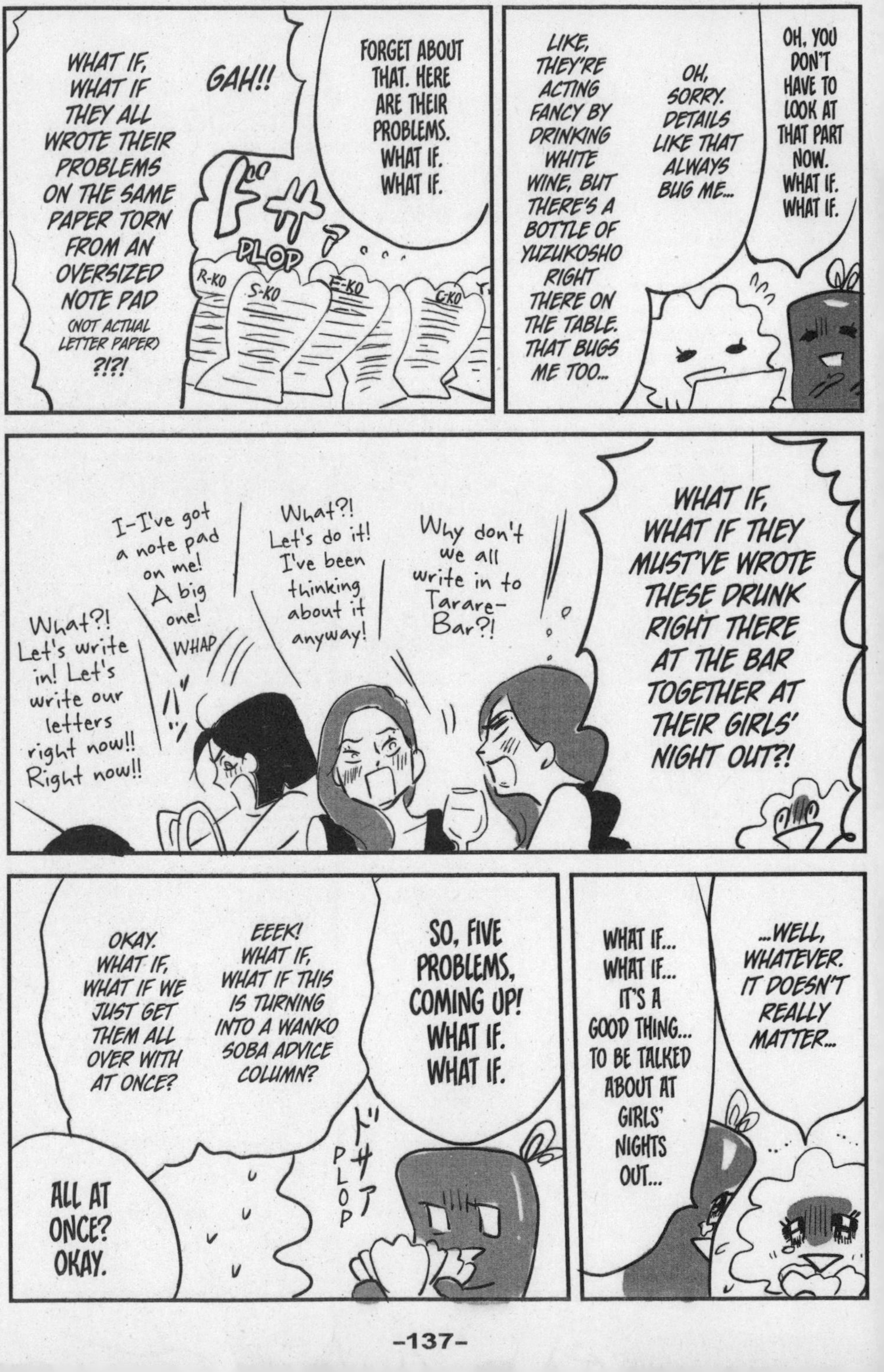
OH, YOU DON'T HAVE TO LOOK AT THAT PART NOW. WHAT IF. WHAT IF.
OH, SORRY. DETAILS LIKE THAT ALWAYS BUG ME...
LIKE, THEY'RE ACTING FANCY BY DRINKING WHITE WINE, BUT THERE'S A BOTTLE OF YUZUKOSHO RIGHT THERE ON THE TABLE. THAT BUGS ME TOO...
FORGET ABOUT THAT. HERE ARE THEIR PROBLEMS. WHAT IF. WHAT IF.
GAH!!
PLOP
R-KO
S-KO
E-KO
C-KO
WHAT IF, WHAT IF THEY ALL WROTE THEIR PROBLEMS ON THE SAME PAPER TORN FROM AN OVERSIZED NOTE PAD (NOT ACTUAL LETTER PAPER) ?!?!
WHAT IF, WHAT IF THEY MUST'VE WROTE THESE DRUNK RIGHT THERE AT THE BAR TOGETHER AT THEIR GIRLS' NIGHT OUT?!
Why don't we all write in to Tarare-Bar?!
What?! Let's do it! I've been thinking about it anyway!
I-I've got a note pad on me! A big one!
WHAP
What?! Let's write in! Let's write our letters right now!! Right now!!
...WELL, WHATEVER. IT DOESN'T REALLY MATTER...
WHAT IF... WHAT IF... IT'S A GOOD THING... TO BE TALKED ABOUT AT GIRLS' NIGHTS OUT...
SO, FIVE PROBLEMS, COMING UP! WHAT IF. WHAT IF.
EEEK! WHAT IF, WHAT IF THIS IS TURNING INTO A WANKO SOBA ADVICE COLUMN?
OKAY. WHAT IF, WHAT IF WE JUST GET THEM ALL OVER WITH AT ONCE?
PLOP
ALL AT ONCE? OKAY.

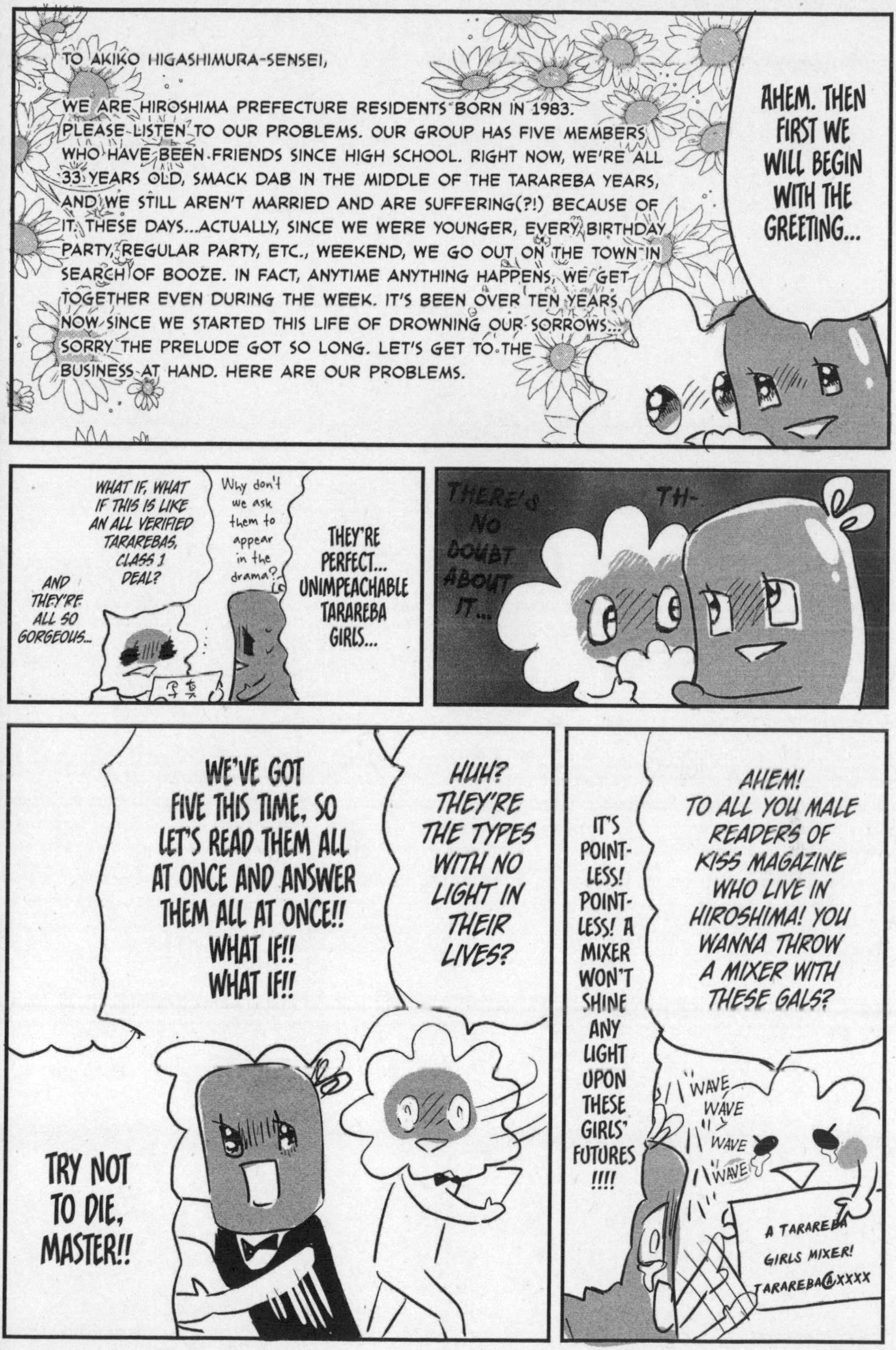
AHEM. THEN FIRST WE WILL BEGIN WITH THE GREETING...
TO AKIKO HIGASHIMURA-SENSEI,
WE ARE HIROSHIMA PREFECTURE RESIDENTS BORN IN 1983. PLEASE LISTEN TO OUR PROBLEMS. OUR GROUP HAS FIVE MEMBERS WHO HAVE BEEN FRIENDS SINCE HIGH SCHOOL. RIGHT NOW, WE'RE ALL 33 YEARS OLD, SMACK DAB IN THE MIDDLE OF THE TARAREBA YEARS, AND WE STILL AREN'T MARRIED AND ARE SUFFERING(?!) BECAUSE OF IT. THESE DAYS...ACTUALLY, SINCE WE WERE YOUNGER, EVERY BIRTHDAY PARTY, REGULAR PARTY, ETC., WEEKEND, WE GO OUT ON THE TOWN IN SEARCH OF BOOZE. IN FACT, ANYTIME ANYTHING HAPPENS, WE GET TOGETHER EVEN DURING THE WEEK. IT'S BEEN OVER TEN YEARS NOW SINCE WE STARTED THIS LIFE OF DROWNING OUR SORROWS... SORRY THE PRELUDE GOT SO LONG. LET'S GET TO THE BUSINESS AT HAND. HERE ARE OUR PROBLEMS.
TH-
THERE'S NO DOUBT ABOUT IT...
THEY'RE PERFECT... UNIMPEACHABLE TARAREBA GIRLS...
Why don't we ask them to appear in the drama?
WHAT IF, WHAT IF THIS IS LIKE AN ALL VERIFIED TARAREBAS, CLASS 1 DEAL?
AND THEY'RE ALL SO GORGEOUS...
AHEM! TO ALL YOU MALE READERS OF KISS MAGAZINE WHO LIVE IN HIROSHIMA! YOU WANNA THROW A MIXER WITH THESE GALS?
IT'S POINTLESS! POINTLESS! A MIXER WON'T SHINE ANY LIGHT UPON THESE GIRLS' FUTURES!!!!
WAVE WAVE WAVE WAVE
A TARAREBA GIRLS MIXER! TARAREBA@XXXX
HUH? THEY'RE THE TYPES WITH NO LIGHT IN THEIR LIVES?
WE'VE GOT FIVE THIS TIME, SO LET'S READ THEM ALL AT ONCE AND ANSWER THEM ALL AT ONCE!! WHAT IF!! WHAT IF!!
TRY NOT TO DIE, MASTER!!

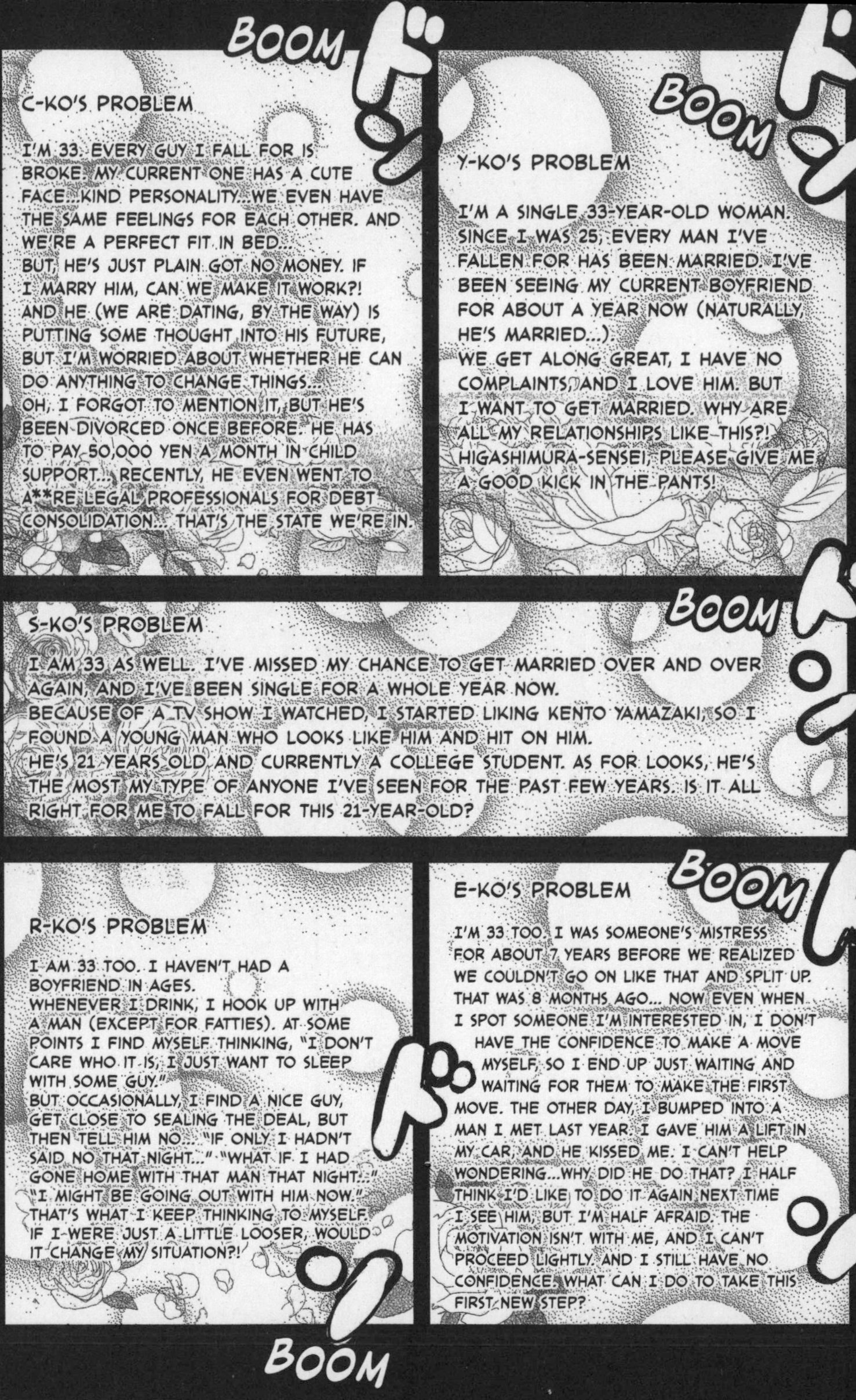
BOOM
Y-KO'S PROBLEM
I'M A SINGLE 33-YEAR-OLD WOMAN. SINCE I WAS 25, EVERY MAN I'VE FALLEN FOR HAS BEEN MARRIED. I'VE BEEN SEEING MY CURRENT BOYFRIEND FOR ABOUT A YEAR NOW (NATURALLY, HE'S MARRIED...).
WE GET ALONG GREAT, I HAVE NO COMPLAINTS, AND I LOVE HIM. BUT I WANT TO GET MARRIED. WHY ARE ALL MY RELATIONSHIPS LIKE THIS?! HIGASHIMURA-SENSEI, PLEASE GIVE ME A GOOD KICK IN THE PANTS!
BOOM
C-KO'S PROBLEM
I'M 33. EVERY GUY I FALL FOR IS BROKE. MY CURRENT ONE HAS A CUTE FACE...KIND PERSONALITY...WE EVEN HAVE THE SAME FEELINGS FOR EACH OTHER. AND WE'RE A PERFECT FIT IN BED...
BUT, HE'S JUST PLAIN GOT NO MONEY. IF I MARRY HIM, CAN WE MAKE IT WORK?! AND HE (WE ARE DATING, BY THE WAY) IS PUTTING SOME THOUGHT INTO HIS FUTURE, BUT I'M WORRIED ABOUT WHETHER HE CAN DO ANYTHING TO CHANGE THINGS...
OH, I FORGOT TO MENTION IT, BUT HE'S BEEN DIVORCED ONCE BEFORE. HE HAS TO PAY 50,000 YEN A MONTH IN CHILD SUPPORT... RECENTLY, HE EVEN WENT TO A**RE LEGAL PROFESSIONALS FOR DEBT CONSOLIDATION... THAT'S THE STATE WE'RE IN.
BOOM
S-KO'S PROBLEM
I AM 33 AS WELL. I'VE MISSED MY CHANCE TO GET MARRIED OVER AND OVER AGAIN, AND I'VE BEEN SINGLE FOR A WHOLE YEAR NOW.
BECAUSE OF A TV SHOW I WATCHED, I STARTED LIKING KENTO YAMAZAKI, SO I FOUND A YOUNG MAN WHO LOOKS LIKE HIM AND HIT ON HIM.
HE'S 21 YEARS OLD AND CURRENTLY A COLLEGE STUDENT. AS FOR LOOKS, HE'S THE MOST MY TYPE OF ANYONE I'VE SEEN FOR THE PAST FEW YEARS. IS IT ALL RIGHT FOR ME TO FALL FOR THIS 21-YEAR-OLD?
BOOM
E-KO'S PROBLEM
I'M 33 TOO. I WAS SOMEONE'S MISTRESS FOR ABOUT 7 YEARS BEFORE WE REALIZED WE COULDN'T GO ON LIKE THAT AND SPLIT UP. THAT WAS 8 MONTHS AGO... NOW EVEN WHEN I SPOT SOMEONE I'M INTERESTED IN, I DON'T HAVE THE CONFIDENCE TO MAKE A MOVE MYSELF, SO I END UP JUST WAITING AND WAITING FOR THEM TO MAKE THE FIRST MOVE. THE OTHER DAY, I BUMPED INTO A MAN I MET LAST YEAR. I GAVE HIM A LIFT IN MY CAR, AND HE KISSED ME. I CAN'T HELP WONDERING...WHY DID HE DO THAT? I HALF THINK I'D LIKE TO DO IT AGAIN NEXT TIME I SEE HIM, BUT I'M HALF AFRAID. THE MOTIVATION ISN'T WITH ME, AND I CAN'T PROCEED LIGHTLY. AND I STILL HAVE NO CONFIDENCE. WHAT CAN I DO TO TAKE THIS FIRST NEW STEP?
R-KO'S PROBLEM
I AM 33 TOO. I HAVEN'T HAD A BOYFRIEND IN AGES.
WHENEVER I DRINK, I HOOK UP WITH A MAN (EXCEPT FOR FATTIES). AT SOME POINTS I FIND MYSELF THINKING, "I DON'T CARE WHO IT IS, I JUST WANT TO SLEEP WITH SOME GUY."
BUT OCCASIONALLY, I FIND A NICE GUY, GET CLOSE TO SEALING THE DEAL, BUT THEN TELL HIM NO... "IF ONLY I HADN'T SAID NO THAT NIGHT..." "WHAT IF I HAD GONE HOME WITH THAT MAN THAT NIGHT..." "I MIGHT BE GOING OUT WITH HIM NOW." THAT'S WHAT I KEEP THINKING TO MYSELF. IF I WERE JUST A LITTLE LOOSER, WOULD IT CHANGE MY SITUATION?!
BOOM

Y-KO RESPONSE "WHAT IF, WHAT IF YOU'RE BEING USED?"

WHAT IF, WHAT IF THE VERY FACT THAT HE'S MARRIED MEANS HE'S HANDSOME AND CHARMING?! WHAT IF, WHAT IF YOU DON'T LIKE "MARRIED MEN," YOU LIKE "GOOD MEN"?! SURELY EVEN YOU REALIZE THAT A MAN WHO LIVES CONSTANTLY WITH A WOMAN (HIS WIFE) IS GONNA BE BETTER AT HANDLING WOMEN THAN A RANDOM SINGLE GUY?! APOLOGIZE TO ALL THE SINGLE MEN IN HIROSHIMA!! WHAT IF, WHAT IF YOU'RE BEING USED BY A MARRIED MAN AND NEED TO OPEN YOUR EYES?!

C-KO RESPONSE "WHAT IF, WHAT IF IT WON'T WORK OUT EVEN IF YOU GET MARRIED?"

MONEY! IT'S REALLY ROUGH IF YOU DON'T HAVE ANY!! WHAT IF, WHAT IF I THINK YOU UNDERSTAND THAT BETTER THAN ANYONE, C-KO-SAN?! WHAT IF, WHAT IF 50,000 A MONTH IS HUUUGE?! WHAT IF, WHAT IF YOU COULD WORK YOUR BUTT OFF TO SUPPORT HIM, SURE, IF YOU'RE PREPARED TO DO THAT, BUT LIFE IS LONG? WHAT IF, WHAT IF ONCE YOU HIT 40, YOU WON'T BE ABLE TO WORK LIKE YOU CAN IN YOUR 30S? YOU'LL WRECK YOUR BODY. MARRIAGE IS ALL ABOUT HOW YOU SUPPORT EACH OTHER WHEN YOU'RE DOWN. WHAT IF, WHAT IF THE REST IS UP TO A**RE?!

S-KO RESPONSE "YEAH, FALL FOR HIM!"

SURE, WHY THE HELL NOT?! WHAT IF, WHAT IF THAT'S GREAT?! WHAT IF, WHAT IF THIS IS THE FIRST STEP TO CHANGING YOUR SITUATION?! WHAT IF, WHAT IF I THINK IT'S JUST FINE?! THERE ISN'T A BOY OUT THERE WHO DOESN'T LIKE A PRETTY OLDER LADY SHOWING HIM SOME AFFECTION, AND THE BEST VITAMIN(?) COLLAGEN(?) HORSE OIL(?) FOR YOU AT THE MOMENT IS REMEMBERING HOW FUN IT IS TO BE IN LOVE!! GO DATE THIS YOUNG GUY, MAKE YOURSELF EVEN PRETTIER, AND ENJOY YOUR THIRTIES!! WHAT IF, WHAT IF YOU CUT DOWN ON YOUR GIRLS' NIGHTS OUT, GO TO THE BEACH OR SOMETHING WITH YOUR KENTO YAMAZAKI, AND SEND US SOME PICTURES?! WHAT IF, WHAT IF WE'LL BE WAITING?!

E-KO RESPONSE "TO THE HURT E-KO"

WHAT IF, WHAT IF AFTER A LONG, LONG STRETCH AS A MISTRESS, YOU ARE SIMPLY EXHAUSTED? WHAT IF, WHAT IF UNLIKE THE OTHER FOUR, YOU ARE A DELICATE WOMAN? SO EVEN WHEN YOU KISS A NEW MAN, YOU GET A LITTLE FREAKED OUT INSTEAD OF EXCITED. WHAT IF, WHAT IF THAT'S PERFECTLY NORMAL? WHAT IF, WHAT IF YOU SHOULD TAKE A YEAR TO A YEAR AND A HALF OFF TO HEAL YOUR WOUNDS, THEN TRY TO MOVE FORWARD AGAIN SLOWLY? BUT THOSE FOUR FRIENDS OF YOURS ARE WILD, HUH? HOW DID YOU MAKE FRIENDS WITH THEM IN THE FIRST PLACE? ARE YOU OKAY? WHAT IF, WHAT IF YOU'VE GOTTA EAT AND DRINK PLENTY TO MAKE SURE YOU GET YOUR MONEY'S WORTH WHEN YOU SPLIT THE CHECKS EVENLY AT YOUR GIRLS' NIGHTS OUT? HANG IN THERE, E-KO!

R-KO RESPONSE "YOU'RE THE MOST NORMAL"

SETTING ASIDE ALL THE "WHAT IF, WHAT IF YOU EXPLAIN HOOKING UP WITH MEN (EXCEPT FATTIES)?! WHY DON'T YOU GET INVOLVED WITH OUR FATTY FRIENDS?!" STUFF... THE FACT THAT YOU'RE QUICK ON THE POUNCE BUT NOT IN THE SHEETS IS KIND OF CUTE, NO? WHAT IF, WHAT IF THERE'S NO REASON TO SLEEP AROUND MORE? JUST TRY TO BECOME A WOMAN GOOD MEN WILL FIND "INTERESTING" TO TALK TO WHEN YOU MEET THEM. TO MAKE IT SIMPLER TO UNDERSTAND, BECOME FRIENDS WITH THEM. WHAT IF, WHAT IF THAT'S THE SHORTCUT TO SUCCESS OVER ONE-NIGHT STANDS? YOUR DRINKING HABIT MAY BE A BIT OF A PROBLEM, BUT YOU JUST NEED TO MAKE MORE GUY FRIENDS WHO THINK IT'S FUNNY. WHAT IF, WHAT IF IT'S OKAY? WHAT IF, WHAT IF YOU SHOULD START WITH JUST REDUCING YOUR GIRLS' NIGHT OUT ATTENDANCE?!?!

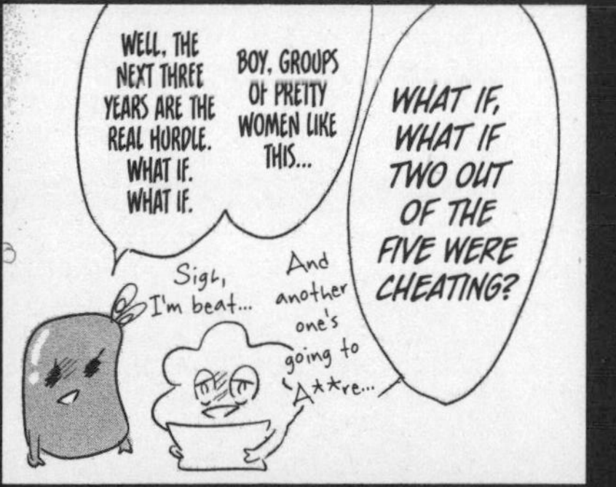
WHAT IF, WHAT IF TWO OUT OF THE FIVE WERE CHEATING?
BOY, GROUPS OF PRETTY WOMEN LIKE THIS...
WELL, THE NEXT THREE YEARS ARE THE REAL HURDLE. WHAT IF. WHAT IF.
And another one's going to 'A**re...
Sigh, I'm beat...

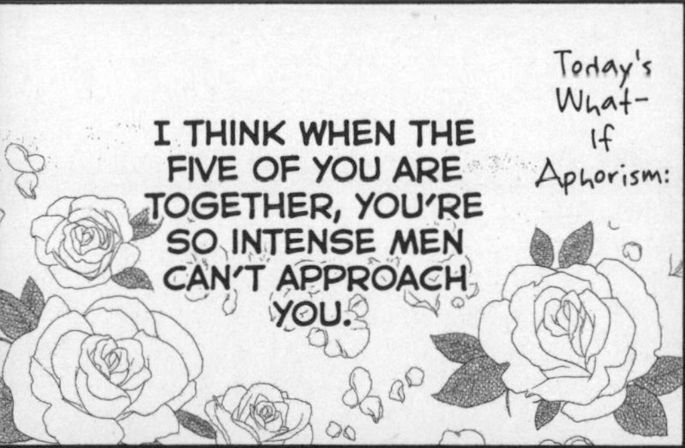
Today's What-If Aphorism:
I THINK WHEN THE FIVE OF YOU ARE TOGETHER, YOU'RE SO INTENSE MEN CAN'T APPROACH YOU.

★ NIGHT 16 ★

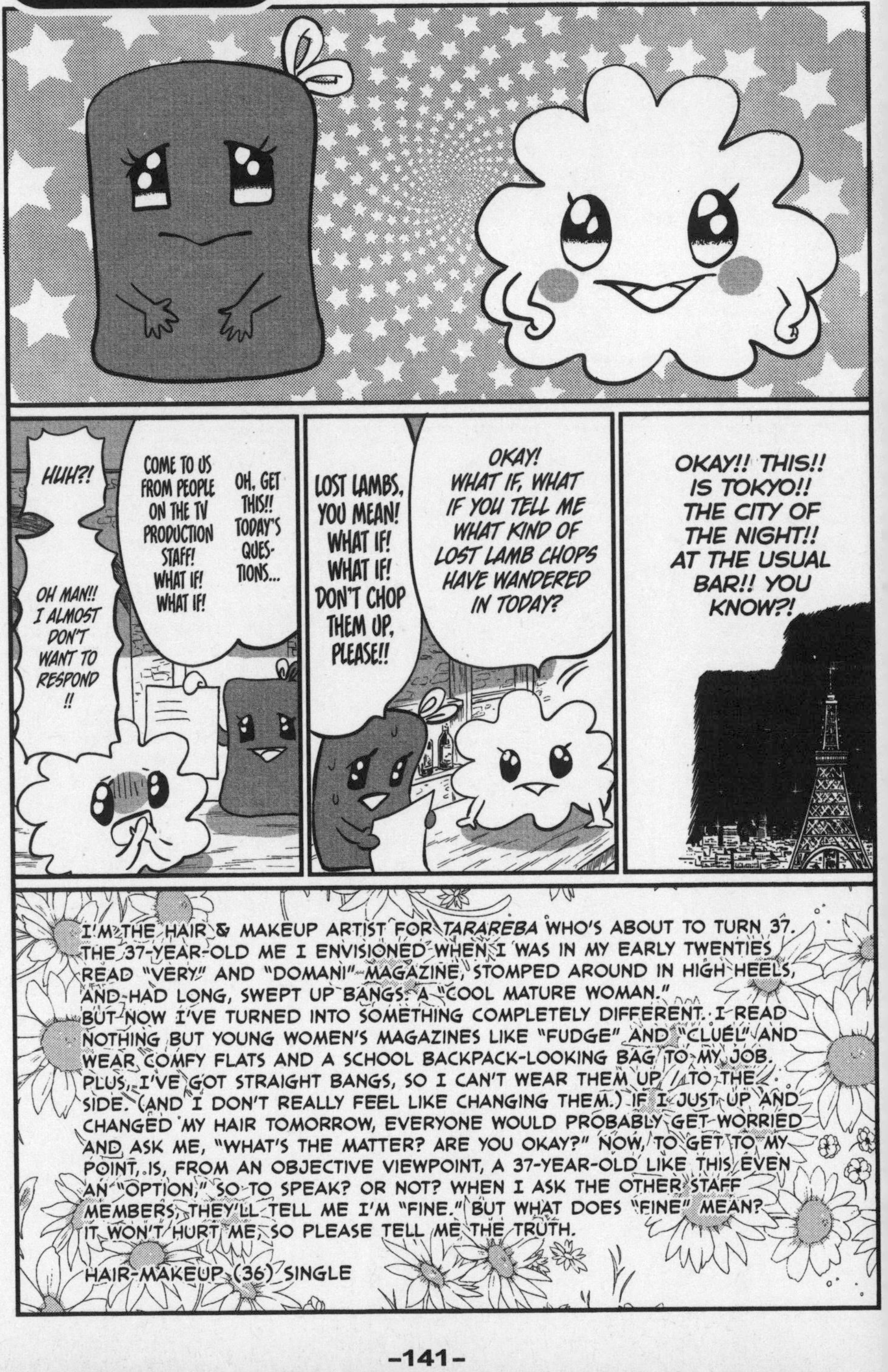
OKAY!! THIS!! IS TOKYO!! THE CITY OF THE NIGHT!! AT THE USUAL BAR!! YOU KNOW?!
OKAY! WHAT IF, WHAT IF YOU TELL ME WHAT KIND OF LOST LAMB CHOPS HAVE WANDERED IN TODAY?
LOST LAMBS, YOU MEAN! WHAT IF! WHAT IF! DON'T CHOP THEM UP, PLEASE!!
OH, GET THIS!! TODAY'S QUESTIONS...
COME TO US FROM PEOPLE ON THE TV PRODUCTION STAFF! WHAT IF! WHAT IF!
HUH?!
OH MAN!! I ALMOST DON'T WANT TO RESPOND !!

I'M THE HAIR & MAKEUP ARTIST FOR *TARAREBA* WHO'S ABOUT TO TURN 37. THE 37-YEAR-OLD ME I ENVISIONED WHEN I WAS IN MY EARLY TWENTIES READ "VERY" AND "DOMANI" MAGAZINE, STOMPED AROUND IN HIGH HEELS, AND HAD LONG, SWEPT UP BANGS. A "COOL MATURE WOMAN." BUT NOW I'VE TURNED INTO SOMETHING COMPLETELY DIFFERENT. I READ NOTHING BUT YOUNG WOMEN'S MAGAZINES LIKE "FUDGE" AND "CLUEL" AND WEAR COMFY FLATS AND A SCHOOL BACKPACK-LOOKING BAG TO MY JOB. PLUS, I'VE GOT STRAIGHT BANGS, SO I CAN'T WEAR THEM UP / TO THE SIDE. (AND I DON'T REALLY FEEL LIKE CHANGING THEM.) IF I JUST UP AND CHANGED MY HAIR TOMORROW, EVERYONE WOULD PROBABLY GET WORRIED AND ASK ME, "WHAT'S THE MATTER? ARE YOU OKAY?" NOW, TO GET TO MY POINT, IS, FROM AN OBJECTIVE VIEWPOINT, A 37-YEAR-OLD LIKE THIS EVEN AN "OPTION," SO TO SPEAK? OR NOT? WHEN I ASK THE OTHER STAFF MEMBERS, THEY'LL TELL ME I'M "FINE." BUT WHAT DOES "FINE" MEAN? IT WON'T HURT ME, SO PLEASE TELL ME THE TRUTH.

HAIR-MAKEUP (36) SINGLE

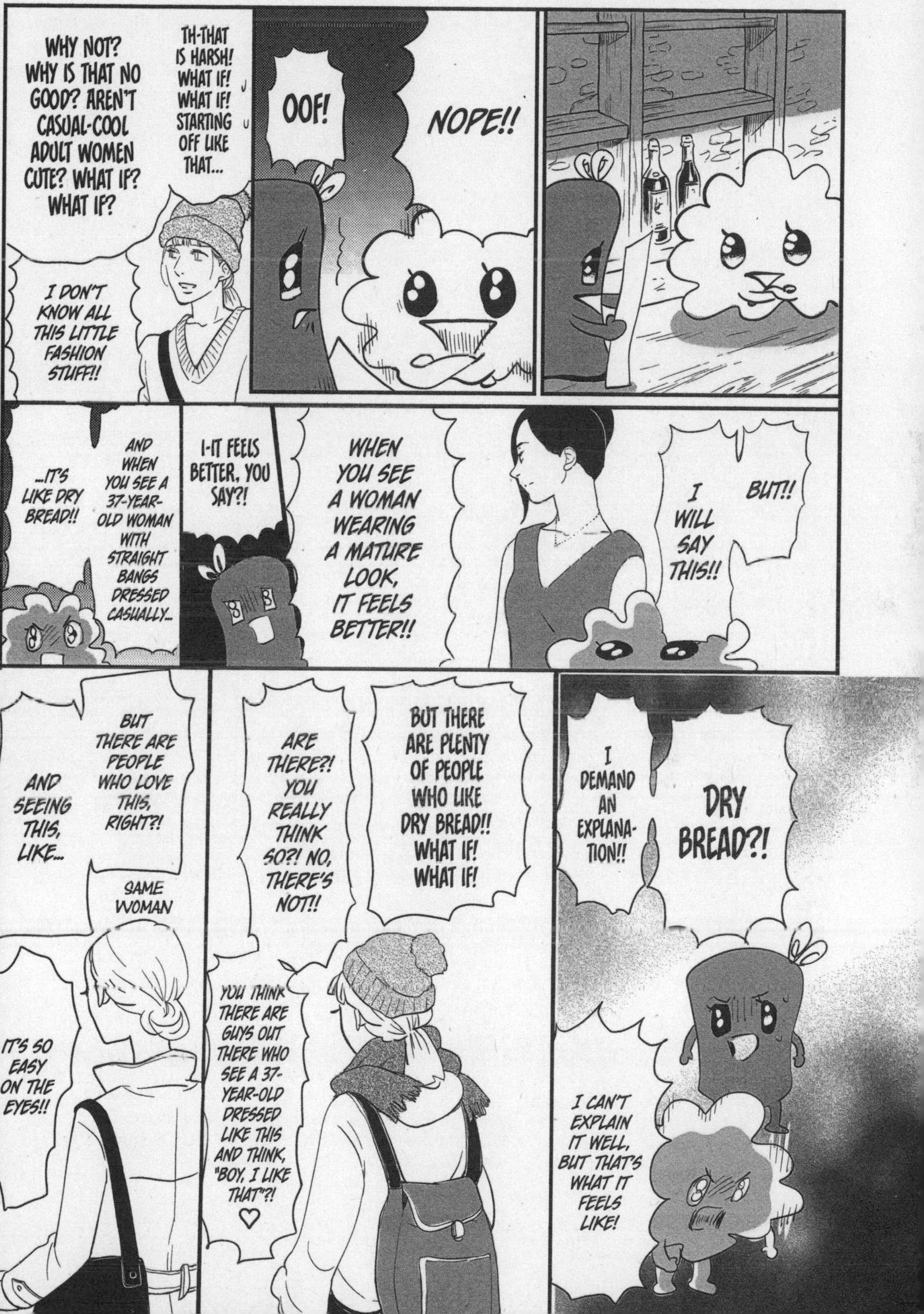
NOPE!!
OOF!
TH-THAT IS HARSH! WHAT IF! WHAT IF! STARTING OFF LIKE THAT...
WHY NOT? WHY IS THAT NO GOOD? AREN'T CASUAL-COOL ADULT WOMEN CUTE? WHAT IF? WHAT IF?
I DON'T KNOW ALL THIS LITTLE FASHION STUFF!!
BUT!!
I WILL SAY THIS!!
WHEN YOU SEE A WOMAN WEARING A MATURE LOOK, IT FEELS BETTER!!
I-IT FEELS BETTER, YOU SAY?!
AND WHEN YOU SEE A 37-YEAR-OLD WOMAN WITH STRAIGHT BANGS DRESSED CASUALLY...
...IT'S LIKE DRY BREAD!!
DRY BREAD?!
I DEMAND AN EXPLANATION!!
I CAN'T EXPLAIN IT WELL, BUT THAT'S WHAT IT FEELS LIKE!
BUT THERE ARE PLENTY OF PEOPLE WHO LIKE DRY BREAD!! WHAT IF! WHAT IF!
ARE THERE?! YOU REALLY THINK SO?! NO, THERE'S NOT!!
YOU THINK THERE ARE GUYS OUT THERE WHO SEE A 37-YEAR-OLD DRESSED LIKE THIS AND THINK, "BOY, I LIKE THAT"?! ♡
BUT THERE ARE PEOPLE WHO LOVE THIS, RIGHT?!
AND SEEING THIS, LIKE...
SAME WOMAN
IT'S SO EASY ON THE EYES!!

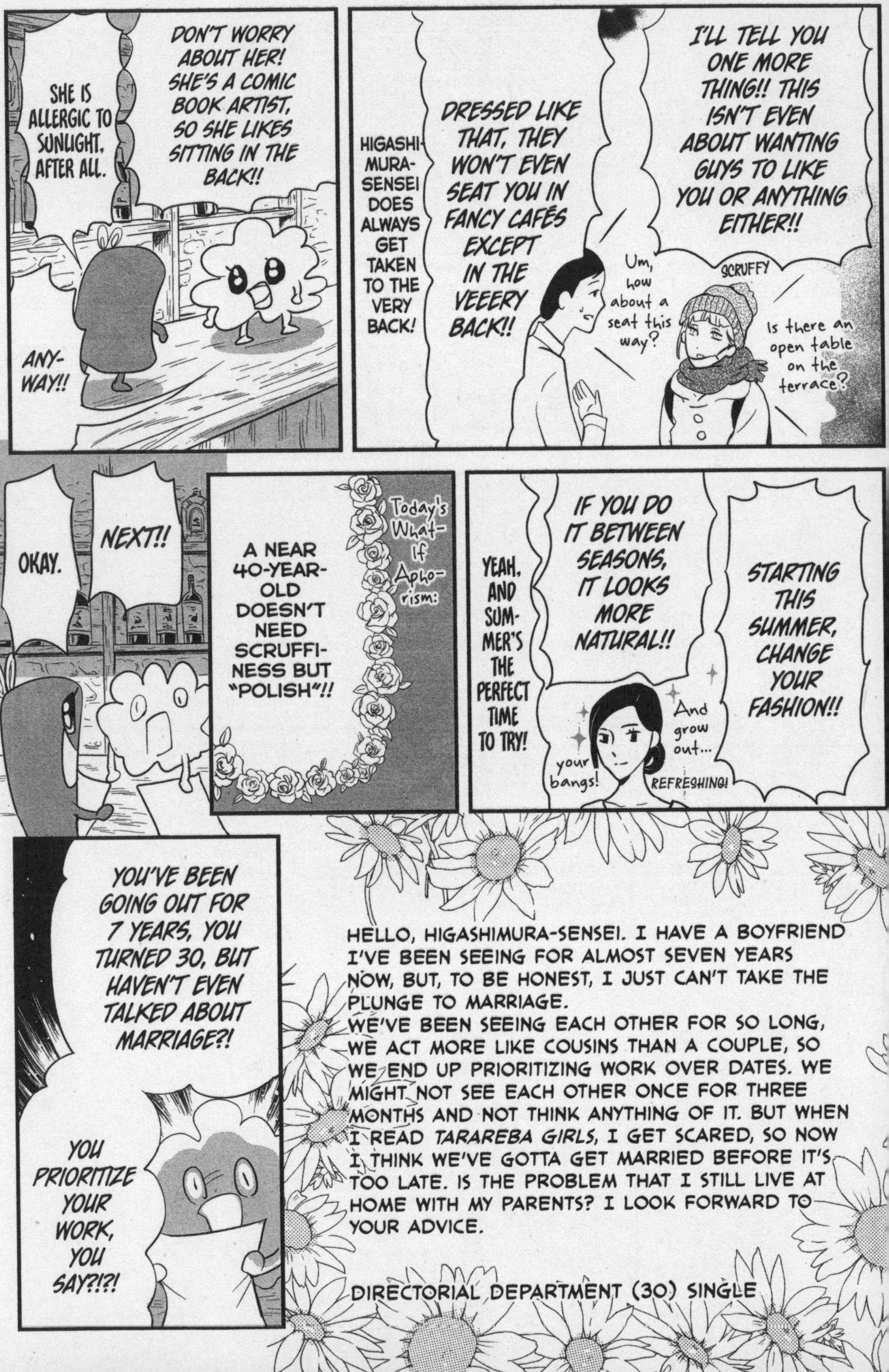
I'LL TELL YOU ONE MORE THING!! THIS ISN'T EVEN ABOUT WANTING GUYS TO LIKE YOU OR ANYTHING EITHER!!
DRESSED LIKE THAT, THEY WON'T EVEN SEAT YOU IN FANCY CAFÉS EXCEPT IN THE VEEERY BACK!!
HIGASHIMURA-SENSEI DOES ALWAYS GET TAKEN TO THE VERY BACK!
SCRUFFY
Is there an open table on the terrace?
Um, how about a seat this way?
DON'T WORRY ABOUT HER! SHE'S A COMIC BOOK ARTIST, SO SHE LIKES SITTING IN THE BACK!!
SHE IS ALLERGIC TO SUNLIGHT, AFTER ALL.
ANYWAY!!
STARTING THIS SUMMER, CHANGE YOUR FASHION!!
IF YOU DO IT BETWEEN SEASONS, IT LOOKS MORE NATURAL!!
YEAH, AND SUMMER'S THE PERFECT TIME TO TRY!
And grow out...
your bangs!
REFRESHING!
Today's What-If Aphorism:
A NEAR 40-YEAR-OLD DOESN'T NEED SCRUFFINESS BUT "POLISH"!!
NEXT!!
OKAY.
HELLO, HIGASHIMURA-SENSEI. I HAVE A BOYFRIEND I'VE BEEN SEEING FOR ALMOST SEVEN YEARS NOW, BUT, TO BE HONEST, I JUST CAN'T TAKE THE PLUNGE TO MARRIAGE.
WE'VE BEEN SEEING EACH OTHER FOR SO LONG, WE ACT MORE LIKE COUSINS THAN A COUPLE, SO WE END UP PRIORITIZING WORK OVER DATES. WE MIGHT NOT SEE EACH OTHER ONCE FOR THREE MONTHS AND NOT THINK ANYTHING OF IT. BUT WHEN I READ TARAREBA GIRLS, I GET SCARED, SO NOW I THINK WE'VE GOTTA GET MARRIED BEFORE IT'S TOO LATE. IS THE PROBLEM THAT I STILL LIVE AT HOME WITH MY PARENTS? I LOOK FORWARD TO YOUR ADVICE.
DIRECTORIAL DEPARTMENT (30) SINGLE
YOU'VE BEEN GOING OUT FOR 7 YEARS, YOU TURNED 30, BUT HAVEN'T EVEN TALKED ABOUT MARRIAGE?!
YOU PRIORITIZE YOUR WORK, YOU SAY?!?!

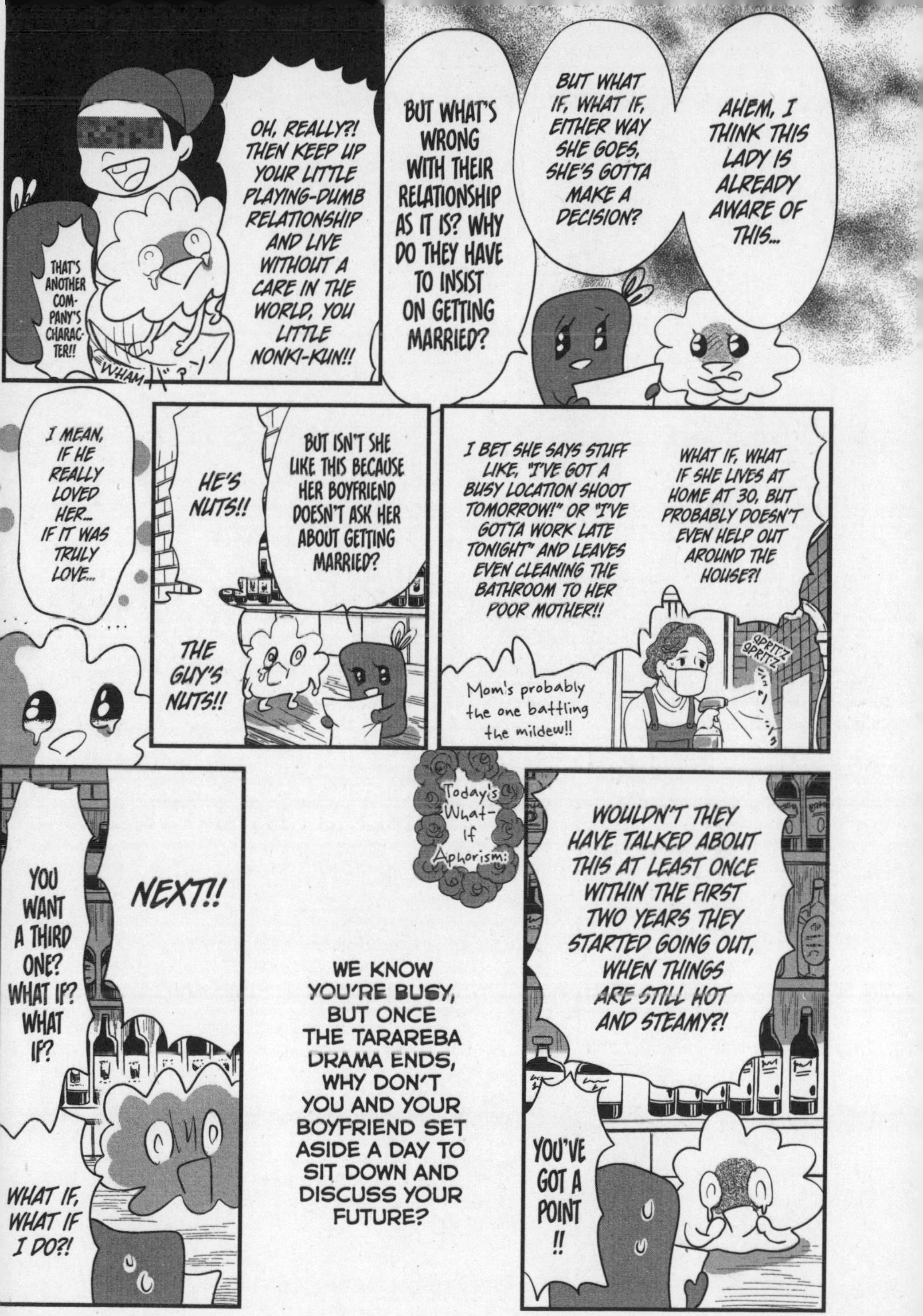
AHEM, I THINK THIS LADY IS ALREADY AWARE OF THIS...
BUT WHAT IF, WHAT IF, EITHER WAY SHE GOES, SHE'S GOTTA MAKE A DECISION?
BUT WHAT'S WRONG WITH THEIR RELATIONSHIP AS IT IS? WHY DO THEY HAVE TO INSIST ON GETTING MARRIED?
OH, REALLY?! THEN KEEP UP YOUR LITTLE PLAYING-DUMB RELATIONSHIP AND LIVE WITHOUT A CARE IN THE WORLD, YOU LITTLE NONKI-KUN!!
THAT'S ANOTHER COMPANY'S CHARACTER!!
WHAM
WHAT IF, WHAT IF SHE LIVES AT HOME AT 30, BUT PROBABLY DOESN'T EVEN HELP OUT AROUND THE HOUSE?!
I BET SHE SAYS STUFF LIKE, "I'VE GOT A BUSY LOCATION SHOOT TOMORROW!" OR "I'VE GOTTA WORK LATE TONIGHT" AND LEAVES EVEN CLEANING THE BATHROOM TO HER POOR MOTHER!!
SPRITZ SPRITZ
Mom's probably the one battling the mildew!!
BUT ISN'T SHE LIKE THIS BECAUSE HER BOYFRIEND DOESN'T ASK HER ABOUT GETTING MARRIED?
HE'S NUTS!!
THE GUY'S NUTS!!
I MEAN, IF HE REALLY LOVED HER... IF IT WAS TRULY LOVE...
WOULDN'T THEY HAVE TALKED ABOUT THIS AT LEAST ONCE WITHIN THE FIRST TWO YEARS THEY STARTED GOING OUT, WHEN THINGS ARE STILL HOT AND STEAMY?!
YOU'VE GOT A POINT!!
Today's What-If Aphorism:
WE KNOW YOU'RE BUSY, BUT ONCE THE TARAREBA DRAMA ENDS, WHY DON'T YOU AND YOUR BOYFRIEND SET ASIDE A DAY TO SIT DOWN AND DISCUSS YOUR FUTURE?
NEXT!!
YOU WANT A THIRD ONE? WHAT IF? WHAT IF?
WHAT IF, WHAT IF I DO?!

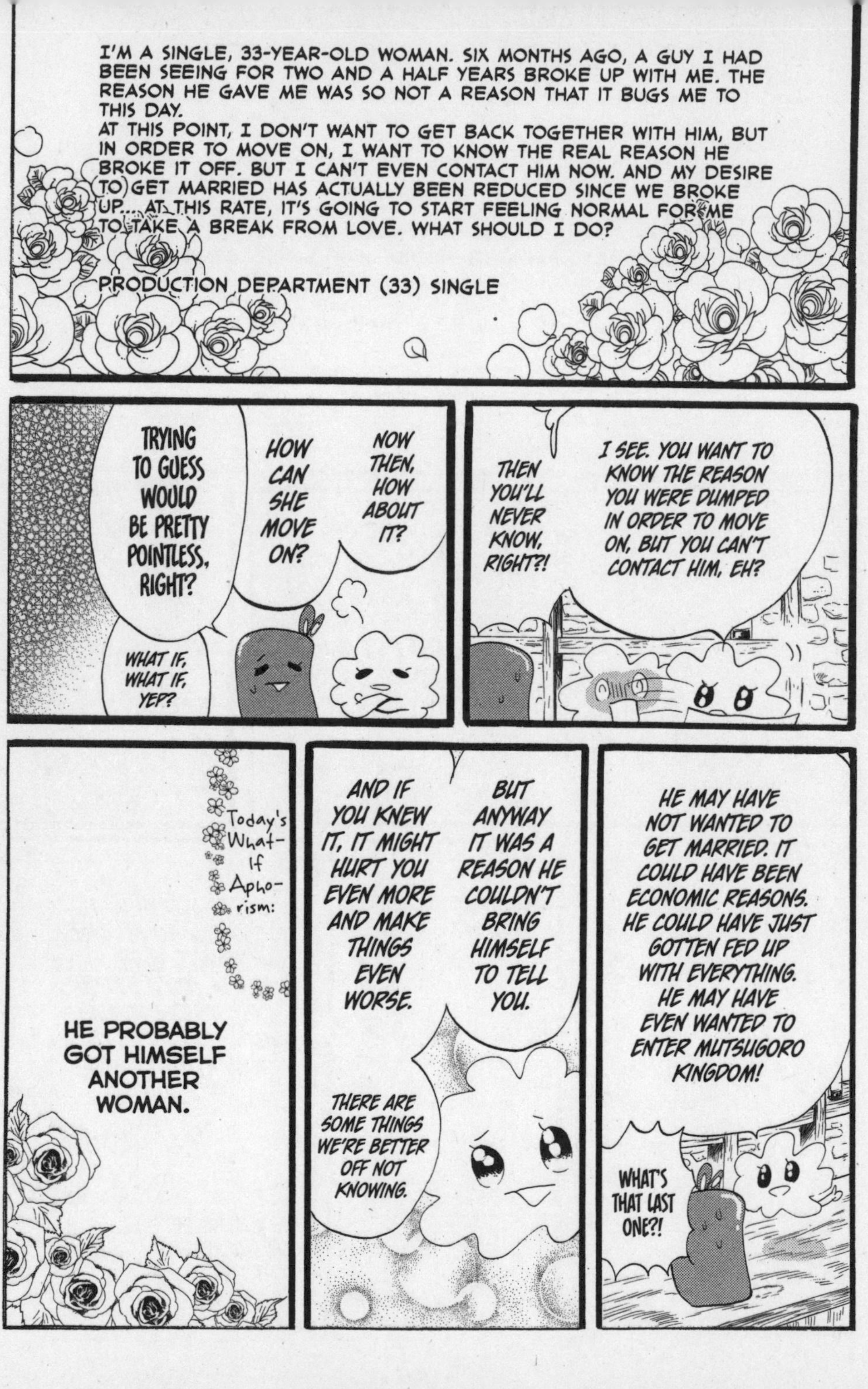
I'M A SINGLE, 33-YEAR-OLD WOMAN. SIX MONTHS AGO, A GUY I HAD BEEN SEEING FOR TWO AND A HALF YEARS BROKE UP WITH ME. THE REASON HE GAVE ME WAS SO NOT A REASON THAT IT BUGS ME TO THIS DAY.
AT THIS POINT, I DON'T WANT TO GET BACK TOGETHER WITH HIM, BUT IN ORDER TO MOVE ON, I WANT TO KNOW THE REAL REASON HE BROKE IT OFF. BUT I CAN'T EVEN CONTACT HIM NOW. AND MY DESIRE TO GET MARRIED HAS ACTUALLY BEEN REDUCED SINCE WE BROKE UP... AT THIS RATE, IT'S GOING TO START FEELING NORMAL FOR ME TO TAKE A BREAK FROM LOVE. WHAT SHOULD I DO?
PRODUCTION DEPARTMENT (33) SINGLE
I SEE. YOU WANT TO KNOW THE REASON YOU WERE DUMPED IN ORDER TO MOVE ON, BUT YOU CAN'T CONTACT HIM, EH?
THEN YOU'LL NEVER KNOW, RIGHT?!
NOW THEN, HOW ABOUT IT?
HOW CAN SHE MOVE ON?
TRYING TO GUESS WOULD BE PRETTY POINTLESS, RIGHT?
WHAT IF, WHAT IF, YEP?
HE MAY HAVE NOT WANTED TO GET MARRIED. IT COULD HAVE BEEN ECONOMIC REASONS. HE COULD HAVE JUST GOTTEN FED UP WITH EVERYTHING. HE MAY HAVE EVEN WANTED TO ENTER MUTSUGORO KINGDOM!
WHAT'S THAT LAST ONE?!
BUT ANYWAY IT WAS A REASON HE COULDN'T BRING HIMSELF TO TELL YOU.
AND IF YOU KNEW IT, IT MIGHT HURT YOU EVEN MORE AND MAKE THINGS EVEN WORSE.
THERE ARE SOME THINGS WE'RE BETTER OFF NOT KNOWING.
Today's What-If Aphorism:
HE PROBABLY GOT HIMSELF ANOTHER WOMAN.

AND FINALLY!!

NOW THAT I'VE MOVED ON FROM THIRTY-SOMETHING INTO FORTY-SOMETHING, LONG AFTER PASSING FORTY, MY TROUBLE IS THERE ARE SO MANY TYPES OF LOVE I CAN'T TELL WHO I'M REALLY INTO FOR SURE. THE ONE WHO'S JUST MY TYPE THAT I'M INTERESTED IN? OR MY BEST GUY FRIEND?
THERE'S A GUY I'M INTO, BUT I NEVER REALLY TRIED TO CONTACT HIM. I'M INTERESTED IN HIM, SO I'D LIKE TO TALK, BUT I DON'T KNOW HOW TO, AND WHILE I SPUN MY WHEELS DOING NOTHING, NEARLY A WHOLE YEAR PASSED.😅 A YEAR LATER, HE'S STILL TOTALLY MY TYPE.
AND MY BEST GUY FRIEND HAS A GIRLFRIEND, WHO'S SOMEONE YOU CAN TALK TO ABOUT ANYTHING AND A RELATIONSHIP BUILT ON TRUST. BUT ON OCCASION, I'VE DETESTED THIS GIRLFRIEND SO MUCH I'VE WANTED TO KILL HER. BUT MY JOB ALWAYS WINS OUT IN THE END, AND I PUT LOVE ON THE BACK BURNER.
I DON'T REALLY CARE ABOUT GETTING MARRIED, BUT HOW CAN I ESCAPE FROM WHATEVER IT IS I'VE GOTTEN MYSELF INTO?

STYLIST (40's) SINGLE

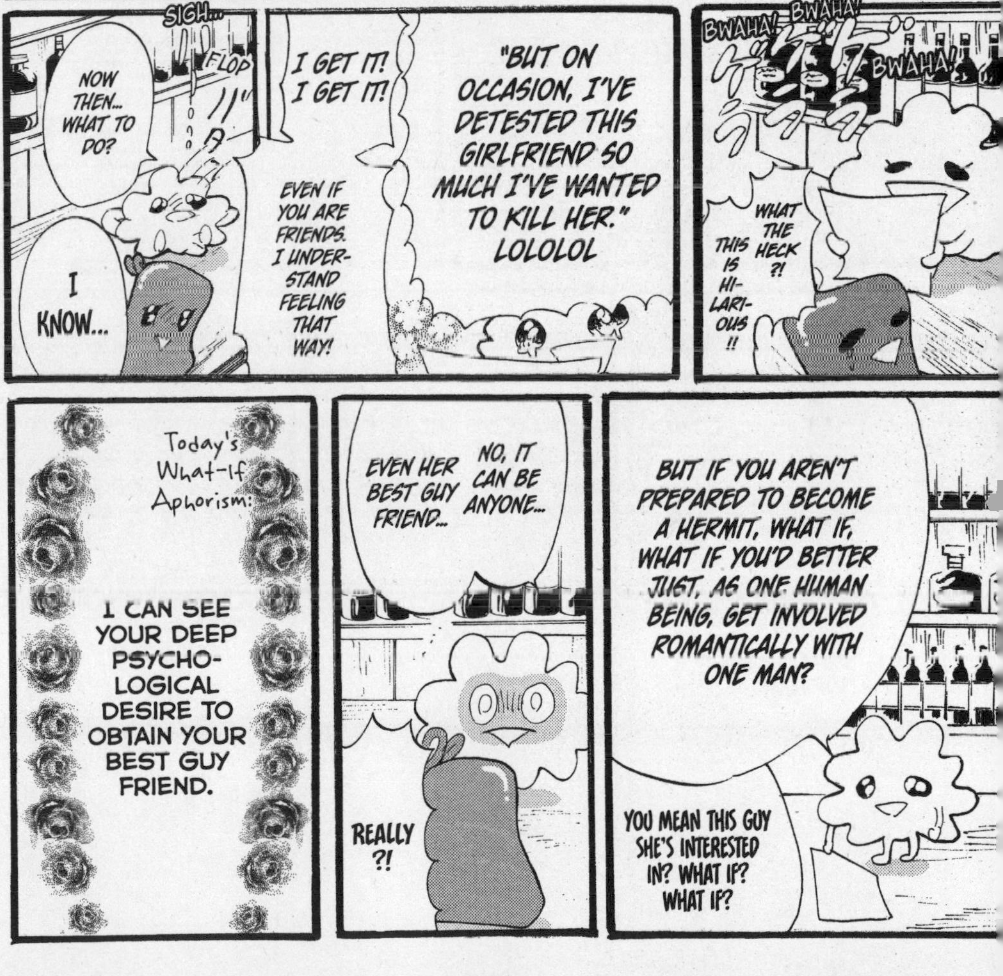
BWAHA! BWAHA! BWAHA!
WHAT THE HECK?!
THIS IS HILARIOUS!!
"BUT ON OCCASION, I'VE DETESTED THIS GIRLFRIEND SO MUCH I'VE WANTED TO KILL HER." LOLOLOL
I GET IT! I GET IT!
EVEN IF YOU ARE FRIENDS. I UNDERSTAND FEELING THAT WAY!
SIGH...
FLOP
NOW THEN... WHAT TO DO?
I KNOW...
BUT IF YOU AREN'T PREPARED TO BECOME A HERMIT, WHAT IF, WHAT IF YOU'D BETTER JUST, AS ONE HUMAN BEING, GET INVOLVED ROMANTICALLY WITH ONE MAN?
YOU MEAN THIS GUY SHE'S INTERESTED IN? WHAT IF? WHAT IF?
NO, IT CAN BE ANYONE...
EVEN HER BEST GUY FRIEND...
REALLY?!
Today's What-If Aphorism:
I CAN SEE YOUR DEEP PSYCHOLOGICAL DESIRE TO OBTAIN YOUR BEST GUY FRIEND.

TOKYO

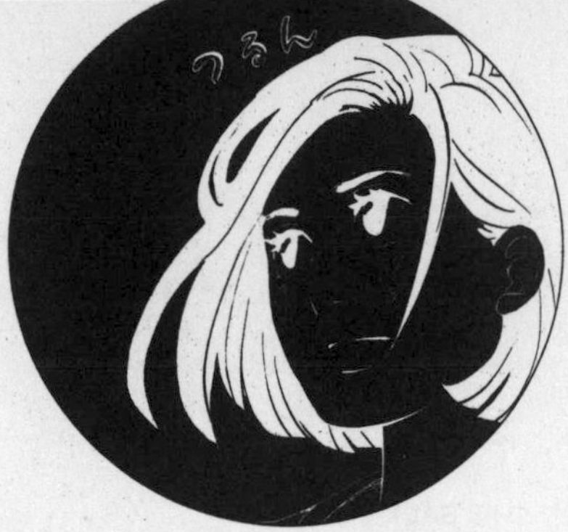
つるん

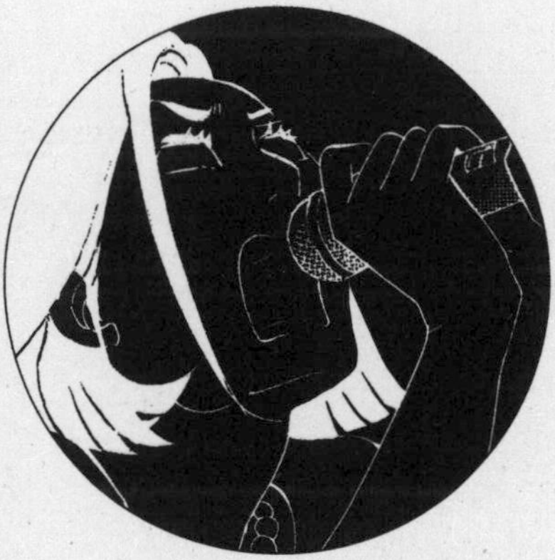

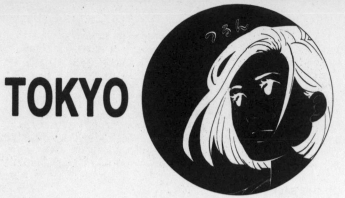

TARAREBA

GIRLS

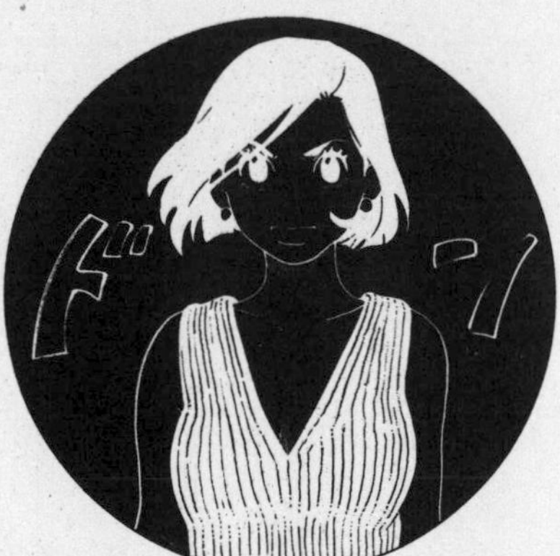

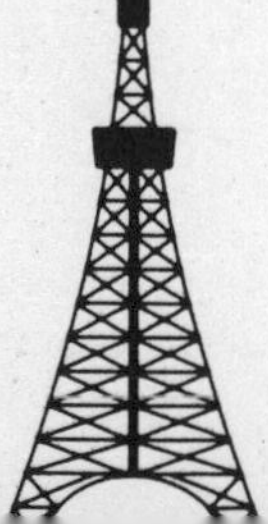

TOKYO

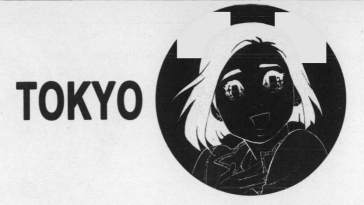

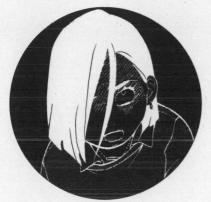

TARAREBA

GIRLS

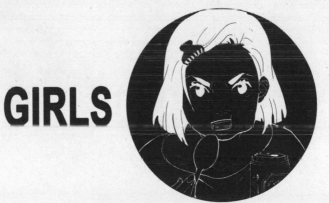

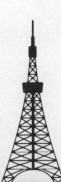

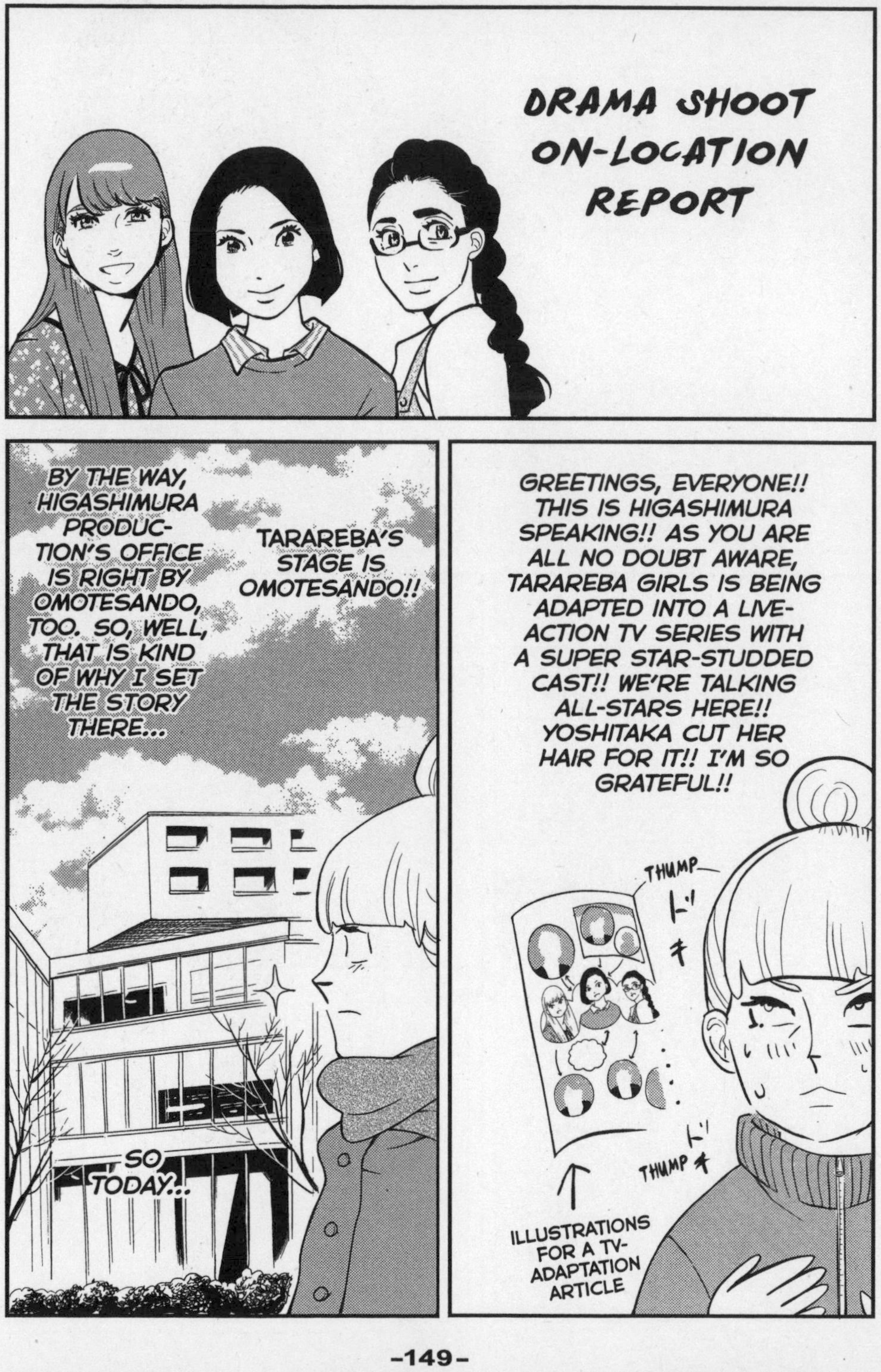
DRAMA SHOOT ON-LOCATION REPORT
GREETINGS, EVERYONE!! THIS IS HIGASHIMURA SPEAKING!! AS YOU ARE ALL NO DOUBT AWARE, TARAREBA GIRLS IS BEING ADAPTED INTO A LIVE-ACTION TV SERIES WITH A SUPER STAR-STUDDED CAST!! WE'RE TALKING ALL-STARS HERE!! YOSHITAKA CUT HER HAIR FOR IT!! I'M SO GRATEFUL!!
THUMP
THUMP
ILLUSTRATIONS FOR A TV-ADAPTATION ARTICLE
TARAREBA'S STAGE IS OMOTESANDO!!
BY THE WAY, HIGASHIMURA PRODUCTION'S OFFICE IS RIGHT BY OMOTESANDO, TOO. SO, WELL, THAT IS KIND OF WHY I SET THE STORY THERE...
SO TODAY...

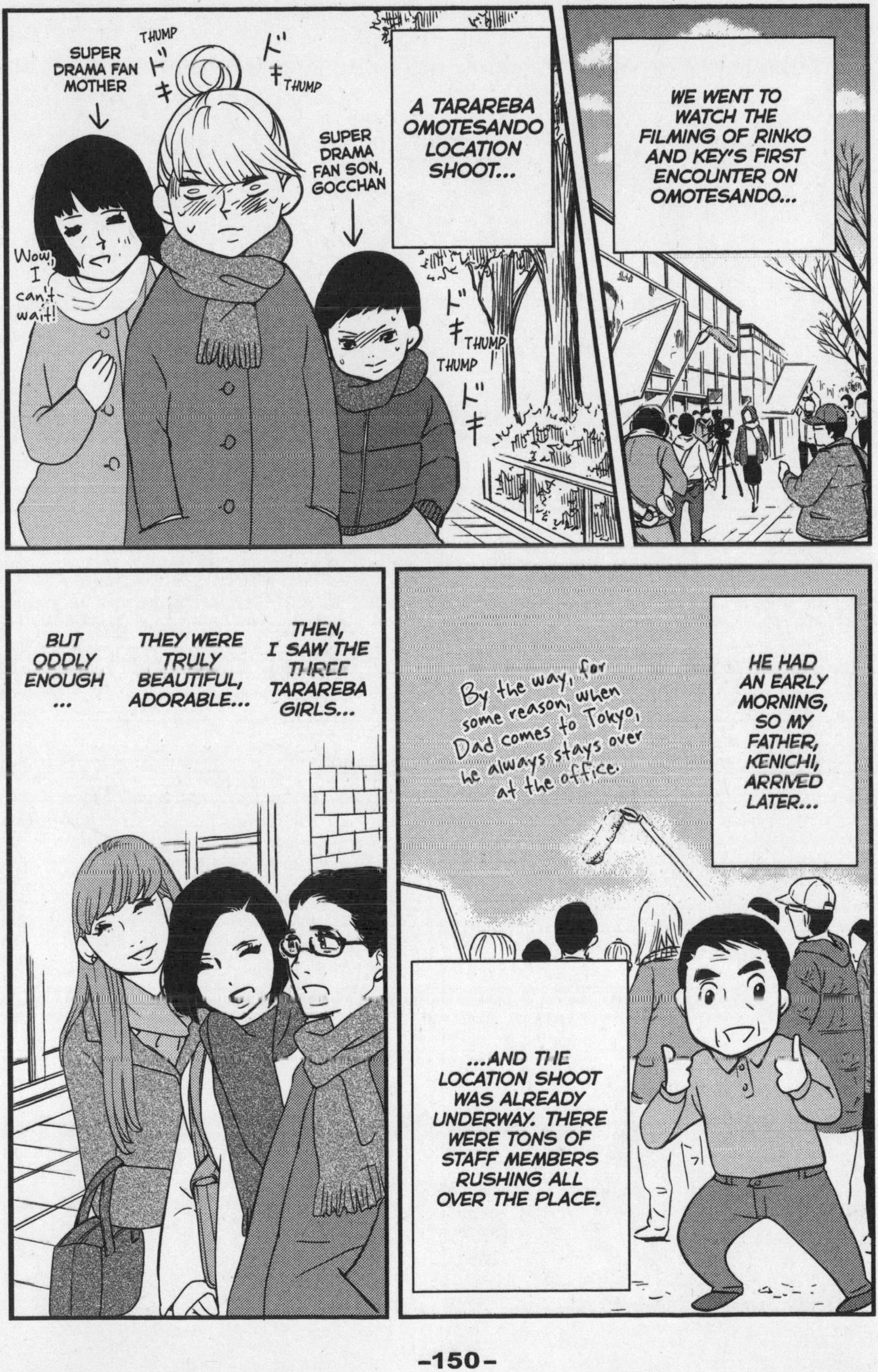
WE WENT TO WATCH THE FILMING OF RINKO AND KEY'S FIRST ENCOUNTER ON OMOTESANDO...
A TARAREBA OMOTESANDO LOCATION SHOOT...
ドキ THUMP
ドキ THUMP
SUPER DRAMA FAN SON, GOCCHAN
ドキ THUMP
ドキ THUMP
SUPER DRAMA FAN MOTHER
Wow, I can't wait!
HE HAD AN EARLY MORNING, SO MY FATHER, KENICHI, ARRIVED LATER...
By the way, for some reason, when Dad comes to Tokyo, he always stays over at the office.
...AND THE LOCATION SHOOT WAS ALREADY UNDERWAY. THERE WERE TONS OF STAFF MEMBERS RUSHING ALL OVER THE PLACE.
THEN, I SAW THE THREE TARAREBA GIRLS...
THEY WERE TRULY BEAUTIFUL, ADORABLE...
BUT ODDLY ENOUGH ...

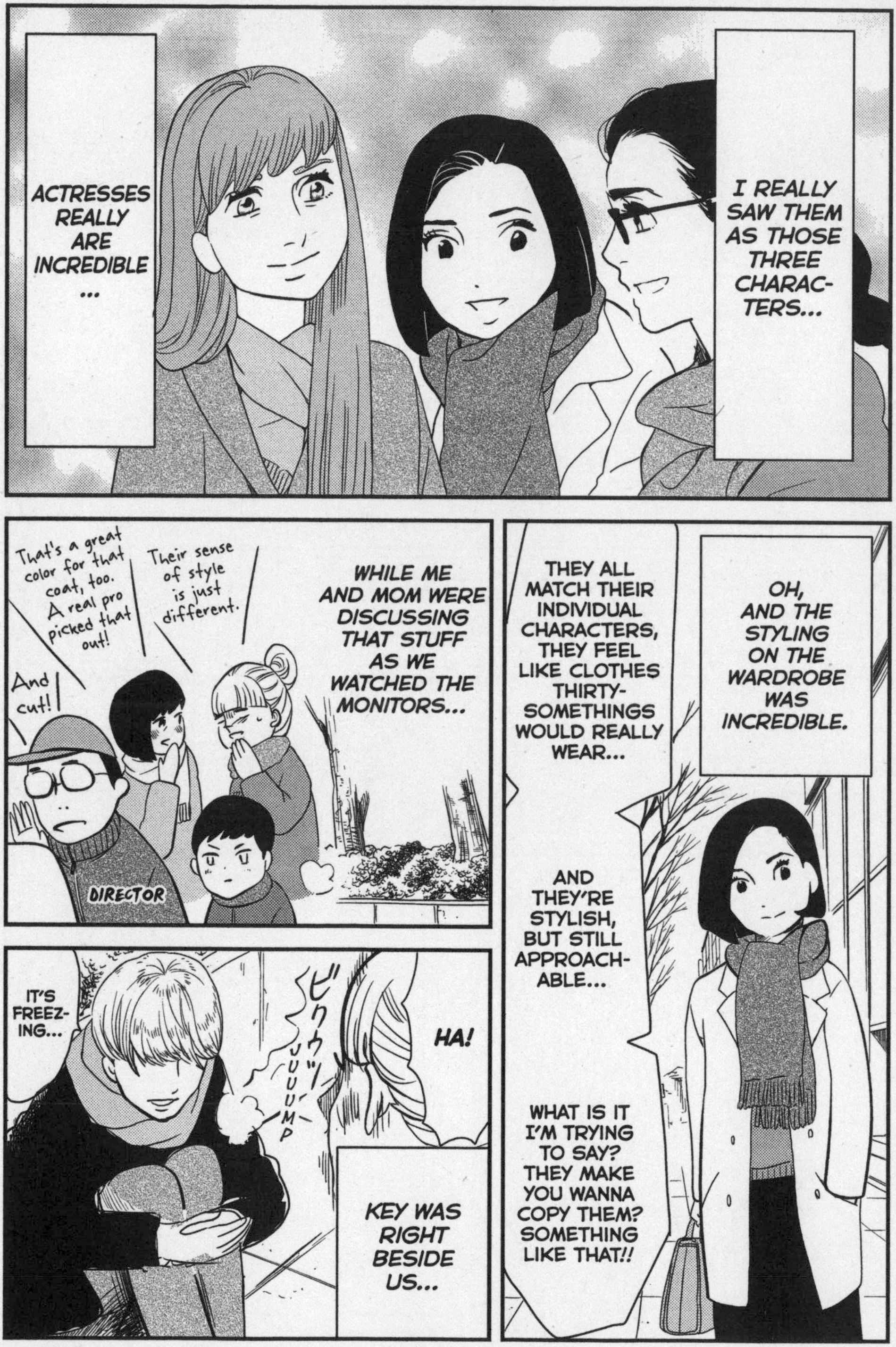
I REALLY SAW THEM AS THOSE THREE CHARAC-TERS...
ACTRESSES REALLY ARE INCREDIBLE...
OH, AND THE STYLING ON THE WARDROBE WAS INCREDIBLE.
THEY ALL MATCH THEIR INDIVIDUAL CHARACTERS, THEY FEEL LIKE CLOTHES THIRTY-SOMETHINGS WOULD REALLY WEAR...
AND THEY'RE STYLISH, BUT STILL APPROACH-ABLE...
WHAT IS IT I'M TRYING TO SAY? THEY MAKE YOU WANNA COPY THEM? SOMETHING LIKE THAT!!
WHILE ME AND MOM WERE DISCUSSING THAT STUFF AS WE WATCHED THE MONITORS...
Their sense of style is just different.
That's a great color for that coat, too. A real pro picked that out!
And cut!
DIRECTOR
HA!
ビクゥッ
JUUUUMP
IT'S FREEZ-ING...
KEY WAS RIGHT BESIDE US...

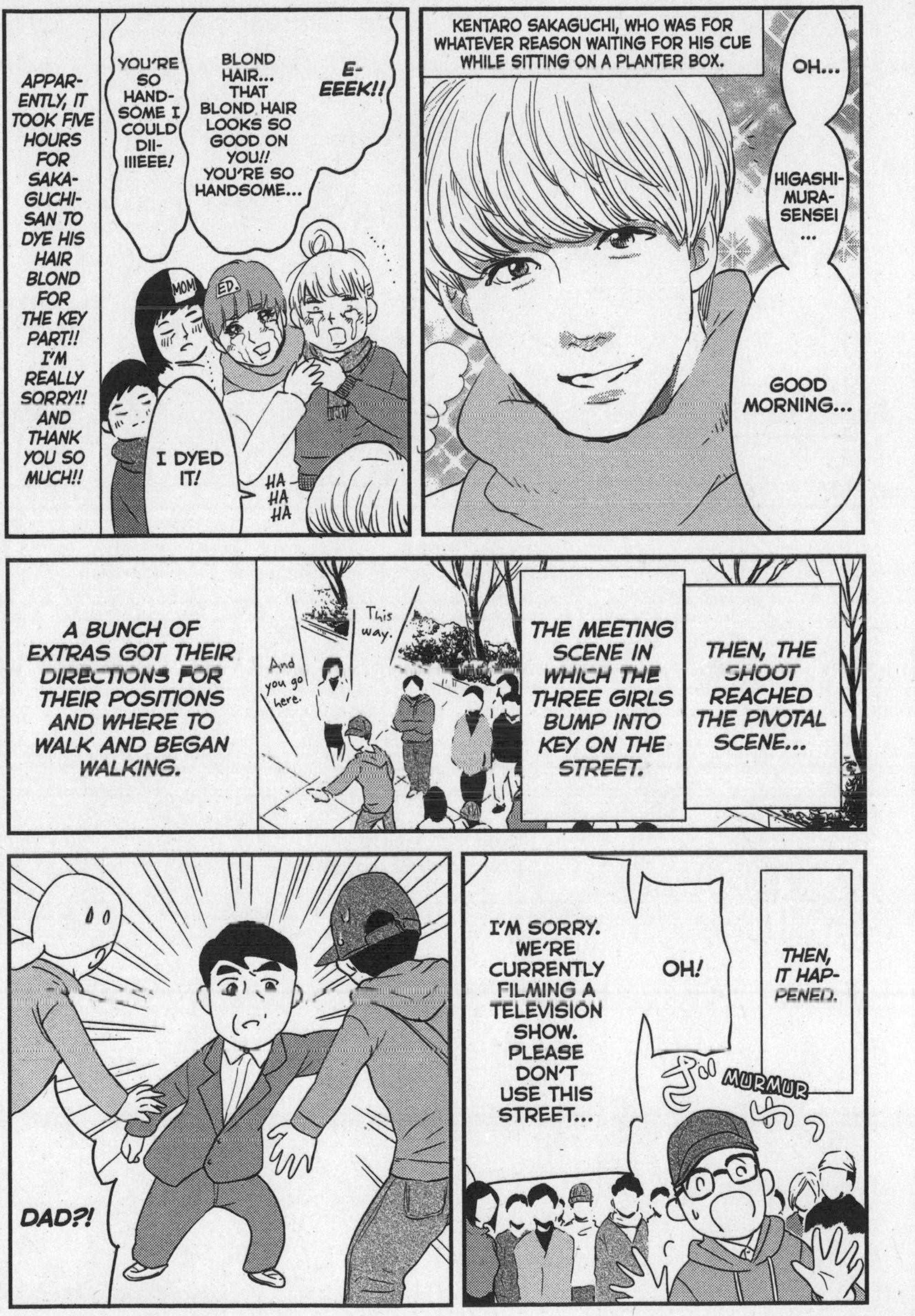

KENTARO SAKAGUCHI, WHO WAS FOR WHATEVER REASON WAITING FOR HIS CUE WHILE SITTING ON A PLANTER BOX.
OH... HIGASHIMURA-SENSEI ...
GOOD MORNING...
E-EEEK!!
BLOND HAIR... THAT BLOND HAIR LOOKS SO GOOD ON YOU!! YOU'RE SO HANDSOME...
YOU'RE SO HANDSOME I COULD DII-IIIEEE!
APPARENTLY, IT TOOK FIVE HOURS FOR SAKAGUCHI-SAN TO DYE HIS HAIR BLOND FOR THE KEY PART!! I'M REALLY SORRY!! AND THANK YOU SO MUCH!!
MOM
ED.
I DYED IT!
HA HA HA
THEN, THE SHOOT REACHED THE PIVOTAL SCENE...
THE MEETING SCENE IN WHICH THE THREE GIRLS BUMP INTO KEY ON THE STREET.
This way.
And you go here.
A BUNCH OF EXTRAS GOT THEIR DIRECTIONS FOR THEIR POSITIONS AND WHERE TO WALK AND BEGAN WALKING.
THEN, IT HAPPENED.
OH!
I'M SORRY. WE'RE CURRENTLY FILMING A TELEVISION SHOW. PLEASE DON'T USE THIS STREET...
MURMUR
DAD?!

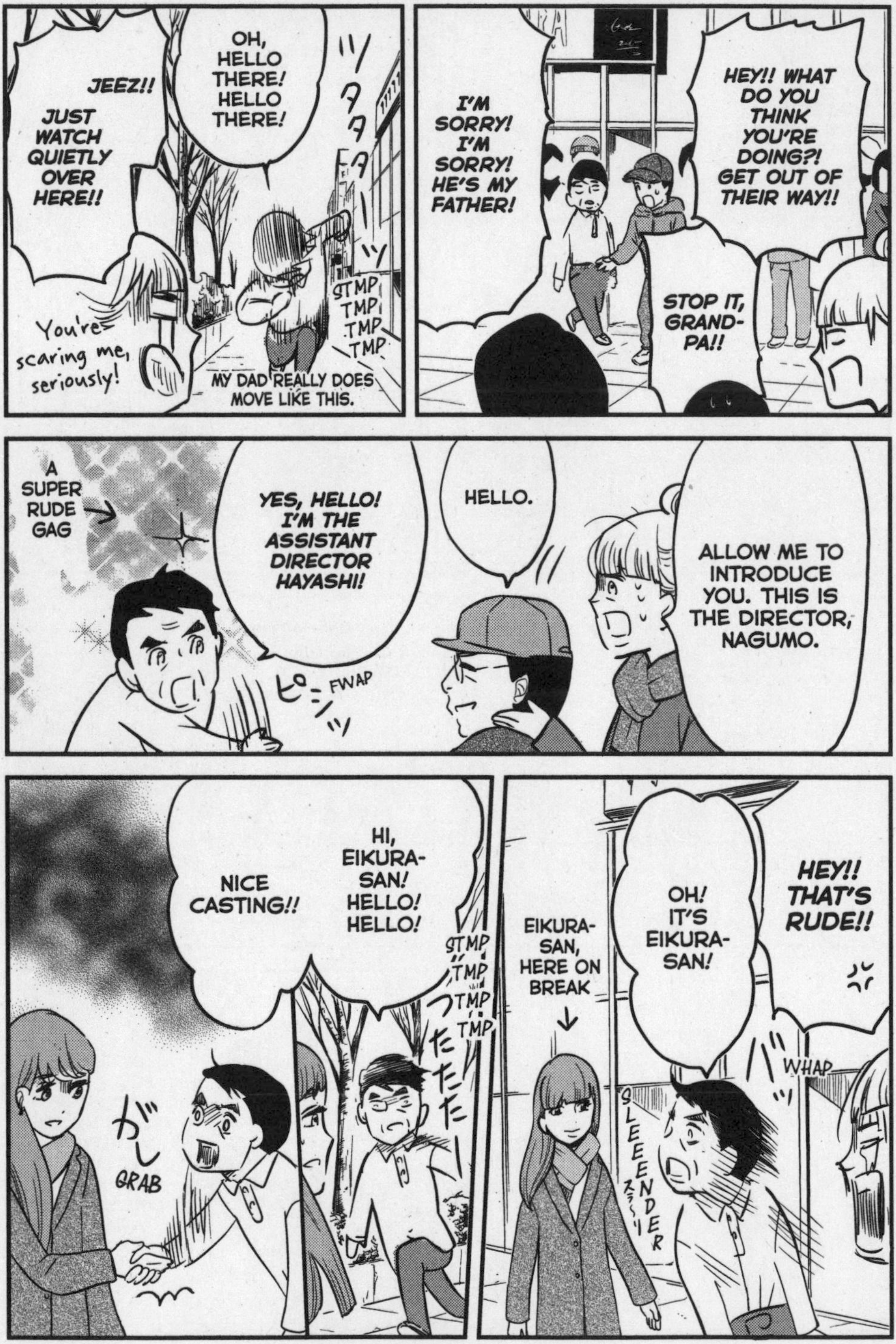
HEY!! WHAT DO YOU THINK YOU'RE DOING?! GET OUT OF THEIR WAY!!
I'M SORRY! I'M SORRY! HE'S MY FATHER!
STOP IT, GRAND-PA!!
OH, HELLO THERE! HELLO THERE!
JEEZ!! JUST WATCH QUIETLY OVER HERE!!
STMP TMP TMP TMP
You're scaring me, seriously!
MY DAD REALLY DOES MOVE LIKE THIS.
ALLOW ME TO INTRODUCE YOU. THIS IS THE DIRECTOR, NAGUMO.
HELLO.
YES, HELLO! I'M THE ASSISTANT DIRECTOR HAYASHI!
FWAP
A SUPER RUDE GAG
HEY!! THAT'S RUDE!!
OH! IT'S EIKURA-SAN!
EIKURA-SAN, HERE ON BREAK
WHAP
SLEEEENDER
HI, EIKURA-SAN! HELLO! HELLO!
NICE CASTING!!
STMP TMP TMP TMP
GRAB

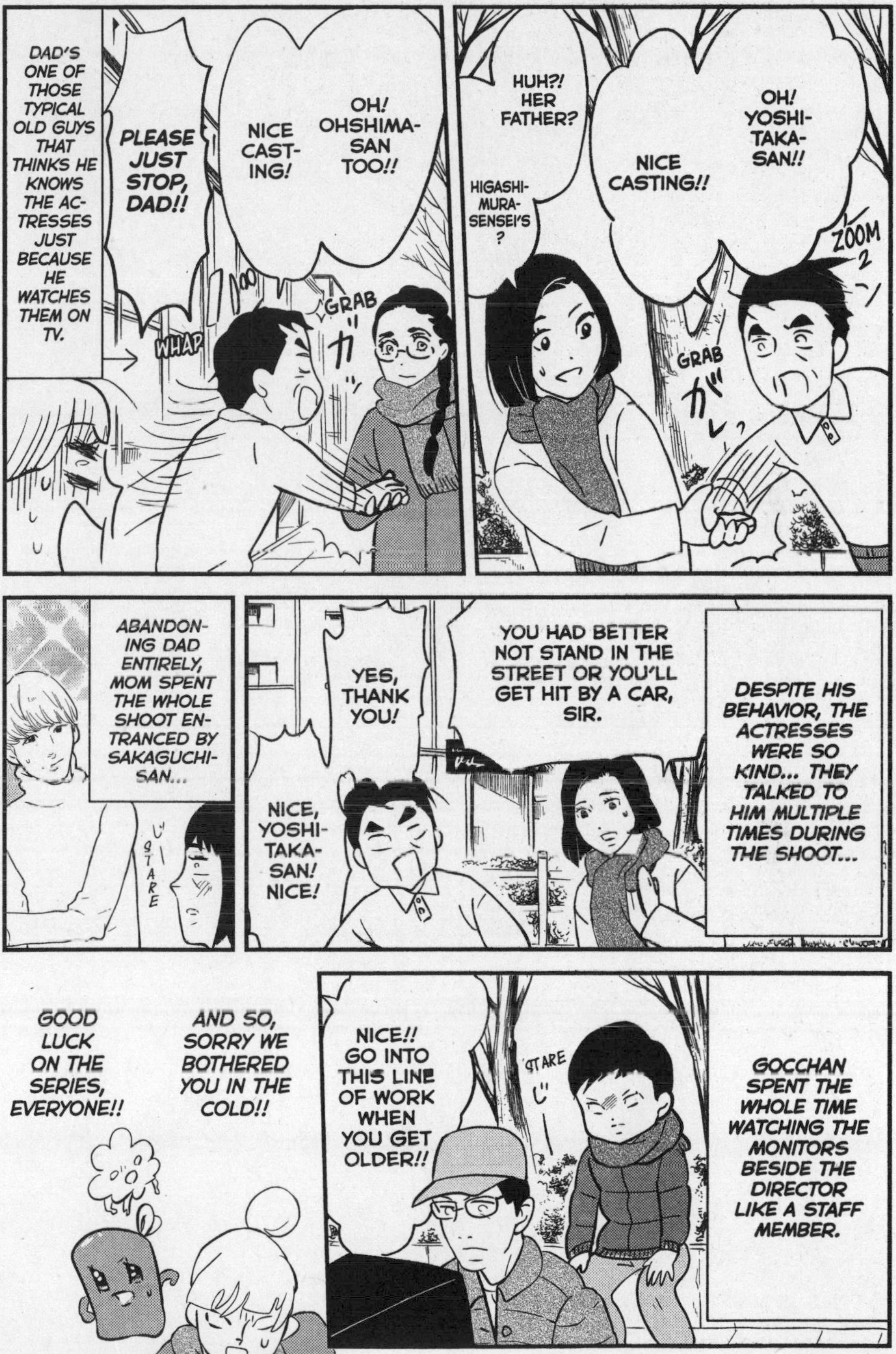
OH! YOSHI-TAKA-SAN!!
NICE CASTING!!
HUH?! HER FATHER?
HIGASHI-MURA-SENSEI'S ?
ZOOM
GRAB
OH! OHSHIMA-SAN TOO!!
NICE CAST-ING!
PLEASE JUST STOP, DAD!!
DAD'S ONE OF THOSE TYPICAL OLD GUYS THAT THINKS HE KNOWS THE AC-TRESSES JUST BECAUSE HE WATCHES THEM ON TV.
GRAB
WHAP
DESPITE HIS BEHAVIOR, THE ACTRESSES WERE SO KIND... THEY TALKED TO HIM MULTIPLE TIMES DURING THE SHOOT...
YOU HAD BETTER NOT STAND IN THE STREET OR YOU'LL GET HIT BY A CAR, SIR.
YES, THANK YOU!
NICE, YOSHI-TAKA-SAN! NICE!
ABANDON-ING DAD ENTIRELY, MOM SPENT THE WHOLE SHOOT EN-TRANCED BY SAKAGUCHI-SAN...
STARE
GOCCHAN SPENT THE WHOLE TIME WATCHING THE MONITORS BESIDE THE DIRECTOR LIKE A STAFF MEMBER.
STARE
NICE!! GO INTO THIS LINE OF WORK WHEN YOU GET OLDER!!
AND SO, SORRY WE BOTHERED YOU IN THE COLD!!
GOOD LUCK ON THE SERIES, EVERYONE!!

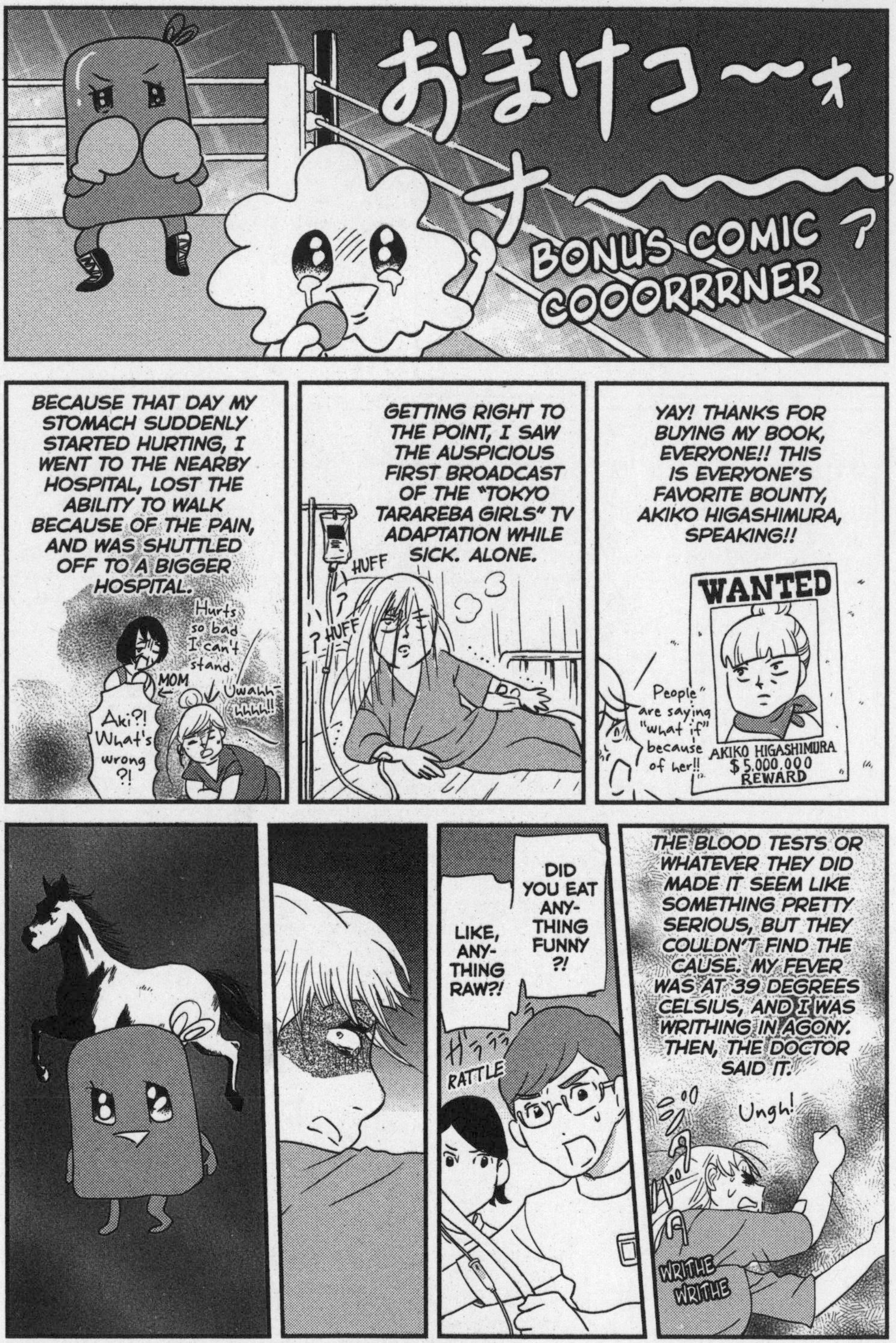
おまけコ〜〜ォ
ナ〜〜〜ア
BONUS COMIC COOORRRRNER
YAY! THANKS FOR BUYING MY BOOK, EVERYONE!! THIS IS EVERYONE'S FAVORITE BOUNTY, AKIKO HIGASHIMURA, SPEAKING!!
WANTED
AKIKO HIGASHIMURA
$5,000,000 REWARD
People are saying "what if" because of her!!
GETTING RIGHT TO THE POINT, I SAW THE AUSPICIOUS FIRST BROADCAST OF THE "TOKYO TARAREBA GIRLS" TV ADAPTATION WHILE SICK. ALONE.
HUFF
HUFF
BECAUSE THAT DAY MY STOMACH SUDDENLY STARTED HURTING, I WENT TO THE NEARBY HOSPITAL, LOST THE ABILITY TO WALK BECAUSE OF THE PAIN, AND WAS SHUTTLED OFF TO A BIGGER HOSPITAL.
Hurts so bad I can't stand.
MOM
Uwahh-hhhh!!
Aki?! What's wrong?!
THE BLOOD TESTS OR WHATEVER THEY DID MADE IT SEEM LIKE SOMETHING PRETTY SERIOUS, BUT THEY COULDN'T FIND THE CAUSE. MY FEVER WAS AT 39 DEGREES CELSIUS, AND I WAS WRITHING IN AGONY. THEN, THE DOCTOR SAID IT.
Ungh!
WRITHE WRITHE
DID YOU EAT ANY-THING FUNNY?!
LIKE, ANY-THING RAW?!
RATTLE

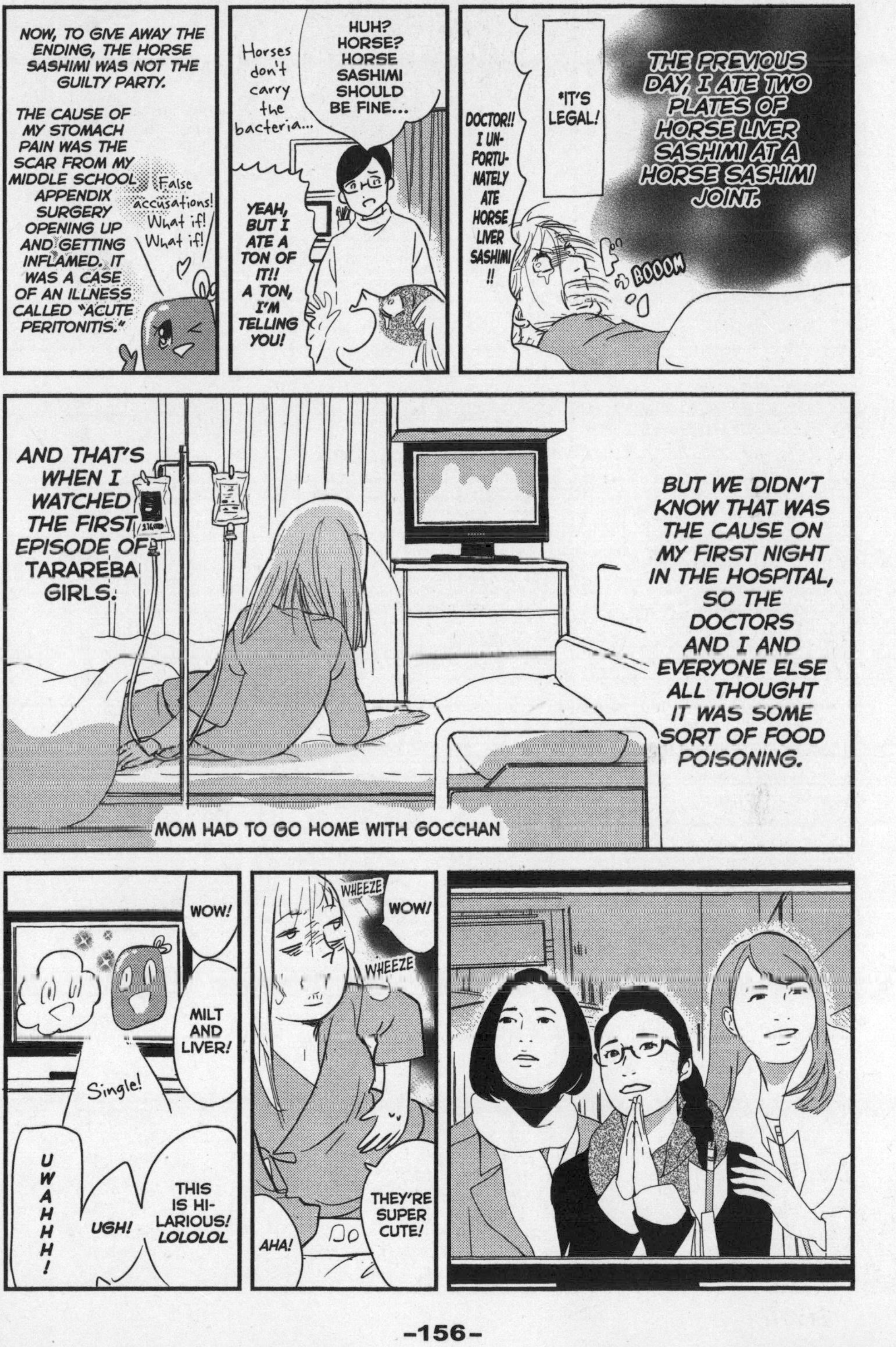
THE PREVIOUS DAY, I ATE TWO PLATES OF HORSE LIVER SASHIMI AT A HORSE SASHIMI JOINT.
*IT'S LEGAL!
DOCTOR!! I UNFORTUNATELY ATE HORSE LIVER SASHIMI!!
BOOOM
HUH? HORSE? HORSE SASHIMI SHOULD BE FINE...
Horses don't carry the bacteria...
YEAH, BUT I ATE A TON OF IT!! A TON, I'M TELLING YOU!
NOW, TO GIVE AWAY THE ENDING, THE HORSE SASHIMI WAS NOT THE GUILTY PARTY.
THE CAUSE OF MY STOMACH PAIN WAS THE SCAR FROM MY MIDDLE SCHOOL APPENDIX SURGERY OPENING UP AND GETTING INFLAMED. IT WAS A CASE OF AN ILLNESS CALLED "ACUTE PERITONITIS."
False accusations! What if! What if!
BUT WE DIDN'T KNOW THAT WAS THE CAUSE ON MY FIRST NIGHT IN THE HOSPITAL, SO THE DOCTORS AND I AND EVERYONE ELSE ALL THOUGHT IT WAS SOME SORT OF FOOD POISONING.
AND THAT'S WHEN I WATCHED THE FIRST EPISODE OF TARAREBA GIRLS.
MOM HAD TO GO HOME WITH GOCCHAN
WHEEZE
WOW!
WHEEZE
THEY'RE SUPER CUTE!
AHA!
WOW!
MILT AND LIVER!
Single!
THIS IS HILARIOUS! LOLOLOL
UGH!
UWAHHH!

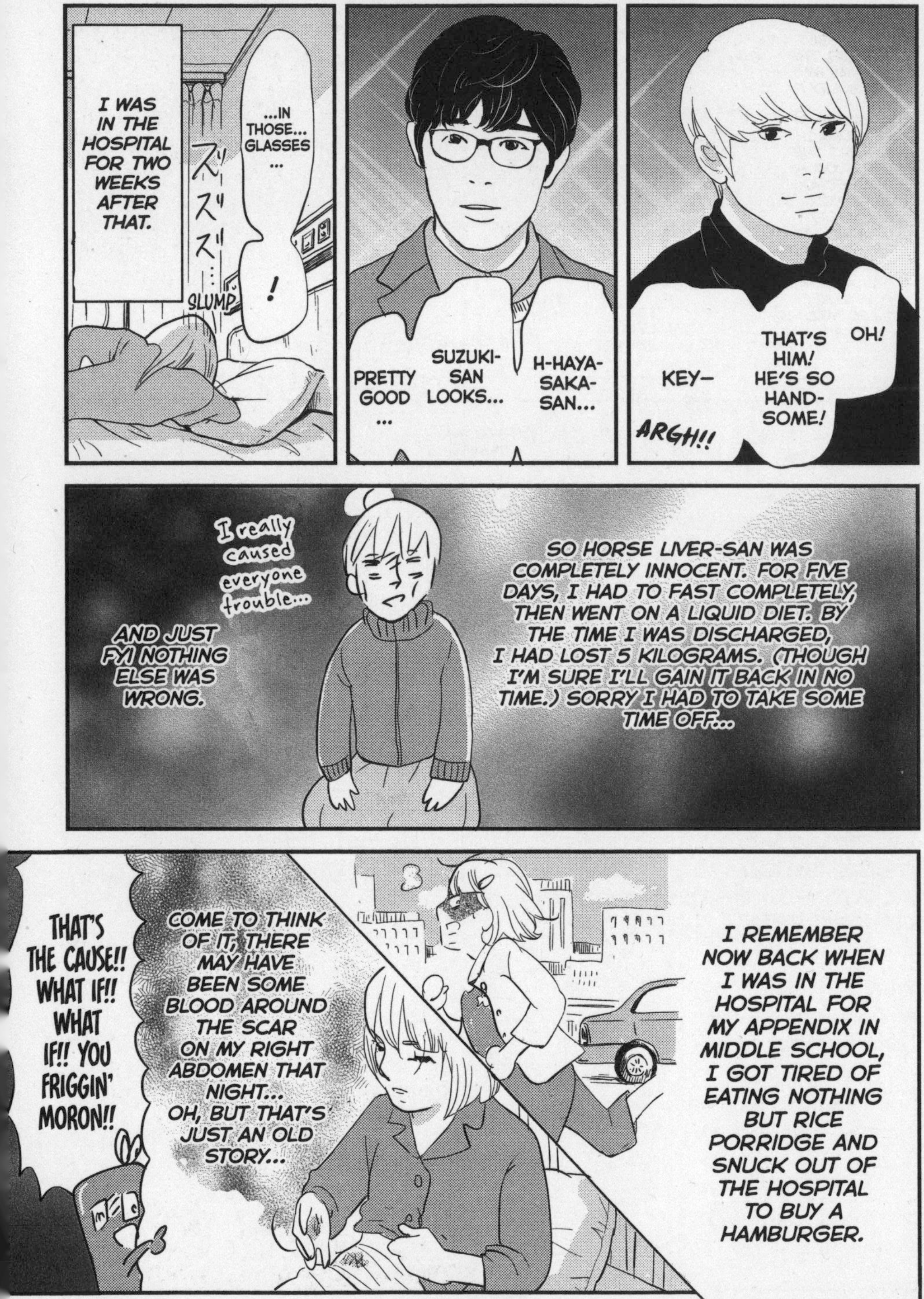

OH!
THAT'S HIM! HE'S SO HANDSOME!
KEY—
ARGH!!
H-HAYASAKA-SAN...
SUZUKI-SAN LOOKS...
PRETTY GOOD ...
I WAS IN THE HOSPITAL FOR TWO WEEKS AFTER THAT.
...IN THOSE... GLASSES ...
!
ズッズズ…
SLUMP
SO HORSE LIVER-SAN WAS COMPLETELY INNOCENT. FOR FIVE DAYS, I HAD TO FAST COMPLETELY, THEN WENT ON A LIQUID DIET. BY THE TIME I WAS DISCHARGED, I HAD LOST 5 KILOGRAMS. (THOUGH I'M SURE I'LL GAIN IT BACK IN NO TIME.) SORRY I HAD TO TAKE SOME TIME OFF...
I really caused everyone trouble...
AND JUST FYI NOTHING ELSE WAS WRONG.
I REMEMBER NOW BACK WHEN I WAS IN THE HOSPITAL FOR MY APPENDIX IN MIDDLE SCHOOL, I GOT TIRED OF EATING NOTHING BUT RICE PORRIDGE AND SNUCK OUT OF THE HOSPITAL TO BUY A HAMBURGER.
COME TO THINK OF IT, THERE MAY HAVE BEEN SOME BLOOD AROUND THE SCAR ON MY RIGHT ABDOMEN THAT NIGHT... OH, BUT THAT'S JUST AN OLD STORY...
THAT'S THE CAUSE!! WHAT IF!! WHAT IF!! YOU FRIGGIN' MORON!!

END!!

Tokyo Tarareba Girls Translation notes

Tokyo Tarareba Girls: *"Tarareba"* means "What if," like the "What-if" stories you tell yourself about what could be or could have been. The name is also taken from the names of the two food characters in the series, *tara* (codfish milt) and *reba* (liver) who always say *"tara"* and *"reba"* respectively at the end of their sentences in Japanese, referencing the "what-if" meaning of *"tarareba."*

Frisk, page 26
A brand of breath mints with a strong mint flavor. Very popular in Japan.

Unbelievable, page 95
A human-interest TV series starring Beat Takeshi.

Gyaru, page 107
Gyaru, though initially borrowed from the English term "girl" and "gal" has since become a subculture of Japanese street fashion. Gyaru typically bleach and dye their hair lighter and wear a lot of make up and gaudy accessories. The excessive and fun femininity that gyaru put on is at once an indulgent performance and also a statement that catches one's eyes. Because of this, gyaru are sometimes thought of as vain, shallow, or airheaded.

Bagna Càuda, page 113:
An italian dish similar to fondue.

Feeling Couples 5 vs. 5, page 115
A segment on a TV show that ran from the mid-'70s to the mid-'90s in which a group of men and women from competing colleges would meet for a televised singles party. The final portion would take place in front of the presenters on opposite sides of a large table.

Email addresses, page 117
In Japan, messages like texts on a phone, are sent through email addresses, rather than by phone number.

Yukhoe and Ponzu, page 120
Yukhoe is a Korean raw beef dish. Ponzu is a Japanese sauce made of citrus and soy sauce.

Gopchang, page 121
Another Korean dish: grilled beef intestine.

Wanko Soba, page 137
A style of serving soba noodles served in small bowls which are repeatedly refilled, rather than the usual method of a single serving in a large bowl.

KISS Magazine, page 138
Tokyo Tarareba Girls was initially serialized by chapter in KISS Magazine.

Nonki-kun, page 144
A manga by Yoji Katakura about a lazy elementary school boy. *Nonki* means "carefree" or "happy-go-lucky."

Mutsugoro Kingdom, Page 145
An animal park founded by zoologist and essayist Masanori Hata, who wrote under the pen name "Mutsugoro."

Tokyo Tarareba Girls volume 8 is a work of fiction. Names, characters, places, and incidents are the products of the author's imagination or are used fictitiously. Any resemblance to actual events, locales, or persons, living or dead, is entirely coincidental.

A Kodansha Comics Trade Paperback Original.

Published in the United States by Kodansha Comics,
an imprint of Kodansha USA Publishing, LLC, New York.

Publication rights for this English edition arranged through Kodansha Ltd., Tokyo.

First published in Japan in 2017 by Kodansha Ltd., Tokyo, as *Tokyo Tarareba Musume* volume 8.

ISBN 978-1-63236-801-0

Printed in the United States of America.

www.kodanshacomics.com

9 8 7 6 5 4 3 2 1

Translation: Steven LeCroy
Lettering: Thea Willis and Paige Pumphrey
Editing: Sarah Tilson and Paul Starr
YKS Services LLC/SKY Japan, INC.
Kodansha Comics Edition Cover Design: Phil Balsman